THE WORLD ENCYCLOPEDIA OF

DESTROYERS AND FRIGATES

68

THE WORLD ENCYCLOPEDIA OF DESTROYERS AND FRIGATES

A fully illustrated history of naval vessels from the early torpedo boats of the 1890s through to the modern ships of the missile age

BERNARD IRELAND

LORENZ BOOKS

This edition is published by Lorenz Books
an imprint of Anness Publishing Ltd
www.lorenzbooks.com
www.annesspublishing.com
info@anness.com
twitter: @AnnessLorenzBks

Publisher: Joanna Lorenz
Senior Editor: Felicity Forster
Cover Design: Nigel Partridge
Production Controller: Ben Worley

The nationality of each ship is identified in the specification box by the national flag that was in use at the time of the vessel's commissioning and service.

PAGE 1: ***Nastoychivyy*, Sovremennyy class.**
PAGE 2: ***Anzio* (CG.68), Ticonderoga class.**
PAGE 3: ***Daring*, Type 45 (Daring) class.**

Contents

DIRECTORY OF FRIGATES

ABOVE: **Typifying World War II-built destroyers were the American Fletchers. USS *Cowell* retains her heavy surface and Anit-Submarine (AS) armament in the 1950s, but electronics are already proliferating.**

Introduction

On its introduction, followed by rapid development and proliferation in the late 19th century, the self-propelled torpedo made a tremendous impression on the world's navies. The measure of sea power remained the heavy-calibre gun, deployed in battleships heavily armoured to enable them to absorb damage inevitable in the gunnery exchanges that decided an encounter. Gunnery was still an art as much as a science and, with the concept of fire control still in the future, engagement ranges tended to be short. Hence the menace of the torpedo, whose effective range soon exceeded that acceptable to traditional gunnery men.

There is an old adage among designers that, to sink a ship, it is necessary to admit water. History abounds with examples of well-built ships, grievously damaged topside, that have survived through their watertight integrity remaining intact. The torpedo was invented expressly to defeat this capacity to endure such punishment, simply by delivering a powerful explosive charge beneath all protective armour and opening the hull to the sea.

In those pre-*entente cordiale* days, the French in particular saw in the torpedo an affordable means of offsetting the preponderance of British sea power. The result was a horde of torpedo boats of various sizes. As was customary, the British responded in kind.

In practice, these fragile craft, although manned by young men with boundless enthusiasm, posed little threat in a seaway but were, for instance, instrumental in obliging the British to abandon their time-honoured strategy of close blockade. Specialist yards in both Britain and France, then Germany, made a very good living as any fleet with pretentions to effectiveness felt obliged to follow suit.

Concerned, however, at an obviously emerging threat to their naval dominance, the British introduced the torpedo boat destroyer. Larger, and sufficiently well-armed to run down and eliminate a torpedo boat at sea, such "destroyers" were themselves able to carry torpedoes. A new class of warship had been born.

Fast, operating in great flotillas and popularly described as "maids of all work", classic destroyers possessed innate glamour and were very popular commands for young officers keen to make their mark.

The very versatility of destroyers eventually, however, exposed their shortcomings. Modern examples were exercised endlessly in fleet escort and in flotilla torpedo attacks. In the

LEFT: **With the coming of missiles and helicopters, destroyers became volume-critical and rapidly increased in size. Accommodated in a Vertical Launching System (VLS), the area-defence missiles are invisible and, with just one gun, a large Spruance (USS *Deyo*) appears underarmed.** ABOVE: **Faced with tight peacetime budgets, smaller navies have the perennial choice of quality or quantity. The Italian *Luigi Durand de la Penne* and her sister are very capable ships but are just two.** BELOW: **To increase numbers, the British Type 22s (*Brazen* seen here) were designed to a budget. The result was over-tight and unsatisfactory, with later ships having to be considerably stretched.** BOTTOM: **Current destroyers and frigates are dominated by measures designed to reduce radar reflection. The German *Hessen* is designed along MEKO (MEhrzweck KOmbination or, roughly, multi-purpose) principles to allow systems to be more easily interchanged or upgraded.**

former role they proved to be deficient against the newer threats of aircraft and submarine attack while, for all the torpedoes carried around the world's oceans, they were relatively little-used except, perhaps, in the Pacific.

Both great wars of the 20th century demonstrated the critical importance of mercantile shipping and its defence. The major threat to national security thus came, in large measure, not from the battle fleets but from submarines, natural successors to the early torpedo boats. In the absence of sufficient alternatives, older destroyers were drafted in for the vital drudgery of convoy escort. Designed for other tasks, however, they lacked the endurance, capacity and habitability inseparable from such escort duties.

For these, the simple corvette was already in production but, intended primarily for coastal duty, proved, in turn, inadequate for ocean work. Assuming a famous generic name from the days of sail, the frigate, once introduced, developed rapidly into an efficient submarine killer.

Post-war, technology advanced rapidly with fast conventional, then nuclear-propelled, submarines demanding larger frigates with stand-off weapons, notably helicopter-based. The threat from jet-propelled aircraft, themselves carrying stand-off weapons, was such that the guided missile inevitably transcended the gun.

Destroyers and frigates alike necessarily evolved from their "classic" forms in a process that remains continuous. This book endeavours to chart the full story to date. The lists of names of individual classes are so extensive as to require inclusion in a six page section at the back of the book.

21

The History of Destroyers and Frigates

The history of war at sea is largely one of weapon and antidote. The locomotive torpedo quickly gained the status of "wonder weapon", able to strike the heaviest capital ship below its armour. Every maritime nation had to have its flotillas of torpedo boats which, themselves, were quickly eclipsed by the torpedo boat destroyer, itself a torpedo carrier.

By the end of World War II destroyers were routinely discharging salvoes of eight or more torpedoes in the course of furious, mainly nocturnal, encounters. Already, however, their effectiveness, expressed as torpedoes launched per ship sunk, was less than that for those dropped by aircraft. As the primary torpedo platform, the destroyer had already peaked, been surpassed and had begun the metamorphosis to the specialist anti-aircraft escort that she is today.

On the way, largely as a consequence of being available, destroyers had been pitted against the rapidly evolving threat of the submarine. Despite the development of sonar and depth charges, the destroyer, designed for speed, lacked the range, weapon capacity and habitability necessary for essentially low-speed convoy escort. Thus was introduced the frigate, specifically anti-submarine in concept.

LEFT: **Guided missiles resulted in some confusion in categorization of escorts. The 5,670-ton, double-ended USS *Gridley*, here seen firing an Anti-Submarine Rocket missile, served 12 years as a frigate before being reclassed a cruiser.**

LEFT: **At what appears to be his factory at Fiume, Italy, Robert Whitehead ponders one of his experimental failures. It appears to be one of the "14-foot" weapons of 1870, the damage consistent with its having sunk beneath its crush depth.**

BELOW: **Better known for his successful development of the steam-driven paddle wheel, Robert Fulton also experimented with towed torpedoes, seeking patronage from both the United States and France during their wars with Britain.**

The early development of the self-propelled torpedo

The *raison d'être* of the Torpedo Boat and its eventual nemesis, the Torpedo Boat Destroyer (TBD or, more simply, Destroyer), was the deployment of the torpedo, a brief look at the early development of the weapon will assist in the understanding of the craft themselves.

The American engineer Robert Fulton is generally credited with introducing the term "torpedo" during the Napoleonic Wars, its early meaning embracing any underwater explosive device intended to sink a surface ship. These could be static (later termed "mines") or mobile. The latter included "spar torpedoes" projecting ahead of steam launches or, such as the Harvey torpedo, towed like a paravane. All such variants required a human in the loop, it was a very hazardous operation in what was, unavoidably, close-quarter manoeuvring against an opponent.

About 1862, Commander Johann Luppis of the Austrian Navy built a model of a small steamboat, armed with an explosive charge and steered remotely by lines connected to its rudder. His idea was taken up by Robert Whitehead, who managed an engineering concern in Fiume (now Rijeka). Whitehead saw immediately the huge potential of submerging such a vehicle, to render its approach invisible. Thus was born the idea of the Locomotive (or "Automobile") Torpedo, ancestor of all such weapons used today.

"The use of the torpedo still constituted a greater danger to the man who launched it than to his enemy" – Alfred, later Grand Admiral von, Tirpitz on the Whitehead Torpedo (which he did not like) in 1877

The prototype was run in 1866 and was a neutrally buoyant, spindle-shaped body with long parallel fins for longitudinal stability. It was of 14in maximum diameter and was driven by compressed air. An improved model was run two years later, incorporating Whitehead's patented arrangement of a balance chamber which, via a heavy pendulum, controlled horizontal surfaces for the maintenance of a selected depth.

In 1870, Whitehead demonstrated the weapon to British Admiralty officials. Carrying a 30kg/66lb warhead, it ran over 250m/273yd at 8 knots. The Admiralty soon afterwards bought the rights of manufacture, an endorsement that guaranteed the device's success.

Whitehead retained the patents, selling them to the French in 1873. Although the latter pronounced Whitehead's performance claims to be exaggerated, both they and the

LEFT: **An early 20th-century picture of an American torpedo boat launching a "Mark 3 Whitehead". The change in shape will be evident, development being conducted independently by each purchaser of Whitehead's patent.**

LEFT: **Accepted by the US Navy in 1899, the USS *Holland* successfully married the torpedo to the submersible. The round cap to the single torpedo tube is visible on the axis of the pressure hull. Above it, in the "bullnose", is the cap of a Zalinsky pneumatic dynamite gun.** ABOVE: **Between 1885 and 1889 the British carried out a protracted series of experiments, simulating the effects of exploding shells and torpedoes against the obsolete ironclad *Resistance*. Important conclusions were drawn about the use of anti-torpedo nets and watertight compartments.**

British worked independently to improve the weapon even as more fleets acquired its principles. Both worked officially on deploying it from small, semi-submersible craft similar to the "Davids" used by the Confederates during the American Civil War. The specialist British builders, Thornycroft and Yarrow, each, however, produced superior fast steam launches of conventional design.

By the late 1870s, contra-rotating propellers had been introduced, neutralizing torque effects and providing for improved straight running. This was vital to improving range, which currently stood at 1,000m/1,094yd at 7 knots, or 300m/328yd at 12 knots.

To improve directional stability the American Howell torpedo used a heavy internal flywheel, but the device was inferior to Ludwig Obry's addition of a gyroscope to directly control a pair of vertical rudders. This improvement of 1894 allowed the weapon to be increased in diameter to 45cm/18in, giving it a range of 3,000m/3,282yd with a good chance of hitting a target. As this was comparable with the effective battle ranges for gunfire at this time, the torpedo now had to be considered a real threat.

Frank Leavitt of the Bliss Company in the United States then developed the technique of burning fuel in the presence of enriched compressed air to deliver greatly increased energy. This was applied to a miniature reciprocating engine, later a turbine for smoother performance.

A torpedo was first used offensively in 1877. Its ability to be deployed from almost any type of warship, particularly small, inexpensive craft, inspired the French Admiral Théophile Aube to develop his ideas of what became known as the *Jeune École*. This propounded the concept that swarms of small, torpedo-carrying flotilla vessels could neutralize the mightiest conventional battle fleet. Although later proved specious, the philosophy led directly to the rapid development of the torpedo boat and, rather more slowly, the technologically more challenging submarine, or submersible.

ABOVE: **"Davids" of the American Civil War were not submersibles in the true sense, but were designed to be ballasted down with only the vestigial casing and funnel visible above the water. Their usual weapon was a spar torpedo.**

ABOVE: **Lieutenant William B. Cushing successfully used a spar torpedo to sink the rebel ironclad *Albemarle* in the Roanoke River on October 27, 1864. In this impression, Cushing is holding the lanyard to detonate the charge.**

The origins of the torpedo boat

When, in 1871, the British government purchased the rights to manufacture Whitehead's torpedo, the weapon could be launched from tubes above or below water, and under the impulse of either compressed air or a powder charge. Alternatively, it could be run-up and released from "dropping gear". To decide on how to deploy it, the Admiralty set up a Torpedo Committee. This recommended that, besides putting it aboard existing and specially designed warships, it would best be carried by ships' boats and "torpedo launches".

Larger, purpose-built warships were indeed built, but fast launches rapidly predominated in that they could be afforded in considerable numbers while, being nimble and of low profile, they were ideal for stealthy nocturnal attack. Smaller ("2nd Class") variants could even be carried aboard larger warships for both defensive and offensive purposes.

British builders, particularly Thornycroft and Yarrow, had already amassed considerable experience in constructing steel-hulled launches with compact steam machinery for private use. In 1873 Thornycroft built one, armed with a spar torpedo, for the Norwegian government and then, on approaching the British Admiralty, was rewarded with an order for a 27-tonner. About 25.6m/84ft long, she made over 19 knots on trials in 1877, whereupon she was commissioned as *Torpedo Boat No.1*. She was the first to be built specifically to deploy locomotive, as opposed to spar or towed, torpedoes.

ABOVE: The Thornycroft-built *Lightning* of 1877 was based on a river launch design. She was purchased by the Royal Navy as *1st Class Torpedo Boat No.1*, or TB No.1. In this picture, she is yet to be fitted with sided dropping gear for locomotive torpedoes. BELOW LEFT: The British Admiralty ordered from many ship yards for warship construction. The resulting non-uniformity that resulted is clear in this undated photograph. Also evident is the fine craftsmanship in their thin metal hulls. BELOW: One of a batch of 20 1st Class Torpedo Boats from Thornycroft was TB No.50, dating from 1886. Note the protected position for the helmsman, the turtledeck forward and the disproportionate size of the 18in torpedo tube.

As built, TB No.1 was equipped with two dropping frames, but these were found to be difficult to operate, requiring the craft to be slowed. They were, therefore, replaced by a single, trainable tube on the foredeck. The vessel was also renamed HMS *Lightning*.

Over the next two years, Thornycroft built 11 more, slightly longer, craft (TB Nos.2–12, not named). It is significant that similar vessels acquired by foreign navies quickly exchanged the spar-and-towed torpedoes, for which they had been designed, for Whitehead's weapons.

Lacking freeboard and superstructure, the early torpedo boats had limited seakeeping qualities. France and others were, however, also building enthusiastically, with yards such as Normand and Schichau beginning to establish reputations.

ABOVE: **An important intermediate step between torpedo boat and destroyer was the 125-ton *Swift*, conceived by J. Samuel White and built speculatively in 1885. Purchased by the Admiralty as TB No.81, she showed superior seakeeping qualities.** RIGHT: **Instantly recognizable by her enormous goose-neck hydraulic cranes, the cruiser HMS *Vulcan* was designed around stowage for a flotilla of 2nd Class torpedo boats. These, armed with 14in torpedoes, were supposed to be set afloat in the vicinity of an enemy battle line.**

In 1884, J. Samuel White produced a speculative "one-off" which he named *Swift*. Displacing 125 tons and of 45.7m/150ft overall length, she showed improved seaworthiness and was acquired by the Admiralty. Renamed TB No.81 she was fitted with not only three torpedo tubes but also six 3pdr quick-firing (QF) guns. Capable of nearly 21 knots in the light conditions, she was designated a "torpedo boat catcher".

She resulted in the Admiralty building a disparate collection of boats between 41.1–44.2m/135–145ft long. Designed to have a broadly interchangeable armament of guns and torpedoes, they proved totally inadequate to the task of catching other torpedo craft. Nonetheless, this concept was also used abroad, notably in Germany, where the larger craft were termed "division boats". These were commanded by a more experienced officer, charged with maintaining order in often large flotillas of small craft, each with enthusiastic lieutenants enjoying their first command.

The French also began to construct larger and more seaworthy craft, known as "Haute Mer" torpedo boats. Their leaders, or division boats, were for a time armed with a single 14cm gun. Termed "bateaux-canon" they were intended to both lead and to support torpedo attacks but it proved impossible to fire their big gun accurately from so small and lively a platform.

To counter the threat of a flotilla of torpedo boats, the British Admiralty (still favouring the time-proven procedures of close blockade) sought a suitable design of vessel to screen major warships. These, in their evolutionary stage, were referred to variously as "catchers", "hunters" or, on occasion, "torpedo boat destroyers".

Probably inspired by the 15.24m/50ft semi-submersible "Davids", independent innovators persevered with developing an alternative form of stealthy torpedo carrier. Their endeavours would shortly produce the submersible which, with its ability to navigate both invisibly and undetectably, would become the most effective solution of all.

> **"We lived on ham, sardines and tinned soups … it was as much as we could do to get a little water boiled. We had a table … but there was no point in laying it, for nothing would stay on it."**
> **From an account of life aboard a 33m French torpedo boat**

ABOVE: **In the tranquillity of a dockyard basin an early French torpedo boat appears stylish. She proved, however, inadequate in a Mediterranean "blow". Note the pair of torpedo tubes located beneath the turtle deck forward.**
BELOW: **With only basic facilities of their own, torpedo boats depended upon their depot ships. This division of 2nd Class French boats are designed to be awash in any sea, their crews being confined largely to the light, elevated spar decks.**

FAR LEFT: **The three Hawthorne-Leslie boats of the 1898–99 Programme were highly rated, being "far superior" to the remaining 30-knotters. "Fine sea boats, combining strength, economy of coal consumption and seagoing qualities", the incomplete *Racehorse* is seen undergoing trials.** LEFT INSET: **In his various senior posts in the Admiralty, Admiral Sir John ("Jackie") Fisher may be truly said to have revolutionized the Royal Navy. As Controller and Third Sea Lord in 1892, he initiated the concept of the "torpedo boat catcher".** BELOW: **Of the first six 27-knotters, the Thornycroft pair (*Daring* seen here) were marginally the fastest. Note the pronounced tumblehome of the hull, the turtleback forecastle and the watch officer sharing the "bridge" with a 12pdr gun.**

The torpedo boat destroyer in the Royal Navy

The Torpedo Boat Destroyer (TBD) was inevitable. The torpedo boat was too small to be effective, while the larger Torpedo Gun Boats (TGBs) and their foreign equivalents, although an improvement, were still incapable of catching them.

To maintain speed in a seaway, length is the most important parameter. Having brought this fact to the attention of the Controller, then Rear Admiral John Fisher, Alfred Yarrow and John I. Thornycroft were involved in 1892 in discussions regarding larger craft. These resulted in six interested companies being invited to tender costed design proposals for a "large, seagoing torpedo boat".

The draft specification required the craft, of about 200 tons displacement, to maintain 27 knots over a three-hour trial, possible only under ideal conditions. A single 12pdr was to be carried to deal with French "haute mer" boats, in addition to a 6pdr and an 18in bow-mounted torpedo tube. Space and weight margins were to be allowed for either two more 6pdrs or a pair of deck-mounted torpedo tubes. Invitations to build were confined to private yards, as Royal Dockyards had not the expertise to design and build such lightly constructed craft.

A complication was that this was the very period in which the old-style locomotive boiler was being challenged by various types of water-tube boiler. While more compact and lighter, these still lacked the older boiler's reliability.

Before the initial order was placed – two each with Yarrow, Thornycroft and Laird – the craft, initially referred to as Torpedo Boat Catchers, had been redesignated Torpedo Boat Destroyers. Between them, they had installed three types of water-tube and one locomotive boiler for the purpose of evaluation. The six boats (like submarines, they were still commonly termed "boats") were significant in being the first real TBDs and were known officially as the A-class 27-knotters of the 1892–93 Programme.

All managed 27–27.7 knots on trials except for the locomotive-boilered *Havock*, which could make only 26.2. This obsession with high potential speed was totally academic, for even a fairly moderate sea was sufficient to cause progressively more severe damage to any TBD venturing to make better than about 15 knots. Conditions aboard remained little better than those in the torpedo boats. Vibration at speed was intense, while to hit anything with guns usually meant stopping the ship. They could, however, overhaul torpedo boats.

With the French still building numbers of large torpedo boats, the Admiralty quickly ordered six, then 30 more

> **"Although the forebridge and chart house are a decided advantage, the close proximity to [the] top of [the] foremost funnel is most inconvenient ... a positive danger. Twice ... at a critical moment I was completely and suddenly enveloped in smoke and burning ashes."**
> **From a 1904 report by the Commanding Officer of the River-class *Itchen***

LEFT: **Essentially a modified 30-knotter, the *Viper* was a testbed for Parsons' new steam turbine. She could make 36 knots with more compact machinery and with much reduced vibration. She had eight propellers on four shafts and was coal-fired.** BELOW LEFT: **Realistic night exercises confirmed the menace that flotillas of torpedo craft posed to capital ships. The immediate answer was additional searchlights and quick-firing guns. Jutland showed that the Germans were better prepared.** BELOW: **The German armoured ship *Ägir* of 1896, escorted by what appears to be a Germania-built "large torpedo boat" of 1902. With her long forecastle, the latter was much dryer than her British contemporaries and better able to maintain her speed.**

27-knotters. Although also referred to as the A-class, they were of the 1893–94 Programme, with contracts being spread over no less than 14 private yards. All were in the water by the end of 1895.

The Admiralty, by now, was pressing for a minimum of 75 TBDs. Because some contractors were having difficulty reaching guaranteed performance, some earlier boats were late in delivery. This left funds available to commence work on a new class, slightly enlarged and capable of 30 knots. (Some of the A class had made 29 knots.) Known as the B, C and D classes, they were ordered under successive programmes between 1894 and 1901. They totalled 66 in all.

The expanding German fleet was now also causing concern. Between 1898 and 1901 it acquired its first true TBDs, building 12 of the Schichau-designed S.90 class. Shorter but beamier than the British 30-knotters, they were given a proper forecastle, as opposed to the British ships' very wet turtledecks. Designed less with regard to speed, they enjoyed superior seakeeping and greater endurance. Obviously better ships, they stimulated the British Admiralty to pay 40 per cent more for what became the River or E class, built between 1902–06. These followed work with several experimental turbine-driven boats, and some of the Rivers were similarly powered. Like their German peers, the Rivers traded excessive speed for a raised forecastle and an enclosed bridge structure. Seen as a great improvement, they are generally considered to have been the Royal Navy's first true destroyers,

BELOW: **Yarrow's contributions to the six "special" 27-knotters of 1892–93 were the *Havock* and *Hornet*. They were similar except that *Havock*, seen here, was powered by two locomotive boilers, requiring two close-spaced funnels.** BOTTOM: ***Hornet* was fitted with eight, more compact water-tube boilers and four funnels. She was the first vessel to be accepted into the Royal Navy in 1894 as a torpedo boat destroyer, quickly abbreviated to TBD.**

Destroyers at the Dardanelles

Although conceived for torpedo attack and defence, destroyers exhibited their versatility in other tasks during the Dardanelles operations, the first major campaign of World War I, which involved both French and British fleets.

A beguilingly simple War Council directive of January 1915 stated that the Navy would "bombard and take the Gallipoli Peninsula, with Constantinople as its objective". To achieve this aim an Anglo-French fleet would have to penetrate the 30km/18-mile long strait of the Dardanelles. Narrowing progressively from five miles to one, the waterway is subject to fierce currents. Ably assisted by their German ally, the Turks had created a near-impregnable defensive system. The ancient forts that dotted the arid and often steep shorelines were rearmed with considerable numbers of modern guns. Then lines of moored mines barred the Narrows. Fixed and mobile batteries, with searchlights, covered the minefields. Further mobile batteries ranged either shore.

Forcing a passage thus posed something of a conundrum. The considerable assembly of pre-Dreadnoughts could not transit the strait before the mines were cleared. Minesweepers, however, could not work under close-range gunfire from the numerous batteries. Top-level opinion was divided, some insisting that naval forces could do the job alone, others that military forces would need to secure the shore as the Navy advanced up the waterway by stages.

The lower, wider part of the strait, below the minefields, was largely subdued by naval bombardment, followed by landing demolition parties to destroy individual batteries.

"The responsibility for the ultimate failure of the Fleet to force a passage ... lies on the shoulders of those who would not allow us to accomplish our task after ... efficient minesweepers [ie the destroyers] had been provided". Commodore Roger Keyes, Chief-of-Staff to the Admiral Commanding

TOP: **Seen off Toulon, the Claymore-class destroyer *Massue* was one of a considerable force of French ships reinforcing the British fleet during the World War I Gallipoli campaign. Although capable of minesweeping, she was never so employed.** ABOVE: **Significant numbers of French and British pre-Dreadnoughts, considered expendable, were employed in the Dardanelles. The one-off French *Bouvet*, dating from 1898, hit a mine on March 18, 1915, and sank with great loss of life.**

Tackling the mine barriers was, however, a different matter. With the fleet were 21 North Sea fishing trawlers, converted to sweep in pairs. Low-powered, they could manage only 5 knots with sweeps streamed and, as adverse currents could run as fast as 4 knots, they made near-stationary targets for the Turkish gunners. Sweeping was thus conducted at night, but under the glare of numerous searchlights and a hail of fire. Even with their civilian crews assisted by naval volunteers, the trawlers had little to show for numerous attempts and considerable damage. They were simply inadequate for the task.

Attending the fleet was a flotilla of 550-ton River-class destroyers. They were small ships, limited in both power and available space, but were used in pairs, linked by a cable secured to their after bitts. Thus encumbered, they preceded several major warships engaged on support duties. The wire was insufficient to cut any mine cable that it encountered but would provide warning. (It might be noted that the paravane and the serrated sweep wire were still in the future.)

LEFT: **In the absence of proper port facilities, troop movements had to be conducted in the time-honoured fashion, using ships' boats. This picture gives an idea of the vulnerability of such craft in the face of an opposed landing.** ABOVE: **Beaches on the Gallipoli peninsula were little more than coves backed by high ground which, once secured, gave protection from direct Turkish artillery and small-arms fire. With the eventual arrival of U-boats, ships could no longer loiter offshore.**

Fortunately for the destroyers, which were not free to manoeuvre, the larger ship following attracted the majority of the fire. The system worked well below the mine barriers, but several old British and French battleships manoeuvred out of the main stream, blundering into a hitherto unsuspected line of mines. Their loss caused despondency in the C-in-C.

Also available were two flotillas of 975-ton Beagle, or G-class, destroyers. Larger, and with 60 per cent more propulsive power, they drew considerably less water than the trawlers, giving them a good chance of being able to pass over the moored mines with impunity. With the assistance of Malta Dockyard, the Beagles were fitted to work in pairs, streaming a 2.5in steel cable. Trials showed that this could be towed at 14 knots, enabling destroyers to sweep against the tidal stream, relying on sheer power to snag a mine cable and, if not to cut it, to drag it clear.

Preliminary sweeps in the strait itself proved the efficacy of the system, but too late. To the great disappointment of the destroyer crews, they were never to have the distinction of leading the battle fleet through the Narrows. Successive C-in-Cs had been too concerned about losses, more feared than actual, and their pessimism led to the decision to take the Gallipoli peninsula by military force.

Following the landing, the Beagles were kept busy sweeping offshore on the Army's flanks, ensuring the safety from mines of fire support ships.

LEFT: **HMS *Redpole* was a 755-ton Acorn- or H-class destroyer, seen here probably at the fleet base on Mudros. She has lifelines rigged along the starboard side of the hull and has a Carley float stowed at the break of the forecastle.** ABOVE: **Destroyers, as usual, were called upon to handle all the fleet's "odd jobs". These crew members, suitably armed, are using rifle fire to explode floating mines, which posed a considerable menace in the strait.** LEFT: **Britain's then-large fishing fleet was a valuable source of modern trawlers and drifters which, with their superb seaman crews, performed as auxiliaries to the fleet. The *Seaflower*, seen here, was unusual in being owned by the Admiralty.**

LEFT: This picture of *Royal Sovereign* gives a good idea of why the director positions needed to be located so high and on vibration-resistant tripod masts. Even in a calm sea, the low freeboard sees the bow wave almost over the deck edge. ABOVE: Three British battlecruisers were lost at Jutland. As their armour protected them only against the gunfire of armoured cruisers at these ranges, it amounted to foolishness to expose them to the fire of capital ships.

Destroyers at Jutland

Admiral Sir John Jellicoe framed his Battle Orders around the premise that the preservation of the British Grand Fleet was more important than the destruction of the German High Seas Fleet. He forecast, correctly, that the latter, under severe pressure, would make a "battle turn away" to disengage. This would be made under cover of a smoke screen and a massed destroyer torpedo attack. It might also be to entice the Grand Fleet into a "submarine trap". Jellicoe made it clear beforehand that he would not directly follow a battle turn away but, at Jutland, this was a primary cause for the fleets to lose touch at a critical phase, just as daylight was fading.

For his destroyers (50 boats of three flotillas), Jellicoe's instructions were "not to miss a favourable opportunity for a successful [torpedo] attack on the enemy's battle fleet". Their "primary duty", however, was to prevent enemy flotillas from disturbing the Grand Fleet's gunfire. Their role was, thus, primarily defensive, with Scheer's battle fleet of secondary importance, a target of opportunity.

Not so with the destroyers (27 from four flotillas) of Vice Admiral Sir David Beatty's Battle Cruiser Fleet. Beatty believed that, by launching his torpedo attack first, he would oblige the enemy's destroyers to protect their own fleet, disrupting any plan to attack Jellicoe.

During the first phase of the battle, the battlecruisers "run to the south", the hard-pressed Beatty and his opponent, Hipper, unleashed their destroyers simultaneously. About 30 ships thus became involved in furious and confused close-range action between the lines, ended only by the sudden appearance of Scheer's main battle fleet. Each side lost two destroyers, only one to torpedo.

Most of the heavy fighting at Jutland was between the battle cruiser forces. With the second phase, the "run to the north", Beatty successfully enticed Scheer's battle fleet into Jellicoe's waiting gunnery trap. With Scheer's successful disengagement in the gathering gloom, Jellicoe eschewed the uncertainties of night action, intending to renew the action at dawn.

The main battle fleets lost touch in the darkness but British light forces fought a series of deadly skirmishes with various parts of the German line. Nineteen destroyers of the 4th Flotilla, led by the *Tipperary*, challenged strange ships, which replied with a hail of fire at close range. Unsure still of the stranger's identity, some responded with torpedoes, some held their fire. None thought it necessary to inform Jellicoe that they had discovered the position of the German main body.

LEFT: The 14 battleships of the High Seas Fleet's 1st and 2nd Battleship Squadron drawn up in the Kiel Fiord. Closest is probably *Thüringen*, second ship of the 1st Division of the 1st Squadron. She was probably responsible for sinking the armoured cruiser *Black Prince*.

LEFT: **German destroyers steaming at high speed in quarter line. Note the day shapes on the masts; circular, triangular or rectangular in outline, they were carried in addition to painted pennant numbers on the bows.** BELOW: **Attached to the screen of Hood's ill-starred 3rd Battle Cruiser Squadron, the destroyer *Shark* was disabled by gunfire in a mêlée with enemy destroyers. She was torpedoed and finished off, sinking with heavy loss of life.**

LEFT: **German destroyers were organized in flotillas of eleven boats, comprising a leader and two "half flotillas" of five boats apiece. These were numbered in sequence so that, for instance, the 4th Flotilla (absent at Jutland) comprised the 7th and 8th Half Flotillas.** BELOW: **The Germania-built G.96 of 1916 was a final, modified unit of the G.85–95 batch, differing from them in that her forecastle was extended to the bridge structure. Only G.86, 87 and 88 were at Jutland, the G.96 was mined and sank off Ostend in 1917.** BOTTOM: **Jellicoe made clear beforehand that, in the event of a massed German destroyer torpedo attack, he would turn his battle line away, rather than towards, the enemy. He did, lost contact and valuable time, and, with it, a victory.**

Several such skirmishes cost the British a further six destroyers. The nature of the actions is well borne out by the high-speed collisions between the British *Spitfire* and the German battleship *Nassau*, the British destroyers *Broke* and *Sparrowhawk*, and the German light cruiser *Elbing* and battleship *Posen.* Although reluctant to fire torpedoes in the circumstances, British destroyers succeeded in sinking the pre-Dreadnought *Pommern* and the light cruiser *Rostock*.

In the course of that night, the British light forces, including light cruiser squadrons, saw more action than the whole of Jellicoe's main body in the earlier daylight encounter. Scheer was bent on escape, while Jellicoe needed to find him in order to renew the action with daylight. One of the enduring mysteries of Jutland is how few ships with vital information felt it necessary to inform their C-in-C. This included capital ships of his main body which observed the night encounters at considerable distance without being involved. With too little information upon which to base a judgement, Jellicoe failed to re-establish contact, and Jutland was over, destined to become one of the great "what ifs" of history.

Post-battle analysis reached the conclusions that the British destroyers were organized in over-large flotillas, and were poorly trained in attack procedures. Valour and aggression were not lacking, but attacks were not co-ordinated and they were "simply overwhelmed by the enemy's searchlights, star shells ... and secondary armament".

Swift and *Broke* in the Dover Patrol

With the Western Front hopelessly stagnated, the Allies could conduct operations from Dunkerque while the Germans used Ostend and Zeebrugge, the former less than 48km/30 miles up the coast. By early 1917, British shipping lost to U-boat torpedoes had reached crisis level, although the armies in France depended upon uninterrupted cross-channel shipments of troops and supplies.

The British Dover Command was thus of crucial importance, having as its main responsibilities the protection of shipping in the eastern English Channel, and the denial of U-boat's passage to the Atlantic via the shortest route.

A little over 32km/20 miles in width, the Dover Strait had been "closed" by a mine barrier. Except for shallow waters and shipping gates, mines had been laid in rows set at depths of 9–30m/30–100ft below low water. Most shipping could cross it quite safely, but submerged submarines were at great risk. Some 32km/20 miles to the north-east, a second barrier of mined nets ran between the South Goodwin and Dyck lightships, the latter near Dunkerque.

To be effective, both barriers had to be patrolled and tended by large numbers of drifters requisitioned from the fishing fleet. These unarmed craft and, indeed, the whole Command area, were subject to sudden attack by German destroyers, of which their Flanders Flotilla, together with coastal U-boats, were based on the inland port of Bruges. Emerging via Zeebrugge on a dark night, the destroyers could arrive at the barriers in a couple of hours. With no warning, they could not fail to encounter the drifter line, and they could operate with the confidence of knowing that every vessel met with would be hostile.

There were two leaders and sixteen destroyers attached to the Dover Command, most of the latter being older and smaller boats. These conducted deterrent patrols at irregular intervals, but had been unable to prevent several incursions by the

> **"It was like an excerpt from a Marryat story, an echo of the spar-to-spar combats at Trafalgar."**
> **Reginal Pound, Evans's biographer**

TOP: **An inspiration of Admiral Sir John Fisher when Controller, the *Swift* was an expensive one-off, part Scout, part Leader. The sided 4in forecastle guns, seen here, had been replaced by a single 6in by the date of the action described here.**
ABOVE: **Wreathed in steam, a 21in torpedo leaves one of *Broke*'s sided tubes. In so close a mêlée, torpedoes may not get sufficient time to arm, and may be a hazard to either side.**

ABOVE LEFT: **The exultant crew of the *Swift* pose for a decidedly informal picture on "the morning after". Note how the previously open bridge has gained an enclosed wheelhouse, with appliqué protection. Note also the 6in gun and semaphore.** ABOVE: **The Dover Barrage had the dual purpose of contraband control and submarine deterrent. The latter role was mainly through deep mining and nets, since depth charges of the power shown here were still under development.** MIDDLE LEFT: **The *Broke*, together with her sisters *Botha*, *Faulknor* and *Tipperary*, had been building to Chilean account when taken over in 1914. Badly damaged at Jutland (where *Tipperary* was sunk), she suffered severely at Dover.** LEFT: **Miles of steel netting, supported by floats, effectively closed the Dover Strait from the Goodwins to the Ruytingen Bank. Tended by a force of 132 drifters, such as the *Lorraine*, they were deployed as an anti-submarine measure.**

Flanders Flotilla, which had sunk several ships and bombarded coastal towns before withdrawing rapidly. Public opinion over the latter activities was outraged.

In April 1917, regular rotation of Flanders Flotilla boats saw the arrival of two dozen from the High Seas Fleet. Half of these were new craft, fast and well-armed. On the night of April 20/21 six each were despatched to Calais and Dover. Both towns were briefly shelled but, on withdrawing, the Dover force ran into the two big British leaders, *Swift* and *Broke*. The Germans were in line ahead, encountering their opponents on an almost reciprocal course, port bow to port bow. Both sides opened fire, the larger British ships turning hard to ram their enemy,

It was extremely dark and, blinded by her own gun flashes, the *Swift* just missed, running close astern of the G.42, the German tail-under. Both British ships also fired a single torpedo, one of which hit the G.85, the next in line. With both ships making 30 knots, the *Broke* then slammed into the G.42. Locked together, the two swung through 100 degrees. This brought the unfortunate G.85, already dead in the water, abeam of the *Broke*, which hit her with a second torpedo.

The *Swift* disappeared in pursuit of the four remaining enemy ships, receiving considerable punishment from their gunfire before finally having to abandon the chase.

The *Broke*, meanwhile, remained in the embrace of the stricken G.42. She was obviously settling, and her crew boldly attempted to board the *Broke*. As there had been no question of surrender, they were met with fixed bayonets, cutlasses, pistols and even "cups of hot cocoa". Also still under accurate fire from the nearby disabled G.85, *Broke* wrenched herself free and decided the issue with a third torpedo.

Her bows shattered, with just one serviceable gun remaining, the *Broke* took aboard as many survivors as she was able to locate, but had to be towed to Dover. Her commanding officer, Commander "Teddy" Evans was, thereafter, eulogized in the popular press as "Evans of the *Broke*", an incubus that he bore with good humour.

Further developments in destroyers to 1918

Warship development proceeded rapidly during World War I, driven by the dynamics of necessity and with the British and Germans, in particular, greatly influencing each other.

The destroyer (smaller examples of which were still termed "torpedo boats" by the Germans) was already by 1914 large enough to carry guns capable of disabling its opponents, while carrying torpedoes as the weapon of opportunity.

Torpedoes themselves were becoming more effective. The 21in "heater" torpedo, for instance, was available to the Royal Navy by 1910. It could range to 5,030m/5,500yd at 30 knots, carrying a 100kg/225lb warhead. Experimental weapons, however, were managing up to 9,144m/10,000yd at 30 knots, or 4,572m/5,000yd at 40 knots.

These increasing ranges led designers to give capital ships more powerful secondary armaments to keep destroyers beyond effective range. It seems to have been insufficiently appreciated, however, that even at 30 knots, a torpedo would take about 10 minutes to travel 9,144m/10,000yd. Its target would have moved a considerable distance in this time, making a hit by a single weapon unlikely. Only a mass torpedo attack against a battle line (so feared by Jellicoe at Jutland) would likely constitute real danger.

Pre-war French exercises suggested that close-range torpedo attack would be a different matter. This was partly confirmed at Jutland although, overall, the results here were unspectacular (the British firing a total of 94 torpedoes for six hits, the Germans 105 for two, possibly three).

> **"Boats are continually out of action with minor defects due to bad materials, workmanship and inefficient personnel … suppose due to shortage of skilled labour and good material … more easily met if we turned out fewer destroyers." February 1918 report by Captain (D) of the 13th Flotilla on his Modified R-class boats**

ABOVE: **The radiussed sheer strake on these German destroyers suggests that they are of the Vulkan-built T 150 type, although lacking a gun on the forecastle. These still have their peacetime pennant numbers painted up.**

BELOW: **The French *Commandant Bory* was one of the twelve-strong *Bouclier* class of 1911–13. Only the Bordeaux-built pair, *Bory* and *Boutefeu*, had equi-spaced funnels, the remainder having theirs in two distinct pairs.**

Raised forecastles greatly improved seakeeping. Having introduced the feature with the "Rivers", in 1903, the British retained it thereafter. The Germans had preceded this with a half-height forecastle in 1902 but full height only in 1908. The Americans were ambivalent, adopting it in 1909 with the *Smith* but abandoning it again, presumably to reduce topweight, in 1917. French boats carried forecastles from 1911.

The adoption of oil firing was not only a boon to weary crews, for it also influenced the size and cost of a destroyer. One ton of oil would take the ship as far as 1.32 tons of coal while occupying less space and being able to be accommodated in remote tanks. Space otherwise devoted to bunkers could be saved, although British destroyers had mediocre endurance.

LEFT: **A British 21in torpedo, showing its contra-rotating propellers. The single tube located between second and third funnels, together with what appears to be stowage for a spare torpedo in the foreground, suggests an Acasta, or K-class boat of 1912–13.** ABOVE: **American flush-deckers were notoriously narrow aft. Note the resulting limited number of depth charges that could be accommodated and the 4in gun trained on the beam to give space in which to work.** BELOW: **The late war-built "V & Ws" introduced superimposed main armament but they were deemed large and expensive, resulting in a reversion to a Modified Trenchant, or S-class, one of 67 such actually survived until 1947.**

Steam turbines, although compact and reliable, had the drawback of driving the shafts at undesirably high revolutions. Reduction gearing was complex and expensive, first going to sea in the L-class *Leonidas* in 1913. Propulsive efficiency was, thereby, much improved and less power was required for the same speed.

Destroyers grew inexorably in size, most being better than 1,000 tons displacement by 1918. Philosophies differed somewhat, with the British tending toward superior gun armament; the Germans, torpedoes. Most war-built German boats carried six tubes of 500mm diameter. Until the Improved W-class, late in the war, British equivalents had four of 533mm. American destroyers tended to be larger, due to the oceanic conditions in which they had to operate. Their flush-deckers carried 12 tubes, but with guns limited to 4in calibre. With the Improved W-class, the British increased gun calibre from 4 to 4.7in. This increased projectile weight from 14.1 to 22.7kg/ 31 to 50lb, overtaking the Germans, most of whose war-built boats carried the 10.5cm weapon, firing a 17.3kg/38lb shell.

To save on ship length the British introduced superimposed gun positions in what became generally known as "V & Ws". In them, they had a design which, with surprisingly little modification, would serve the Royal Navy and many foreign fleets for the next 20 years.

During hostilities, the British completed no less than 28 leaders and 255 other destroyers. Experience in war showed the need for two separate types, large and long-legged for fleetwork; smaller, and more heavily gunned elsewhere. Such specialization was not possible in wartime but, with the "Hunts" of World War II, one may discern a partial realization of the ideal. British destroyers were often later criticized for their conservative structural and machinery design, but they rarely suffered major breakdown and none was lost to stress of weather.

BELOW: **Several classes of slightly enlarged leaders were built or commenced during World War I, including the eight Scotts. Note the distinguishing black top to *Stuart*'s forefunnel and the fifth 4.7in gun between the funnels.**

RIGHT: **Nameship of her class of 1910, the 700-ton USS *Smith* was the first of what the Americans referred to as "flivvers". Ships of this size quickly proved to be too small, being superseded by the "thousand-tonners".**

LEFT: **Two Js and an F class at sea. With six rather than the eight 4.7in guns, the Javelins were introduced as cheaper diminutives of the Tribals. Their main armament could elevate only to 40 degrees, saving nearly 4 tons weight per mounting.**
ABOVE: **Otherwise excellent ships, the Js, in common with all other British destroyers, had totally inadequate anti-aircraft firepower. Most traded their after torpedo tubes for a single 4in High-Angle (HA) whose elevated barrel is here visible.**

Destroyer developments between the wars

World War I found destroyers playing roles for which they had never been designed. Catastrophic shipping losses due to the depredations of U-boats obliged a reluctant British Admiralty finally to adopt a convoy system during 1917. Where this improved matters dramatically it also gave destroyers, the only effective means to hand, a major new task as escorts.

Designed for speed rather than endurance, destroyer machinery was uneconomic and inefficient at continuous convoy speed. Depth charges, undergoing continuous improvement, accounted for 30 U-boats in the course of the war but hydrophones, as a means of detection, proved next to useless. Active sonar, then called ASDIC, was under development but, despite an enormous inter-allied effort, would not be available in practical form until the 1920s. Older destroyers, superseded for fleet work, would continue to find adequate employment as escorts.

LEFT: **Slightly enlarged versions of the war-built Admiralty Ws, the two Amazons of 1926 were designed to incorporate all wartime engineering improvements, particularly in machinery. They proved to be prototypes for the steadily evolving "A" to "I" classes, adding a flotilla annually until 1938.**

Destroyers also found a role in offensive minelaying, although the extra topweight had often to be compensated through the temporary removal of other armament or equipment.

Replacement British destroyer construction began in 1924, the two *Amazon* prototypes being essentially 1,350-ton improvements of the war-built W-class. Conservatively, the Admiralty then kept to much the same design for more than a decade, with the A to I classes improved only in detail, their torpedo outfit increasing from six to eight, then ten.

This persistence was contrary to developments abroad, where the United States, France, Italy Japan and, later, Germany, were building larger and faster ships, with comparable torpedo armament but with guns of 5in calibre or larger. The Admiralty followed suit in 1935–36 with the Tribal (eight guns, four torpedo tubes) and several six-gun classes (J to N inclusive) with ten tubes.

To complement these expensive "fleet" destroyers the Admiralty in 1938, again identified the need for numbers of smaller and less-capable vessels. The result was the four-gun "emergency" flotillas with full destroyer specification, beginning with the O-class of 1941, together with slower "escort" destroyers with little or no torpedo armament but with a

ABOVE LEFT: As built, the 16 Tribals of 1938 were held by many to be the most handsome destroyers ever. In light grey Mediterranean Fleet livery, the *Mohawk* also exhibits the red-white-blue recognition bands adopted during the Spanish Civil War. ABOVE: The USS *Maury* (DD.401) closes with battleship *South Dakota* in the Pacific. Single-funnelled, raised forecastle destroyers were unusual in the US Navy and were confined to designs of the late 1930s. LEFT: Although the British Nelsons were equipped with 24in torpedoes during the late 1920s, there was disbelief in the West, even as late as 1942, that the Japanese had brought a similar calibre into general use at the same time.

"It is not performance on trial which is in doubt, but operational reliability at sea." Wise words from the Engineer-in-Chief to the Admiralty Board in 1931, when asked to consider new-pattern auxiliary machinery for the C-class boats

powerful dual-purpose (DP) gun battery. Begun in 1939, these became the extensive Hunt classes.

Although during the 1930s the growing potency of air attack was becoming well-recognized, destroyer armaments, British or foreign, did not reflect it. Main armaments were of insufficient elevation to engage aircraft, while multiple machine guns and "pompom" type cannon were inadequate to deter dive-bombers, which were to prove deadly against them.

Throughout the 1930s American and Japanese developments were mutually influential. As early as the late 1920s, Japanese destroyers were carrying six 5in guns and nine 21in (soon to be uprated to 24in) torpedo tubes. Although their contemporary classes were faster, the Americans had no directly comparable ships until 1939–40.

An unusual feature of Japanese boats was an armoured box, adjacent to each bank of torpedo tubes and containing a full outfit of reloads. Despite the cost of torpedoes, Japanese commanding officers were trained to use them readily and aggressively. American ten-tube destroyers were given allocated space for a few reloads but, surprisingly, no weight margins, their design already being tight.

British destroyer design remained conservative and, by not attempting too much on limited displacements, produced reliable and seaworthy ships that were also able to survive severe battle damage. German and American designers were experimenting with advanced steam conditions to produce compact but powerful machinery developing up to 52,200kW/70,000shp for speeds of up to a claimed 38 knots. In contrast, the six-gun British J class of 1936 had a relatively simple 29,828kW/40,000shp installation that, with little further refinement, was repeated for all war-built "emergency" flotillas. With steadily increasing deep displacements, this resulted in speeds falling off to about only 32 knots maximum. As full power was rarely used, this was adjudged a fair price to pay for reliability.

A major problem for all would be the wartime accumulation of heavy equipment (reducing stability and endurance) and the overcrowding produced by many extra personnel.

ABOVE: The German *Leberecht Maass* and her sister *Max Schultz* were sunk in error by friendly aircraft off Borkum in February 1940. There was a heavy loss of life, the incident being officially attributed to mining.

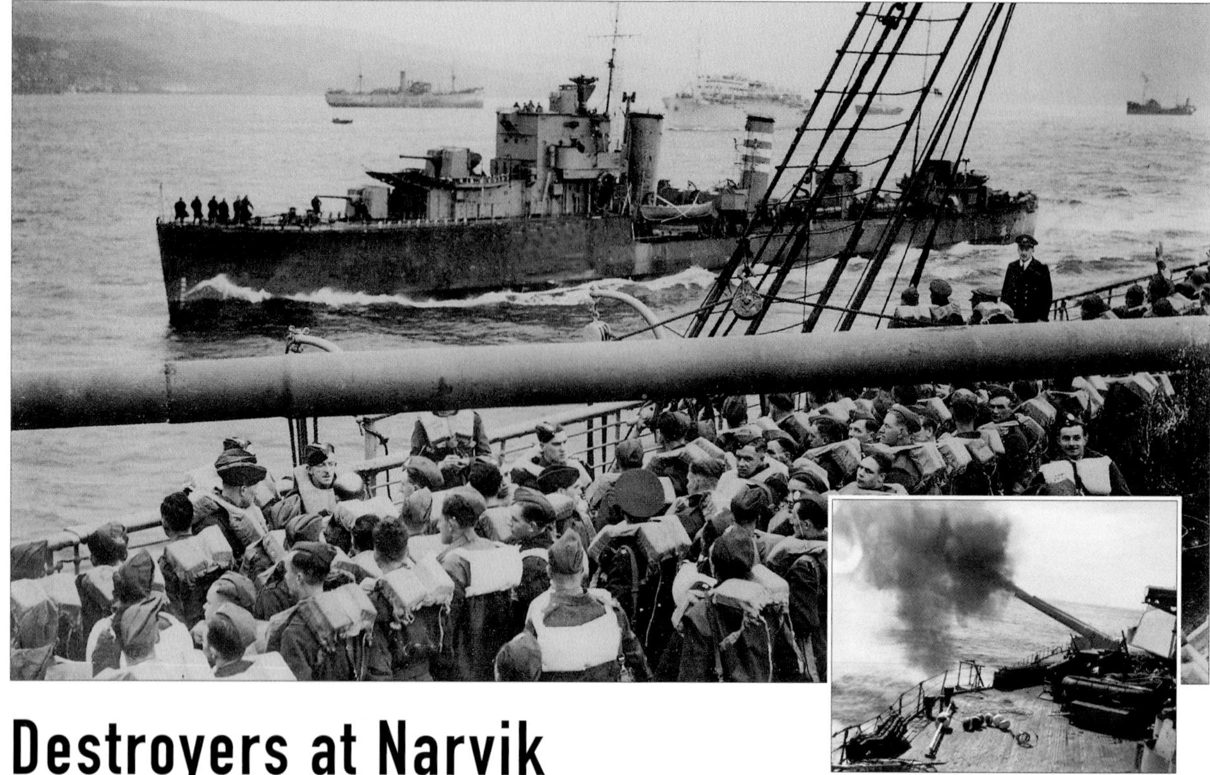

Destroyers at Narvik

Brilliantly executed, the German invasion of Norway demanded the mobilization of every available warship. Spearhead troops were landed simultaneously at Bergen, Kristiansand (South), Narvik, Oslo and Trondheim. There was considerable disparity in the length of sea passages involved and the British Home Fleet presented a major threat. Surprise was achieved, however, but, once in Norway, the German warships were open to attack.

Most remote was Narvik, over 1,609km/1,000 miles distant from Wilhelmshaven. Ten destroyers, covered by the battleships *Scharnhorst* and *Gneisenau* and transporting 20,000 troops, arrived on the evening of April 8, 1940. Alone, the destroyers then made the 160km/100-mile passage up the Vestfjord to Narvik. At dawn on the 9th they overwhelmed two elderly Norwegian warships and landed their force.

Powerful British forces were at sea and reaction was swift, Captain B. Warburton-Lee being ordered to Narvik with five destroyers of the 2nd. Flotilla. He had discretion to recapture the port but, at 16:00 on the 9th, during the long passage up the Vestfjord, he learned from Norwegian pilots that the enemy was there in strength. Warburton-Lee was, in fact, very considerably outgunned for, between them, the German ships could muster fifty 5in guns and eighty torpedoes against his twenty-one 4.7in guns and forty torpedoes. The enemy was also reported to have established shore batteries.

Screened by blindingly dense snow showers, the British arrived off Narvik at 04:30 on the 10th to find visibility there of about 1.6km/1 mile. Five enemy destroyers were present, their exact disposition not immediately obvious.

TOP: As troops in life jackets form up prior to disembarking from the transport *Oronsay*, they are passed by one of their destroyer escort, the *Fury* of 1935. The censor has removed the pennant number from her hull but has left her flotilla markings. ABOVE INSET: Admiral Whitworth's decision to take the veteran battleship *Warspite* into very restricted waters for the Second Battle of Narvik was a bold one, for his reconnaissance aircraft had proven the presence of U-boats and the enemy destroyers were torpedo-armed. The loss of eight fleet destroyers at Narvik, in addition to losses and damage incurred elsewhere, would affect German surface fleet operations for the remainder of the war.

Warburton-Lee attacked immediately with his ship, *Hardy*, leading *Hunter* and *Havock*. *Hotspur* and *Hostile* held back to engage shore defences. Totally surprised, two German ships were torpedoed alongside the pier, their commodore being among the many fatalities. The other three were damaged by gunfire before the British force rapidly drew back to regroup for a second attack. Stopping to destroy half-a-dozen enemy transports, however, they achieved little more before commencing their retirement.

It was now about 05:40 and, suddenly, the hitherto unsuspected remaining five enemy destroyers fell on the British from two directions. In a fierce manoeuvring action, swept by snow squalls,Warburton-Lee's destroyers now suffered from the Germans' heavier armament, the *Hardy* being driven ashore and the *Hunter* sunk before the three survivors escaped. In the Vesfjord, however, they encountered and destroyed a large enemy merchantman which was carrying the Narvik force's reserve ammunition. Warburton-Lee was awarded a posthumous Victoria Cross.

Only three German destroyers remained undamaged, with four more still in fighting condition. At the head of a long, many-branched fjord they were, however, trapped in a dead-end and vulnerable to further attack. This came on the 13th and in overwhelming force, the battleship *Warspite* being accompanied by nine destroyers.

Advancing up the fjord, the *Warspite* launched her Swordfish reconnaissance aircraft. This performed valuable service in warning the force of two enemy destroyers located in side fjords and positioned to ambush with torpedoes. Incredibly, the aircraft also sank one of two U-boats that had been sent in support.

The first would-be ambusher was overwhelmed without registering any torpedo hits. She did, however, raise the alarm. Of the remaining six, all but one were able to get under weigh.

Visibility was still indifferent and patchy and this, together with the destroyers' funnel and gun smoke, largely offset the value of the *Warspite*'s massive firepower. In a series of close and hard-fought exchanges the Germans, increasingly short of ammunition, were divided, confined and knocked out. Several British destroyers were hard-hit, the *Eskimo* losing her bows to a torpedo.

Without the necessary strength to reoccupy Narvik and aware of the *Warspite*'s own vulnerability, 161km/100 miles from the open sea, the Senior Naval Officer, Vice Admiral Whitworth, withdrew on the 15th. Three destroyers, particularly *Eskimo*, required temporary repair in a nearby "safe" area before their return.

The Germans retained Narvik but had lost half their fleet's total destroyer strength.

LEFT: As the background ship is the light cruiser *Emden*, these German troops must have been disembarking at Oslo. The cowl ventilators in the foreground are typically German mercantile, the vessel probably being one of two accompanying whalers. ABOVE: HMS *Hunter*, together with her sisters, *Havock*, and Captain Warburton-Lee in *Hardy*, penetrated Narvik harbour to engage enemy shipping. At point-blank range, the heavier German armaments proved decisive, *Hunter* and *Hardy* being disabled. BELOW: Warburton-Lee's ship at First Narvik was the H-class leader, *Hardy*. In this pre-war shot, she wears neutrality markings on "B" gunshield and her full leader's black forefunnel top. Leaders never painted up pennant numbers.

ABOVE: In 1940, "H" boats formed the Royal Navy's Second Destroyer Flotilla, identified by the two black bands on their after funnels. Being also a divisional, ie. half-flotilla, leader, *Hotspur* also carries a single band on her forward funnel. BELOW: The Fairey Swordfish, shown launching from a battleship catapult, could be fitted either with wheeled undercarriage or with floats. It could carry an 18in torpedo or 680kg/1,500lb of bombs. Armed with the latter, the *Warspite*'s Swordfish sank the *U-64* in the Herjangsfjord.

The raid on St. Nazaire

In the event that the great German battleship *Tirpitz* ventured into the Atlantic and had been damaged, the only dock available to her would have been the double-ended Normandie Lock at St. Nazaire. To reduce her options, the British Combined Operations Command was tasked with destroying the facility.

The resulting plan was to ram the outer lock gate (or "caisson") with an explosive-filled destroyer. This floating bomb would be timed to explode some 2½ hours after impact, during which time commandos would secure the immediate area while demoltion squads destroyed all auxiliary machinery. Despite a 644km/400-mile passage from Falmouth and 8km/5 miles up a shoal-strewn estuary with no operative navigation aids, surprise was essential, for the port was heavily defended.

Selected for immolation was the ex-American "four-piper" *Campbeltown* (late USS *Buchanan*), prone to machinery problems and transferred to the Royal Navy in November 1940. To reduce her draught, she was stripped of all expendible weight. Three tons of explosive, in the shape of two dozen depth charges, were packed into her bows. Topside she was given light armouring and a more suitable armament of light automatic weapons. Her aftermost two funnels were removed and the forward pair given angled tops to superficially resemble those of a German Möwe-class torpedo boat, of which five were based in the port.

Two companies of commandos, totalling 268 officers and men, were to be embarked, both aboard the *Campbeltown* and on 16 Motor Launches (MLs) accompanying her. There were in addition Motor Gun Boat (MGB) 314, acting as headquarters ship, and Motor Torpedo Boat (MTB) 74, charged with torpedoing the caisson should the *Campbeltown* be sunk. Four Hunt-class destroyers were available to provide passage escort, but not participating in the raid.

TOP: Key to the raid, the great German battleship *Tirpitz* could be accommodated in only one dry dock on the whole Atlantic seaboard of Europe. This, the Normandie dock in St. Nazaire, had to be denied her. ABOVE: Thoroughly wrecked, the *Campbeltown* lays with her crumpled bows overhanging the lock gate and her scuttled after end on the bottom. Apparently not having checked for explosives, a knot of Germans have gathered forward.

Having followed a circuitous route, screened by low cloud, the little armada arrived after dark on March 27, 1942. A British submarine, posted as a navigational mark, confirmed its position and the escort left, leaving the force to head into the estuary, and the hazards of its unlit shoals.

Covered by a diversionary air raid the force was within two miles of its objective before being challenged from the shore. The correct signal was flashed back (furnished by Ultra radio decryption operations intelligence), giving a few more precious minutes before the force, in the glare of searchlights, came under fire. Light and uncertain at first, this grew to a storm of multicolour tracer as the British replied.

LEFT: **Awaiting transfer to the British flag are seen three of fifty vintage American destroyers. Left to right, the USSs *Buchanan, Crowninshield* and *Upshur* became *Campbeltown, Chelsea* and *Clare* respectively.** ABOVE: **Taken some weeks after the raid, this aerial reconnaissance picture shows a useless dock, empty of water again but enclosed by an earth dam. The remains of the *Campbeltown* give an idea of the installation's vast dimensions.** BELOW: **The task of the British commandos was to hold a perimeter while demolition teams targeted and destroyed key features of the dock installation. With their means of withdrawal destroyed, the individual choice was simply between surrender or death, a choice already made by many.**

"There were tracer bullets going in every direction, a very colourful sight because the British tracers were all orange in colour and the German's were all a blue green." Lt Frank Arkle RNVR, ML177

ABOVE: **A major U-boat base, St. Nazaire was powerfully garrisoned by mainly German naval personnel who proved adept at street fighting. Here, a rating with a submachine-gun guards a wounded British Commando.**

Already badly holed, the old destroyer headed into an inferno, hitting the lock gate at 01:34 on the 28th. Her troops swarmed ashore to establish a perimeter, but those from the MLs experienced great difficulties. Their wood-built craft were literally being shot to pieces even before reaching the high walls of the dock entrance.

Expecting the *Campbeltown* to detonate at about 04:00, the surviving MLs and the MGB withdrew in good time, laden with wounded and any others available. Most of those ashore, however, had to be left for capture once their resistance was overcome.

Campbeltown's fuses malfunctioned. Abandoned, her stern submerged, her ruined bows rearing above the buckled caisson, she attracted the curious enemy, who were aboard in force when she exploded at 11:35. A wall of water smashed into the vast dock.

Earlier, just seven MLs cleared the estuary with the MGB to rendezvous with their waiting sea escort. They tangled briefly with German warships, which sank one, while two more and the MGB had to be scuttled. Just four MLs made it back to Plymouth, their damage bearing testimony to the action's ferocity.

Back in St. Nazaire, some 36 hours after the raid, the delayed-action torpedoes from MTB 74 exploded against the Old Entrance, causing further mayhem among the already jittery enemy garrison.

In terms of dead and missing, 24 per cent of naval and 22 per cent of total army personnel were casualties. The majority of army survivors were captured. Five Victoria Crosses, Britain and the Commonwealth's highest award for bravery, were awarded for individual and collective acts of valour. The dock remained inoperable for the remainder of the war, while the *Tirpitz* wasted the remainder of her short life in the North.

The "Tokyo Express"

Hot, humid and malarial, the Solomon Islands form a double-chain, aligned north-west/south-east. Some 1,086km/675 miles in length, they are separated by a channel that became known as "The Slot" to those who fought there.

During 1942 the Solomons were occupied by the Japanese who, in the July, began building an airfield on Guadalcanal. Its position flanked the vital Allied line of communication between Hawaii and Australia.

Admiral Ernest King, Chief of Naval Operations, well recognized the island's significance to the Japanese, it being their farthest point of advance through South-east Asia. Their communications and resources were already stretched, and King reasoned that an attritional campaign fought over Guadalcanal might well cost the Americans as much as their enemy, but the latter, with its greatly inferior industrial base and manpower reserves, would be less able to afford the loss. Accordingly, in their first Pacific amphibious operation, US Marines seized the still lightly defended island on August 7, 1942, in an ad hoc operation codenamed Watchtower.

The Japanese reacted quickly and effectively, badly defeating a joint Allied cruiser force off Savo Island, the first of what would be several major engagements.

> **"Tokyo Express' no longer has terminus on Guadalcanal."**
> **Signal from General Alexander M. Patch to Admiral William Halsey, February 9, 1943**

ABOVE LEFT: **For the Americans, Guadalcanal was the theoretical "line in the sand", beyond which the Japanese would not be permitted to advance. This wrecked A6M2 Zero/Zeke fighter is symbolic of the gruelling campaign of attrition that followed.** ABOVE RIGHT: **Following the disastrous Battle of Savo Island, an American destroyer division weaves in tribute to lost ships and men. The reconquest of the Solomons would result in a naval war of attrition in which the Japanese were ultimately defeated.**

The Marines, nonetheless, were firmly dug in and quickly completed the half-finished airstrip, proudly renamed Henderson Field. Wildcat (F4F) fighters and Dauntless (SBD) dive-bombers were flown in by carrier, allowing the Americans local superiority by day but, as their Official Historian so well put it: "As the tropical daylight performed its quick fadeout and the pall of night fell … Allied ships cleared out like frightened children running home from the graveyard … [for] then the Japanese took over".

The night belonged to the Japanese who, immediately following the Guadalcanal landing, began nightly destroyer forays down The Slot, sometimes accompanied by the odd light cruiser. They were mounted from their base at Rabaul in New Britain, at the head of the Solomons archipelago. Their function was to run in troop detachments and supplies, and they were timed to arrive after dark, discharge rapidly and be away, beyond the 400km/250-mile range of the SBDs, by dawn. These high-speed visitations, often accompanied by bombardment, were so regular that they were known to the weary Marine defenders of Guadalcanal as the "Tokyo Express".

The Japanese were skilled night fighters, with nocturnal vision that often out-performed American radar, and with a worrying readiness to loose a salvo of their feared 24in "Long Lance" torpedoes in the direction of perceived trouble. To avoid betraying their position they were rarely first to open gunfire. New to this type of warfare, the US Navy had much to learn but, absorbing the inevitable reverses, learn it did.

Seemingly refusing to accept the strength in which the Americans held Guadalcanal, the Japanese continued to use destroyer detachments to build their numbers a few hundred at a time. Any attempt by day did, however, prove disastrous, with their opponent enjoying air superiority.

To assist in daylight air control the Americans tended to station a carrier group away to the south. This also proved to be a magnet for the Japanese, a catalyst for several major engagements that well contributed to King's philosophy of attrition – a risky philosophy in truth for the US Navy was badly short of carriers.

On Guadalcanal, too, the Americans could never quite achieve the numbers necessary for a decisive push. Despite giving the campaign the highest priority, the Japanese were likewise constricted. To escape the lash of air attack, they operated largely beneath the fetid jungle canopy, where they suffered terribly from tropical diseases and malnutrition. With the "Tokyo Express" increasingly challenged by American forces, supplies had to be dumped offshore in buoyant containers, most of which were lost.

In February 1943, having lost 23,000 men, the Japanese admitted defeat, their indefatigable destroyers spiriting away the remaining 12,000. Japan's first major setback, Guadalcanal cost either side a total of 130,000 tons of warships, a total which only the Americans could fully replace.

TOP: American and British peacetime doctrine had been to conserve torpedoes, which were relatively expensive. It came as an unpleasant shock that the Japanese, seen here, were very ready to launch them in full salvoes and at considerable ranges. ABOVE: Hove-to and rescuing personnel from a stricken troop transport off Guadalcanal, the Japanese destroyer *Mutsuki* made a simple target for US Marine Corps SBDs which sank her by horizontal, rather than dive-bombing. LEFT: That the Japanese could dispute possession of Guadalcanal for over six months was due mainly to the valiant and persistent resupply runs made by Rear Admiral Raizo Tanaka and his light forces, whose activities instigated several actions.

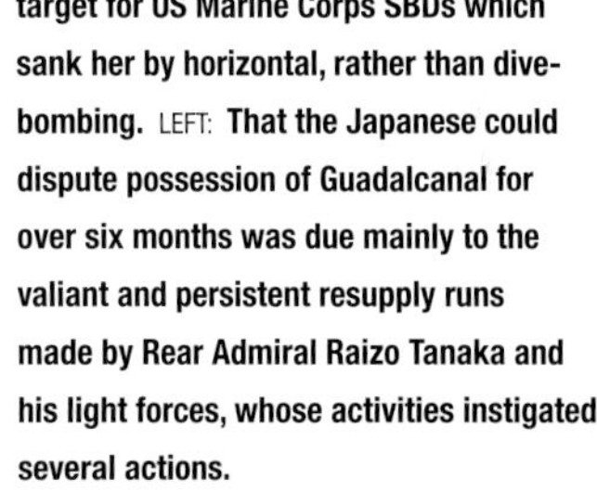

LEFT: The first Marine Corps aircraft alighted on Guadalcanal's Henderson Field 11 days after its capture and transformation from " a wallow of viscous mud". The key construction material was the perforated steel strip known as Marston Mat. ABOVE: Because of the element of chance, most fleets sought to avoid night actions. The Japanese, however, positively provoked them, obliging the Americans to follow suit in what was a painful learning process.

LEFT: ***Jamaica*, spruce again in post-war paint. Her electronic fit has been considerably augmented, "X" turret has been landed and 40mm Bofors AA gun barrels bristle her profile. She was scrapped early in 1961.** ABOVE: **Rear Admiral R.L. Burnett commanded the *Sheffield/Jamaica* cruiser force covering Convoy JW. 51B. In the prevailing conditions he was unaware of its precise position. Here, *Sheffield*'s bridge watch survey typical Atlantic weather.**

The action off the North Cape

In addition to U-boats, Arctic convoys were menaced by heavy German surface units and air power based by the enemy in northern Norway. As far as possible, therefore, convoys were run during the dark, winter months.

Such was JW.51B, which left Loch Ewe on December 22, 1942. Its close escort comprised six (later five) destroyers and five smaller vessels.

By December 30 the convoy was at about 73 degrees North and was headed eastwards, beyond the North Cape of Norway. The senior officer of the escort, Captain R. St. V. Sherbrooke in HMS *Onslow*, had ordered that, in the event of surface attack, he would leave his older destroyer, *Achates*, to screen the convoy with smoke while, with his modern ships, he would threaten the enemy directly with torpedoes.

Alerted to a convoy in the area, the German Vice Admiral Oskar Kummetz sailed from Altenfjord the same day with the 8in cruiser *Hipper* (flag), the 11in "pocket battleship" *Lützow* and six destroyers. His intention was to run eastwards along the convoy's anticipated route and, upon locating it, split his force, the *Hipper* attacking from the left flank, the *Lützow* from the right, making use of the uncertain visibility.

Kummetz was delayed by the *Lützow* being en route to an Atlantic foray, he being ordered to decline action with equal or superior forces to avoid her incurring damage. He was also unaware that two British 6in cruisers, *Sheffield* and *Jamaica*, had left North Russia to reinforce the convoy, which they were also trying to locate. At about 08:30 on the 31st the cruisers were actually about 48km/30 miles to the north of the convoy

LEFT: **Carrying her leader's black funnel top, the *Onslow* is seen in northern waters. Even in a moderate sea, she is continually swept by spray, penetrating every aperture and encouraging the formation of ice topside.**

LEFT: **Named after the faithful friend of Aeneas, HMS *Achates* equally kept faith with her convoy. Crippled and fatally damaged by the *Hipper*'s gunfire, her commanding officer dead, she continued to shield the merchantmen with smoke until she foundered.**

when one of the latter's escort sighted three enemy destroyers crossing its wake.

Visibility was about seven miles when, shortly after 09:30, the *Hipper* made her appearance. Sherbrooke transmitted an enemy contact report and moved against Kummetz with two destroyers, while interposing two more between the enemy destroyers and the convoy, now being covered by smoke from the *Achates*.

Sherbrooke's signal had been received by Rear Admiral R.L. Burnett in the *Sheffield* and, shortly before 10:00, and already under heavy fire, the escort commander was relieved to learn that the cruisers were bending on full speed to come to his aid. Shortly afterward, the *Onslow* received four direct hits, Sherbrooke being blinded and forced to devolve command of the escort force.

With the situation on the convoy's north side looking critical, the *Lützow* group then approached from the south. The *Hipper* was concentrating on the hard-working *Achates* and had already inflicted fatal damage when suddenly, at about 11:30, she was bracketed by 6in salvoes from Burnett's cruisers. Hit badly in a boiler room and in two further places, the *Hipper* hauled off. Totally surprised, Kummetz ordered a general retirement.

The *Lützow* had barely come into the action and had succeeded in damaging only one merchant ship but the *Hipper* was already being pursued by Burnett, who sank one of his destroyers. Despite having radar, Burnett lost the enemy in deteriorating weather conditions.

Burnett's tardy intervention had retrieved an unpleasant situation but the convoy's surviving without loss had been due primarily to Kummetz's constricting orders, obliging him to attack without conviction. Despite this, the badly mauled escort had defended their charges valiantly, Sherbrooke being awarded a well-deserved Victoria Cross.

TOP: **By far the most powerful warship involved, the "pocket battleship" *Lützow* (seen here pre-war) was subordinate to Vice Admiral Kummetz's *Hipper*, and was handled with a distinct lack of determination. She was herself sunk by bombing in Kiel in April 1945.** ABOVE: **Intended as the first of a class of five, of which two were never completed, the *Admiral Hipper* differed from her sisters in her straighter bow profile. At her bows she carries the arms of her namesake, commander of the scouting forces at Jutland.**

The action had an important and unforeseen repercussion in that Hitler, on learning of the outcome, was enraged. Despite the fact that he himself had ordered that his few remaining heavy units be used with circumspection, he accused Grand Admiral Raeder of running a supine service. Raeder, who had been Commander-in-Chief for 14 years, resigned in protest when the Führer ordered the decommissioning of all remaining major warships. He was replaced by Admiral Dönitz, who would concentrate primarily on pursuing a submarine war. There was an interesting historical precedent in that the same decision resulted from the inconclusive Battle of Jutland in 1916.

The sinking of the *Haguro*

Of the 16 heavy cruisers with which the Imperial Japanese Navy went to war, just six remained by May 1945. Of these, the *Haguro* was a marked ship, having participated in the heavy Allied defeat in the Java Sea early in 1942 when the British cruiser *Exeter*, the Australian *Perth* and several other American, British and Dutch ships had been lost.

In May 1945 the British East Indies Fleet again exercised sea control in the Bay of Bengal, and the landing at Rangoon in Burma isolated Japanese garrisons in the island chains of the Andamans and Nicobars. It was known that the Japanese intended to evacuate these forces and, on May 9, signals intelligence indicated that a "Nachi-class cruiser" would depart Singapore for the Andamans on the following day. Only just returned from Rangoon, a powerful force under Vice Admiral H.T.C. Walker sailed from Trincomalee on the 10th with the intention of making an interception.

Also on the 10th, two Royal Navy submarines patrolling the Malacca Strait reported the position of the *Haguro* and her accompanying destroyer, *Kamikaze*. Both were laden with supplies for those personnel that they could not evacuate.

During the next day a Japanese reconnaissance aircraft sighted Walker's force, submarines reporting that the *Haguro* had turned back as a result. Walker deliberately altered course to give the impression that he was engaged on another mission and signals intelligence duly indicated that, on May 14, the *Haguro* had sailed again.

"She was very large, and very black against a very dark monsoon cloud. An enormously impressive sight, just as a warship ought to look." Report by Lt Cdr Michael Fuller, pilot of the Avenger from HMS *Shah* which first located the *Haguro* [Note: The *Haguro* was actually painted pink]

TOP: **HMS *Khedive* was one of four CVEs involved in the hunt for the *Haguro*. This picture illustrates well the often windless conditions of the Indian Ocean, where heavily laden aircraft would experience difficulty in taking off.**
ABOVE: ***Shah*'s Avengers on this day were operating from HMS *Emperor*, as their own ship's catapult became defective. Because of the range, they were carrying no torpedoes, nor could they be supported by Hellcat fighters.**

The British had four escort carriers (CVEs) in company and, at 10:50 on the 15th, the *Haguro* was sighted by an Avenger, flying at maximum range. A small, follow-up bombing mission was unsuccessful but already Walker had sent on ahead the 26th Destroyer Flotilla, four V-class ships led by Captain M.L. Power in the *Saumarez*.

Spaced at 8km/5-mile intervals, and advancing on a line of bearing, Power's destroyers maintained 27 knots both to close their quarry and to get between him and his base. At 19:00 the *Haguro* was estimated to be 120km/75 miles distant to the north-west.

ABOVE: ***Saumarez* was, at the time, leader of the 26th Destroyer Flotilla. She had spent her earlier career with the Home Fleet, supporting Arctic convoys. Late in 1943 she was battle-damaged while participating in the sinking of the *Scharnhorst*.**

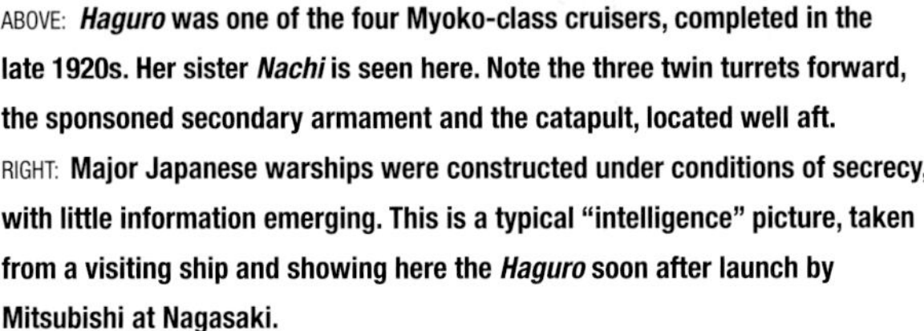

ABOVE: ***Haguro* was one of the four Myoko-class cruisers, completed in the late 1920s. Her sister *Nachi* is seen here. Note the three twin turrets forward, the sponsoned secondary armament and the catapult, located well aft.**
RIGHT: **Major Japanese warships were constructed under conditions of secrecy, with little information emerging. This is a typical "intelligence" picture, taken from a visiting ship and showing here the *Haguro* soon after launch by Mitsubishi at Nagasaki.**

All unsuspecting, the Japanese maintained a steady course and, at 22:45 and benefiting from exceptional radar conditions, the *Venus* reported a contact at 55km/34 miles. Soon after midnight the *Saumarez* acquired the target, and Power ordered a torpedo attack for 01:00, reorganizing his destroyers into a five-pointed star formation.

Just 6 minutes before the attack was due, the *Haguro* and her consort suddenly reversed course, closing the British at a relative speed of about 50 knots. The *Venus* passed within 1.6km/1 mile but was unable to retrain her torpedo tubes quickly enough to fire.

Before the British force could reorganize itself, the *Haguro* then abruptly turned eight points (i.e. 90 degrees) to port, probably to avoid torpedoes that she incorrectly assumed the *Venus* to have discharged.

Although in a position to attack, the *Saumarez* had to apply full helm to avoid the *Kamikaze*. Passing close under the latter's bow, she exchanged fire with both main battery and automatic weapons. As the *Saumarez*'s torpedo crews worked frantically to keep up with the changes of heading, their ship was suddenly brightly illuminated by a starshell from the *Haguro*, which then opened up with both main and secondary armament. The destroyer quickly took hits in the boiler space, the forecastle and through the funnel. As she lost speed, she slewed sufficiently to release a full outfit of eight torpedoes at about 1,829m/2,000yd range.

Power's dispositions had been sound for whichever way the *Haguro* headed she was menaced by torpedo. *Verulam*, undisturbed, fired at about the same time as *Saumarez* and, some ten minutes later, *Venus* and *Virago* coordinated their attack. Hit an unknown number of times, the *Haguro*, her decks cluttered with stores for the Andamans, sank at 02:09. The *Kamikaze* made good her escape as Power's destroyers, by now uncomfortably close to Japanese airfields near Penang, pulled out to the west to avoid dawn retribution.

ABOVE: **Seen post-war at Malta, the *Verulam* was built by Fairfield during 1943. She is here in full destroyer configuration but would shortly be completely remodelled as a Type 15 anti-submarine frigate.** BELOW: **By April 1945, Japanese defences were disintegrating, and Allied warships were able to undertake direct bombardment with little risk. Here, the *Verulam* is seen within easy 4.7 range of the port of Kotaraja, now in Indonesia.**

LEFT: **The *Laffey*'s conspicuous performance earned her a complete repair, although damage sustained would have justified writing her off as a constructive total loss. She is seen here in typical late 1950s Sumner-class configuration.**

ABOVE: **Struck by two enemy bombs on March 19, 1945, the USS *Franklin* survived what was reported to be the most severe fire damage experienced by any American warship. Cruisers USS *Santa Fe* and *Pittsburgh* stood by.**

Radar picket at Okinawa

Despite being subjected to weeks of preliminary softening-up and attrition by American carrier-based air strikes, the Japanese air force reacted strongly and with persistence to the former's amphibious landing on Okinawa on April 1, 1945.

A mass of offshore shipping, vital to progress on the island, lay vulnerable to attack from the air. For the previous six months such orthodox attack had been supplemented with kamikaze suicide missions. At Okinawa, the Japanese went further with mass suicide attacks, called *kikusui* and involving hundreds of aircraft.

Shore airstrips not yet being properly operational, defensive aerial countermeasures had to be mounted by the Fifth Fleet Carriers. To give early warning of incoming Japanese raids, a ring of radar picket destroyers was posted. These also carried fighter control teams, which worked to such good effect that the enemy identified the pickets as primary targets. This was countered by posting the ships, where possible, in pairs, supported by Landing Craft, Support (LCS), small vessels bristling with 20 and 40mm guns and rockets.

Over the ten weeks or so of the Okinawa operation, the Japanese mounted ten kikusui, involving an incredible 1,465 aircraft. No surprise then that the odd dozen or two could be directed at a picket destroyer, many of which suffered horrendous damage, sometimes fatal.

"Stands out above the outstanding."
***Laffey*'s performance, from the report of Rear Admiral C. Turner Joy, Commanding Officer of Unit Two, Task Force 54 Gunfire and Covering Force at Okinawa**

ABOVE: **Nimble ship handling ensured that most of the *Laffey's* kamikaze strikes were sustained well aft, while the Japanese pilot's tendency to aim for the superstructure meant that there were few solid hits to cause major failure of watertight integrity. Fires were kept well under control.**

On April 16 the Sumner-class destroyer *Laffey* (DD.724) was just one that suffered, this in the course of the third *kikusui* onslaught. Shortly before 08:00 she easily drove off a single "bandit", only to have her radar displays suddenly saturated with 50 or more contacts, spread over a 90-degree sector. By ill fortune, the standing US Navy Combat Air Patrol (CAP) was in the process of handing over to its relief, and response to this major threat was tardy. The attackers split to approach from a variety of directions, the CAP not intercepting until they were over their target, and having to fly through "friendly" fire in their pursuit. They accounted for several but were defeated by sheer numbers.

Over the next 80 frantic minutes the *Laffey* underwent 22 separate attacks, was hit by six kamikaze aircraft, four bombs and thoroughly raked by strafing.

Four suiciders opened proceedings by each crashing close aboard, one grazing the ship while the blast from the explosion of another deranged her fire-control radar. The first to hit clipped the hull with a wing, spinning around into the superstructure, its fuel causing a major fire. Another, damaged, "belly flopped" before bouncing into the after 5in gun mounting. The resulting inferno acted as a magnet, an aiming point for three further bomb-armed aircraft. The *Laffey*'s whole after end was, by now, a ruin from which no gun was left firing. Surprisingly, however, the hull was not yet badly holed.

Laffey's remaining electronics were written off when a Japanese attacker, with a CAP Corsair on its tail, flew through the mast. Both aircraft spun into the sea. Now dead in the water, the *Laffey* fought back, with LCS-51 doing her utmost to defend her charge. Those aboard the destroyer who were not manning her remaining guns were engaged in rescuing their mates from the nightmare of fire and searing steam that had been their ship.

At 09:47 the ordeal ended with a Japanese attacker, already shredded with automatic fire, exploding close enough aboard to shower the ship in flaming debris. The attackers had expended an unknown number of aircraft – nobody had time to count, but the *Laffey*'s diminished gun crews claimed nine. Just four 20mm weapons remained operable.

For 3 hours damage-control parties plugged holes and shored-up straining bulkheads to save their ship while surviving engine room personnel maintained steam although, with a jammed rudder, the *Laffey* was uncontrollable.

Eventually salvage tugs arrived, pumping and towing her to a safe anchorage. She had suffered 31 dead and 72 wounded but, more fortunate than others, she eventually returned to service.

TOP: Beach Yellow 3 on Okinawa. Four Landing Craft, Tank (LCT(6)) are at the tide line, with a Landing Ship, Medium (LSM) immediately behind and a Landing Ship, Tank (LST) beyond. Visible is a bulldozer, held by Admiral Halsey to be the third most important contributor to American victory in the Pacific.

ABOVE: Covered by a Fletcher-class destroyer, two Landing Craft, Support, Large (LCS(L)) move into the Okinawa beach area, April 1945. These Mark 3s were converted from Landing Craft, Infantry, Large (LCI(L)) and were heavily armed.

BELOW: *Laffey* was sufficiently sound to serve until 1975. As with all surviving operational Sumners, she underwent a major FRAM modernization, being reconfigured as shown here. In the foreground is the 2,200-ton Coast Guard cutter *Ingham* of 1936.

The submarine threat in 1939

Still, more correctly, a submersible, the submarine of 1939 spent most of its time on the surface. Conserving both power and air, it might remain submerged for 24 hours or more but would then be obliged to surface to recharge its batteries and its internal atmosphere.

Submarines were slow compared with surface ships, even though the latter were subject to weather conditions. For instance, the German Type VIIC boat, workhorse of the U-boat fleet, could make 17 knots on the surface (half the speed of a destroyer) but only 7½ knots submerged. Restraining her submerged speed to just 4 knots (a smart walking pace) she could travel a maximum of 128km/80 miles. It followed that a submerged submarine could not escape an escort by flight, only by stealth.

A further limitation of a VIIC was that she could carry only 14 torpedoes. As "spreads" were frequently launched to guarantee a hit, these could be quickly exhausted. A U-boat thus had to be resupplied at sea or spend most of her time on passage. A network of ocean re-supply ships was thus established, and these could be targeted.

To offset all these shortcomings, the submarine retained the enormous advantage of invisibility. While she could not be seen, she could, however, be heard. Machinery, propeller cavitation and water flow over the hull's many excrescences could, in quiet conditions, be detected on a sensitive hydrophone, the only method available during World War I. The sea, however, is never quiet, while the vessel carrying the hydrophone would, herself, generate noise. Work was already in progress in Great Britain, the United States and France to build an oscillator that would produce pulses of acoustic energy. These, transmitted through the water, would result in some of the energy being reflected from a solid body, such as a submarine. The reflected pulse would be detected by a hull-mounted hydrophone.

"We have got to the stage when the hitherto 'undetectable craft' is detectable ... the time is coming when we shall have to re-balance our theories as to the tactical use of submarines."
Minute by Rear Admiral Chatfield, Assistant Chief of Naval Staff, July 1921, following Asdic trials

TOP: **A sight to stir any destroyerman's heart. Destroyers, however, were designed for fleet screening and proved to be deficient submarine hunters, being short-legged and with insufficient accommodation, particularly for equipment.** ABOVE: **Woefully unprepared for submarine warfare, the Americans seemed powerless to prevent a handful of Dönitz's U-boats creating mayhem off the eastern seaboard early in 1942. Here, the tanker *Dixie Arrow* burns herself out.**

LEFT: **By 1945, the chance of a depth charge attack being successful had increased from five to seven per cent. Hedgehog, however, subject to less "dead time" eventually improved to about 30 per cent. Squid was even better, but arrived too late to affect the outcome.** ABOVE: **The 1930s-trained U-boat skippers were resourceful and dedicated. They enjoyed their initial "Happy Time" but, once they had been accounted for, their replacements deteriorated in quality as that of Allied escort commanders improved.**

Refinement of the system took time and the first production sets of what was termed Asdic (later Sonar) appeared in fleet destroyers only in the early 1930s. Acoustic transmission in the sea column is capricious but Asdic, in the hands of a trained operator, could determine the range and bearing of a submerged target. Importantly, however, it could not, at this stage, register its depth.

Ignoring the limitations of Asdic itself, but taking into account those of the U-boat, naval opinion, especially in Great Britain, greatly underestimated the threat that submarines again posed. This was encouraged further by Germany entering the war in 1939 with just 57 boats.

The primary anti-submarine (AS) weapon remained the depth charge, which had accounted for 30 U-boats during the earlier war. It was a simple drum, containing several hundred pounds of explosive and triggered by a hydrostatic switch at a predetermined depth.

This Asdic/depth charge combination had its own weaknesses. Fitted in a streamlined dome below a ship's forward keel, the Asdic transmitted pulses in a focused "beam", aimed downward at a fixed angle. For search purposes, it could be rotated in azimuth. Probing ahead at a fixed angle of declination, the Asdic inevitably lost contact some distance short of a submerged target. The attacker thus had to estimate the point, directly over the target, to release depth charges. Because the target's depth was not known, a "pattern" had to be dropped, set to explode at various depths. The charges themselves took time to sink and the cumulative "dead time" was sufficient to allow an astute submarine commander to manoeuvre clear of the lethal zone in good time, usually by a radical change of course.

What was required was a mortar-type weapon to project charges ahead of the ship, while the target was still "in the beam". The need for this had been identified by British scientists between the wars but, due to budget restrictions, the concepts did not progress beyond the prototype stage. As a result, ahead-throwing weapons, in the shape of such as Hedgehog, Mousetrap and Parsnip, did not enter general service before the end of 1941.

ABOVE: **Early depth charges were simple cylindrical containers that sank to the required depth painfully slowly. For any chance of success they were released in "patterns", being rolled over the stern from traps and fired on the beam from projectors.** LEFT: **An excellent example of the US Navy's graphic art, but note the "handraulic" loading and enlisted men apparently in dress suits. Reality in the Atlantic is more closely portrayed by the rig of the German ratings above.**

LEFT: **Although many commercial trawlers were hired by the Royal Navy, the service built several extended classes of "Admiralty Trawler", based on designs with proven seakeeping qualities. The censor has obliterated the pendant numbers of the A/S trawler *Turquoise.*** ABOVE: **In order to confuse an enemy as to her true heading, a British "Kil"-class patrol craft was given a near-symmetrical profile. The *Kildare*, seen here, was one of about 40 such 900-tonners, constructed during 1917–18.**

Escort vessels to World War II

Between the wars, Great Britain was an enthusiastic supporter of naval limitation agreements even though many of the adopted clauses proved to be more detrimental to her own interests rather than to those of her peers and, increasingly, prospective enemies.

Following Jutland, the unrestricted German U-boat campaign had brought Britain to the brink of disaster before the timely institution (or, historically more correct, reinstitution) of the convoy system. The British failed, before the cessation of hostilities, to develop a viable detect-and-destroy means of countering the enemy submarines. Intense effort at the 1921–22 Washington Conference to dispose of the threat simply by banning submarine warfare was negated by late allies intent in preserving it as "the weapon of the weaker navy". In response, the British clung to the unsubstantiated belief that the introduction of Asdic (Sonar) on a general scale would remove the submarine as a major threat.

Even after the hard cull of destroyers following World War I, the Royal Navy still operated a total of 16 flotillas, or 144 ships. These were considered insufficient to both screen the battle fleet and to escort convoys, a situation made considerably worse by the London Naval Treaty of 1930, at which Britain and the United States agreed to capping global destroyer tonnage at 150,000 imperial tons apiece. Japan negotiated an improved 10:7 ratio for a total of 105,500 tons.

For the purpose of the Treaty, a "destroyer" was defined simply as having a standard displacement of less than 1,850 tons and mounting guns of under 130mm calibre. The agreed ceiling represented something like a further 25 per cent reduction in the Royal Navy's 16 flotilla establishment, exacerbating the convoy-escort situation.

ABOVE: **The German Navy continued to build both "destroyers" (for fleet work) and "torpedo boats" (effectively light destroyers) for general escort duties. Of the latter, four of the six Möwe class are seen pre-war with the two modernized Schlesiens behind.**

Fortunately, Article 8 of the Treaty stated that no limit would be placed on vessels of under 2,000 tons provided that, *inter alia*, they:

i) mounted no gun of greater than 155mm calibre;
ii) mounted no more than four of greater than 3in calibre;
iii) carried no apparatus for launching torpedoes; or
iv) were powered for no more than 20 knots' speed.

Within these stipulations are found the basic parameters of contemporary escorts ("sloops" in British parlance), particularly once (ii) was dropped at the largely ineffective Second London Naval Conference of 1936.

Britain, still in recession, required large numbers of inexpensive convoy escorts, and divided them between trawlers, dual-role mine-sweeping sloops, (e.g. Bangor, Halcyon and Algerine classes), true sloops (Grimsby, Bittern, Black Swan) and corvettes (Flowers), of which only the Bitterns and derivatives were governed by treat limits.

Largely locked in internal rivalry, the French and Italians pursued different roles, the former opting for fewer, but larger, destroyers and the latter more numerous escort destroyers. These, confusingly, were termed Torpedo Boats (*Torpediniere*). Fast and generally below 1,000 tons, they were well-suited to Mediterranean conditions.

Through the Anglo-German Naval Agreement of 1935, the Germans were legally permitted to build to 35 per cent of current British strength. In destroyers, that represented 52,000 tons. Disturbing though German rearmament was, this total, in conjunction with the rest of their naval programme, was unattainable. The Kriegsmarine likewise opted for a mix of fleet destroyers and "torpedo boats".

With war looking inevitable by 1938 the British Admiralty looked to expand the destroyer force, complementing the large and expensive six- and eight-gun fleet destroyers with smaller vessels designed specifically for escort duties. These "Intermediate Destroyers", the extensive Hunt class, were really the equivalent to foreign torpedo boats. Like the sloops, they mounted an effective high-angle armament but had a greatly superior speed and a modest torpedo battery.

The Americans had also been looking to produce an escort destroyer but, with the US Navy's inherent dislike for small ships (which in the words of the naval historian Norman Friedman "saved very little money at a great cost in capability") made little headway until the British requested 100 hulls in June 1941, effectively crash-starting the excellent Destroyer Escort (DE) programme.

TOP: **The Italian Navy rarely receives credit for its effective AS operations, 1940–43. These Spica-class torpedo boats (*Libra* and *Climene*) were typical of those which accounted for many Malta and Gibraltar-based British submarines.** ABOVE: **Although launched in 1921, the Italian *Generale Achille Papa* could almost pass as a three-funnelled Royal Navy "L" boat of some seven years earlier. Constructed as destroyers, the Generali were demoted to torpedo boats in 1929.** BELOW: **An early example of a "Flower" with a long forecastle, HMS *Nasturtium* was one of three ordered from the design originators, Smiths Dock, to French account but purchased by the Admiralty in June 1940.**

ABOVE: **Classed as sloops by virtue of being relatively fast and being rated anti-aircraft escorts, the Black Swans proved to be most efficient anti-submarine ships. *Starling*, seen here, sank three U-boats and participated in the destruction of eleven others.** RIGHT: **The British equivalent of foreign torpedo boats were the very useful Hunt classes (this is the Type I *Garth*). Their dual-purpose armament made them effective against aircraft.**

Atlantic experience – the emergence of the frigate

On the basis that slow-moving U-boats would waste too much time travelling to and from the deep ocean, it was assumed pre-war that they would concentrate around traffic nodal points fairly close to land. Convoy escort was, therefore, considered largely in coastal terms. Even so, restricted budgets had resulted in little being done before 1939 to develop prototypes suitable for emergency series production.

During that year an earlier proposal, to use a modified whaling ship, was reconsidered. Designed to operate independently in the Southern Ocean, these little ships were supremely seaworthy and, produced to commercial standards, were of a size that could be built by many small yards. These were not only in the United Kingdom but also in the less-developed marine industry of Canada.

In view of the looming inevitability of war as the 1930s progressed, it appears remarkable in retrospect that the orders for the first tranche of what were to become the Flowers were placed only in the late July of 1939.

In practice, Dönitz's U-boats did not operate entirely as expected, working ever further out into the Atlantic, not least to keep beyond the range of ASW aircraft. Intended for coastal escort, the Flowers thus found themselves in conditions to which they were not suited. Seaworthiness was not a problem for, although wet, a Corvette (as she became officially termed) could ride the worst of seas. In doing so, however, she had a motion that induced nausea and fatigue in crews already tolerating the spartan conditions inseparable from small ship life. Mess decks were rarely dry, often flooded.

> **"I was half-sitting and half-lying ... my shoulders wedged ... with the pitching of the ship, I seemed to be alternately reclining with my feet higher than my head, and then bending over so that I tended to fall forward." Alan Easton, shipper of the Canadian Flower-class corvette *Sackville*, from his autobiography *50 North***

TOP: **By mid-1943, a high proportion of any Atlantic convoy would comprise standard, war-built ships. Laden with a low-density cargo and riding high, this unidentified Liberty ship was only one of over 2,700 built to the basic EC2-S-C1 specification.** ABOVE: **In addition to a huge Destroyer Escort (DE) programme, the Americans built about 100 Patrol Frigates (PFs) based on the British "River" design. *Anguilla* is one of 21 transferred to the Royal Navy, all of which were named after minor colonies.**

The usual track from the British west coast to the Canadian convoy terminal of Halifax was 4,023km/2,500 miles. Routed evasively to avoid known U-boat concentrations, however, a convoy could cover nearer 4,828km/3,000 miles. A slow convoy could thus be 2½ weeks in transit, while the frequency of the convoy cycle saw several on passage simultaneously. Until more ships were forthcoming, the strain on an inadequate escort force was thus considerable.

Early Asdics (Sonars) were not of great range, perhaps 1.8km/1 mile in reasonable conditions and, as the periphery of even a small convoy was considerable, the two or three

ABOVE: **Where the 761/865-ton Type VIIC was Dönitz's general purpose, "workhorse" U-boat, the various larger Type IX were designed for lengthy patrols to say, the US eastern seaboard or the Caribbean. The ultimate IXC/40 displaced 1,144/1,257 tons.** RIGHT: **To those participating, convoys appeared to present enormous targets to enemy submarines. They were, however, mere specks in the immensity of the ocean and, with intelligence-based evasive routing, could be safely shepherded around known U-boat concentrations.**

LEFT: **Symbolically No.100, the American Destroyer Escort (DE) *Christopher* hits the Delaware River at Wilmington on June 19, 1943. Many DEs served with the Royal Navy, which considered them very satisfactory, but with a violent motion.** BELOW: **HMCS *Sackville*, preserved as a museum ship, is the sole surviving "Flower" and fittingly commemorates the enormous contribution in men and ships that Canada made toward ultimate victory in the bitterly contested Battle of the Atlantic.**

typically available escorts had to work hard to give effective cover. This meant working at speeds considerably greater than that of their charges, consuming extra fuel and diminishing endurance as a consequence.

To extend the escorts' range, Replenishment-At-Sea (RAS) was adopted. This in turn, however, exacerbated the problems of their over-crowded accommodation, the Flowers' designed complement of 29 having grown under operational conditions to no less than 74. The extended forecastle of the modified design improved matters in terms of both space and wetness, but the steady consumption of fuel oil and of topweight, represented by sixty 136kg/300lb depth charges, served only to increase a corvette's liveliness.

Because they could be built at so many yards (a total of 23 British and 12 Canadian yards was involved), Corvettes – Flowers, Modified Flowers and, later, Castles – were being completed right up to early 1945.

Despite their numbers, however, Corvettes had effectively been superseded from April 1942, with the entry into service of the first River. Of a size and speed with a Black Swan-class sloop, this type was initially termed a Twin-screw Corvette before being reclassed as a Frigate (a title which, like Corvette, had been dormant since the days of the sailing navy). Still built to commercial standards, it was nearly half as long again as a Flower, with greatly reduced motion. Although the crew was larger, its amenities were much improved. To their considerable capacity of 150 depth charges was later added the forward-firing Hedgehog as it became available.

Operating on the surface, a U-boat could out-run a Flower, but not a 20-knot River, which also had better endurance. The simple but reliable 4-cylinder triple-expansion engine was, rather than the more complex turbine, selected for the great majority of both British- and Canadian-built escorts.

Convoy action – Battle of the Atlantic

Dönitz's tactics in the Atlantic included concentrating U-boats into groups or "Wolf Packs" which would form a patrol line across the anticipated track of a convoy. The boat making contact did not attack immediately but would vector-in the remainder to mount a simultaneous assault. Allied strategy, in turn, used intelligence to route convoys "evasively", around known U-boat concentrations. Although effective, this procedure did not always work.

On October 29, 1942, the 42-ship slow, east-bound SC 107 was nearing Cape Race, Newfoundland when it was seen and reported by *U-522*. The German radio intercept service had already discovered a mid-ocean rendezvous point for the convoy, and Dönitz now brought 14 boats together as Group *Veilchen* (Violet). These formed a line of search north-east of Newfoundland, awaiting the arrival of three further submarines.

On the 30th the local escort force handed responsibility for SC 107 to its ocean escort, the Canadian C-4 escort group. Even three years into the war, this comprised only one destroyer and four Flower-class corvettes, one of which was British. It was short of two units, one of which was the destroyer of the usual senior officer.

ABOVE: **The Royal Navy's "C" class of 1931 was curtailed at four ships. All were transferred to the Royal Canadian Navy, the *Comet* being renamed *Restigouche*. As an Atlantic escort, she has landed "Y" gun and her after tubes. Note the High Frequency Direction Finding (HF/DF) and Type 286 air search radar antennae.**

At this point, the convoy was still covered by land-based air and, working ahead, the Royal Canadian Air Force scored a notable opening success in exploiting German radio transmissions to surprise and sink the *Veilchen* boat *U-659* and the independent *U-520*.

Unfortunately, the short-range radio net used by the Allies to coordinate a convoy's defence was easily monitored by the attacking U-boats.

During the morning of November 1, SC 107 ran into the patrol line, whose *U-381* transmitted sighting reports. The escorts reacted immediately to make her submerge and to lose contact, but there were so many others in the area that, by dusk, five were in attacking positions.

German practice was to work on the surface by night, when their submarines' full speed could be utilized. The few early radar sets deployed by C-4 should have countered this, but all were unreliable or defective. Despite starshell illumination and determined intervention by individual escorts (two of whose COs had only five weeks' command experience), the enemy attacked boldly and continuously, torpedoing eight ships in 7 hours. Only one boat, *U-437*, was damaged sufficiently to oblige her retirement.

During November 2, the convoy was enveloped in thick fog and, despite being dogged by ten U-boats, lost only two further ships. A further Canadian corvette and a British destroyer arrived to buttress the escort.

LEFT: **Where a convoy might advance at only 8 knots or so, its escort, in rescuing survivors or investigating contacts, might fall well behind. A fast burst of speed to regain station could greatly deplete already limited bunkers.**

"Against such a scale of attack, a group of this kind cannot be expected to suffer other than heavy losses." Captain Hewlett Thebaud, US Navy, Senior Officer of US escorts based at Londonderry, commenting in writing on the report of SC 107's experience

Group *Veilchen* had not yet finished with SC 107. Attacking during the night of November 3/4, they took four more victims. One, an ammunition ship, exploded with such violence that it is believed to have destroyed her assailant, *U-132*, which disappeared without trace.

On November 4, the convoy's dedicated rescue vessel, loaded to capacity with over 300 survivors, was detached to Iceland with two escorts that were very low on fuel. One last ship was torpedoed and lost, but six U-boats had also to withdraw, themselves requiring fuel and torpedoes.

Finally having crossed the mid-Atlantic "air gap" on November 5, the convoy came under continuous air cover from Iceland, whence also arrived three American escort vessels. It proved to be the end of SC 107's travails, but the loss of 15 ships was serious and resulted in the British Admiralty, rather unfairly, severely criticizing the Canadians. SC 107's slow progress – it covered only 1,770km/1,100 miles in seven days, averaging 6 knots exposed it to a week of attack by up to 15 U-boats working together. C-4's ships were inadequate in numbers and, except for the destroyers, too slow. Their experience was limited and their defence was simply overwhelmed, just as Dönitz's tactics had intended.

The most effective procedure was to keep U-boats submerged, to prevent them using their relatively high surface speed and, thus, to lose contact. For this, more long-range maritime aircraft were urgently required.

RIGHT: By October 1942 the battle against the U-boat was being won. Early aces such as Kretschmer (seen here), Schepke and Prien had been eliminated, and operational effectiveness was declining.

ABOVE LEFT: Designed as a heavy bomber, the B-24, or Consolidated Liberator, proved to be an outstanding success as a maritime patrol aircraft. Stripped to accommodate extra fuel, it could cover the notorious mid-Atlantic gap. ABOVE: From a small, peacetime nucleus, the Royal Canadian Navy expanded rapidly by its own effort to become a major force in the Western Atlantic. British and American criticism of its early shortcomings was, in retrospect, unduly harsh. BELOW: Dönitz's single-minded objective in targeting every possible merchant ship was, militarily, a brilliant strategy. A single ship might, for instance, be carrying more armoured vehicles than could be lost in a major tank battle.

"Johnny" Walker and the Anti-submarine Support Group

In September 1941, Commander Frederick J. Walker was ordered to Liverpool to take command of HM sloop *Stork*, as a senior officer of the Western Approaches Command's 36th Escort Group.

Escort groups were a comparatively new concept, possible only with increasing numbers of escorts. Ideally homogeneous in terms of ship types, groups underwent brief but intensive training at Tobermory on Mull, Scotland, thereafter being kept together to develop a high degree of mutual understanding.

The primary duty of the senior officer of a convoy escort lay in the "safe and timely arrival" of his charges. With too few escorts, each stretched to its limit, the destruction of U-boats was secondary to just "keeping them down", where their low speed prevented their further intervention. Escort groups, however, comprised about eight ships (although, at any time, two might expect to be in dock) and the odd unit or two might usually be spared to prosecute a contact to conclusion. This was made clear in the Operational Instructions issued by Walker to his commanding officers. "The particular aim of the Group", he wrote, "is ... the destruction of any enemy which attacks the convoy." Walker's preferred methods involved several ships and a generous expenditure of depth charges.

It was already recognized that the presence of an Escort Carrier (CVE) acted as a force multiplier to enable an escort force to adequately cover the long perimeter of a convoy. The prototype British CVE, HMS *Audacity*, had already made her mark when, in December 1941, she was allocated, together with Walker's group, to the Gibraltar-UK convoy HG 76.

The 32-strong convoy passed beyond Gibraltar-based air cover on December 17, and, for four days, until it came within UK-based air cover, depended upon *Audacity*'s half-dozen fighters for local support. Besides forcing U-boats to submerge, the Martlets could also direct escorts to the spot. During four days of almost continuous action, Walker's ships were able to sink five U-boats. Although the carrier, a prime target, was lost, together with a destroyer and two merchantmen, it was a decided victory for the defence. In recognition, Walker was awarded the first of his eventual four Distinguished Service Orders.

LEFT: **During one of Walker's "rolling carpet" depth charge attacks, *Starling*'s after end could be a very busy place. The rapid replenishment of 136kg/300lb depth charges required dedicated team work, although conditions here are relatively benign.** ABOVE: **Stark though it was, Liverpool's Gladstone Dock was always a welcome sight to a weary Western Approaches escort. Admiral Sir Max Horton has "cleared lower decks" to cheer in the returning *Starling*. Her upper mast detail has been censored.**

LEFT: **Built to full naval, rather than mercantile, standards, the Black Swans and their improved successors were necessarily built in fewer numbers. Conspicuous on *Starling* is the aft-mounted "lantern" of her Type 271 surface-search radar.**
ABOVE: **No "gift horse" was ever better utilized. The first British escort carrier, *Audacity*, was remodelled from the captured German merchantman *Hannover.* Her career was short but she proved the value of a CVE in the defence of convoys.**

"No officer will ever be blamed by me for getting on with the job in hand." From Walker's Operational Instructions to the 36th Escort Group

A series of convoy actions confirmed his methods and his determination but, already exhausted when promoted Captain in July 1942, Walker was rested in a shore billet for six months. Following his repeated requests for a further sea command, however, he was given the new sloop *Starling* in January 1943, transferring to her the experienced crew of the *Stork.*

With five others of her class, *Starling* formed the Second Support Group. Support groups differed from escort groups in being intended to reinforce the escort of any convoy that found itself strongly attacked.

Besides drilling his ships into a state of high efficiency, Walker developed new attack tactics. A problem with contemporary Asdic (Sonar) was that it lost contact for the final stage of an attack approach. Depth charges were thus dropped on an estimated position, with additional error being possible through "sinking time". Walker's method was to follow the target, at the same speed and at about 1,829km/2,000yd range. Aware of his Asdic, the submarine had no immediate reason to evade. One thousand yards ahead of Walker, however, steering the same course at a silent 5 knots, and with Asdic secured, was a second sloop. Under Walker's direction, this vessel slowly overtook the unsuspecting target, rolling over a large depth charge pattern. Its detonation would be U-boat's first intimation of danger, usually too late to allow effective evasive action.

For deep-diving or "difficult" targets, a variation was to use three sloops in line abreast to release a lethal, rolling carpet of depth charges, saturating the whole target area.

Improved Sonars and ahead-throwing weapons largely cured the problem but Walker's ingenuity proved that it was possible to work effectively within the limitations of then-current equipment.

An inspirational leader, slated for flag rank but worn out by constant sea service, "Johnny" Walker collapsed and died in July 1944. He was just 48 years old.

ABOVE: **Known to the US Navy as the Grumman F4F Wildcat, the Martlet entered service with the British Fleet Air Arm in 1940. Tough enough to withstand the rigours of carrier life, it served both with the fleet and, as here, on CVEs.**
LEFT: **The 2nd Escort Group seen from the *Starling. Loch Fada* is followed in order by *Wren*, *Dominica* and *Loch Killin.* The tall pole mast of the US-built *Dominica* contrasts with *Wren*'s tripod and the *Loch*'s sturdy lattice masts.**

Escort carrier Support Groups – taking the fight to the enemy

ABOVE: **During 1943 the US Navy formed five anti-submarine groups based on CVEs such as the *Block Island* (CVE-21). Known to the Americans as hunter-killer groups, they could operate independently by virtue of Ultra information.**

The first three years on the North Atlantic were all about survival, with inadequate and dangerously extended Allied AS resources covering UK-bound convoys in the face of unremitting submarine attack. This was Admiral Dönitz's chosen battleground, where his forces could destroy the greatest amount of tonnage for the least effort. Only reluctantly did he deploy extended-range boats farther afield, notably to the Caribbean and West Africa. In general, these forays resulted in fewer sinkings but were useful for their nuisance value, diverting scarce Allied defence resources.

With Allied war production getting into its stride, however, the North Atlantic and the Bay of Biscay transit area were, by mid-1943, becoming dangerous for U-boats. Dönitz responded by temporarily moving the centre of gravity of his operations southwards. Land-based aircraft from Bermuda, Morocco and Brazil proved inadequate (the Azores were not yet available) and the US Navy decided to allocate some of its earlier Escort Carriers (CVEs) to the theatre.

U-boats despatched to remote areas expended much time and fuel in transit and, to keep them on station longer, replenishment was required. It had been standard procedure for homeward-bound boats to transfer spare fuel or torpedoes to those remaining but the procedure was difficult. Special resupply submarines were thus built, notably the Type VIIF "torpedo carrier" and the Type XIV "U-tanker", which cruised the area, meeting depleted boats by appointment. They were particularly valuable targets and, as their activities were frequently identified through Ultra signals intelligence, advantage was taken by the Allies now that the means had become available.

During the latter half of 1943 the US Navy created the first half-dozen "hunter-killer" groups, each based on an 18-knot CVE with about two dozen aircraft, usually Wildcats and Avengers. Four to six escorts were provided, latterly new Destroyer Escorts (DEs) but, initially, veteran "four pipers". Like the already constituted British Support Groups, the Americans were intended to reinforce dedicated convoy escorts when particularly threatened (notably on the US–Gibraltar route) but, otherwise, to seek out and destroy U-boats wherever they could be found. Before the advent of information from Ultra, such speculative hunts in a vast ocean were an impractical waste of resources but high-grade intelligence made specific targeting possible. Ultra, however, was neither guaranteed nor continuous, and the U-boats' greatest enemy continued to be the endless radio chatter generated by Dönitz's centralized control. All Allied AS vessels now sported the birdcage antenna of "Huff-Duff" (High Frequency Direction Finding, or HF/DF), which could give an accurate bearing on a transmitting boat.

LEFT: **Successor to the F4F Wildcat, the F6F Hellcat became the US Navy's standard fighter from 1943. Working from CVEs, they strafed surface U-boats to suppress defensive fire while an Avenger approached with depth charges or homing torpedoes.** BELOW: **The Avenger torpedo-bomber built by Grumman was designated TBF or TBM depending upon its source of manufacture. Its cavernous ventral compartment could accommodate a full-sized 18in torpedo or 907kg/2,000lb of bombs.**

"Presence of escort aircraft carriers with the convoys make operating conditions so difficult for the U-boats that they are not likely to meet with success." Dönitz's Command War Diary, extract from entry for July 11, 1943

First on line was American Support Group 6, comprising the carrier *Bogue* and two veteran destroyers. They were joined at intervals by further groups based on the CVEs *Card*, *Core*, *Santee*, *Croatan* and *Block Island*. Their Wildcat fighters would typically surprise and strafe a surfaced U-boat to suppress return fire for a follow-up Avenger to deliver a knockout with depth charges or, increasingly, a "Fido" homing torpedo.

Allowed to roam freely within support distance of major convoy routes, the CVE groups achieved considerable success. Submarines were frequently caught on the surface in twos, or even threes, in the process of replenishment. It was far from being a turkey shoot, however, for many U-boats were now being armed with quadruple 2cm anti-aircraft guns and, in pressing home their attacks, many aircraft were heavily damaged or destroyed. Against the AS escorts, the Germans were also deploying acoustic torpedoes.

Remarkably, the only CVE lost on these profitable operations was the *Block Island*, destroyed by *U-549* with three conventional torpedoes. With a homing weapon, the latter then blasted the stern off an escort before herself succumbing to Hedgehog salvoes. The *Block Island* group had already accounted for six U-boats.

The CVE groups exploited the technical limitations and over-tight control of U-boats which, ultimately, were responsible for the failure of their campaign.

ABOVE LEFT: **A submariner of World War I, Admiral Dönitz ran a devastating U-boat campaign against the Allies. That it was ultimately adjudged fair was illustrated by Admiral Nimitz's testimonial on Dönitz's behalf during the post-war Nuremburg Tribunal.** ABOVE RIGHT: **Caught on the surface, a Type IX is lashed as she attempts to dive. Unfortunately for her, the aircraft would follow up with a depth charge salvo or a homing torpedo just ahead of the swirl that marked her submergence.** BELOW: **The sort of rendezvous that Support Group pilots dreamed of interrupting. In order to extend their patrols, operational U-boats were directed to meet up with Type XIV resupply boats for fuel, torpedoes and fresh stores.**

LEFT: **The 24 bombs of the Hedgehog were mounted on long spigots, angled so as to place the projectiles in a circular or elliptical pattern. As they exploded only on contact with a submerged target or the bottom, the bombs were not set for a specific depth.**

Improved weapons, sensors and escorts

As noted above, early Asdic (Sonar) had the unfortunate characteristic of losing contact with submerged targets at ranges below 100–150m/109–164yd. An AS vessel thus released depth charges on an estimated position, a shortcoming exacerbated by the time that the weapons took to sink to the desired depth. The result was "dead time", during which the target could take evasive action.

British Admiralty scientists were well aware of the Navy's problem, postulating that the solution lay in a mortar that could fire depth bombs ahead of a ship, while the target was still fixed in the Asdic beam.

During the 1930s a weapon was sea-tested and proved capable of throwing a small bomb up to a half-mile ahead. Although it was progressed no further, it led to proposals for two further weapons, a triple-barrelled mortar capable of firing three 200kg/440lb bombs, and a multi-way ejector throwing up to twenty smaller projectiles. From 1941 both concepts were given high priority.

The latter idea was the simpler, entering service late in 1941 as the Hedgehog. It fired 24 contact-fused bombs loaded on to spigots. Because of the powerful recoil forces, the bombs were electrically ripple-fired, the spigots aligned so as to drop them in a circle of some 35m/38yd diameter, centred about 200m/218yd ahead of the ship. Each 30kg/65lb bomb contained half its weight of explosive, sufficient to hole a submarine hull. Somewhat more streamlined, the bomb sank twice as fast as a depth charge.

"Anti-Dive Bombing Equipment."
Officially, the explanation to be given to casual enquirers of the purpose of Hedgehog during its secret introductory phase

ABOVE: **Converted to a radar picket (DER), the American destroyer escort *Thomas J. Gary* retained her Hedgehog in the superfiring position forward. Further to a massive electronics upgrade, she has received an enclosed bridge and long amidships deckhouse.**

Hedgehog was initially very unpopular. Mounted on an exposed foredeck, it required constant maintenance. There was no reassuring "big bang" of a depth charge, unless the bombs actually contacted the target.

Hedgehog's first "kill", nonetheless, was in February 1942 and, by the end of the year, over 100 British ships had been so fitted. It was also adopted wholeheartedly by the US Navy.

ABOVE LEFT: **The American Mousetrap was Hedgehog redesigned for smaller craft. The fierce recoil forces associated with firing the Hedgehog bombs was nullified by making the Mousetrap rounds rocket-propelled** TOP: **Designed around a double Squid installation, the British Lochs were given spacious accommodation for it forward of the bridge. *Loch More* was completed just before the war's end, but the class was greatly curtailed by cancellations.** ABOVE: **Compared with that of a Loch (see above) the platform for a Castle-class single Squid was much shorter. "Castles" were too large to be built in Canada and were transferred from the Royal Navy. The Royal Canadian Navy's *Tillsonburg* was thus built as HMS *Pembroke Castle.*** BELOW: **The triple-barrelled Squid was built into a compact frame which allowed the weapon to be automatically roll-compensated. Barrels were angled to place the bombs in an equilateral triangle, and were lowered to the horizontal for loading.**

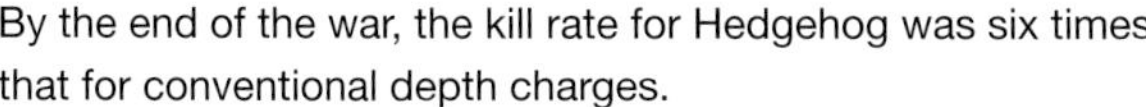

By the end of the war, the kill rate for Hedgehog was six times that for conventional depth charges.

Improvements to U-boats included tougher hulls for deeper diving. There began to be doubts that the Hedgehog bomb was sufficiently lethal, and work was accelerated on the triple-barrelled mortar. Called Squid, this entered service in September 1943. Like that of the Hedgehog, the launcher was roll-stabilized, and its three bombs each weighed 180kg/390lb, again half of which was explosive. The projectiles fell in an equilateral triangle of side 35m/38yd, and centred some 250m/273yd ahead of the ship. They sank four times as rapidly as depth charges.

"Double Squid" proved to be particularly effective as, in plan, the two triangles formed a six-pointed star (i.e. with a relative offset of 60 degrees), with the two salvoes separated by about 20m/65ft in depth.

Squid was teamed with new Type 147 Asdic. This generated a precise, fan-shaped beam that could be depressed through a vertical range of 45 degrees. A specially adapted pen recorder gave a visual readout of range and depth of the contact. This data was communicated directly to Squid, which was fused and aligned automatically.

By the end of the war, Double Squid's kill rate was nudging 40 per cent. It was supplied to the US Navy, which service did not pursue it, preferring to rely on Hedgehog while it developed its own weapons.

A probable reason was that the system, with its magazines and handling spaces, was too demanding in space and weight to retrofit economically into large numbers of war-built ships. A major shortcoming was the tight design of the otherwise excellent destroyer escorts (DEs), making them unsuitable for modifications to accept Squid.

Fully committed to the weapon, the British designed the Loch-class frigate around the Double Squid and the Castle-class corvette around a single. Their firsts-of-class commissioned in December 1943 and September 1943 respectively. To accelerate the programme, Lochs were assembled from modules prefabricated in numerous facilities.

LEFT: **Type XXIs in the Blohm and Voss yard in Hamburg in May 1945. The fast electric boats, assembled from modules to production-line principles, posed a serious threat to the Allies but, fortunately, came too late to have any impact.**
ABOVE: **The head of an extensible Schnorkel for a Type XXI featured what was effectively a large ball-valve. The small stub on the top was to support a radar detector, and surfaces are meshed to reduce radar reflection and to improve flow.**

The emergence of the fast frigate

Early in 1943 the Germans acknowledged that convoy defences were getting the better of U-boats, and looked for a radical solution. The major shortcomings of existing boats were their very limited submerged endurance and speed, making it necessary to surface daily to recharge batteries, to renew the internal atmosphere, or to keep station on a convoy. Surfaced, and despite warning devices, they were vulnerable to detection and attack by increased numbers of aircraft, both shore-based and from escort carriers.

The resulting Type XXI U-boat was a major step forward in submarine design. Its large and deep hull contained three times the battery power of earlier boats while, externally, the hull was "cleaned-up" to minimize hydrodynamic drag. Schnorkel (or "Snort") was also under urgent development to permit extended submerged operation.

Tests predicted a Type XXI to be capable of submerged speeds of 18 knots for 1½ hours, or 12–14 knots for 10 hours. Hampered by surface conditions and the need to operate Asdic/Sonar, conventional convoy escorts would be unable to cope with such performance.

The Type XXI was assembled from large, prefabricated modules. These came from widely dispersed facilities and depended upon transport via inland waterways that were vulnerable to strategic bombing. This, together with acute shortages in skilled labour and materials, saw the production schedule slip to the point that the first-of-class "went operational" just four days before close of hostilities.

ABOVE: **Following the construction of two "hydrogen peroxide boats" to German principles, the Royal Navy abandoned the idea as impracticable. The ultimate goal would have been an atmosphere-independent boat, requiring no "Snort".**

Any relief at this, however, was short-lived for, with the immediate onset of the Cold War, the Soviet Union utilized captured German technology to produce a large submarine fleet of which the backbone were 236 Project 613, 644 and 665 known to NATO as the "W", or Whisky-class submarines and a near copy of the Type XXI.

Escalation to full hostilities would, once again, see Atlantic convoys as the keystone of Allied strategy, and a cash-strapped Royal Navy had to respond. The only new buildings that could be afforded were four each of Anti-Aircraft (AA) and Aircraft-Direction (AD) frigates. To provide fast frigates, capable

ABOVE: **A double Limbo installation in the after well of what appears to be a British Type 12 frigate. A major difference from Squid was that the weapons, fully stabilized in both roll and pitch, lifted their bombs over the ship's superstructure.** BELOW: **Converted to a Type 15 fast frigate, the British destroyer *Grenville* shows her Limbo installation. She was fitted with a small flight pad for initial experiments with a helicopter, in the interests of increasing stand-off capability.**

of meeting the new submarine threat, it was decided to convert some of the 32-knot war-built fleet destroyers, many of which had seen little service.

Suitably strengthened, these were capable of being driven at 25 knots in Atlantic conditions, while realizing a range of 5,311km/3,300 miles at 15 knots. The full conversion (Type 15) had an AS armament including Double Squid (or its successor, Limbo) and eight fixed tubes to launch the new Mark XX homing torpedo, which could work to the limit of range of contemporary sonars. Even these ships proved to be too expensive, so a limited conversion (Type 16) was produced in parallel. About two dozen destroyers were so modified between 1950 and 1958, but proved that speed alone did not provide the complete solution.

ABOVE: **The Type 81s (Tribals) were the first British frigates designed around a shipborne helicopter. The elevated flight pad, located well forward, formed the roof of deckhouse which became, via an elevator, the hangar for the aircraft.**

> **"Sometimes, the exhaust clouds would turn from grey to black and then, to the stupefaction of all who saw them, suddenly erupt into cataclysmic fireballs of smoke and flame as the oxygen in the atmosphere completed the combustion begun inside *Explorer*."**
> **Report of surface trials with Britain's first hydrogen peroxide-fuelled submarine HMS *Explorer* (known to the Navy as *Exploder*!), quoted in *Daily Telegraph* of November 18, 1999**

During the war, the Germans had persevered, but failed, in their attempts to produce a hydrogen peroxide-fuelled, turbine-driven submarine capable of bursts of very high submerged speed. The Soviets had also inherited this technology. All attempts to make it work failed ultimately, due to the dangerous instability of the fuel but, from 1954, emerged the even greater threat of the nuclear attack submarine (SSN). Somewhat slower than the abortive German hydrogen peroxide-fuelled "Walter" boat, the SSN had an effectively infinite submerged endurance and posed a far more serious problem.

As no affordable AS ship could realistically hope to track an SSN bent on evasion, the adopted solution was to build a slower frigate that deployed a rapid-reaction stand-off weapon. For a ship acting alone, the range of such equipment was limited to the useful range of the ship's sonar. The US Navy opted for a rocket-propelled missile (that became ASROC) which could compensate for long-range inaccuracy by its ability to carry a small nuclear warhead. The more radical British solution was to put a light helicopter aboard the ship. Since initial trials in 1956, frigate design has become ever more driven by helicopter requirements.

Into the missile age

World War II, and the ensuing Cold War, redefined the destroyer. For instance, in 1939 the Royal Navy began commissioning its J-class destroyers. Designed for surface warfare, their six 4.7s and ten torpedo tubes resulted in a 23 per cent increase in legend displacement. Their main armament, with its 40-degree elevation, could hardly be termed "high angle", however, while their few minor weapons proved to be no deterrent to a dive-bomber. Even using small patterns, their full outfit of 30 depth charges could be exhausted in prosecuting a single submarine contact.

By 1945, armaments reflected the fact that the major killers of destroyers were aircraft and submarines, not other ships. In the Royal Navy, this had brought about two, separate evolutionary lines.

Launched from 1943, the Battles were intended for Pacific operations, with about 20 per cent greater endurance than a J-class boat. Designed around the air threat, their four 4.5s were truly dual-purpose, housed in two, forward-facing gunhouses and capable of 80-degree elevation. Eight torpedo tubes were carried but the after end was dominated by two fully stabilized, twin 40mm mountings.

The second development, launched from 1945, was directed at the new threat of the fast submarine. Smaller than the Battles, the Weapons were designed around four 4in High-Angle (HA) guns and an ahead-firing Anti-Submarine (AS) mortar (first a Hedgehog, latterly a Squid). They carried a full outfit of torpedo tubes but also up to 70 conventional depth charges. "Conventional" submarines were, by now, the business of frigates but the German Type XXI "Elektroboote" were capable of bursts of submerged speed which, at that time, only a destroyer could match.

The dedicated AS destroyer proved, however, to be an evolutionary dead-end, displaced by rapidly improving frigate design. The finale of the Pacific war, meanwhile, had shown that it was not sufficient to shoot down a suicide aircraft – it had to be disintegrated, preferably at a safe distance. The one required at least 3in, proximity fused ammunition, the other a Surface-to-Air guided Missile (SAM).

With the Cold War, the Soviet Union built on captured German technology to create fleets of high-speed submarines and long-range strike aircraft, armed with ship-busting, Air-to-Surface Missiles (ASMs). These were aimed at the West's potent amphibious warfare capability and the vulnerability of still-vital convoys. They prompted development of SAM-armed escorts, deploying also stand-off AS missiles. The size of such escorts was driven by the dimensions of missile stowage and handling facilities plus the large electronic systems necessary both to "illuminate" the target and to steer the missile to interception.

TOP: **The flotilla attacks in the Surigao Strait (Leyte Gulf), and in the sinking of the *Haguro*, were effectively the last for which the classic destroyer had evolved. These three British war-built "Emergencies" were already obsolescent by 1945.**
UPPER LEFT: **With her 17-knot submerged burst speed the Type XXI U-boat arrived too late to cause problems to Allied escorts. The post-war acquisition of the technology by Soviet Russia, however, led directly to the fast escort, such as the British Type 15.**
LOWER LEFT: **The 1942 Battle class (*Cadiz* seen here) were designed to address the aerial threat. Main armament, all forward, elevated to 80 degrees. Two stabilized, radar-laid twin 40mm mountings were located aft but displacement grew to over 2,900 tons.**

LEFT: **Despite the Terrier SAM's being successfully installed in the Gearing-class *Gyatt* as early as 1956, the series conversion of other war-vintage hulls did not prove practicable. The optimum platform proved to be the custom-designed 4,500-ton Coontz-class DLGs.**

ABOVE RIGHT: **The British Squid mortar proved to be a deadly killer of U-boats but, unlike the Hedgehog, was not adopted by the US Navy, which preferred to develop its own Mk.108 Weapon Able/Alfa, which could fire 12 single rounds per minute.** LEFT: **A shipborne helicopter has an enormous impact on ship layout and size. The DASH (Drone AS Helicopter) was a bold attempt to reduce helicopter dimensions and weight by deleting its crew. It proved to be ahead of contemporary technology.** BELOW: **ASROC, the US Navy's Anti-Submarine Rocket, can release a homing torpedo out to the practical range of a large sonar. All launcher versions, such as that illustrated, have been retired in favour of interchangeable vertical-launch rounds.**

The US Navy had large numbers of nearly new, war-built destroyers and, to avoid block obsolescence, sought to convert them to SAM escorts. A single, prototype conversion (USS *Gyatt* in 1956) was successful in deploying a medium-range Terrier system, but no general conversion programme resulted. The destroyers were instead remodelled around the ASROC (AS Rocket) stand-off AS system. It was apparent that viable Anti-Aircraft (AA) escorts would need to be designed, bottom-up, around specific weapon systems.

With greater standardization and inter-operability becoming the norm within NATO, destroyers (in the West, at least) came to be considered primarily anti-aircraft-oriented, frigates anti-submarine. The Soviet Union then technically behind the West and still concentrating on anti-ship warfare, opted for destroyers large enough to carry large Surface-to-Surface Missiles (SSMs). As the weapons were bulky, reloading at sea was not considered practical, so more launchers were accommodated, further forcing up dimensions.

The US Navy tried to improve its AS stand-off capability with unmanned, torpedo-carrying helicopters, called DASH (Drone AS Helicopter). Ahead of its time, however, the programme failed, leading to a life-extension for ASROC and the adoption of the manned helicopter. Two of these are better than one. Each new type is larger and more capable. "Destroyers" continue to grow larger.

LEFT: **The superb all-round capability of large modern frigates, such as the German *Sachsen*, disguises their still-potent anti-submarine potential and tends to blur the distinction between destroyer and frigate as separate categories.** ABOVE: **An Australian-designed anti-submarine guided weapon, Ikara was purchased for the Royal Navy, with several Leander-class frigates being modified to deploy it. It works to maximum sonar range, releasing an American Mk 46 torpedo over the target's computed position.** BELOW: **Her duty done, the British Type 12 *Lowestoft* is expended as a submarine target. Anti-ship torpedoes are designed, not to hit a target, but to detonate under its keel. The shock of the explosion whips the ship in a longitudinal mode, breaking its back and causing structural failure.**

Frigates in the missile age

An obvious indication that, post-war, frigates were in a new age, was the virtual disappearance of superstructure in British designs. The thinking of the early Cold War included using nuclear warheads against groups of ships such as convoys or task groups. By the late 1950s, however, the need for useful topside space ensured that superstructures returned to something like normal.

With NATO standardization, frigates became Anti-Submarine (AS) specialists and destroyers Anti-Aircraft (AA). Both types, however, were expected to contribute to the firepower of a group while being able to defend themselves.

Heavy, tube-launched AS torpedoes soon lost favour, replaced by small, lightweight weapons which could be deployed effectively by shipboard helicopter as well as by tube. The helicopter became the ship's primary AS system, directed by the ship's hull-mounted and Variable Depth Sonars (VDSs).

As a less space-consuming alternative to the helicopter, the stand-off, shipboard AS missile looked attractive. The French, Soviet Union and United States developed their own, the British adopted the Australian Ikara. With ranges of 20km/12.5 miles or more, however, such weapons worked beyond the reliable range of the ship's sonar and the helicopter, instead of being made redundant, found a necessary alternative role in carrying a dipping (or "dunking") sonar to assist in targeting. There was then, of course, immediate pressure to increase the machine's size in order to carry weapons as well, a complex data link, and a crew of two to work it all. For a submarine hunt, two helicopters are infinitely

more effective, while conferring a measure of redundancy. The effect on frigate size was dramatic.

The introduction of the gas turbine as a main propulsion unit in the 1960s was a revolution. Its great advantages include its ability to start from cold in a matter of minutes, its compactness and relatively light weight. It suffers from a higher initial cost and its narrow efficiency bands, necessitating separate main and cruising turbines. Repair is by replacement, much reducing time spent in dockyard hands. An extra bonus is the reduction in engine room personnel, representing a considerable saving in through-life costs as well as in accommodation space.

LEFT: **The impact of a shipborne helicopter on a frigate's design is enormous, fully 30 per cent of the *Iron Duke*'s length being devoted to the upkeep and operation of her Merlin helicopter. Fully loaded, the aircraft weighs 14.3 tons, compared with a Lynx's 4.6 tons.** ABOVE: **The current American Littoral Combat Ship project will result in an unconventional multi-purpose, high-speed vessel with interchangeable weapons systems. The General Dynamics *Independence* trimaran is shown here, one of three contenders.**

Frigates continue to provide designers with a dilemma. Ideally, a design is compact and inexpensive, necessary for series production in an emergency. In reality, however, all modern systems are demanding in volume, driving up size and cost. The more valuable the ship, the greater the case for comprehensive "defensive armament", so space is made for up to eight canister-launched anti-ship missiles. Earlier attempts to save space by eliminating the sole remaining dual-purpose gun came to nought when, in 1982, the Falklands War was a reminder of just how indispensable it was, and remains.

Anti-ship missiles are getting ever more sophisticated and, currently, considerable effort is being devoted to "stealth" measures to reduce frigates' radar signatures. While this produces some striking designs it is possible that the effectiveness of the measures will be outweighed by their inhibiting effects on a ship's utility.

Bearing in mind that the helicopter remains the frigate's primary AS weapons and targeting platform, it makes sense to configure the ship to facilitate the operability of the aircraft across the greatest range of sea states. Since the inception of the shipborne helicopter, however, it has been the practice, almost without exception, to locate the helicopter right aft, where it is subject to the maximum accelerations and amplitude of movement. Experimental trimaran ship forms promise a steadier platform with considerable amidships deck space, hulls of reduced resistance and significantly reduced heat signatures.

ABOVE: **One of the 46-ship Knox class of frigate, the USS *Aylwin* (FF-1081) is seen launching an ASROC missile. The 8-cell Mk.116 launcher was modified to launch Harpoon SSMs in addition, but has been superseded by Vertical Launching System (VLS).** BELOW: **The acutely raked stem of the Russian *Neustrushimyy* indicates a sizeable, low-frequency bow sonar. The hump right aft, abaft the flight pad, covers the winch and stowage for a variable-depth sonar and passive towed array. As with German frigates, freeboard is generous.**

56
55

Directory of Destroyers

Up to 1918

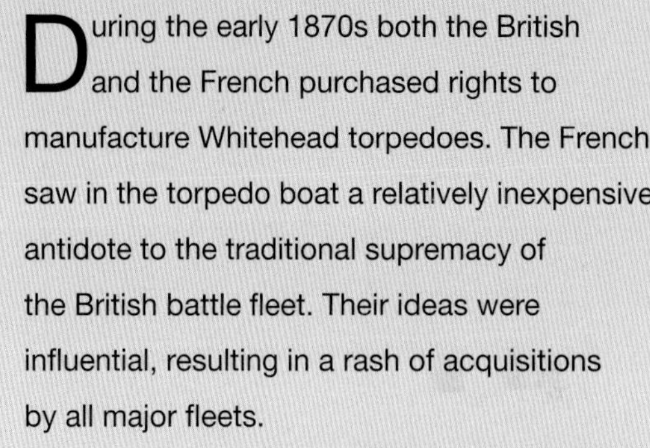

During the early 1870s both the British and the French purchased rights to manufacture Whitehead torpedoes. The French saw in the torpedo boat a relatively inexpensive antidote to the traditional supremacy of the British battle fleet. Their ideas were influential, resulting in a rash of acquisitions by all major fleets.

The American Admiral Alfred Thayer Mahan, however, in several major writings, examined the historical relationship between imperial greatness and an effective battle fleet. By thus reaffirming the pre-eminence of the capital ship, he directly influenced the ambitious German Kaiser Wilhelm II and, through him, the architect of his new navy, Admiral Alfred Tirpitz. For long, therefore, the latter pursued the gun rather than the torpedo in the developing "naval race" with the British.

Initially concerned at the threat from the French, the British Admiralty sought an antidote to the torpedo boat, finding it in the "Torpedo Boat Destroyer" (TBD). Itself little more than a large torpedo boat, its design was prioritized for seakeeping rather than for sheer speed. It could, therefore, in anything but calm sea, exploit the torpedo boat's poor seakeeping, running it down and destroying it by superior firepower.

LEFT: **A careworn pod of Vulcan-built torpedo boats in the lock at Wilhelmshaven. The bracket on the stem is for streaming paravanes. The amount of glazing to the wheelhouses is surprising, and all foremasts have been lengthened.**

LEFT: **If this is, indeed, Thornycroft's original *Lightning*, then her riverine steam launch limitations are all too obvious. As the Royal Navy's purchased TB.1, however, she carried a single 14in torpedo tube on the foredeck, with two reloads amidships.**

Early torpedo boats

Like the static, explosive mine, the new locomotive torpedo was considered by the British Admiralty to be a weapon for a lesser fleet. Despite this element of disdain, however, it could not be ignored and considerable funds were committed to its development. The "lesser fleets" certainly seized upon the torpedo boat as an inexpensive force multiplier, in theory capable of knocking out a battleship, and companies specializing in its construction enjoyed full order books.

Name	Builder*	Year	Displacement (tons)	Dimensions (ft)	Torpedo tubes
TB.1	T	1877	27	84.5 x 11	1
TB.21–22	T	1885	63	113 x 12.5	3
TB.41–60	T	1886	60	127.5 x 12.5	4
TB.61–79	Y	1886	75	125 x 13	5
TB.81	W	1885	125	150 x 17.5	3
TB.91–97	T, W, L	1893–94	130	140 x 15.5	3
TB.98–99	T	1901	178	160 x 17	3
TB.109–113	T	1902–03	200	166 x 17.5	3

*Builder: T= Thornycroft; Y = Yarrow; W = White; L = Laird

While mindful of the need to acquire torpedo boats to assess their value in attack, the British Admiralty was more concerned with protecting the battle fleet against such craft. Where, in 1877, it purchased its first torpedo boat in Thornycroft's *Lightning*, therefore, it was already thinking in terms of "torpedo catchers, hunters or destroyers", acquiring White's *Swift* in 1885.

Divergent evolutionary lines were, thus, already evident. The *Lightning*, or TB.1, was no more than a steam-engined river launch which, in sheltered waters, could manage barely 18 knots with torpedoes aboard. She, and her 11 sisters of 1878–79, had a single, rotatable tube on the foredeck, and "dropping gear" on either side amidships for single torpedoes.

The *Swift*, or TB.81, however, was 45.7m/150ft overall against 25.6m/84ft, enabling her to maintain speed in open water. She mounted three tubes, one in the stern and, emphasizing her "catcher" role, six 3pdrs (difficult to lay accurately in a seaway).

In an effort to produce the smallest craft with the necessary combination of speed, self-sufficiency and ability to accompany the fleet, the Admiralty evolved a 61m/200ft design, with four torpedo tubes, one 4in gun and six 3pdrs. This was the beginning of the "torpedo-gunboat" concept, which proved to be something of an evolutionary dead-end, largely because of the poor power-to-weight ratio of contemporary machinery, which was bulky and heavy.

BELOW: **Torpedo Boat No.27, or TB.27, was built in 1886, one of a group of five boats from Thornycroft. Less than a decade after the *Lightning*, displacement has more than doubled, with length increased by some 50 per cent. Already a small warship.**

The 27-knotters, or "A" class

As can be seen from the data opposite, Torpedo Boats, numbered in a continuous sequence, but varying in specification, were acquired by the Admiralty until after the turn of the century. Unimpressed by their performance, particularly compared with that attributed to examples from Normand and Schichau, the Controller of the Navy, Rear Admiral John ("Jackie") Fisher, had invitations to tender sent to a group of leading builders. The requirement was simply for 27-knot craft with a substantial gun armament. The Board of Admiralty was hoping that this brief might be satisfied within a 200-ton displacement, but the three best proposals showed 240–280 tons. Orders were thus placed, early in 1893 for two Torpedo Boat Catchers from each of Yarrow, (*Havock* and *Hornet*), Thornycroft (*Daring* and *Decoy*), and Laird (*Ferret* and *Lynx*). For every quarter-knot under the stipulated 27 there was a substantial financial penalty, with rejection for less than an averaged 25 knots.

Except for widely differing funnel arrangements, the six were very similar, flush-decked with a raised, turtleback forecastle. The recessed conning position was roofed by a bandstand supporting a 12pdr gun, while a 6pdr was mounted aft.

One fixed torpedo tube was located to fire through the stem, with two rotatable single tubes being sited on the centreline aft of amidships. The latter tubes were interchangeable with two further 6pdrs. All six ships were accepted, with only *Havock* (having older-style locomotive boilers rather than water-tube) failing to make 27 knots.

ABOVE: **The Fairfield-built *Hunter* made the requisite 27 knots on trials but it was some time before the Admiralty came to realize that, while high trial speeds were very expensive to attain, they were relatively unimportant compared with seakeeping.**

All were now referred to as Torpedo Boat Destroyers or, simply "Destroyers".

Such was the perceived threat from France that the six prototypes, once seen as satisfactory, formed the basis for contracts for no less than 36 repeats, the orders spread among 14 yards. Officially the "A" class, but universally known as "27-knotters", all were launched in 1894–95.

ABOVE: ***Salmon*, from Earle, had an entirely different boiler/funnel layout. Note the navigating platform shared with the 12pdr gun. The airing hammocks remind of the eternal problem of wetness and condensation, a cause of major health problems in destroyermen.**

Havock (27-knotters slightly larger but variable in specification)

	Built	Commissioned
Havock	Yarrow, Poplar	January 1894

Displacement: 240 tons (light); 275 tons (full load)
Length: 54.8m/180ft (bp); 56.4m/185ft (oa)
Beam: 5.6m/18ft 6in
Draught: 2.3m/7ft 6in
Armament: 1 x 12pdr gun, 3 x 6pdr guns; 3 x 18in torpedo tubes
Machinery: 2 x 3-cylinder triple-expansion engines, 2 boilers, 2 shafts
Power: 2,650kW/3,550ihp for 26.2 knots
Endurance: 47 tons coal for about 1,666km/900nm at 11 knots
Protection: None
Complement: 42

LEFT: **An extra 10m/32.8ft on length certainly improved the 30-knotters' seakeeping as compared with that of the preceding class, but the turtledeck forward in no way compensated for what was inadequate freeboard. This is *Flying Fish*.**

ABOVE: **On the four-funnelled "B" class (*Spiteful* seen here), the two centre boilers, back-to-back, exhausted through separate uptakes. Two more Palmer's boats, *Albacore* and *Bonetta*, were the only ones to be fitted with experimental Parson's turbines.**

The 30-knotters, or "B", "C" and "D" classes

Some of the trials speeds achieved by the 27-knotters led the Admiralty to believe that 30 knots were easily attainable. The Board was anxious to acquire a force of at least 80 TBDs quickly but, lacking sufficient funds, had to delay other projects while pushing shipbuilders hard, even to bankruptcy.

The 30-knotters were built under programmes from 1894 to 1901. After 1913 they were classed according to numbers of funnels, there being 21 four-funnelled "B" class, 37 three-funnelled "C" class, and 20 two-funnelled "D" class. Builders were allowed to interpret the specification quite freely as long as their price was acceptable and certain criteria were met. Besides a 30-knot speed, the latter included a metacentric height of at least 60cm/2ft when in the deep condition, a minimum of 80 tons of coal was to be carried and, at 15 knots, a ship should steam 15nm to the ton.

In achieving these requirements, Thornycroft's D-class *Desperate* and *Fame* displaced only 310 tons on 63.4m/208ft hulls, while John Brown's C-class *Thorn*, *Tiger* and *Vigilant* were of 380 tons and 66.4m/218ft respectively. With no standard hull form, some builders met the speed requirement with no problem while others went bankrupt in having to undertake many expensive trials with varying loading, alternative propellers, etc., in order to have their ships accepted.

Beyond the extra length and displacement allowing for a further pair of 6pdrs to be shipped, the 30-knotters were much like the preceding "A" class. The earlier ships' stem torpedo tube was, however, abandoned as it created excessive wetness and induced a forward trim.

In full seagoing condition, no "30-knotter" ever made more than 27. High speed induced a pronounced stern trim ("squat"), shifting the centre of buoyancy aft and creating instability. Hence the requirement for a generous metacentric height.

LEFT: **The *Fame* and *Whiting* spent their careers in the Far East. They made their name in 1900 during the Boxer Rebellion when, following the seizure of the Taku forts by an international force, the pair cut out and captured four new German-built Chinese destroyers.**

C-class *Cheerful*, average for class

	Built	**Commissioned**
Cheerful	Hawthorn Leslie, Hebburn	June 1899

Displacement: 355 tons (light); 400 tons (full load)
Length: 64.1m/210ft 6in (bp); 65.5m/215ft (oa)
Beam: 6.4m/21ft
Draught: 2.5m/8ft 2in
Armament: 1 x 12pdr gun, 5 x 6pdr guns; 2 x 18in torpedo tubes (2x1)
Machinery: 2 x 3-cylinder triple-expansion engines, 4 boilers, 2 shafts
Power: 4,550kW/6,100ihp for 30.3 knots
Endurance: 87 tons coal for 2,400km/1,300nm at 15 knots
Protection: None
Complement: 63

LEFT: **With the Royal Yacht on South Railway Jetty as backdrop, the *Eden* makes her way up Portsmouth Harbour. The additional freeboard conferred by the forecastle made the Rivers reportedly "wonderfully dry", but difficult to berth in a side wind.**

BELOW: **The Rivers' four water-tube boilers were accommodated in two back-to-back pairs. Deck space could thus be saved by exhausting them through just two wide funnels or two pairs of thin funnels.**

River, or "E" class

Opportunities arose during 1901 for British destroyer officers to visit their German counterparts, and their reports were full of praise for the Kaiser's ships, particularly in standards of accommodation. In British ships, "hard lying" was religion, with fatigue and cold stoically accepted, the endless wetness and commonly resulting diseases just another aspect of small-ship existence. German conditions were a revelation, relatively spacious, internally wood-lined, steam-heated, electrically lit and with real washing facilities. Worse, the ships' greater size conferred superior seakeeping and endurance.

The general specification for the next British ships, the "E" class took this to heart. Earlier structural weakness would be rectified through the greater use of high-tensile steel. A full-height forecastle would both improve seakeeping and increase internal volume. The 12pdr gun would still be located above the conning position but there would be, abaft it, an enclosed charthouse with open bridge above. Set farther aft, this benefited from reduced motion and wetness for watchkeepers.

Trials were to be run in the more realistic deep condition, with 25½ knots being stipulated. One ship, the *Eden*, was to be fitted with experimental steam turbines (she proved complex, but the fastest, at 26.23 knots). The class was spread over three programmes, the later ships being fitted for stowing oil fuel, permitting boiler room personnel to be reduced by 11.

The designers resisted burdening the larger Rivers with heavier armament, but the fact that they carried no more than their "30-knotter" predecessors attracted much adverse comment, particularly as they were 40 per cent more expensive. Their seagoing performance was, in fact, far superior and, while being popular with their crews, they are considered to have been the Royal Navy's first successful destroyers. They gave good service during World War I, some exchanging their 6pdrs for three more hard-hitting 12pdrs.

RIGHT: **Probably post-war, the *Welland* is seen in a cooler grey paint scheme, which better emphasizes detail. Note the built-up bridge structure, high mast with W/T aerials, recessed anchor bed and 6pdrs in sponsons at the break of the forecastle.**

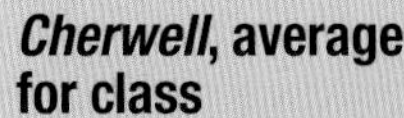

Cherwell, average for class

	Built	Commissioned
Cherwell	Palmer, Hebburn	November 1904

Displacement: 549 tons (light); 620 tons (full load)
Length: 68.5m/225ft (bp); 70m/229ft 6in (oa)
Beam: 7.2m/23ft 6in
Draught: 3m/10ft
Armament: 1 x 12pdr gun, 5 x 6pdr guns; 2 x 18in torpedo tubes (2x1)
Machinery: 2 x 3- or 4-cylinder triple-expansion engines, 4 boilers, 2 shafts
Power: 5,222kW/7,000ihp for 25.26 knots
Endurance: 130 tons coal for 3,140km/1,700nm at 11 knots
Protection: None
Complement: 61

Beagle, Acorn and Repeat Acorn, or "G", "H" and "I" classes

With persistent reports of German destroyers making speeds of 33 and even 34 knots with steam turbines and coal-firing, the Beagles, like the Rivers, were influenced at an early stage. Oil-firing had been proposed but, with doubts as to its reliable supply in time of war, the Beagles stayed with coal.

This apparently simple option had considerable consequences for the ships' design. A further dozen stokers would need to be accommodated. Coal bunkers had to flank the boiler spaces to be accessible, where oil could be stowed in tanks of variable shape almost anywhere in the hull. Coal is nearly half as dense as oil. Extra space was required for stokers to work, while a coal-fired boiler developed less energy than one fed by oil. In short, the Beagles' fuel weight penalty through using coal was 45 tons, or about 5 per cent of legend displacement.

In earlier classes, builders were permitted to interpret a fairly general specification, leading to a wide variation in the appearance and, to some extent, layout of individual ships. Checking each variation imposed heavy work on the Department of Naval Construction. To reduce this, the Beagle specification was tighter, resulting in less individuality.

ABOVE: **The Beagles were coal-fired (note *Racoon*'s smoke), an advantage in the Mediterranean, where oil fuel was always in rather short supply. A "first" for the class was the fitting of stockless anchors, which would stow directly against the hawse, in a much simplified procedure.**

ABOVE: **With the bridge structure of the early Beagles set farther forward (and correspondingly wetter) the gap between it and the forward funnel was greater, permitting the funnels to be of equal height. Note the *Pincher*'s after torpedo tube carried at the extreme after end.**

ABOVE: **HMS *Wolverine* is seen at Malta during World War I, with French warships in the background. The three Cammell-Laird built boats – the others being *Racoon* and *Renard* – had a pleasing (if inefficient) stern profile.**

LEFT: **With the Beagles came a far greater uniformity of design, with individual builders allowed less independence of Admiralty requirements. To improve their lethality against enemy torpedo boats they were the first to be given 4in guns.**

The proposed gun armament was five 12pdrs, two of which would be forecastle-mounted. In view of the German boats' 8.8cm weapons, this conservatism drew criticism, and a single forward 4in gun was substituted.

First to deploy 21in torpedoes, the Beagles had two centreline tubes, one of them right aft in a most unsatisfactory location. One spare torpedo was carried for each.

The steam turbine installation required a three-shaft arrangement, but all but one of the class comfortably exceeded the required 27-knot trial speed. All 16 Beagles were launched between October 1909 and March 1910, nine yards participating. Their final appearance varied widely.

Destroyers of this era were built in large numbers and in a rolling programme, the first of 20 follow-on Acorns going into the water just three months after the last of the Beagles. Progress will not be denied, and the principal difference was that the new ships were oil-fired. This was largely responsible for average displacement being reduced from about 950 to 760 tons, with a saving of some 12 per cent on initial cost, and with speed improved by nearly an extra knot.

"H" and "I" classes proved excellent seaboats. They served widely during World War I, particularly with the Grand Fleet and in the Mediterranean. In all, these groups totalled 59 boats yet, by the early 1920s, all had been scrapped.

ABOVE: **Like the *Larne* (above), the *Sheldrake* was actually an Acorn, or "H" class. Ships of the class were equipped with two single 21in torpedo tubes and they were oil-fired. Following only ten years of service, the class was sold as a block for scrapping.** BELOW: **The Royal Australian Navy was, at this time, dependent upon British-designed and built warships. Denny, at Dumbarton, Scotland, which had already built two Repeat Acorns and a "special", launched the similar HMAS *Yarra* in April 1910.**

ABOVE: **To encourage innovation, the Admiralty ordered nine "specials" from three builders. One of a pair from Yarrow, the *Archer*, like the remainder, had so many contract strictures that very little improvement was effected.**

Repeat Acorn, or "I" class

Displacement: 760 tons light
Length: 73.1m/240ft (bp); 74.9m/246ft (oa)
Beam: 7.8m/25ft 8in
Draught: 2.7m/8ft 9in
Armament: 2 x 4in guns, 2 x 12pdr guns; 2 x 21in torpedo tubes (2x1)
Machinery: Direct-drive steam turbines, 3 shafts
Power: 11,040kW/14,800shp for 28 knots
Endurance: 178 tons oil for 4,260km/2,300nm at 13 knots
Protection: None
Complement: 71

LEFT: **Given the loose specification, and allowing seven builders considerable freedom in interpretation, while spreading the orders over three consecutive programmes, it is little wonder that the Tribals were something of a ragbag. Cammell Laird's *Cossack* is seen here.** ABOVE: **To achieve the requisite 33 knots, some Tribals had five boilers, others, such as the four-stack *Nubian* (seen here), six. Their puny 12pdr guns were criticized as being like "going elephant hunting with a snipe gun".**

Tribal, or "F" class

Always revolutionary, Admiral Sir John Fisher, on becoming First Sea Lord in 1904, demanded big destroyers. Not only big, but fast. His requirements were stated simply – they should make 33 knots in a "moderate" sea, be oil-fired and self-sufficient for 7 days. To save weight, the heaviest guns would be 12pdrs.

Considering that yards at this time were constructing 25–26-knot Rivers of about 550 tons, this was a considerable evolutionary step. To realize the speed steam turbines, of which few builders yet had experience, were required. The necessary power demanded five or six boilers. For the sake of both speed and internal volume, a long hull was needed. For good seakeeping, a forecastle was desirable. Weight, however, was a problem, so in three cases (the seven builders were permitted considerable latitude), a turtledeck was substituted. In the remainder, forecastles were kept short and the hull scantlings very light – so light that all initial proposals were rejected pending further strengthening. Threatened with rejection for trials speeds of under 32 knots, builders' estimates were twice those for the Rivers.

The 12 hulls of what became the Tribals were launched between February 1907 and September 1909. As finished, they varied considerably, most having four funnels but one, the Palmers-built *Viking,* being the Navy's only-ever six funneller, with one for each boiler.

All exceeded 33 knots on trials, the *Tartar* actually making 35.36 knots. Their fuel economy was, however, poor, and for this reason the class found itself with the Dover Command rather than with the Grand Fleet. Here, they found themselves badly outgunned by the 10.5cm weapons of the German Flanders Flotilla. The Tribals were, therefore, upgunned to two 4in guns, although trials with a single 6in proved unsatisfactory.

Very much "specials", the nine surviving ships were quickly scrapped after the war.

ABOVE: **Hawthorn Leslie's *Ghurka* was a short-hulled Tribal of the first batch. On a 6-hour trial she averaged over 33.9 knots but, as can be seen clearly, suffered excessively from "squat", which reduced speed in shallow water. She was sunk by a mine off Dungeness in February 1917.**

Amazon, average for class

	Built	Commissioned
Amazon	Thornycroft	1909

Displacement: 970 tons (light)
Length: 85.4m/280ft 4in (bp)
Beam: 8.1m/26ft 8in
Draught: 3.1m/10ft 1in
Armament: 2 x 4in guns; 2 x 18in torpedo tubes (2x1)
Machinery: Direct-drive steam turbines, 6 boilers, 3 shafts
Power: 18329kW/24,570shp for 33.2 knots
Endurance: 200 tons oil for 3,890km/2,100nm at 15 knots
Protection: None
Complement: 67

LEFT: As the "K" class, the Acastas were intended originally to take "K" names. Thornycroft's *Porpoise* was thus allocated the name *Kennington*. Although dropped, the system was revived with the following "L" class. ABOVE: The Acastas were designed to screen the battle squadrons of the Grand Fleet. Three 4in guns were thus specified to stop enemy torpedo boats. *Unity*, here, shows the characteristic torpedo tube between second and third funnels. BELOW: The three John Brown boats could be distinguished by their shorter after funnels. *Achates* was one of the few to achieve the required 32 knots, although trials were run at displacements that varied between 903 and 1,071 tons.

Acasta, or "K" class

Gunnery trials showed that a single hit from a 4in weapon did more damage than six from 12pdrs. One 4in gun weighed no more than two 12pdrs but required five fewer gun crew. As a single calibre also simplified logistics. The 12pdr disappeared in the Acasta class in favour of a third 4in, located between the after torpedo tube and the diminutive mainmast of the Acastas.

Experience had showed that over-running machinery through forced, rather than natural, draught for the boilers caused unreliability and mechanical failure. To achieve a required 29½ knots in the deep condition it was thus accepted that four boilers and three funnels would be necessary. The two boiler spaces were adjacent, the thicker centre funnel exhausting one boiler of each. The forward funnel was usually raised in order to keep products of combustion clear of the bridge.

Twelve Acastas (three from each of four builders) were ordered to a standard design, together with eight "specials" to allow the best builders to incorporate their own ideas. Complaints of inadequate endurance led several builders to suggest diesel engines for cruising. The extra complications – clutches, shafting, weight and cost – enthused neither the Navy's Engineer in Chief nor the Controller but, in the event, the still-nascent diesel industry proved unable to deliver what was required.

The *Ardent* was interesting in that Denny's framed her longitudinally, as opposed to the usual transverse construction. The Admiralty agreed to fund the extra work involved, the end result being a slightly lighter hull, whose enhanced stiffness reduced vibration.

During the course of World War I, several of the class surrendered an after 4in gun in favour of such as twinned torpedo tubes, anti-aircraft guns, kite-balloon arrangements or, increasingly, depth charges and throwers. Seven Acastas became war casualties.

ABOVE: *Garland* has sent her whaler away for some rowing practice, boatwork then being more important than it is today. Note that, where her sisters here display no identifiers, *Garland* carries the "K" class letter. *Acasta* herself had "OO" painted up.

Acasta class, standard design, as built

Displacement: 935 tons (light); 1,072 tons (full load)
Length: 79.2m/260ft (bp); 81.5m/267ft 6in (oa)
Beam: 8.2m/27ft
Draught: 2.8m/9ft 3in (deep)
Armament: 3 x 4in guns; 2 x 21in torpedo tubes (2x1)
Machinery: Direct-drive steam turbines, 4 boilers, 2 shafts
Power: 18,650kW/25,000shp for 30 knots
Endurance: 258 tons oil for 5,090km/2,750nm at 15 knots
Protection: None
Complement: 75

Laforey, or "L" class

Essentially repeat Acastas, with a slightly increased beam, the 22 "L" class were still completing at the outbreak of World War I. They were the first destroyer class to adopt names based on the class letter.

In the Laforeys, No.2 4in gun was moved to an amidships position, the advantage of which is obscure, for its tubular, underdeck support now intruded into the after boiler space, while its ammunition supply had to be manhandled all the way from the forward magazine. The torpedo tubes were thus displaced farther aft and were, for the first time, twinned. No reloads were carried but all four weapons could now be fired at one time. For safety, their warheads were normally stowed below in a dedicated magazine space.

Despite the policy of greater standardization, there were still variations. Most apparent was, where the majority had three boilers and two funnels, some had four boilers and three funnels, displacing some 20 more tons on the same dimensions.

A significant technical advance lay in that two ships, *Leonidas* and *Lucifer*, had single-stage reduction gearing added downstream of their steam turbines. At normal full speed, this reduced shaft revolutions from an average of some 630rpm to about 370rmp. At lower rotational speeds, propellers can be designed for higher efficiency and the *Leonidas* was able to achieve the required trials performance while developing about 8 per cent less power. Comparative trials were run against *Lucifer*.

ABOVE: ***Lucifer* was one of the class selected to trial single-stage gearing for the turbines. This nearly halved propeller speed for a significant increase in hydrodynamic efficiency. A further innovation in the Ls was twinned 21in torpedo tubes.**

A further proposal, to provide a steadier fighting platform through the installation of passive, anti-roll tanks, was not progressed owing to the urgency of mobilizing the class for war.

The Laforeys saw much action, with the Harwich Force, at the Heligoland Bight, at the Dardanelles and at Jutland. Despite incurring heavy damage, however, none was lost to direct enemy action, but two to mines and one wrecked.

ABOVE: **In other respects identical, "L" boats were either two- or three-funnelled, reflecting whether they had three or four boilers respectively. Both types had the same nominal power. *Liberty*, seen here, stemmed from J. Samuel White's yard at Cowes.**

"L" class, average for class

Displacement: 995 tons (light); 1,115 tons (full load)
Length: 79.2m/260ft (bp); 81.9m/268ft 10in (oa)
Beam: 8.4m/27ft 8in
Draught: 2.9m/9ft 8in
Armament: 3 x 4in QF guns; 4 x 21in torpedo tubes (2x2)
Machinery: Direct-drive steam turbines, 3/4 boilers, 2 shafts
Power: 18,277kW/24,500shp for 29 knots
Endurance: 268 tons oil for 4,445km/2,400nm at 15 knots
Protection: None
Complement: 72 (3 boilers); 76 (4 boilers)

"M" class

ABOVE: **The Ms were the first class since the 30-knotters to include ships with two, three or four funnels, the greater majority having three. The Admiralty "standards", such as *Murray*, had triple shafts, while the seven "specials" had twins.**

The destroyers of the 1913–14 Programme were important in that they were the last major pre-war design, greatly influencing the many war-built "standards" that followed. Again to match the reported speeds of German destroyers, they were required to make 34 knots, yet have a docking displacement small enough to allow two to be stemmed simultaneously in the Harwich floating dock.

A speed of 34 knots represented an increase of 4.5 knots on that of the still-building L-class boats, yet on a length of only about 1.2m/4ft greater and an extra 500shp. It was possible only by running trials with just 75 tons of oil (about 27 per cent) aboard, equivalent to 2½–3 knots extra.

With specifications based on those of preceding classes, three yards were building speculatively, on the understanding that orders would be forthcoming. Although they varied in length by about 0.5m/1ft 8in and in deep displacement by 172 tons, six of these boats (designated M-class "specials") were purchased by the Admiralty which went on to produce a standard M-class design, very much a mean of the above. Orders for seven of these were then placed with three builders.

The three Yarrow "specials" were, on average, the slowest of that group, but were of lighter and stiffer construction. Displacement, trim, the quality of stoking and the depth of water on the measured mile course all greatly influenced speed, Thornycroft's *Mastiff* returning over 37 knots. The "specials" were of twin-screw design, the "standards", triple. Only one standard, *Moorsom*, bettered 34 knots.

Most boats had three boilers and three funnels. Four had four boilers, two boats having four funnels. The three Yarrow "specials" had only two funnels, that forward being heavily trunked to allow the bridge to be sited advantageously farther aft.

LEFT: **Heaviest of the first batch of Ms, *Mansfield* was a "special" from Hawthorn Leslie. Flying a Red Ensign, she is seen on trials. As with most Ms, the Admiralty's over-optimistic hopes for speed were not realized, *Mansfield* making only 33.7 knots average.**

Admiralty "standard" "M" class

Displacement: 900 tons (light); 1,150 tons (full load)
Length: 80.7m/265ft (bp); 83.3m/273ft 4in (oa)
Beam: 8.1m/26ft 8in
Draught: 2.9m/9ft 7in (deep)
Armament: 3 x 4in QF guns; 2 x 1pdr pompoms on HA mountings (2x1); 4 x 21in torpedo tubes (2x2)
Machinery: Direct-drive steam turbines, 3 boilers, 3 shafts
Power: 18,650kW/25,000shp for 34 knots
Endurance: 278 tons oil for 4,685km/2,530nm at 15 knots
Protection: None
Complement: 79

ABOVE: ***Kempenfelt*** **seen manoeuvring in company. Leaders were enlarged sufficiently to include accommodation for Captain (D) and his staff, an extra ten personnel. The greater size permitted increased power and a fourth main-calibre gun.**

Contemporary Destroyer Leaders

Early Grand Fleet destroyer flotillas of World War I comprised twenty boats, organized in five divisions. Each four-boat division was divided into two subdivisions. Attached were two "scouts", 2,900-ton light cruisers with 4in armament and, usually, a Boadicea- or Gem-class light cruiser as Senior Officer's ("Captain (D)'s") ship. With the maximum speeds expected of the M-class destroyers, however, it was obvious that an attendant cruiser would be inhibiting. Designs were, therefore, called for an enlarged destroyer, not exceeding 1,800 tons but capable of over 33 knots and with an endurance superior to that of the boats that she would lead. Accommodation would be required for Captain (D) and his staff of eight or nine. Signalling arrangements were to be the equal of those in the latest light cruisers. Four 4in guns would be supplemented by "two anti-airship pompoms".

The initial pair, at a little over 1,600 tons, were launched early in 1915. Their names, *Lightfoot* and *Marksman*, repeated the initial letters of their flotillas, but a repeat pair, *Kempenfelt* and *Nimrod*, made for an alphabetical sequence. As built, with a low bridge and four funnels of equal height, they had the purposeful appearance of miniature light cruisers, spoiled somewhat by sea experience necessitating the addition of an upper bridge and the raising in height of the forward funnel.

Before any of these ships was launched a further three were ordered, all from Cammell Laird, who were already building the *Kempenfelt*. These were given the angelic names of *Abdiel, Gabriel* and *Ithuriel*, and had a slightly larger displacement.

Abdiel's extra size saw her converted into a high-speed minelayer (as, later, was *Gabriel*). With torpedo tubes and two 4in guns landed, she could stow 80 contact mines on deck, although the resulting deeper draught reduced her maximum speed and endurance.

LEFT: **With increasing numbers of leaders becoming available, several, including *Abdiel* (seen here), were converted to fast minelayers. To accommodate two rows, each of forty 682kg/1,500lb mines, two guns and all torpedoes had to be sacrificed.**

Lightfoot class

Displacement: 1,440 tons (light); 1,605 tons (full load)

Length: 96m/315ft (bp); 98.9m/324ft 10in (oa)

Beam: 9.7m/31ft 9in

Draught: 3.3m/10ft 9in (normal)

Armament: 4 x 4in QF (4x1); 2 x 2pdr pompoms (2x1); 4 x 21in torpedo tubes (2x2)

Machinery: Direct-drive steam turbines, 4 boilers, 3 shafts

Power: 26,856kW/36,000shp for 34.5 knots

Endurance: 515 tons oil for 7,960km/4,300nm at 15 knots

Protection: Thickened shell plating 11.1mm/$\frac{7}{16}$in over machinery spaces

Complement: 105

Emergency "M" class

The various options resulting from the 1913–14 M-class programme enabled the Admiralty to order large blocks of additional construction in order to rapidly expand the Grand Fleet destroyer force. Ninety hulls were acquired in five tranches; of these, eleven were "specials" from Thornycroft and Yarrow.

To achieve high speed, destroyers were very lightly built and, except where heavily stressed, plating was thin. Much was of only 6.35mm/¼in thickness, some even 4.76mm/3⁄16in. It was essential to galvanize such plating before assembly, but war quickly brought shortages, including that of the necessary zinc. In the presence of salt water, ungalvanized 6.35mm/¼in plate could be penetrated by rust within three years. Weight considerations precluded any increase in thickness and the resulting poor condition of many destroyers by 1918 contributed to their rapid disposal.

Sixteen Admiralty "standards" and four Yarrow "specials" were ordered in September 1914. For the sake of rapid delivery, most lacked cruising turbines. The Yarrow boats had two, rather than the remainder's three, funnels, were slightly longer, and were capable of trial speeds of up to a reported 39 knots.

TOP: ***Orpheus* features the straight, vertical hance at the break of the forecastle, common to early destroyers. This sudden discontinuity resulted in a high-stress concentration in an already stressed shallow hull girder.** ABOVE: **Two of eight stemming from the Sunderland yard of Doxford, *Opal* is identical to her sister *Orpheus*. No standard pendant-numbering system existed at this time, with ships changing numbers on switching service.**

Nine further "standards" and one Yarrow "special" were ordered in November 1914, quickly followed by contracts for 22 more "standards". Most could, with a little coaxing, make 34 knots. Superficially, all were very similar, but the experienced eye could usually identify the products of individual builders through subtle variations in funnel section, rake of bow, stern profile, etc.

Orders for the fourth group, comprising 16 "standards" and two Thornycroft "specials" followed in February 1915, with 16 more "standards" and two each Thornycroft and Yarrow "specials" in the May. Thirteen yards were involved and all hulls bar one were in the water by November 1916.

Although still termed "M" class, destroyers of later groups carried names commencing "N" to "R".

ABOVE: **With the introduction of the blimp came aerial photography, as with this picture of *Patrician*. As a Thornycroft "special", she was given thicker, raking funnels. Note the two-stage hance, rendered less obvious by a canvas "dodger".**

Emergency, later Admiralty "standard" "M" class

Displacement: 1,025 tons (standard)
Length: 80.7m/265ft (bp); 83.4m/273ft 8in (oa)
Beam: 8.2m/26ft 10in
Draught: 2.6m/8ft 6in (light); 2.9m/9ft 6in (deep)
Armament: 3 x 4in QF guns; 1 x 2pdr pompom on HA mounting; 4 x 21in torpedo tubes (2x2)
Machinery: Direct-drive steam turbines, 3 boilers, 3 shafts
Power: 18,600kW/25,000shp for 34 knots
Endurance: 300 tons oil for 4,630km/2,500nm at 15 knots
Protection: None
Complement: 79

"R" and Modified "R" classes

Even before hostilities commenced in 1914 the Controller, obviously concerned at the rapid growth in destroyers, and their increasing emphasis on gun, rather than torpedo, armament, proposed a smaller type of just 700 tons, with five torpedo tubes but only 12pdr guns. Essential builders were, however, desperately short of work and the quickest solution was to order further M-class vessels rather than develop a new concept.

As noted earlier in this section, two L-class destroyers had been completed with geared steam turbines. These were proving economical, so it was decided to put a similar installation into an M-type hull form, which would require only two shafts. The overall length would be slightly greater, as a slightly raked stem, combined with moderate flare and adequate freeboard, greatly improved seakeeping and dryness.

The initial order was for nineteen "standards" and seven "specials" from Thornycroft and Yarrow, the latter with direct-drive turbines proving to be faster but less efficient. All were launched in 1916–17, overlapping the orders for the second and third blocks. The second, placed in December 1915, was for eight "standards" and two "specials"; the third, of March 1916, was for twelve "standards" and three "specials".

The final block was for 11 Modified "R" class. All Rs had three boilers, necessitating one single and one double boiler space. In the modified design, these were transposed, the larger space now being the farther aft, adjacent to the engine room. This arrangement reduced survivability but, requiring only two funnels, permitted both bridge and forecastle to be located farther aft.

Despite many complaints from the crews about deteriorating standards of workmanship, which affected reliability and availability, the Rs proved to be good seaboats and were vital to the support of the battle fleet. Again somewhat perversely, the class names commenced with "R" through "U".

ABOVE: **The war-built classes were so numerous that, typically, these classes had names spanning "R", "S", "T" and even "U". *Tyrant* was one of seven Yarrow-built "specials" and is seen post-war, disarmed and with added structures for trials duties.**

LEFT: **The R-class *Raider* with pendants painted up post-war. The view emphasizes the very shallow depth of the hull. The two pairs of torpedo tubes are clearly shown, as is the afterdeck, now crowded with paravane gear and depth charges.**

Standard "R" class

Displacement: 890 tons (light); 1,223 tons (full load)
Length: 80.7m/265ft (bp); 84.1m/276ft (oa)
Beam: 8.1m/26ft 8in
Draught: 3m/9ft 10in (full load)
Armament: 3 x 4in QF guns; 1 x 2pdr pompom on HA mounting; 4 x 21in torpedo tubes (2x2)
Machinery: Single-reduction geared steam turbines, 3 boilers, 2 shafts
Power: 20,142kW/27,000shp for 36 knots
Endurance: 296 tons oil for 6,297km/3,400nm at 15 knots
Protection: None
Complement: 82

LEFT: **The "S" class, whose names again commenced confusingly with either "S" or "T", marked a reversion to cheaper, simpler destroyers as an alternative to the very expensive "Admiralty Vs" then building. Note *Torbay*'s long forward sheerline.** BELOW: **Not the Mediterranean of the travel brochures – *Tryphon* stranded in the Aegean during May 1919. Despite being towed to Malta, she was declared a total loss, and sold locally for scrapping.**

"S" class

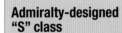

Continual reports and rumours of the speed and firepower of German destroyers quickly brought about the evolution of the British "V" and "W" classes (see next pages). The Controller had earlier, but unsuccessfully, tried to revert to a simpler 700-ton boat with an enhanced torpedo armament and when, early in 1917, indications were that the enemy was, in fact, building only a few larger vessels, he proposed that Modified R-class boats would again be better value. Thus was agreed the Admiralty "S" class, a further derivative.

Sea experience with the Rs had resulted in recommendations for even higher freeboard and greater flare at the forward end. To save weight, the first was satisfied in the Ss with a sharply curved sheerline, which raised the stemhead by 61cm/2ft. To avoid the increased flare causing excessive width of forecastle deck, the sheer strake was given a distinctive radius.

Topweight being a chronic problem, the class reverted to an earlier, but lighter, mark of 4in gun. The pronounced forward sheer prevented the forecastle gun from firing in depression on forward bearings, but approval to locate it on a raised platform was refused.

The bridge structure had, by now, migrated aft to the point where it was all abaft the break of the forecastle, leaving a clear athwartship space beneath. For the high-speed, close-range encounters expected of Dover Command destroyers, two fixed 14in torpedo tubes had been shipped amidships by some. Grand Fleet boats saw little requirement for these but, nonetheless, early examples of the "S" class had two single 18in tubes sided at the break of the forecastle. They traversed through a limited angle and were in addition to the normal 21in torpedo armament.

Eleven Ss (and one R) survived to serve during World War II. Six remained in service in 1945.

Admiralty-designed "S" class

Displacement: 1,075 tons (light); 1,225 tons (full load)
Length: 80.7m/265ft (bp); 84.1m/276ft (oa)
Beam: 8.1m/26ft 8in
Draught: 3.1m/10ft 4in (full load)
Armament: 3 x 4in/102mm QF guns (3x2); 1 x 2pdr pompom on HA mounting; 4 x 21in torpedo tubes (2x2); 2 x 18in torpedo tubes (2x1)
Machinery: Single-reduction geared steam turbines, 3 boilers, 2 shafts
Power: 20,142kW/27,000shp for 36 knots
Endurance: 300 tons oil for 5,090km/2,750nm at 15 knots
Protection: None
Complement: 84

LEFT: ***Sardonyx*, with four other Ss, survived the mass scrappings of the depression years to serve during World War II as Atlantic escorts, for which duty they were ill-suited. This 1920s picture shows her in a typical destroyer "nest".**

"V" and "W" classes

By 1916 the growth of the fleet destroyer was such that yet another, even larger, leader was required. The earlier Lightfoots had been considered over-expensive, and the Admiralty now approved two, five-ship series for the purpose of comparison. Both were to prove influential.

Five (the Shakespeare class) were all by Thornycroft to their own design, which effectively set the pattern for British destroyers for nigh on two decades. Their major innovation was in the adoption of superimposed guns which, with suitable blast shielding, could be centreline-mounted, maximizing broadside fire without undue penalty in overall length.

On an identical trials displacement with the *Lightfoot*, the lead ship mounted the heavier 4.7in gun. While having a lower rate of fire, this weapon used a ship-stopping 50lb projectile in place of the 31lb shell of the 4in gun. With a fifth 4.7in carried between their two tall funnels, the Shakespeares were imposing ships, their size permitting also a single 3in High-Angle (HA) gun for use against aircraft or for firing starshell, and two triple banks of torpedo tubes.

ABOVE: ***Viceroy*, together with the *Viscount*, were a pair of Thornycroft "specials", recognizable through their larger after funnel. They boasted 10 per cent more power than could the Admiralty design, and were slightly beamier and deeper.**

TOP: ***Versatile*, marked up as a divisional leader of the then Atlantic Fleet's Fifth Destroyer Flotilla, was typical of a large number of near-identical "V & Ws", as they were invariably known. Note the minelaying track in a sponson right aft.**
ABOVE: **Retaining her full power but refitted with radar-equipped director, two twin 4in High-Angle (HA) mountings and multiple pompoms, *Verdun* gave valuable service to the east coast convoys as one of the "Wair" escorts.**

More modest in scale (and 6.1m/20ft shorter on the waterline) were the five Admiralty-designed boats. Originally considered "300-foot leaders", they lost this distinction and adopted "V" names when it was decided to order 25 more. The original five were all launched between March and May 1917. They carried two pairs of superimposed 4in guns, and the two paired torpedo tubes of earlier classes.

Previous argument had revolved around the relative importance of gun and torpedo armament, but a new role had emerged in the need for anti-submarine escort. Space and weight margins thus had to be allowed, while 17 of the class were fitted for carrying over 50 mines apiece.

The initial order of "V"-named boats was followed in December 1916 by another for 21, mostly beginning with "W".

The primary difference lay in their respective twinned and tripled torpedo tubes.

The "V & Ws", with their various combinations of thick and thin funnel, proved to be capable ships and, early in 1918, two blocks of what became known as "Modified V & Ws" were ordered. These differed in carrying the larger 4.7in gun. Of these later blocks, of 16 and 38 hulls respectively, only 9 and 7 were completed, the remainder being cancelled at the armistice, although many were well advanced.

Thornycroft "specials" continued to influence official opinion. Externally, they differed in having funnels of equal size, the after one flat-sided. They also had increased freeboard, although the bridge was already higher by virtue of having to maintain adequate vision over the superimposed "B" gun.

Barely a handful of the class was scrapped between the wars and when, in 1939, they entered what was for most their second war, the newest hull was 20 years old, and had deteriorated from years in reserve. No longer fleet destroyers and now, in their turn, considered small, the majority underwent conversion.

Fifteen became anti-aircraft escorts (generally known as "Wairs"), primarily to supplement the Hunts protecting the strongly contested English east coast convoys. These ships retained full propulsive power but landed at least one bank of torpedo tubes. Their four single guns were exchanged for a twin High-Angle, Dual-Purpose, (HA, DP) 4in mounting forward and aft, with multiple machine-guns or pompoms amidships. A more substantial bridge was fitted, supporting a radar-laid director, extra topweight which made for an easier roll movement.

Sixteen more of the class became long-range escorts for Atlantic convoys. The forward boiler was removed, still leaving adequate power for 24½ knots but releasing space for extra fuel tanks and accommodation for crews which, in wartime, increased from 115 to as many as 170. In this service they presented a very different appearance. The forward funnel was removed and at least one set of torpedo tubes and the two guns in "A" and "Y" positions landed. Air and surface-search radars, depth charges and throwers were added.

ABOVE: One of the later "Repeat Ws", *Worcester* mounts the noticeably larger 4.7in gun. She is seen in about 1942 leading the earlier *Walpole*; by this time she had an enlarged bridge structure and forward funnel, even early radar. BELOW: *Watchman* as converted for long-range escort. Forefunnel and forward boiler have been removed. After torpedo tubes, and "A" and "Y" guns landed. Radar and "bow-chaser" added, the latter probably indicating coastal convoy attachment.

LEFT: Although by World War II considered small and obsolescent, the V & Ws played a noble role as Atlantic escorts, usually landing "A" and "Y" guns, together with after torpedo tubes, for increased capacity. Here, the radar-fitted *Wanderer* refuels at sea.

ABOVE: Immaculate in pre-war paint, *Whirlwind* has the lighter grey then worn by Mediterranean Fleet destroyers, to whose First Flotilla she is attached. Note the harbour "gash chute", rigged by the galley amidships.

"W" class, as built

Displacement: 1,100 tons (light); 1,460 tons (full load)
Length: 91.4m/300ft (bp); 95.1m/312ft (oa)
Beam: 9m/29ft 6in
Draught: 3.6m/11ft 8in (full load)
Armament: 4 x 4in QF guns (4x1); 1 x 3in HA gun; 6 x 21in torpedo tubes (2x3)
Machinery: Single-reduction geared steam turbines, 3 boilers, 2 shafts
Power: 20,142kW/27,000shp for 34 knots
Endurance: 370 tons oil for 4,815km/2,600nm at 15 knots
Protection: None
Complement: 115

Early torpedo boats

Well before Tirpitz began to make his name as the architect of the Kaiser's new battle fleet, he was, as a Captain, appointed to be Inspector of Torpedo Development. At this time he was an enthusiastic supporter of the French *Jeune École* philosophy of defeating a major seapower with larger numbers of inexpensive torpedo craft. Instrumental in the establishment of a state torpedo factory and development facility, he also pressed for gun-armed "high seas" torpedo boats to be built in addition to coastal craft.

Prototype examples were obtained from domestic and foreign – including British – builders. Tirpitz's comment, on having been made responsible for developing a doctrine for their use, was that they "proved to be either unsuitable or inefficient".

Between 1890 and 1896 the Danzig firm of Schichau was given a monopoly of torpedo boat construction for the Imperial Navy, a period which saw displacements increase from generally 100 tons or less, to about 180 tons, with resulting improvements in seakeeping, in which the type was singularly deficient.

Even after other yards were permitted to build to official account, Schichau continued to turn out some of the best examples. A considerable advance over small, earlier craft was the S.67 design of 1894, of which seven were constructed, with nine improved follow-ons.

The writer Erskine Childers' description of a "low, grey rat of a vessel" in *Riddle of the Sands*, well fits the appearance of these craft, turtledeck forward with a depressed, protected conning position ahead of a single funnel. Two rotating centreline tubes aft were separated by a mast with torpedo derrick. A third tube was located in the forecastle, launching through the cutaway forefoot.

They were the last to be powered with the old-style locomotive boiler, pending the introduction of Thornycroft small-tube units.

ABOVE: **Completed in 1894, S.71 had three 45cm torpedo tubes. Later renamed T.71, she was given a second funnel and mast, serving throughout World War I as a tender and minesweeper. She was sold out in 1921.** BELOW LEFT: **Showing the flag on a Rhein cruise are three early Schichau torpedo boats of the numerous S.7 type, of which 50 were built. Less than 38m/124ft in length, they are fitted with a pronounced forward turtledeck.**

S.67–73

Displacement: 135 tons (light); 163 tons (full load)
Length: 47.9m/157ft 3in (oa)
Beam: 5.4m/17ft 9in
Draught: 1.6m/5ft 4in (light); 2.6m/8ft 6in (full load)
Armament: 1 x 5cm gun; 3 x 45cm torpedo tubes (3x1)
Machinery: 1 x 3-cylinder triple-expansion engine, 1 boiler, 1 shaft
Power: 1,194kW/1,600ihp for 22 knots
Endurance: 30 tons coal for 2,025km/1,100nm at 15 knots
Protection: None
Complement: 21

Divisionsboote

By 1887 the Imperial German Navy had completed, or had under construction over 40 torpedo boats, with plans for many more. To control the, otherwise, unwieldy formations there was introduced the so-called "Division Boat", or flotilla leader. Although of twice the displacement of their charges, they suffered the usual shortcoming of contemporary small-scale reciprocating machinery not being capable of delivering sufficient power to make them significantly faster. Neither were they of much greater endurance.

Compare, for instance, the first, D.1, with S.41 of the same year (1887). Some 40 per cent larger, and with a second boiler, she had about 84 per cent more power yet, at 20.6 knots, had an advantage of barely half a knot. Succeeding boats, D.2–D.8, used small-tube (rather than locomotive) boilers, increasing speed by up to two knots. D.9 (1894) and D.10 (1896) were increased in size to accommodate a third boiler, the latter boat also adopting twin-screw propulsion to make 27 knots.

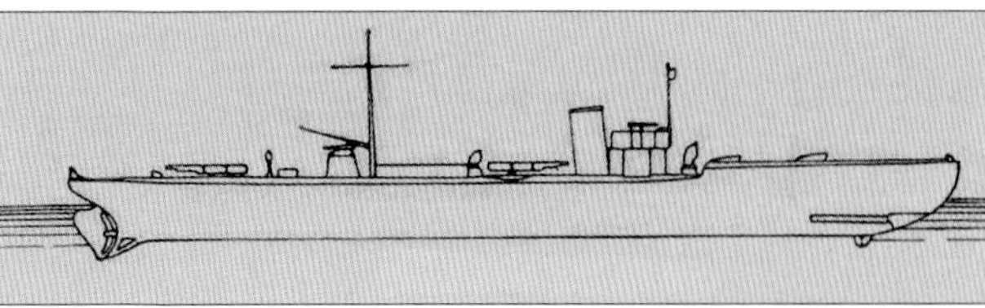

Although, as a type, Division Boats were adjudged disappointments, one can see in them quite clearly the genesis of the *Grosse Torpedoboote* (equivalent to Torpedo Boat Destroyer), which title was generally adopted after D.10.

Until D.8, Division Boats maintained the configuration of the smaller torpedo boats. Their forward turtle decks were very wet, and D.9 introduced the great improvement of a full-height forecastle. This terminated short of the bridge structure, leaving a diminutive well deck, somewhat lengthened in D.10. Their size also permitted them to carry further small-calibre guns.

In common with all early German flotilla craft, the D-boats had bow rudders, not held very effective when going ahead. All except D.1 had steel hulls, zinc-clad below water level.

As a comment on seakeeping, D.10 was known by her crew as *Schlingerpott* (roughly "rolling tub").

TOP: **This picture of the 56m/184ft D.1 may show her disarmed and acting as the Baltic "station yacht", or inspection vessel. Her mainmast is unusually low and a flimsy bridge has been added.**

ABOVE: **D.9 dated from 1894. Note the bow torpedo tube and diminutive bow rudder. The unusual rudder arrangement was necessitated by the large-diameter single screw.**

ABOVE: **The Thornycroft-built D.10 shows British characteristics in appearance. The turtleback forms a low forecastle, abaft which is a gun platform which, unfortunately for the gun crews, creates an excellent breakwater.**

D.10, as built

	Built	Completed
D.10	Thornycroft, Chiswick	1898

Displacement: 305 tons (light); 364 tons (full load)
Length: 64.3m/211ft 1in (wl); 66.1m/217ft (oa)
Beam: 6m/19ft 6in
Draught: 2.3m/7ft 6in (mean)
Armament: 5 x 5cm guns (5x1); 3 x 45cm torpedo tubes (3x1)
Machinery: 2 x 4-cylinder triple-expansion engines, 3 boilers, 2 shafts
Power: 4,290kW/5,750ihp for 27 knots
Endurance: 79 tons coal for 3,890km/2,100nm at 14 knots
Protection: None
Complement: 40

LEFT: **The Schichau-built S.120–124 dated from 1903–04, with S.123 seen here. Two of her three 45cm torpedo tubes were sided in the forward well deck. This arrangement allowed them to be used at finer angles on the bow.** BELOW: **Seen in what might be termed "fairly average" conditions for the North Sea, the Germania-built G.110 was one of a group of six built from 1900–02. Slightly larger than the S.123 (left), she was capable of the then high speed of 29.2 knots.**

Grosse Torpedoboote (1902)

Good seakeeping is greatly influenced by length and by forward freeboard. Later Division Boats proved the point with short, full-height forecastles and the extra length necessary to accommodate a third boiler. They thus established the basic form of the German Large Torpedo Boat, i.e. Destroyer, which persisted through to the end of World War I.

On much the same length as a Division Boat, succeeding classes had their bridge structure moved a little farther aft. This made for drier bridges and also a forward well deck long enough to locate a single, centreline torpedo tube, capable of being trained on to either beam.

Three-boiler ships usually had two boiler spaces sited forward of the engine room, and one abaft it. There were two funnels, spaced widely to permit two more centreline tubes to be located between. The forward funnel and bridge were effectively a single structure, leading to a peculiar arrangement whereby the forward boiler exhausted via a curving trunk, which emerged from the well deck and passed beneath the bridge to join the forward funnel.

Sterns were subject to considerable variation in form in efforts to improve water flow across the propellers; "cruiser" sterns, "spoon" sterns and sloping profiles were all common.

German destroyers of this era were not named, being designated by the prefix "T" followed by a number allocated in order of construction. In general use, however, were the alternative prefixes "S", "V" or "G", denoting the major builders Schichau, Vulcan or Germania. Only the final two digits of the number were painted-up on the bows. Flotilla/division letters or numbers might be carried temporarily on the after funnel, or distinguishing day marks, e.g. triangles or rings, hoisted on the signal mast.

ABOVE: **Persistent reports of 30-plus knot speeds by German torpedo boats proved to be a great spur to British development. The S.143 was one of twelve 70.7m/232ft boats dating from 1906–08, armed with 8.8cm guns and four 50cm torpedoes.**

Grosse Torpedoboote, typical for type, as built

	Built	Completed
G.108–113	Germania Werft, Kiel	1902

Displacement: 324 tons (light); 432 tons (full load)
Length: 65.5m/215ft (wl); 65.8m/216ft (oa)
Beam: 6.7m/22ft
Draught: 2.3m/7ft 7in (light); 2.9m/9ft 6in (full load)
Armament: 3/4 x 5cm guns (3/4x1); 3 x 45cm torpedo tubes (3x1)
Machinery: 2 x 3-cylinder triple-expansion engines, 3 boilers, 2 shafts
Power: 4,476kW/6,000ihp for 29 knots
Endurance: 108 tons coal for 1,850km/1,000nm at 17 knots
Protection: None
Complement: 55

LEFT: **Vulcan at Stettin also produced many torpedo boats, including the two very similar groups V.150–155 and V.156–160, dating from 1907–08. Note how, although the bridges were well set back, they remained low to minimize silhouette.** ABOVE: **V.180 shows her generous forward freeboard. The forward well greatly reduced the amount of solid water impacting the bridge structure, though at a considerable price to the forward torpedo crews. Note the rounded, stress-reducing sheer strakes.**

Grosse Torpedoboote (1907–08)

The first destroyers to be ordered from the Vulcan yard at Stettin were V.150–161, completed in 1908. They were the last German boats to rely solely on coal-firing, while the last of the series, V.161, was the first to be propelled by steam turbines.

Similar in layout to earlier groups, they nonetheless had developed a more robust appearance. The well deck, with its single torpedo tube, was considered as a feature by the Royal Navy but was rejected on the grounds that the torpedo crew would be continuously inundated with water driving over the forecastle. Certainly the Germans tried various configurations of forecastle and breakwaters. The bridge structure, with its enclosed navigating bridge, extended the full width of the ship, its forward side slightly rounded to shed solid water the more easily. The two funnels were of large, round section, the forward one capped. Between them the hull was bare to allow the training of the two amidships torpedo tubes, themselves separated by a pair of massive engine room ventilators. A torpedo derrick was stepped on the tall mainmast, used for all flag signals. A vestigial foremast and large searchlight (the Germans took night-fighting seriously) crowned the wheelhouse roof. One 8.8cm gun was located on the forecastle, another right aft.

Spare torpedoes were often carried, unprotected, on the upper deck. Six of the class were later upgraded, the forward tube being twinned, and all changed for the heavier 50cm torpedo.

The experimental V.161 (later, T.161, all torpedo boats acquiring the standard "T" prefix) was propelled by two AEG direct-drive steam turbines. Her size and displacement were unchanged but her four boilers were of higher output, permitting speeds of up to 33 knots.

Vulcan followed up in 1909 with V.162–164, slightly enlarged and with one of their four boilers fired by diesel oil.

ABOVE: **Still bearing her original H.190 pendant number, the Howaldt-built *Claus van Bevern* is seen as rebuilt for a "research vessel" in the late 1930s. Rearmed, she participated in the invasion of Denmark in April 1940.**

V.150–160, as built

	Built	Completed
V.150–160	AG Vulcan, Stettin	1907–08

Displacement: 548 tons (light); 670 tons (full load)
Length: 72.2m/237ft (wl); 72.5m/238ft (oa)
Beam: 7.8m/25ft 7in
Draught: 2.8m/9ft 3in (light); 3m/9ft 11in (full load)
Armament: 2 x 8.8cm guns (2x1); 3 x 45cm torpedo tubes (3x1)
Machinery: 2 x 3-cylinder triple-expansion engines, 4 boilers, 2 shafts
Power: 8,131kW/10,900ihp for 30 knots
Endurance: 161 tons coal for 3,700km/2,000nm at 14 knots
Protection: None
Complement: 81

LEFT: **The G.37 of 1915 survived what must have been a spectacular collision, not uncommon with fast-manoeuvring torpedo boats. On November 4, 1917, however, she was destroyed by a mine off the Dutch Friesian islands, and four of the crew were lost.** BELOW **Despite their very crowded appearance, the V.25 type (V.26 seen here) were able to accommodate 24 mines as deck load. As built, the bridge and forefunnel were considerably lower than seen here in their post-1916 reconfiguration.**

Torpedoboote (1914–15)

Confusingly, all pre-1912 German torpedo boats, irrespective of builder, were renumbered in the coherent series to T.197 but, from 1912, the numbered series began again, each group assuming a prefix appropriate to one of the four major builders.

Between 1909 and 1911, successive groups had increased displacement to about 810 tons full load but the first three groups completed in 1912 (V.1–6, G.7–12 and S.13–24) retrenched to some 700 tons. All were turbine-propelled, the Schichau ships being consistently faster as well as carrying the heavier 10.5cm gun, which fired a 15kg/33lb shell.

The British Admiralty's continued concern at the reported performance of German destroyers appears well grounded for, while the Schichau boats were smaller than the contemporary Acherons, their legend speed was greater by about 5 knots. Their gun armament was also superior.

In 1914, the next group to be delivered, V.25–30, marked a further increase in size, being no less than 7m/30ft longer than the preceding class. This allowed them to carry six torpedo tubes, the after two mountings being twinned. The 8.8cm gun was, however, readopted, assisting in giving a stability margin sufficient to carry a deck load of 24 mines.

The final groups of the earlier series (T.186–191 and T.192–197) had adopted a "long forecastle" layout, the forecastle being narrowed on either side, forward of the bridge structure, sufficient to permit the location of a single torpedo tube per side, each training through a limited forward angle. This arrangement was adopted again in the 1914 Schichau boats, S.31–36. Four more, S.49–52, delivered in 1915, differed in having single-reduction geared turbines. Slightly larger than contemporary British M-class boats, they were of similar power but, reportedly, were some 2 knots faster. It is not certain, however, whether trials were conducted in the same deep condition as British ships.

ABOVE: **Despite her odd appearance, S.49's layout is practical. She has a short, high forecastle for dryness. The prominent casing exhausts the forward boiler and passes beneath the bridge to the forward funnel, allowing the bridge to be positioned well aft.**

V.25–30, as built

	Built	Completed
V.25–30	AG Vulcan, Stettin	1914

Displacement: 798 tons (light); 958 tons (full load)
Length: 77.8m/255ft 4in (wl); 78.5m/257ft 8in (oa)
Beam: 8.33m/27ft 4in
Draught: 3.33m/10ft 9in (light); 3.63m/11ft 11in (full load)
Armament: 3 x 8.8cm guns (3x1); 6 x 50cm torpedo tubes (2x1/2x2); 24 mines
Machinery: Direct-drive steam turbines, 3 boilers, 2 shafts
Power: 17,531kW/23,500shp for 36 knots
Endurance: 221 tons oil for 2,025km/1,100nm at 20 knots
Protection: None
Complement: 80

LEFT: **Howaldt at Kiel came late to German destroyer production, but their initial trio, H.145–147 completed in 1918, were among the largest. Still a new ship, H.145 was scuttled in Scapa Flow, only to be salvaged and scrapped in 1928.**

Torpedoboote (1917)

Wartime experience in the North Sea led, inevitably, to increasing destroyer size and, as in the Royal Navy, individual builders were allowed a degree of freedom to interpret a general specification in a manner totally unknown in the computer-controlled precision of today.

After 1915, Germania-built boats, e.g. G.37–42, had a loftier bridge structure, relocated to the after end of a lengthened forecastle, eliminating the forward well. The after end of the forecastle was tapered in to allow a single torpedo tube to be sited on either side. With the bridge moved, the boiler spaces were closed up and exhausted through two thicker and more closely spaced funnels. These adopted the sloped funnel cap that became a feature of German warships. All destroyers completed after 1914 were fully oil-fired.

After Jutland, in mid-1916, later German destroyers exchanged their 8.8cm guns for 10.5cm weapons carried by all new construction. This kept pace with the British, who had found that a 4in projectile was the smallest that had any chance of stopping a larger, modern destroyer.

Both pairs of torpedo tubes were now located abaft the funnels and separated by a bandstand supporting one of the three main guns. To the searchlights atop the bridge was added a second, conspicuously sited on a small house abaft the tall mainmast. Increased demands on signalling had also seen the foremast considerably heightened.

The bow rudder, a complication of doubtful utility, was being abandoned and a reasonably uniform "cruiser" stern adopted, although the form of this was often unclear due to many boats being fitted for minelaying.

Special "torpedo-boat steel" had been developed to withstand the high tensile stresses developed at sea in long, shallow hulls. Germania-built boats had double bottoms, some compartments of which were fuel tanks. It is not clear whether these could be flooded as ballast tanks.

ABOVE: **H.146 and her sister H.147 (seen here) were ceded to the French Navy post-war, becoming the *Rageot de la Touche* and *Delage* respectively and serving until 1935. The low freeboard, particularly forward, is very evident, while the bridge is located well forward.**

G.37–40, as rearmed

	Built	Completed
G.37–40	Germania Werft, Kiel	1915

Displacement: 807 tons (light); 1,031 tons (full load)
Length: 78.6m/258ft (wl); 79.5m/261ft (oa)
Beam: 8.4m/27ft 5in
Draught: 3.5m/11ft 4in (light); 3.7m/12ft 3in (full load)
Armament: 3 x 10.5cm guns (3x1); 6 x 50cm torpedo tubes (2x1/2x2); 24 mines
Machinery: Direct-drive steam turbines, 3 boilers, 2 shafts
Power: 17,904kW/24,000shp for 34.5 knots
Endurance: 295 tons oil for 3,130km/1,700nm at 17 knots
Protection: None
Complement: 84

ABOVE: **The six ex-Noviks, B.97–98 and B.109–112, were completed in 1915 but, in terms of armament, displacement and speed equated almost exactly to the two British Amazon prototypes, which were not launched until 1926.**
RIGHT: **Although wearing a naval ensign and displaying a circular flotilla day-shape at the mainmast, the B.97 appears to be unarmed in this picture. Of the six, she was the only one to have a post-war career, as the Italian *Cesare Rossarol.***

Expropriated destroyers

Warships building to foreign account are commonly taken over by governments faced with imminent hostilities. The Imperial German Navy thus benefited by the official expropriation of destroyers building for Tsarist Russia and Argentina.

Domestic classes, whether *Kleine* or *Grosse Torpedoboote*, tended to be popularly termed, simply, *Torpedoboote*. The above acquisitions were, however, so much larger that the prefix *Grosse* was invariable. They were, it could be claimed, among the German Navy's first true fleet-type destroyers.

The Hamburg yard of Blohm and Voss, not then associated with destroyer construction, had six of its own design, the Novik class, under construction at the outbreak of war. Under the German flag they were designated B.97–98 and B.109–112. All were completed in 1915 and, despite design deficiencies, emphasized the shortcomings of average size under North Sea conditions, influencing the move toward larger domestic designs. Their size permitted them to be fitted with passive, anti-rolling tanks.

Powered by four boilers, each had three, equispaced funnels, the foremost of which was later raised. As built, four 8.8cm guns were fitted, all on the centreline but in varying positions. In 1916, these were exchanged for 10.5cm weapons. All were of the short forecastle and well deck layout.

Marginally smaller were the four Argentine destroyers building at Germania. Their intended names of *Santiago*, *San Luis*, *Sante Fé* and *Tucuman* became, simply, G.101–104 on their completion in 1915. Although lacking a well deck, their forecastles were still short. They were the only wartime German destroyers with both bridge structure and forward funnel located on the forecastle deck. The navigating bridge was thus substantial and enclosed. As with the Russian boats, all were retrospectively upgunned.

Of the above twelve destroyers, no less than ten terminated their careers in the mass scuttling of the High Seas Fleet at Scapa Flow in 1919.

ABOVE: **Closely resembling, in form and size, the Blohm and Voss boats (above) were the Vulcan-built pair, V.99 and V.100. V.99 was badly damaged in the Baltic, coincidentally by the existing Russian destroyer *Novik*, before sinking on mines.**

B-type, average as rearmed

	Built	Completed
B.97–98 and B.109–112	Blohm and Voss, Hamburg	1915

Displacement: 1,350 tons (light); 1,812 tons (full load)
Length: 96m/315ft 2in (wl); 98m/321ft 8in (oa)
Beam: 9.4m/30ft 9in
Draught: 3.4m/11ft 2in (light); 3.8m/12ft 6in (full load)
Armament: 4 x 10.5cm guns (4x1); 6 x 50cm torpedo tubes (2x1/2x2); 24 mines
Machinery: Direct-drive steam turbines, 4 boilers, 2 shafts
Power: 29,840kW/40,000shp for 36.5 knots
Endurance: 516 tons oil for 4,815km/2,600nm at 20 knots
Protection: None
Complement: 110

LEFT: **Laying astern a Bretagne-class battleship, the size of the *Amiral Sénès* ex-S.113 can be appreciated. She served as a flotilla leader in the French Navy until 1936.** ABOVE: **The S.113 and her completed sister V.116 introduced the 15cm gun to World War I German destroyers. In this shot, again as the French *Amiral Sénès*, her low freeboard is evident. The anchor is recessed to reduce spray.**

S.113-type leaders

Launched in 1907, the British leader *Swift* proved to be an over-ambitious one-off. Her 2,200 tons and her ability to maintain 35 knots were, however, impressive. Less so was the 6in gun that she carried for a trial period.

The advantages of larger hulls were further impressed on the German Navy from 1915 in its operation of expropriated foreign destroyers. In 1916, therefore, all four major builders were each given an order for a trio of ships of exceptional size. Although most were never completed, data suggests that the builders had a degree of freedom in interpreting the specification.

Although probably intended as leaders, they attracted little priority; all were laid down in 1916 but only two were ever completed, a lead ship from each of Schichau (S.113) and Vulcan (V.116). Uniquely, they carried four single 15cm guns, one forward, one amidships and two right aft, one of which was superimposed. Large guns are notoriously difficult to lay accurately from small hulls, while manual loading of the 45kg/100lb projectiles on a lively deck would tax the best of gun crews.

Another "first" was two pairs of 60cm torpedo tubes, one mounting being located between the two funnels, the other forward of the mainmast.

They developed as much power as a contemporary light cruiser, yet failed to meet designed speed. Even without their intended deck load of mines, they were described as "crank". Both completed ships were surrendered as reparation, S.113 serving at the French *Amiral Sénès* and V.116 as the Italian *Premuda*.

LEFT: **Seen at Wilhelmshaven is the 1918-completed S.131, leadship of a class of mine-destroyers that reverted to smaller dimensions and the handier 10.5cm gun. Note how the bridge is elevated to allow solid water to pass beneath.**

S.113-type, as designed

Name	Builder	Displacement*	Length (oa/beam)
S.113–115	Schichau	2,372	106 x 10.2m/347ft 11in x 33ft 6in
V.116–118	AG Vulcan	2,318	107.5 x 10.4m/352ft 10in x 34ft 2in
G.119–121	Germania	2,362	107.5 x 10.3m/352ft 10in x 33ft 9in
B.122–124	Blohm and Voss	2,312	108.8 x 10.3m/357ft 2in x 33ft 9in

* Tons, full load

S.113, as designed

Displacement: 2,023 tons (light); 2,372 tons (full load)
Length: 105.4m/346ft (wl); 106m/347ft 11in (oa)
Beam: 10.2m/33ft 6in
Draught: 3.4m/11ft 2in (light); 4.8m/15ft 9in (full load)
Armament: 4 x 15cm guns (4x1); 4 x 60cm torpedo tubes (2x2); 40 mines
Machinery: Single-reduction geared steam turbines, 4 boilers, 2 shafts
Power: 33,570kW/45,000shp for nearly 37 knots
Endurance: 707 tons oil for 4,630km/2,500nm at 2 knots
Protection: None
Complement: 168

LEFT: **USS *Thornton* (TB.33) belonged to the nine-ship Shubrick class, the last torpedo boats built for the US Navy. Note that the machinery space was located between the boiler rooms. The multi-masted coastal schooners were very much a feature of the American scene.** BELOW: **Threatened by no foreign power, the United States showed little interest in coastal torpedo boats, the appropriately named *Cushing* (TB.1) not appearing until 1890. Although equipped with quadruple-expansion machinery, she was as frail as early European craft.**

Early torpedo boats

The advisory board of the US Navy supported the acquisition of up to 150 torpedo boats for the protection of major bases and seaports. It also appreciated that an American battle fleet, operating in foreign waters, might need to defend itself against hostile torpedo attack. Also recommended, therefore, was that major warships should, themselves, carry torpedo launches, or what elsewhere would be termed Second-class Torpedo Boats.

Funds, however, were scarce, priorities laying elsewhere, and the first torpedo boat, USS *Cushing* (TB.1), was not completed until 1890. She was built largely to the ideas of her constructor, Herreshoff and, although her 23 knots were not impressive, the Navy was determined to develop domestic expertise. The department thus further developed Herreshoff's design for TB.2. Named *Ericsson*, she went to a different builder. Both craft carried three tubes to launch 18in Whitehead torpedoes.

Half a dozen yards quickly became involved each, as in Great Britain, being permitted considerable interpretation of the basic specification. In these pre-Panama Canal days, it was necessary to build ships on the east or west coast where they would serve.

A total of 35 torpedo boats was eventually built, comprising 17 separate designs. Except for the one-off *Rowan* (TB.8), which had a short, full-height forecastle, all followed the general pattern of minimum profile, with a turtledecked forward end. A displacement of 175 tons was considered optimum but, although some boats exceeded 30 knots on trials, it was thought desirable to sacrifice a little on maximum speed in order to strengthen what proved to be fragile hulls.

None had superstructures, the main features being two or three funnels and a light signal mast, all heavily raked, some collapsible. Both forward and aft were low, protected conning positions.

The nine-ship Shubrick class, the only extended group, concluded torpedo boat construction in 1901.

ABOVE: **The Herreshoff-designed *Porter* (TB.6) came early in the sequence, yet it is clear that the Shubricks were only an extrapolation of her design. Despite the turtledeck forward, there is no raised forecastle, the hull having a hogged appearance.**

Shubrick class, average

	Builders	Completed
TB.27–35	Various	1899–1901

Displacement: 165–220 tons
Length: 53.3m/175ft (oa)
Beam: 5.4m/17ft 9in
Draught: 2m/6ft 6in
Armament: 3 x 6pdr guns; 3 x 18in torpedo tubes (3x1)
Machinery: 4-cylinder triple-expansion engines, 2 shafts
Power: 2,238kW/3,000ihp for 25 knots
Endurance: Not known
Protection: Minimal
Complement: 28

Bainbridge (DD.1) class

With little prospect that the US battle fleet would be threatened by hostile torpedo craft, there existed no apparent requirement for the newly developing "torpedo boat destroyer". In the course of the 1898 war with Spain, however, three of the latter's destroyers steamed to Cuba, proving their capacity to cross the Atlantic. Although they were subsequently eliminated, their action was sufficient to galvanize the US Navy into acquiring its own. As politicians periodically have to relearn, warships cannot be conjured up by emergency bills, and the war was history by the time that the first American destroyer was commissioned in 1902.

The sixteen ships of the pioneer Bainbridge class (DD.1–16) comprised four distinct subgroups. The official design, to which nine were built, included a full-height forecastle to improve seakeeping. Sufficient latitude was, however, given to enable other builders to dispense with this feature in favour of a torpedo boat-style turtledeck forward. At the expense of wetness and cramped quarters, this measure saved weight which could be used to work in heavier hull scantlings.

All sixteen had four funnels. Except for those in DD.8 and 9, which were close-grouped, these were arranged in two widely spaced pairs, a visual indication of two boiler spaces separated by the engine room. The two reciprocating engines reportedly vibrated badly at high speeds; this, in conjunction with generally over-weight construction, resulted in their failing contract speed by as much as 1½ knots.

Compared with the Royal Navy's exactly contemporary "30-knotters", the Bainbridges were larger but carried the same scale of armament. Despite their disappointing maximum speed, they proved to have an unexpectedly high endurance at cruising speeds. Their extra size also conferred adequate seakeeping and this, with their robust construction, made them a suitable model for extrapolation.

ABOVE: **The Spanish–American War had been fought before the US Navy received its first true destroyers. These, the 16-strong Bainbridge class, fell into four subgroups. This is *Truxtun* (DD.14).** LEFT: **Detail of one of *Perry*'s (DD.11) two single, revolving 18in torpedo tubes emphasizes the still-simple construction and the continuing spindle shape of the weapons themselves. The tube is located right aft.** BELOW: **The nine-strong "Bainbridge" group differed from the Truxtuns in having a raised forecastle. Although lighter and smaller, they were slower. The *Preble*'s (DD.12) forward 6pdrs are sided, firing ahead along the faceted sides of the forecastle.**

ABOVE: **This shot of *Worden* (DD.16), a sister of *Truxtun*, emphasizes the length and lack of depth of hull common to early destroyers. A corresponding lack of stiffness led to considerable deflection and "working", while machinery-induced vibration was magnified.**

"Official" type

	Builders	Commissioned
DD.1–5/DD.10–13	Various	1902–03

Displacement: 414 tons (light); 450 tons (full load)
Length: 74.4m/244ft 3in (wl); 76.1m/249ft 10in (oa)
Beam: 7.1m/23ft 5in
Draught: 2.1m/6ft 9in (full load)
Armament: 2 x 3in guns; 5 x 6pdr guns; 2 x 18in torpedo tubes (2x1)
Machinery: Triple-expansion steam engines, 4 boilers, 2 shafts
Power: 5,968kW/8,000ihp for 28 knots
Bunkers: 212 tons coal
Protection: None
Complement: 71

LEFT: **Rapidly eclipsed by larger types, the very similar Smith and Paulding classes were popularly known as "Flivvers".** ***Perkins*** **(DD.26), like all built by Fore River, had three funnels rather than four. Note heavy W/T spreaders and World War I camouflage.**

Smith (DD.17) and Paulding (DD.22) classes

An eight-year hiatus followed completion of the Bainbridges. While this was due primarily to lack of funding, it gave the service time to evaluate what it already had, before deciding the way ahead. It was by now accepted that the battle fleet would usually have to be accompanied by destroyers. If the latter were to be asset, rather than liability, ruggedness and reliability had to be their main attributes.

A specially convened board of 1905 recommended that all future destroyers run trials in realistic loaded condition, rather than aiming simply for maximum speed. Seakeeping, strength, wetness and manoeuvrability were emphasized. For survivability, boiler spaces should be separated by the engine room.

While still effectively being stretched Bainbridges, the five Smiths (DD.17–21), authorized in 1906–07, incorporated these requirements. Their four funnels grouped distinctively by builder, the "Flivvers", as they were popularly known, emphasized gun armament at the expense of torpedoes. Of the five 3in guns, three fired forward while two were located on the centreline, aft. One centreline 18in torpedo tube was also sited well aft, with a further single tube on either side amidships. All the class were steam turbine-propelled, the resulting difficulties in designing fast-turning propellers probably accounting for the requirement for a third shaft.

A further eight units, authorized in 1908, became the Paulding (DD.22) class. Two further orders extended this class eventually to 21 ships. During "prohibition" most of these were transferred to the Coast Guard.

Although of the same basic dimensions as the Smiths, the Pauldings were some 50 tons heavier. Their resulting deeper draught was more than compensated by an increase of 20 per cent in power and an extra 1½ knots. Oil firing was also adopted. The same gun armament was carried but all three torpedo tube mountings were twinned.

ABOVE: **During "prohibition", the US Navy transferred 13 of these classes to its Coast Guard sister service. As with** ***Paulding*** **(DD.22), they retained names but adopted new temporary numbers. Note that she has retained the "North Atlantic" front to the bridge structure.**

Paulding class

	Built	Commissioned
DD.22–42	Various	1910–12

Displacement: 742 tons (light); 897 tons (full load)
Length: 88m/289ft (wl); 89.6m/294ft (oa)
Beam: 8m/26ft 2in
Draught: 2.5m/8ft 3in (full load)
Armament: 5 x 3in guns (5x1); 6 x 18in torpedo tubes (3x2)
Machinery: Direct-drive steam turbines, 4 boilers, 3 shafts
Power: 8,952kW/12,000shp for 29.5 knots
Endurance: 241 tons oil for 5,556km/3,000nm at 16 knots
Protection: None
Complement: 89

LEFT: ***Cummings* (DD.44) of the Cassin class. These and the Tuckers were the first "Thousand Tonners". Twin-screwed, they were experimental in machinery, with geared steam turbines, some with auxiliary cruising turbines or reciprocating engines.**

Cassin (DD.43) and Tucker (DD.57) classes

Even before the final "Flivvers" were completed, the characteristics of the succeeding class were being assessed. Having accepted that the very high speeds of some foreign destroyers were unnecessary, the General Board (now responsible for ship definition) looked instead for long endurance. This, ideally would match that of the capital ships that they were intended to escort. Speed (defined as 30 knots for 1 hour) was necessary in order to manoeuvre independently and to regain station, but size was a parameter that really decided a destroyer's ability to *maintain* station.

Size was also of interest in the argument (common with that in other fleets) as to whether a destroyer screen was essentially defensive (emphasizing gun armament) or offensive (torpedoes). The response was to add a further pair of torpedo tubes and to upgrade the 3in gun armament to 4in, better able to stop larger contemporary destroyers.

Problems were still being experienced with matching the high shaft speeds associated with direct-drive steam turbines with efficient propeller design. Some of the next class – the 14 Cassin (DD.43–56) – were thus given auxiliary turbines or reciprocating engines for cruising. The permanent answer lay, of course, in single-reduction gearing for the main turbines, but this was introduced only in the *Wadsworth* (DD.60), a unit of the 12-strong Tucker class (DD.57–68).

Known for obvious reasons as the "Thousand Tonners", the Cassin carried four 4in guns, two of them sided on the main deck at the break of the forecastle. The after, centreline torpedo tubes location having proved impractical, their four twin mountings were now sided farther forward.

About 3m/10ft longer, and displacing an extra 80 tons, the Tuckers differed primarily in having geared turbines and in carrying the heavier 21in torpedo. The final half-dozen of the class were given four triple mountings.

ABOVE: **Taking her place in a fleet review, the *Benham* (DD.49) is seen in peacetime dark Atlantic Fleet grey. Not for the first or last time, the "Thousand Tonners" were heavily criticized as being over-large for destroyer duties, the Tuckers showing growth in size and power over the Cassins.**

Tucker class

	Built	Commissioned
DD.57–68	Various	1916–17

Displacement: 911 tons (light); 1,132 tons (full load)
Length: 94.4m/310ft (wl); 96m/315ft 3in (oa)
Beam: 9.1m/29ft 10in
Draught: 2.9m/9ft 7in (full load)
Armament: 4 x 4in guns (4x1); 8/12 x 21in torpedo tubes (4x2/4x3)
Machinery: Single-reduction geared steam turbines, 4 boilers, 2 shafts
Power: 13,055kW/17,500shp for 29.5 knots
Endurance: 290 tons oil for 4,630km/2,500nm at 20 knots
Protection: None
Complement: 99

The "Flush-Deckers"

If size bought increased comfort and firepower, it failed to please all the destroyer community. They saw their role as offensive. A torpedo attack on an enemy battle line was considered so hazardous that it was likely that only one salvo could be fired before being disabled. Sided torpedo tubes, therefore (ran the argument), were less use than a powerful centreline battery. To reduce the target profile, destroyers should be *smaller*. An 800-tonner with nine centreline tubes was proposed, but the General Board refused it on the grounds that torpedoes could contact the deck edge on being fired, while the ship would be unable to carry 4in guns.

Instead, the Board proposed a ship of the same basic dimensions as the preceding Tucker class, but with a flush deck in place of a raised forecastle. The freeboard at the stem head would be similar but this would decrease in a straight sheerline to the after end, where it would be about 2m/6ft less. This conferred a much higher modulus amidships, with a cross section better suited to improved steadiness.

TOP: *Stockton* (DD.73) of the Caldwell type was one of just three of the many "Flush-Deckers" to have three funnels. She also became one of the 50 to be transferred to the Royal Navy in 1940, becoming HMS *Ludlow*. She was scrapped in 1945. ABOVE: The ambitious programme of Flush-Deckers, otherwise known as "Four Pipers" was meant to triple the US Navy's destroyer strength, but was badly delayed by a shortage of gear-cutting facilities. Converted for minelaying, the *Burns* (DD.171) was scrapped in 1932.

ABOVE: During World War II, 26 Flush-Deckers were converted to Fast Transports (APDs). *Rathburne* (APD.25, ex-DD.113) shows her restyled bridge structure, just two remaining funnels, and four LCPRs (Landing Craft, Personnel, Ramped) in davits in lieu of torpedo tubes.

In keeping four, sided triple torpedo tube mountings, it was necessary to move the two 4in waist guns on to a new amidships deckhouse. As this arrangement proved to be wetter, with solid water in the waist, bulwarks were run forward from the deckhouse to meet the full-width bridge screen.

Six ships (the Caldwell class, DD.69–74) were authorized early in 1915. They had varying combinations of twin- and triple-screw propulsion, and three or four funnels.

The lead ship was launched in July 1917. By this time, the United States had entered the war, only to discover the urgent need for large numbers of Anti-Submarine (AS) ships to defeat the all-out German submarine offensive. Although not designed for this role, the *Caldwell* drawings were immediately available, a staggering 273 hulls being ordered for series production. Only six were eventually cancelled but, having been initiated so late in the war, the programme realized less than 40 new ships by the time of the Armistice.

The building rate was slowed through lack of gear-cutting capacity, so some ships were fitted with cruising turbines, others with direct-drive main turbines. Machinery and boilers were from a variety of sources, affecting reliability and efficiency figures. Rapid yard expansion resulted in widely varying standards of workmanship.

The first block of "flush-deckers" were known as the Wickes class (DD.75–185), which were succeeded by the Clemson type (DD.186–347), which were of higher power and which could stow one-third more fuel.

Ships were completed with a couple of 1pdr Anti-Aircaft (AA) guns, exchanged later for one 3in High-Angle (HA) weapon. Depth charges were a further new addition, their stowage ill-suited to the very narrow sterns of the ships. There were two racks and one projector, known as a "Y Gun". As many were also fitted as high-speed minesweepers, the standard canoe stern was often greatly modified.

Operating closely with their British counterparts, the flush-deckers were inevitably compared. Their crews considered them to ride better in the winter seas encountered around the British Isles, although this was really a matter of the relationship between ship length and wave length at a particular time. They appeared to be more susceptible to structural damage and were definitely less handy, having large turning circles. By 1918, too, the Royal Navy had progressed to the far superior "V & W" classes.

Although already obsolescent, new flush-deckers continued to be commissioned until 1921, their numbers guaranteeing a long domination of the US Navy's destroyer strength. Even with inter-war disposals, sufficient survived for 50 to be transferred to the British flag in 1940, a further 120 serving in the US Navy. Now referred to as "Four Pipers", about two-fifths of them were modified to non-destroyer roles, such as high-speed transports (APDs), or ocean escorts.

ABOVE: **Although completed after World War I, a sub standard block of Flush-Deckers, including the *Selfridge* (DD.320), was scrapped during the early 1930s. The unusual wave formation has probably been caused by the close proximity of another vessel.** BELOW: ***Manley* (DD.74) was the very first Flush-Decker to be completed. Here, she has landed her torpedo tubes, probably to acquire four light assault craft for a Marine company in a pre-war conversion. She became the prototype high-speed transport (APD) during 1940.**

ABOVE: **Long before the days of modularization, the Mare Island Navy Yard was able to commission the *Ward* (DD.139) just 70 days after her laying-down. In sinking a Japanese midget submarine outside Pearl Harbor, she fired the first shots in the Pacific War.**

ABOVE: **Five Clemsons alongside their tender about 1930. Such a spell made a welcome break from "hard-lying". Fires could be drawn and services supplied by "Mother". There were hot baths, and hot food eaten from tables that did not roll and pitch.**

Clemson class

	Built	Commissioned
DD.186–347	Various	1918–21

Displacement: 1,125 tons (light); 1,584 tons (full load)
Length: 94.4m/310ft (wl); 95.7m/314ft 3in (oa)
Beam: 9.4m/30ft 11in
Draught: 2.9m/9ft 7in (full load)
Armament: 4 x 4in guns (4x1); 1 x 3in HA; 12 x 21in torpedo tubes (4x3)
Machinery: Single-reduction geared steam turbines, 4 boilers, 2 shafts
Power: 20,142kW/27,000shp for 35 knots
Endurance: 370 tons oil for 4,630km/2,500nm at 20 knots
Protection: None
Complement: 135

ABOVE: ***Monzambano*, and her sister *Goito*, retained features of "transitional" warships in the bridge structure being amidships and in the rigging detail. The two pedestals aft support a spotlight and the magnetic compass.**

LEFT: **When completed in 1886, the *Tripoli*'s 19 knots was considered very fast. Reciprocating machinery does not, however, tolerate prolonged fast running, and within a decade the ship was one of many to be converted for minelaying.**

Torpedo cruisers

Pre-dating by a decade both its torpedo boats and destroyers, the so-called "torpedo cruisers" of the Italian Navy were, at a little less than 1,000 tons displacement, of about the same size as a 1917 destroyer.

The Elswick cruiser *Giovanni Bausan*, of 1885, impressed the Italians with the potential of her 17 knots and three torpedo tubes. Three domestic versions of the ship were authorized but their expense caused the then Minister of Marine, the gifted Benedetto Brin, to design the same capability into a vessel on one third the price.

His "torpedo cruiser" *Tripoli*, initially capable of 19 knots, was completed in 1886, and carried five 14in torpedo tubes. An attractive little vessel, she featured a ram bow and a mercantile-style counter stern. Her raised forecastle and long, low afterdeck, offset by two capped and boldly raked funnels, gave her a profile that anticipated by over 20 years that of a classic destroyer.

As was common, however, her high-speed reciprocating machinery was trouble-prone and, by 1897, the *Tripoli* was reduced to a minelayer.

In 1888 a class of eight follow-ons had been authorized. These, the Partenope type, were of a similar size but only one of them (*Caprera*) was built with a forecastle. Their two, heavily raked funnels were widely spaced, indicating boiler spaces separated by the engine room. They carried up to six of the heavier 17.7in torpedo tubes; four rotatable tubes were sided on the upper deck, one was fixed and fired through the stem and (in six ships only) another fired through the stern.

Still capable of only 20 knots, they were really too slow for the task and were superseded by torpedo boats. Five had been discarded by 1914 while two of these remaining had been given forecastles in the course of conversion into minelayers.

ABOVE: **As built, *Partenope* was flush-decked, with turtlebacked foredeck, bridge just forward of the after funnel, and two lofty masts. Converted into a minelayer from 1906–08, she gained the prominent forecastle and relocated bridge.**

Partenope type, as built

Displacement: 831 tons (light); 993 tons (full load)
Length: 70m/229ft 9in (bp); 73.9m/242ft 7in (oa)
Beam: 8.2m/26ft 11in
Draught: 3.4m/10ft 2in (light); 3.7m/12ft 2in (full load)
Armament: 1 x 4.7in gun, 6 x 2.2in guns; 5/6 x 17.7in torpedo tubes (5/6x1)
Machinery: 3-cylinder triple-expansion engines, 4 boilers
Power: 2,984kW/4,000ihp for 20 knots
Endurance: 167 tons coal for 3,333km/1,800nm at 10 knots
Protection: 25–40mm/0.98–1.58in protective deck
Complement: 11

LEFT: ***Olimpia*, of the Orione class, shows her attractive lines. Abaft the breakwater is a protected conning tower and two sided torpedo tubes. A second conn and third centreline torpedo tube flank the mainmast.**

High seas torpedo boats

The Italian Navy acquired a force of 29 "high seas" torpedo boats (*torpediniere d'alto mare)* in a commendably short space of time. They were led by six Saffo-class boats, designed and built by the German specialist builder Schichau. Of 206 tons and 50m/164ft on the waterline, they were all launched in 1905 and resembled closely those being built for the Imperial German Navy. Designed with the lowest possible profile, they had a single lofty funnel (necessary with natural draught), two light signal masts and a combined navigation platform and searchlight pedestal atop the low forward conning position. A second conn, also lightly protected, was located aft. A slightly raised forward turtledeck was kept largely clear of spray-inducing clutter. Only three light guns, all of 47mm calibre, were specified. Of these, one was located aft and the others were sided in the waist. The three 17.7in torpedo tubes were all centreline-mounted. The class was later remodelled around two tubes and a pair of 57mm guns.

Italy also obtained a licence to build three groups of Thornycroft-designed craft of virtually the same size as those from Schichau. Slightly finer in form, the four Pegaso type of the first group were built over much the same time scale. Externally they differed primarily in having two funnels and a much shorter turtleback. A very light navigating platform was sited just forward of the forward funnel, well back from the bows. Deck space was saved by siding the forward tubes immediately abaft the turtleback, although this reduced a torpedo salvo to only two, compared with the Schichau boat's three.

They were succeeded by eight similar Cigno (1906–09) and six Alcione (1906–07) types. All coal-burners, they were later converted to oil firing. The four domestically designed Orione type (1906–07) differed mainly in having curved stems.

ABOVE: **The eight Cigno-class torpedo boats pre-dated the Orione type and, like them, were built as coal burners. Most were later converted to oil burning, but although this reduced the crew by some 10 per cent, the programme appeared haphazard.**

RIGHT: **The first group of "high seas" torpedo boats were the six Schichau-built Saffo-class boats, which also initiated the beautiful classical/astronomical name sequences. This is *Serpente*, sunk by collision during 1916.**

Orione class, as built

Displacement: 217 tons (designed)
Length: 51m/167ft 5in (bp); 52.8m/173ft 4in (oa)
Beam: 5.8m/19ft 2in
Draught: 1.6m/5ft 4in (designed)
Armament: 3 x 47mm guns (3x1); 3 x 17.7in torpedo tubes (3x1)
Machinery: 3-cylinder triple-expansion engines, 2 boilers, 2 shafts
Power: 2,238kW/3,000ihp for 25 knots
Endurance: 44 tons coal for 1,260km/680nm at 18 knots
Protection: None
Complement: 38

LEFT: **The 90-plus craft built to basic Schichau design were variously known as Coastal Torpedo Boats, or Torpedo Boats 2nd Class. The identity here is uncertain but it may be 115.S, which served until after World War I.**
ABOVE: **During World War I, Italy made a large investment in coastal torpedo craft, mainly with an eye to service in the adjacent Adriatic. Although generally termed "PN" boats, i.e. Pattison, Napoli, they came from a variety of builders.**

Coastal torpedo boats

The first of Italy's very large fleet of coastal torpedo boats (*torpediniere costiere*) were one each 25-ton craft from Thornycroft and Yarrow. Named *Nibbio* and *Avvoltoio*, they were classified 4th Class and delivered in 1881. Derived from these, the first domestically designed and built 26-tonner, *Clio*, was commissioned in 1885.

At this time the two British yards were also building the 35–40-ton 3rd Class craft of the Sparviero and Aquila classes. These carried two 14in torpedoes in fixed bow tubes. Successful, they led to the slightly larger *Aldebaran*, lead ship of a class of 30, all but 11 of which were domestically constructed under licence. Now becoming too numerous to name, craft adopted sequential numbers, followed by a letter denoting the designer or builder.

In 1886, the German Schichau yard delivered the first 2nd Class boat, a 78-tonner designated 56S. Effectively a scaled-down "high seas" craft, she was the prototype for a class of nearly 100 boats (56S–154S). Built mostly in Italian yards, these were complete by 1894.

During 1887, Yarrow delivered two 100 ton, 2nd Class boats (76YA and 77YA) which were a full 3 knots better than the Schichaus' 22. They were, however, followed by only two domestically built repeats.

ABOVE: **Mediterranean-moored, stern to quay, flotillas of PN craft make a brave show in Taranto's Mare Piccolo. Despite the nature of the threat changing post-1918, these small craft were not discarded until the 1930s.**

It would be 1910 before the next extended series was commenced. Of a size with, but slightly fuller than the Yarrow design, these were the 118-ton 1st Class PN type, the letters representing the Pattison yard at Naples. Capable of 27 knots, the craft were the first coastals to feature two centreline rotatable tubes. Between 1910 and 1918 a large number was ordered in blocks from several yards – Pattison built 30 boats; Odero, Sestri Ponente (OS) built 18; Ansaldo, Genoa (AS) built 14 and Orlando, Livorno (OL) built 6. Many survived until the 1930s.

PN class, second series

Displacement: 106 tons (light); 159 tons (full load)
Length: 42.5m/139ft 6in (wl and oa)
Beam: 4.7m/15ft 3in
Draught: 1.6m/5ft 3in (full load)
Armament: 2 x 3in HA guns (2x1); 22 x 17.7in torpedo tubes (2x1)
Machinery: Triple-expansion engines, 2 boilers, 2 shafts
Power: 2,387kW/3,200ihp for 27 knots
Endurance: 23 tons oil for 1,850km/1,000nm at 14 knots
Protection: None
Complement: 30

Lampo class

Italy's first destroyer, *Fulmine*, was designed and built by Odero. Of about 300 tons (light), she was launched in 1898 and was expected to make 30 knots. Never achieving this, she was deemed a failure. Even before her completion, however, the German Schichau yard at Elbing had launched five of an order for six 320-tonners, to be known as the Lampo class.

At this time, only about 100 tons and 10m/33ft in length separated a destroyer from a "high seas" torpedo boat, but the difference in scale had a considerable effect on seakeeping and the ability to maintain speed in a seaway.

The Lampos were of typical Schichau appearance with their two large funnels of circular section. The sheer strake was radiussed to reduce stress levels in the long, shallow hull. They were given a half-height forecastle, but differed from craft in German service by having no well deck, the very light bridge structure occupying that location immediately ahead of the forward funnel. Only two 14in torpedo tubes were carried, and were located farther aft.

The class was contemporary with, and the equal of, the British 30-knotters. For their size, they were efficient little ships. Less fragile than some, they were nonetheless wet and uncomfortable, with greatly reduced effectiveness in poor conditions. Less accustomed than Northerners to heavy weather, the Italians thought them deficient.

The light navigating bridge was an advance on British practice, enabling a 3in gun to be located on the raised forecastle rather than sharing the navigating platform.

Although the class was useful during the brief war with Turkey in 1911–12, it proved inadequate to the greater demands of World War I. Used briefly for coastal escort duties, the five survivors were converted to take a deckload of 12 mines.

ABOVE: **Not 50 per cent greater in displacement than the torpedo boats, the six Schichau-built Lampos (this is *Strale*) hardly derserved the title of "destroyers". The forecastle-mounted 75mm gun did, however, have a good field of fire.**

LEFT: **This impression of a Lampo does little to refute the reputation of the class as being poor seakeepers. The ram bow was unusual in craft of this size.**

Lampo class, as built

Displacement: 314 tons (light); 348 tons (full load)
Length: 60m/197ft (bp); 62.2m/204ft 1in (oa)
Beam: 6.5m/21ft 4in
Beam: 2.6m/8ft 6in (mean)
Armament: 1 x 3in gun, 5 x 57mm guns (5x1); 2 x 14in torpedo tubes (2x1)
Machinery: Triple-expansion engines, 3 boilers, 2 shafts
Power: 4,476kW/6,000ihp for 30 knots
Endurance: 3,680km/2,000nm at 12 knots
Protection: None
Complement: 56

LEFT: **Following the loss of the *Turbine* to Austro-Hungarian forces in May 1915, the Italians gave the name to her sister *Espero* as a mark of respect.**
ABOVE: **As built, the Nembos were unusual in their mast/funnel arrangement. Converted to oil firing in 1908–12, they gained a third funnel, later removed along with its boiler.**

Nembo class

Keen to acquire the best destroyer technology of the day, Italy followed the Schichau designed-and-built Lampo class with a further half dozen designed by Thornycroft. These, the Nembo class, were slightly larger and, as completed, had four single 14in torpedo tubes, two on the centreline, two sided. Two of the class carried a single 3in gun, the remainder an all 57mm armament.

The design reflected contemporary British practice in being flush-decked, the forward turtledeck having a diminutive breakwater to protect the light navigating bridge. This was built over the usual, lightly protected forward conning "tower", and supported a prominent searchlight platform. Another British feature was the slightly squared-off transom with the upper part of the rudder rather vulnerably exposed. As built, the ships' tall mainmast was stepped between the funnels.

Completed by Pattison, Naples in 1902–05, the ships were upgraded from 1908, with new, oil-fired boilers replacing the original coal-fired equipment. Rather than trunk the existing two funnels, a third was added. Four (later reduced to three) single 3in guns were now shipped, and the four small-bore torpedo tubes were replaced by two single 17.7in models. During World War I the side decks were fitted with rails for laying mines, of which up to 16 could be carried.

As rebuilt, the Nembos were rated fit to operate as front-line units during World War I, in the course of which three were sunk. The powerful Austro-Hungarian fleet was based just across the Adriatic, and the *Turbine* was destroyed (1915) in intercepting a hit-and-run bombardment. *Borea* was also sunk in surface action (1917) while engaged in convoy escort duty. The lead ship, *Nembo*, was destroyed (1916) by Austrian submarine torpedo, the submarine itself being lost.

ABOVE: **The original *Turbine*, seen here, was caught by the scouting division of an Austro-Hungarian bombardment force. Hit in the boiler room, she had to be abandoned. As Italy had just declared war, the loss made an impression.**

Nembo class, as rebuilt

Displacement: 324 tons (light); 379 tons (full load)
Length: 63.4m/208ft 2in (bp); 64m/210ft 1in (oa)
Beam: 5.9m/19ft 6in
Draught: 2.3m/7ft 7in (mean)
Armament: 4 x 3in guns (4x1); 2 x 17.7in torpedo tubes (2x1)
Machinery: Triple-expansion engines, 3 boilers, 2 shafts
Power: 3,730kW/5,000ihp for 30 knots
Endurance: 4,050km/2,200nm at 9 knots
Protection: None
Complement: 54

LEFT: ***Grantiere*'s forecastle party, precariously manning the turtleback, emphasizes just how small these "destroyers" were. Sided 75mm guns are just visible over the canvas dodgers on the bridge wings.** BELOW: **Another unidentified Soldati of the first, coal-burning group. Second group ships could be distinguished by their narrower-section funnels, with caps. Contemporary British Tribals were of twice their displacement.**

Soldati class

In this, the first Italian Soldati class, there were 11 ships, falling into three groups. Six (*Artigliere*, *Bersagliere*, *Corazziere*, *Garibaldino*, *Granatiere* and *Lanciere*) were coal-fired; four (*Alpino*, *Carabiniere*, *Fuciliere* and *Pontiere*) were oil-fired, while one (*Ascaro*) was a hybrid, burning either. The first ten formed a homogeneous class, the major difference being due to no more than that oil was introduced during its construction. Oil reduced the complement by five, this being the saving on stokers.

The *Ascaro* was not commenced until 1911, the year following the completion of the planned ten. She was ordered to Chinese Government account but, with Italy going to war with Turkey over Tripolitania, the ship was acquired by agreement for the Italian Navy. Other than for her "dual-fuel" facility she was, in virtually every respect, another Soldato. Visually, she differed in lacking the funnel caps of the oil-fired quartette. The funnels in all eleven were unequally spaced, the forward two exhibiting the smaller gap.

Although designed and built by the Ansaldo yard at Genoa, the Soldati owed much to the just-completed, Thornycroft-designed, Nembo, with their flush-decked hull and pronounced forward turtleback.

While only 1m/3ft 3in greater in length, the Soldati carried from the outset the four 3in guns for which the Nembo were later modified. Where the latter then carried only two 17.7in torpedo tubes, the Soldati carried three, one centreline, two sided. They were also given the stability reserves to ship a deck-load of 10 mines.

It might be noted that many Italian warships had an auxiliary function in minelaying, as the constricted waters of the Mediterranean include considerable shallow areas well-suited to this form of warfare. According to Italian Navy statistics, no less than 12,293 were laid in the course of the war.

ABOVE: ***Bersagliere*'s crew busying themselves in preparing to raise the old-style stocked anchor. The awnings are a reminder of what a relief it must have been to escape the Mediterranean heat at sea.**

Soldati class, oil-fired

Displacement: 400 tons (light); 416 tons (full load)
Length: 64.5m/21ft 9in (bp); 65.1m/213ft 8in (oa)
Beam: 6.1m/20ft
Draught: 2.2m/7ft 2in (mean)
Armament: 4 x 3in guns (4x1); 3 x 17.7in torpedo tubes (3x1)
Machinery: 4-cylinder triple-expansion engines, 3 boilers, 2 shafts
Power: 4,476kW/6,000ihp for 28.5 knots
Endurance: 2,963km/1,600nm at 12 knots
Protection: None
Complement: 52

Indomito and Pilo classes

Laid down from 1910, the six Indomito-class destroyers represented a great advance on the preceding Soldati. They were 8m/26ft greater in length, and averaged 672 tons displacement (light). Contemporary with, but smaller than, the Royal Navy's Acastas, they superficially resembled them with a full-height forecastle that continued to be a feature of Italian boats. They were the first Italian destroyers with steam turbines and, with 11,900kW/16,000shp behind them, all bettered 33 knots on trials, being able to sustain 29.

As built by Pattison, Naples, they had a forecastle-mounted 4.7in gun, with four 3in sided farther aft. During World War I, this armament was changed to a homogeneous five 4in weapons, the two 17.7in torpedo tubes being increased to four.

Four more, similar ships were built by Orlando at Leghorn. These, the three-funnelled *Ardito* and *Ardente*, and the two-funnelled *Animoso* and *Audace* (slightly larger) appeared to have been less successful.

Following on were eight ships of the Pilo class. Although again of the same basic hull dimensions, they were of somewhat greater displacement, the resulting greater draught costing them about a knot in speed. As built, they reverted to a light armament of four 3in guns but, post-war, these were replaced by five 4in.

Completed 1915–16, the Pilos (except for the *Nievo*, disposed of in 1938) had long and often eventful lives encompassing two major wars. Three (*Abba*, *Mosto* and *Pilo*) served in a reduced minesweeping role until the 1950s. The remainder, together with the Indomito-class *Insidioso*, were lost during World War II. Two of them had the dubious distinction of changing sides twice. These, the *Bronzetti* and *Missori*, came over with the Italian Armistice but, overtaken by events, had to be scuttled at Fiume and Durazzo respectively. Salvaged by the Germans, they were destroyed in 1945.

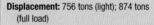

ABOVE: *Ardito* berthed in prime position in the Taranto naval base. Completed in 1913, she has more the appearance of destroyer than torpedo boat. Here, she is still armed with her original single 4.7in gun. BELOW LEFT: The two Animosos were essentially two-funnelled versions of the Arditos. Like them, they originally mounted a forecastle 4.7, as seen here on *Animoso* at Brindisi late in 1917.

Pilo class, as rearmed 

Displacement: 756 tons (light); 874 tons (full load)
Length: 72.5m/238ft 2in (bp); 73m/239ft 8in (oa)
Beam: 7.3m/24ft 1in
Draught: 2.7m/8ft 11in (mean)
Armament: 5 x 4in guns (5x1); 4 x 17.7in torpedo tubes (1x2/2x1)
Machinery: Direct-drive steam turbines, 3 boilers, 2 shafts
Power: 11,563kW/15,500shp for 30 knots
Endurance: 3,700km/2,000nm at 12 knots
Protection: None
Complement: 74

Sirtori and la Masa classes

The last destroyers completed for the Italian Navy before the cessation of hostilities were a dozen from the Odero yard at Sestri Ponente. They were effectively repeats of the preceding Pilo design and, similarly, all had three funnels. These were of unusually slender proportions, the centre one being slightly the largest. Air attack was now seen as a serious threat and some of the class had funnels fitted with umbrella-shaped, open-framed caps to prevent direct damage to the boilers. To the main armament was added two 40mm and two 6.5mm automatic weapons on High-Angle (HA) mountings. These light weapons were later replaced with a pair of 3in HAs.

There appears to be little to differentiate between the four Sirtoris and the eight la Masas which were ordered in two batches. In dimensions, displacement and power they were similar, the only significant variation being that the first group, all laid down on the same day in 1916, were completed with six 4in guns and the remainder only four. All guns were mounted singly, with two sided on the forecastle, two in the waist and two aft.

ABOVE: During World War I Italian destroyers began to carry two-letter identifiers, based on their names. These were far from standard in size or in form. This is the Sirtori-class destroyer *Giovanni Acerbi* in a dark paint scheme. LEFT: *Generale Achille Papa* seen as escort to a Cavour-class battleship. With the remainder of her class she survived to serve as a very efficient anti-submarine escort during World War II.

Other than the la Masa-class *Cairoli*, all survived World War I and, due to the rapid increase in the general size of destroyers, all were reclassified as torpedo boats in 1929.

During World War II the varied experience of the 11 survivors reflected the shifting political affiliations of the nation. Four were destroyed in various locations by Allied air attack and three by German bombs. One was sunk by mine; another was destroyed by her crew on Italy's capitulation in September 1943. The last two, *Carini* and *Fabrizi*, served on until the 1950s, downgraded to minesweepers and finally, in the case of the former, as a harbour training ship.

LEFT: This is *Angelo Bassini* of the la Masa class. Note the flimsy navigating bridge and 4in guns sided on the forecastle. Her armament was reduced to a single 4in during World War II.

la Masa class, as built

Displacement: 771 tons (light); 835 tons (full load)
Length: 72.5m/238ft 2in (bp); 73.5m/241ft 5in (oa)
Beam: 7.3m/24ft
Draught: 2.8m/9ft 2in (mean)
Armament: 4 x 4in guns (4x1); 4 x 17.7in torpedo tubes (1x2/2x1)
Machinery: Direct-drive steam turbines, 3 boilers, 2 shafts
Power: 11,563kW/15,500shp for 30 knots
Endurance: 4,444km/2,400nm at 12 knots
Protection: None
Complement: 78

LEFT: **Discovering that greater speed was possible with longer hulls, the French produced two advanced prototypes in the 27.5-knot, 43.8m *Chevalier* (foreground) and the 31-knot, 44m *Forbin*, completed in 1894 and 1896 respectively.**
ABOVE: **Following the poor showing of the original 35m, 58-ton torpedo boats, a large number of redesigned 37.8m, 80-ton craft, such as No.358 seen here, were built. Many served in a variety of roles until the 1920s.**

Early torpedo boats

Small, unseaworthy and lacking endurance, the limitations of the torpedo boat mattered little in the days when the leading sea powers, particularly Great Britain, made close blockade a major plank of their maritime strategy, thus conveniently stationing major warships close offshore. Spar torpedoes, detonated unexpectedly against the hull of a line-of-battleships, made an appealing "David and Goliath" image and, despite the lamentable performance of large numbers of Russian craft during the war with Turkey (1877–78), French enthusiasm for the concept remained unaffected.

During the late 1870s the French acquired both spar torpedo boats and "torpedo launches", mainly of Thornycroft design, to deploy the yet unproven Whitehead automobile torpedo. With the rapid improvement of the latter came the *Jeune École* movement. Spar torpedo boats were rebuilt with torpedo tubes and, by the mid-1880s, France had not only an eclectic fleet of about 50 craft but also, in Normand, a first-class designer and builder of her own.

Developed in parallel was the "*bateau-canon*", a larger, gun-armed craft which, like a British flotilla leader or German division boat, would both direct and support torpedo craft in attack. France also experimented with the "torpedo boat carrier", transporting small torpedo craft with the fleet for the purposes of offence and defence in an action. This vessel, *Foudre*, was later converted to carry seaplanes.

By 1914, the large numbers (over 100) of 37m and 39m Normands were organized mainly in flotillas, defending ports and bases from Saigon to Dunkirk. In the English Channel the threat from the German Flanders Flotilla, based on Bruges and Zeebrugge, was very real.

The minor force was supported by a few larger craft, such as the 45m Cyclone type, which bridged the gap between the true torpedo boats and the 56m "torpedo boat destroyers" (*torpilleurs d'escadre*) which were, as elsewhere, built almost exclusively after the turn of the century.

ABOVE: **Appropriately named after the renowned French corsair, the *Forbin* was a speculative example of the design genius of Jacques-Augustin Normand, whose contributions rivalled those of J.I. Thornycroft. The greatest limiting factor was reciprocating machinery.**

Cyclone class, as designed

Displacement: 149 tons (light); 177 tons (full load)
Length: 45m/147ft 9in (wl); 46.5m/152ft 8in (oa)
Beam: 4.8m/15ft 9in
Draught: 1.5m/4ft 11in
Armament: 2 x 47mm guns (2x1); 2/3 x 15in torpedo tubes (2/3x1)
Machinery: Triple-expansion engines, 2 boilers, 2 shafts
Power: 2,984kW/4,000ihp for 29 knots
Endurance: 25 tons coal for 1,850km/1,000nm at 14 knots
Protection: Negligible
Complement: 29

The "300-tonners"

By the late 1890s the rapid development of the torpedo had left the traditional maritime strategy of close blockade untenable. Exercises convinced the French Navy that any future blockading would need to keep its distance, maintaining a visual watch using the smallest capable ships. Destroyers, recently introduced by the British, appeared ideal; they were fast and with reasonable endurance, able to threaten capital ships with torpedoes or to subdue torpedo boats with gunfire.

The French entrusted Normand with the design for what would be a considerable programme. At under 300 tons (light), the initial quartette (Durandal class, 1899–1900) were smaller than the "30-knotters" then being built for the Royal Navy. Accepting that they would be awash in maintaining speed at sea, Normand gave them a pronounced forward turtledeck. This terminated at the forward conning tower, atop which was a platform which served as a navigating bridge as well as location for a 65mm gun (later often replaced by a 75mm weapon). The heavily radiussed sheer strake was continued all the way aft and, about 1.5m/5ft above the true upper deck, there ran a light spar deck (called "duckboards" by the French) which remained tolerably dry. Three 47mm guns were spaced along either side and there were two 15in centreline torpedo tubes. The two boiler spaces were separated by the engine room.

Two more quartettes (Pique class, 1900–01 and Pertuisane, 1902–03) of these 56m/184ft craft were followed by the Arquebuse class of 20 (1902–04). By now eight yards were involved in the rapidly evolving programme.

The final groups, of 13 Claymore (1905–08) and 10 Branlebas classes (1907–08), were of 2m/6ft more on the waterline, and mounted two heavier 17.7in torpedo tubes.

TOP: The Normand-built *Fanfare* of the Branlebas class which, at this time, were carrying experimental Italian-style identifiers. Note how the crew are standing on the light, elevated "duckboards". ABOVE: All named after weapons, the Claymore type preceded the Branlebas class and, while very similar, were more lightly built. At the fore the nameship is wearing the "marque distinctive" of a flag officer.

All the so-called "300-tonners" were active during World War I but all were discarded during the 1920s.

ABOVE: An early picture of the Arquebuse-class *Belier* with navigation still being carried out around a 65mm gun. A light bridge was later added abaft the gun. Note the height at which boats need to be carried.

Branlebas class

Displacement: 322 tons (standard); 338 tons (full load)
Length: 58m/190ft 4in (wl); 59.8m/196ft 4in (oa)
Beam: 6.4m/21ft
Draught: 2.4m/7ft 10in max.
Armament: 1 x 65mm gun, 6 x 47mm guns (6x1); 2 x 17.7in torpedo tubes (2x1)
Machinery: Triple-expansion engines, 2 boilers, 2 shafts
Power: 5,073kW/6,800ihp for 27.5 knots
Endurance: 30 tons coal for 2,100km/1,150nm at 14 knots
Protection: None
Complement: 60

LEFT: **One of four Chasseur type, the *Janissaire* was one of the first oil-fired French destroyers. Experimentally, the *Janissaire* was fitted with Foster-Wheeler boilers and Parsons direct-drive steam turbines.** ABOVE: **The Spahi class's two pairs of funnels were distinctive, but varied in proportion and spacing depending upon which of five yards was involved. *Aspirant Herber* came from the old naval yard at Rochefort.**

The "450-tonners"

Compared to the torpedo boats that they came to succeed, the "300-tonners" were large. In actual size, however, they were tiny, their endurance determined by their personnel as much as by mechanical limitations. Wet, uncomfortable and lively, they fatigued crews and reduced efficiency. As the torpedo boats gave way to 300-tonners, so did the latter to 450-ton craft.

A further incentive toward larger dimensions came with the steam turbine. Competent engineers, the French knew of the inefficiency of the high-revving, turbine-driven propeller at cruising speeds. For two prototype craft, therefore, built in parallel with the last of the 300-tonners, they opted for a triple-shaft arrangement with a conventional reciprocating cruise engine on the centreline shaft. For evaluation, two different French-designed turbines were directly coupled to each wing shaft. Four boilers were required, and the two ships (*Voltigeur* and *Tirailleur*), launched in 1908–09, were about 64m/210ft long.

This extra size alone made them more seaworthy, more able to maintain their speed and less wet, so that the idiosyncratic "duckboard" construction was abandoned. With four equispaced funnels, they carried a much-enhanced armament of six 65mm guns and a third torpedo tube, firing through the stem.

Again for comparison, two further groups of similarly sized destroyers were built. The seven-ship Spahi class (1908–12) also had four boilers but featured a conventional arrangement of a reciprocating engine driving each of two shafts. They were instantly recognizable with two pairs of tall funnels, widely separated about the machinery space.

The third class, comprising four ships of the Chasseur type (1909–11) were again of a size but were fitted with a British-designed Parsons turbine on each of their three shafts. They had three funnels, unequally spaced. All three classes were designed to make 28 knots on about 7,500 horsepower.

ABOVE: **The two Voltigeurs were essentially repeat Spahis but, experimentally, were fitted with reciprocating machinery on the centreline shaft and turbines on the wing shafts. *Voltigeur* here passes the old battleship *Hoche*.**

Chasseur type, as built

Displacement: 442 tons (standard); 511 tons (full load)
Length: 64.3m/211ft 1in (bp)
Beam: 6.6m/21ft 8in
Draught: Not known
Armament: 6 x 65mm guns (6x1); 3 x 17.7in torpedo tubes (3x1)
Machinery: Direct-drive steam turbines, 4 boilers, 3 shafts
Power: 5,595kW/7,500shp for 28 knots
Endurance: 133 tons oil or 98 tons coal for 2,685km/1,450nm at 10 knots
Protection: None
Complement: 78

LEFT: **The 800-tonners had a business-like raised forecastle that greatly improved seakeeping. *Cimeterre*, of the 12-strong Bouclier class, shows facets to allow waist guns to fire well forward.**
ABOVE: **During World War I, the *Bouclier* received a modified bridge structure which necessitated a heightened forefunnel. She has a short bulwark in the waist to improve dryness.**

The "800-tonners"

During 1909 the French commenced a group of twelve 800-ton destroyers. There was considerable incentive for this increase in size, as other fleets were discovering. Vibration-free turbines, combined with compact water-tube boilers and oil firing, promised high power in moderate dimensions. Large hulls can be more efficiently driven than small, and are better able to maintain speed in adverse conditions. An obvious choice for fleet escort, large destroyers could both repel enemy craft and conduct attacks of their own.

The French naval constructive department, STCN, did not tightly define the ships' form, allowing no less than seven yards to interpret an open specification that stipulated only the target displacement, armament and type (although not manufacturer) of the main propulsion machinery.

The resulting Bouclìers, although described as a class, thus showed marked differences. All had four boilers but three or four funnels. Two had triple shafts, the remainder twin. All had full-height forecastle but, to allow waist guns to fire forward, some had faceted sides, others small sponsons. As with British experience, wide variations in hull form and propulsive efficiency resulted in trials speeds ranging from 29.3 to 35.5 knots on the same installed power.

Taking the best of the Bouclier-class characteristics, the department added a further couple of feet to the beam of the longest hull for the six more tightly defined Bisson-class ships (1912–14) and the three following Enseigne Roux type (1915–21), most of which were built in naval dockyards.

At 30–32 knots, later ships demonstrated a greater uniformity in speed, suggesting that trials were run in a more realistic loaded condition.

All groups initially had a uniform armament, including a 100mm gun at either end, four 65mm weapons in the waist and two twinned torpedo tubes. This was considerably augmented in the course of World War I.

ABOVE: ***Capitaine Mehl*'s forward funnel carried a distinctive clinker screen to protect personnel on the compass platform, where a searchlight was also mounted. Aft of amidships is a canvas-shrouded Army-pattern 75mm gun.**

Bisson class, as built

Displacement: 850 tons (standard); 1,000 tons (full load)
Length: 78.1m/256ft 4in (bp)
Beam: 8.6m/28ft 2in
Draught: 3.1m/10ft 2in (mean)
Armament: 2 x 100mm guns (2x1), 4 x 65mm guns (4x1); 4 x 17.7in torpedo tubes (2x2)
Machinery: Direct-drive steam turbines, 4 boilers, 2 shafts
Power: 11,190kW/15,000shp for 30 knots
Endurance: 157 tons oil for 2,500km/1,350mm at 14 knots
Protection: None
Complement: 82

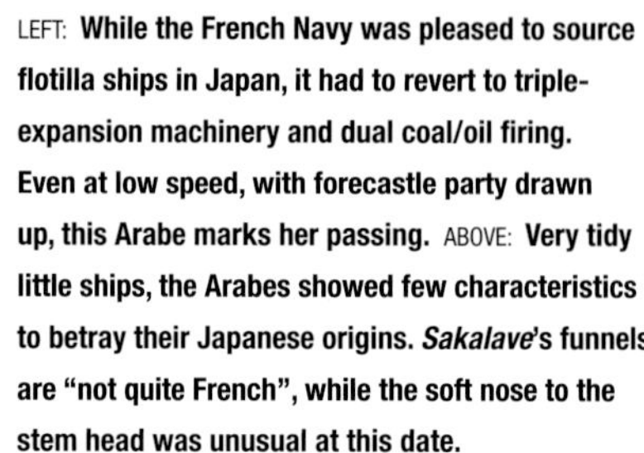

LEFT: **While the French Navy was pleased to source flotilla ships in Japan, it had to revert to triple-expansion machinery and dual coal/oil firing. Even at low speed, with forecastle party drawn up, this Arabe marks her passing.** ABOVE: **Very tidy little ships, the Arabes showed few characteristics to betray their Japanese origins. *Sakalave*'s funnels are "not quite French", while the soft nose to the stem head was unusual at this date.**

Aventurier and Arabe classes

In 1914 the Argentine government had on order four destroyers each from Germany and France. All were requisitioned, the former group becoming the German G.101–104, and the latter the French Aventurier class, which were retained post-war.

In appearance, the Aventuriers were unusual in having not only a full-height forecastle but also a half-height aftercastle, or poop. This greatly improved the officers' accommodation, but at the expense of a higher profile. Their intended armament from the United States was blocked by early neutrality laws and was replaced by four long-barrelled 100mm Canet guns and four single 450mm torpedo tubes, sided in the low waist. Later reboilered, the ships gained a fourth funnel. The four were unequal in size and spacing.

Still short of destroyers in 1917, the French Navy took the unusual step of ordering a dozen from Japan. These were near repeats of the Japanese' own Kaba class, and caused some logistics problems with their mainly British-type weapon calibres.

Known as the Arabe (or Algérien) class, they were built rapidly, one pair by each of six yards. They had a short, half-height forecastle, upon which was a single 4.7in gun. Between the break of the forecastle and the forefunnel was located, German-style a pair of torpedo tubes. These were originally of 18in calibre, as was the second pair, sited well aft. There were also four guns of 3in calibre, two sided in the waist and two on the centreline right aft. The more forward of these was mounted on a bandstand.

By coincidence, Arabes and Kabas served together on convoy escort duty in the Mediterranean at the end of World War I. Both Arabes and Aventuriers served on into the 1930s, by which time the French were building much larger destroyers for fleet work.

ABOVE: **Although relatively small, the Arabes were well built and well thought of as seaboats. Post-war most served with the Atlantic fleet, based on Brest, where they are pictured here. Slow by destroyer standards, they were deleted in the 1930s.**

Arabe class, as designed

Displacement: 673 tons (standard); 835 tons (full load)
Length: 79.4m/260ft 8in (wl); 83m/272ft 5in (oa)
Beam: 7.3m/24ft 1in
Draught: 2.4m/7ft 10in
Armament: 1 x 4.7in gun, 4 x 3in guns (4x1); 4 x 18in torpedo tubes (2x2)
Machinery: 4-cylinder triple-expansion engines, 4 boilers, 3 shafts
Power: 7,460kW/10,000ihp for 29 knots
Endurance: 100 tons coal and 120 tons oil for 2,963km/1,600nm at 14 knots
Protection: None
Complement: 89

Early torpedo boats

By 1904 the Imperial Japanese Navy had acquired over 90 torpedo boats and, by virtue of wars with China (1894–95), Russia (1904–05) and Germany (1914–18), was one of the few major fleets to use them in combat.

The first to enter service were four Yarrow repeats of the Royal Navy 100 footers, shipped in parts for reassembly. Delivered in 1880, they were followed by a slow trickle of larger French-built craft, many from Normand. Three became casualties when the Japanese attacked the Chinese fleet at its Wei-hei-wei anchorage in February 1895, destroying the Chinese battleship *Ting-Yen.*

The war also saw the capture of three Vulcan-built Chinese torpedo boats and the sinking of eight others, stimulating a post-war Japanese programme of 47 boats from Normand, Schichau, Yarrow and domestic yards, building under licence. All were in service by 1903 and closely reflected designs of their countries of origin.

Except for ten 46.5m/152ft Yarrow-built craft, all the foregoing were rated Second- or Third-Class. Several other First-Class boats had also been acquired, including the *Kotaka* (Yarrow 1886, 50.3m/166ft), the ex-Chinese *Fukuryu* (Germania 1886, 42.7m/140ft), *Shirataka* (Schichau 1898, 46.6m/153ft) and the four Hayabusas (Normand 1899–1901, 45.1m/148ft). The last-named were the first with 18in torpedoes.

Newly confident in domestic design and build, the Japanese now produced the 11-strong First-Class Aotaka torpedo boats. Launched in 1903–04, six were built by the Kure Naval Dockyard, the remainder by Kawasaki.

Shortly afterward, hostilities commenced with Russia. At the decisive Battle of Tsushima in May 1905, Admiral Togo used his destroyers and torpedo boats to harry his Russian opponents throughout a long night, several boats sustaining damage. Although a discontinued species, torpedo boats were still useful in the capture of the German enclave at Tsingtao in 1914.

TOP: Designed by Normand, French yards built eleven of their 46.5m/152ft Cyclone class together with four for the Japanese, who called them the Hayabusa class. Seen newly reassembled in Japan in 1901 is the *Chidori*. ABOVE: *Kotaka* was a one-off from Yarrow's Poplar yard, reassembled in Japan in 1886. Her six torpedo tubes were of 15in calibre, only the two forward tubes here being apparent, splayed outward over the extraordinary stem.

Aotaka class

Displacement: 152 tons (design)
Length: 45m/147ft 8in (bp)
Beam: 4.9m/16ft 1in
Draught: 1.5m/4ft 9in
Armament: 1 x 57mm gun, 2 x 42mm guns; 3 x 18in torpedo tubes (3x1)
Machinery: Triple-expansion engines, 2 boilers, 2 shafts
Power: 2,611kW/3,500ihp for 28 knots
Endurance: 26 tons coal for 3,700km/2,000nm at 10 knots
Protection: None
Complement: 30

Harusame and Asakaze classes

With the end of the short war with China, the Japanese ordered their first destroyers, six each from Yarrow and Thornycroft. The former (Ikazuchi class, 305 tons designed) were slightly larger than the latter (Murakumo class, 285 tons), but both approximated to the still-completing British "30-knotters". To follow on, two further boats were ordered from each yard. These, the 345-ton Shirakumos and the 360-ton Akatsukis, were slightly enlarged versions, delivered in 1902.

In the same year, seven destroyers were ordered from the Kure and Yokosuka Naval Yards. The design of these, the Harusame class, was effectively that of the Thornycroft, *Shirakumo,* lengthened by nearly 4m/13ft. The four funnels were similarly disposed, with the second and third more closely spaced and indicating adjacent boilers spaces, ahead of the engine room.

The hull was flush-decked, with freeboard diminishing from forward to aft. A low forward turtledeck terminated at the conning tower, topped by the usual open platform, doubling as navigating position and location for the forward 3in gun. A further 3in weapon was sited right aft. Two 6pdr guns were sided at the break of the turtledeck, with two more sided and staggered in the waist. The two single 18in torpedo tubes were set on the centreline abaft the funnels. The Harusames' machinery was less powerful than that of the earlier Thornycroft boats, costing them about 2 knots.

ABOVE: **Appearing to be on a buoy in Portsmouth, England, prior to her delivery voyage is the Thornycroft-built *Shirakumo* which, with her sister *Asashio*, was completed in 1902. They were models for the seven Japanese-built Harusames.**

By the time that the last of the class was delivered, Japan was at war with Russia. An emergency war programme thus funded no less than 32 further hulls, designated the Asakaze class. These differed mainly in having a heavier gun armament and oil sprayers to boost the performance of the coal-fired boilers. With growing expertise, eight yards were able to participate in this programme.

ABOVE: **The Harusames carried two single 18in torpedo tubes on the centreline abaft the funnels. Although slightly larger than the Shirakumos, they could match neither their power nor speed.**

Asakaze class, as built

Displacement: 380 tons (standard); 450 tons (full load)
Length: 69.2m/227ft (bp); 71.3m/234ft (oa)
Beam: 6.6m/21ft 7in
Draught: 1.8m/6ft
Armament: 4 x 3in guns (4x1); 2 x 3in HA (2x1); 2 x 18in torpedo tubes (2x1)
Machinery: 4-cylinder triple-expansion engines, 4 boilers, 2 shafts
Power: 4,476kW/6,000ihp for 29 knots
Endurance: 150 tons coal and 20 tons oil for 2,220km/1,200nm at 15 knots
Protection: None
Complement: 70

Kaba and Momo/Enoki classes

ABOVE LEFT: ***Tsubaki*** **was of the Enoki class, which were virtual repeats of the preceding Momo type. The forward triple torpedo tubes abaft the break of the short forecastle oblige the bridge to be located uncomfortably far forward.** ABOVE: **Launched in a very advanced stage of completion, *Kaba*, first of ten, is named with full ceremony. In a neat example of pupil teaching master, 12 more were built for France as the Arabe class.**

With the Anglo-Japanese alliance of 1902 bringing Japan into a mainly European war in 1914, her navy found itself short of destroyers. Two 600-ton craft, *Sakura* and *Tachibana*, had been completed by Maizuru Dockyard in 1912, and these provided the basis for the ten Kaba-class boats ordered immediately under an emergency war programme.

Contemporary with the British "M" class, they were of the same length but rather narrower. Their four boilers were housed in adjacent spaces and, by virtue of placing the centre pair back-to-back, it was possible to exhaust them through the same funnel. With only three funnels, deck space was freed, enabling a twin torpedo tube mounting to be located in the well at the break of the half-height forecastle. A second pair was sited just ahead of the mainmast.

Although the Kabas were inferior to the British Ms in having 18in, rather than 21in, torpedo tubes, they were ahead in adopting the harder-hitting 4.7in gun, one of which was carried on the forecastle. Four 3in were mounted in the waist and aft.

Japanese expertise and capacity were increasing rapidly, and they were able to build a further 12 Kabas for the French Navy. The hull had further development potential and, in the four follow-on Momo class, power was increased by about two-thirds for small increases in length and beam. By the adoption of steam turbine propulsion much weight and space was saved. Only two funnels were fitted.

The extra beam permitted three 4.7in guns to be shipped and the torpedo tubes to be tripled. Speed and range were significantly improved.

Six more hulls were completed in 1918 as the Enoki class. They were essentially repeat Momos but with a 10 per cent increase in power.

ABOVE: **In a clear profile, the layout of this Momo-class destroyer can be readily discerned. Seaboats, frequently carried away by heavy rolling, are carried high. Roman letter identifiers indicate Mediterranean service.**

ABOVE: **The 21 Momi-class boats were built post-war, and were developed directly from the Momos. They were the first with 21in torpedoes and, like the *Osu* (ex-*Kaki*) seen here, served throughout World War II.**

Enoki class, as built

Displacement: 850 tons (standard); 1,100 tons (full load)
Length: 83.8m/275ft (bp); 85.8m/281ft 8in (oa)
Beam: 7.7m/25ft 4in
Draught: 2.4m/7ft 9in
Armament: 3 x 4.7in guns (3x1); 6 x 18in torpedo tubes (2x3)
Machinery: Direct-drive steam turbines, 4 boilers, 2 shafts
Power: 13,055kW/17,500shp for 31.5 knots
Endurance: 98 tons coal and 210 tons oil for 4,445km/2,400nm at 15 knots
Protection: None
Complement: 110

D89

Directory of Destroyers

1918 to Date

By 1918 the destroyer had progressed to the classic layout of gun and torpedo armament that, with minor variations, would last until the 1950s. World War II, however, saw the destroyer necessarily adapt to the new roles of anti-submarine and anti-aircraft escort. Rapid wartime development of both submarine and aircraft, together with the lack of opportunity for torpedo attack, found the destroyer form increasingly inadequate, resulting firstly in the introduction of the specialist frigate and, post-war, in a renaissance around the imperatives of guided missiles and helicopters. Such fast-reaction, stand-off weapon systems made very high ship speeds unnecessary, while the gas turbine's supersession of steam machinery resulted in considerable reduction in complement. Today's "destroyer" embraces a wide variety of forms, but is usually configured primarily for area defence against aircraft and missile attack.

The following directory takes the destroyer story from the ship designed for high-speed flotilla torpedo attack against a battle line to a multi-purpose anti-aircraft escort, often the size of an earlier light cruiser. Although the listing is comprehensive, space forbids the inclusion of every class. If selected examples here tend to favour major combatants, it is they that are subject to the greatest evolutionary forces.

LEFT: **A typical modern destroyer, the British Type 42 *Exeter* is configured around an area-defence SAM system combined with good anti-submarine capability.**

LEFT: **In light, pre-war Mediterranean grey, and with awnings rigged, the *Brilliant*, launched in 1930, gives an impression of the standards maintained by the then-Royal Navy, still a major force.** ABOVE: **The *Electra* of 1934 is seen in the darker "Home Fleet" grey that was less flattering than the paler livery. Sent to the Far East, she was lost in the Java Sea battle.**

"A" to "I" classes

With a surfeit of war-built tonnage, Britain built no more destroyers until a pair of "specials", designed in the mid-1920s by Yarrow and Thornycroft. *Amazon* and *Ambuscade* were essentially "W"-class boats, some 3m/10ft longer and incorporating the latest refinements in steam technology and fire control.

Based on these, tenders for a flotilla of eight, plus a leader, were sought in 1927. These, the "A" class, were all launched in 1929, the leader being larger and with a fifth gun between the funnels. All carried quadrupled torpedo tubes.

Nine flotillas were built, roughly one per year, with names commencing "A" to "I". The Cs were restricted to a half-flotilla. Over this period, there were minor variations, which are summarized in the table (right).

Quintuple torpedo tubes were introduced in the "I" class, but it will be noticed that, with the Gs, there was an effort to arrest the progressive growth in size and power.

Flotilla	Launch date	Standard displacement (tons)	Dimensions (LWLxB) (ft)	Designed power (shp)	Designed speed (knots)
A	1929	1,330	320x32.25	34,000	31.25
B	1929	1,360	320x32.25	34,000	31.25
C	1931	1,375	326x33	36,000	32
D	1932	1,375	326x33	36,000	32
E	1934	1,405	326x33.25	36,000	31.5
F	1934	1,405	326x33.75	36,000	31.5
G	1935	1,350	320x33	34,000	31.5
H	1936	1,340	320x33	34,000	31.5
I	1936–37	1,370	320x33	34,000	31.5

Originally criticized for its size, the basic, long-forecastle design proved to have excellent seakeeping and handling. With World War II and the commissioning of larger destroyers, most were converted to long-range, anti-submarine escorts. One or two 4.7in guns were landed and the after torpedo tubes replaced by a 3in high-angle gun. To reduce topweight for greater depth charge capacity, the mainmast was removed and the after funnel shortened.

ABOVE: **The "I" class of 1936 were the last of a continuous line of development that began with the "V & Ws". *Ilex* is seen here as built, marked up as a unit of the 3rd Destroyer Flotilla of the Mediterranean Fleet. She was transferred to Greece in 1945.**

"E" class, as designed

Displacement: 1,405 tons (standard); 1,940 tons (full load)
Length: 99.3m/326ft (wl); 100.2m/329ft (oa)
Beam: 10.1m/33ft 3in
Draught: 3.5m/11ft 5in (standard)
Armament: 44 x 4.7in guns (4x1); 8 x 21in torpedo tubes (2x4)
Machinery: Single-reduction steam turbines; 3 boilers, 2 shafts
Power: 26,856kW/36,000shp for 31.5 knots
Endurance: 470 tons oil for 11,765km/6,350nm at 15 knots
Protection: None
Complement: 145

LEFT: **Only four of the original 16 Royal Navy Tribals survived World War II. Immediately post-war, *Tartar* is seen here in her hostilities paint scheme. Note the addition of radar, lattice masts and a twin 4in gun mounting in "X" position.** ABOVE: **A rather nice impression of *Arunta*, one of the three Tribals built in Sydney for the Royal Australian Navy. These served alongside the US Navy in the Pacific War. Of the eight Canadian Tribals, four were constructed in Halifax, Nova Scotia.**

Tribal class

The London Naval Treaty of 1930 restricted the Royal Navy to a global limit of 150,000 destroyer tons. No individual ship could exceed 1,500 tons (standard), but 16 per cent of tonnage could be allocated to "leaders" not exceeding 1,850 tons. There was concern that large foreign destroyers were being armed with guns of up to the permitted maximum calibre of 130mm. The "A" to "I" flotillas had emphasized torpedo armament and it was now decided to build a double flotilla of primarily gun-armed leaders. Trials with 70lb, 130mm projectiles proved that their weight would slow the rate of fire, so the 4.7in gun with its 50lb shell was retained.

Designed to the 1,850-ton limit, the new Tribals carried eight guns, in two twin-shielded mountings, at either end. Only one quadruple set of torpedo tubes was shipped. The aerial threat was recognized with the requirement for 40 degrees of main battery elevation for long-range barrage fire. Two single-barrelled pompoms and two four-barrelled 0.5in machine-guns were also specified, although still inadequate.

The sheer beauty of the Tribal design was marred by wartime modifications, the most useful of which was the provision of a 4in twin high-angle mounting in lieu of "X" guns. Later, survivors were given a lattice foremast.

Tight design limitations caused the Tribals to be highly stressed and, as they were hard-driven, they tended to suffer bottom damage, which required additional stiffening. They also had a naturally high centre of gravity, giving them a slow, high amplitude roll that could prove unnerving for the uninitiated.

With excellent endurance, seakeeping and armament, the Tribals were very heavily used during World War II. Seldom out of the limelight they lost no less than 12 of their original 16. Eight more were built by or for the Canadians and three by the Australians.

The Tribal design evolved to counter the specific threat posed by foreign destroyers and was far too expensive to be built in large numbers.

ABOVE: ***Mashona* shows the classic Tribal appearance as originally built, with two light tripod masts. The new curved bow profile was adopted not for cosmetic reasons but to increase forecastle deck area without increasing waterline length.**

Tribal class, as built

Displacement: 1,854 tons (standard); 1,959 tons (full load)
Length: 111.1m/364ft 8in (wl); 114.9m/377ft (oa)
Beam: 11.1m/36ft 6in
Draught: 3.3m/10ft 9in (standard)
Armament: 8 x 4.7in guns (4x2); 2 x 2pdr pompom (2x1); 4 x 21in torpedo tubes (1x4)
Machinery: Single-reduction steam turbines, 3 boilers, 2 shafts
Power: 32,824kW/44,000shp for 32.5 knots
Endurance: 525 tons oil for 10,556km/5,700nm at 15 knots
Protection: None
Complement: 195

LEFT: **Cheaper and smaller than a Tribal, the "J" type re-emphasized torpedo armament at the expense of guns. The *Kashmir* shows how the mainmast has been suppressed in order to give the after guns uninterrupted firing arcs.**

ABOVE: **Unlike half the Ls, all of the M class received their designed armament. *Matchless* is shown here in her 1945 paint scheme, and has already acquired a lattice mast. Post-war, she was sold to Turkey.**

"J" to "N" classes

For a smaller and cheaper destroyer to succeed the Tribals, a 10-tube torpedo battery was required, as was a dual-purpose main armament. At the desired elevation of 70 degrees, however, projectiles could not be hand-loaded. The arrangement also set the breech uncomfortably high for low-angle use. Three Tribal-type mountings were thus specified, with no guns in "Y" position. A quadruple 2pdr pompom occupied a bandstand immediately abaft the large single funnel. Sufficient power could be generated by two boilers and, by placing these back-to-back, they could be exhausted through a single large funnel casing.

The speed of these, the "J" and "K" classes, was 32 knots in the deep condition but this was criticized in view of the increasing speeds of capital ships and, indeed, foreign destroyers. The following two flotillas, the "L" and "M"s, were thus designed for a continuous speed of 33 knots. They were given large, fully enclosed twin gunhouses, whose 4.7in weapons were capable of 50-degree elevation while firing a heavier 62lb shell.

The new gun mountings were not an unqualified success, while their extra weight was compensated by the readoption of quadruple torpedo tubes. Slow delivery of the gun mountings also resulted in four L–class boats being fitted instead with four twin 4in HA apiece, and being reclassed as anti-aircraft destroyers.

In 1939, the next flotilla ordered reverted to a repeat of the J/K class, presumably because of the increasing tempo of warship construction. Only one of the "N" class served during hostilities with a British crew. Four were Australian-manned, two Dutch and one Polish (as was one "M").

Several ships of these classes substituted a 4in HA for the after torpedo tube but losses, particularly from air attack, were high, comprising six Js, six Ks, seven Ls, three Ms and one N.

ABOVE: **The extra 50 tons of the L-class's enclosed gunhouses required an extra 0.4m/16in of beam compared with a "J", together with eight torpedo tubes rather than ten. The weather-worn *Lookout* has a Bay-class frigate on her far side.**

"N" class, as designed

Displacement: 1,775 tons (standard); 2,385 tons (full load)
Length: 106m/348ft (wl); 108.6in/356ft 6in (oa)
Beam: 10.9m/35ft 8in
Draught: 4.2m/13ft 9in (standard)
Armament: 6 x 4.7in guns (3x2); 4 x 2pdr pompoms (1x4); 10 x 21in torpedo tubes (2x5)
Machinery: Single-reduction steam turbines, 2 boilers, 2 shafts
Power: 29,840kW/40,000shp for 32 knots
Endurance: 490 tons oil for 10,190km/5,500nm at 15 knots
Protection: None
Complement: 183

LEFT: **Both "O" and "P" classes were instantly recognizable because of their 4in armament and the sharper sheerline at the extreme bow. There were exceptions, the non-minelayers being equipped with 4.7in guns, and *Petard* (shown here) gaining two 4in HA in 1945.**

"O" and "P" classes

The cost, complexity and large complements of recent classes resulted in a requirement for a new-style destroyer with a specification between those of the "I" and "J" classes, and leading to its becoming known as the Intermediate Type. Torpedo armament and speed were to be retained but air defence emphasized. Heavy projectiles (and, thus, a slow rate of fire) and ship movement led to a true dual-purpose armament being thought impracticable. The older 4.7in gun, with a 23kg/50lb shell, was thus specified for the first two groups. These, the "O" and "P" classes, were ordered in September and October 1939 as the First and Second Emergency Flotillas respectively.

None had yet been launched when the experience of Norway and Dunkirk in 1940 highlighted the true level of the air threat, particularly from dive-bombing. The first four of the Os were fitted with four 4.7in guns apiece, as planned, but the second division received four single 4in HAs. With the "Y" gun removed they could also carry a deck load of 60 mines. The second flotilla (i.e. "P" class) might have received twin 4in HA mountings, had production permitted. All, however, were completed with singles, capable of 80 degrees elevation.

With the same machinery as the "J" class the O/P classes were slower, their shorter hulls being hydrodynamically less efficient. Inferior speed and broadside excepted, the ships were well praised for their handling and seakeeping, although progressive weight accumulation necessitated some ballasting in order to restore an acceptable stability range.

The Os, particularly, behaved extremely well when escorting Arctic convoys but, as the first to be constructed to reduced war standards, they showed high rates of deterioration if maintenance was allowed to slip. Despite this, surviving P-class hulls were the oldest to be converted in the crash post-war AS frigate programme.

ABOVE: ***Opportune* (seen here) and three sisters were fitted as minelayers. Their normal armament in this role was three 4in weapons, but here "A" gun has been landed. Sixty mines could be carried, laid over the mine chutes visible right aft.**

ABOVE: **An end-of-war picture of *Offa* which, despite not being fitted for minelaying, has landed her torpedo tubes in addition to "A" and "Y" gun mountings. In 1949 she was transferred to the Pakistan flag.**

"P" class, as built

Displacement: 1,550 tons (standard); 2,250 tons (full load)
Length: 102.7m/337ft (wl); 105.1m/345ft (oa)
Beam: 10.7m/35ft
Draught: 4.1m/13ft 6in (standard)
Armament: 4 x 4in guns (4x1); 1 x 2pdr pompom; 8 x 21in torpedo tubes (2x4)
Machinery: Single-reduction steam turbines, 2 boilers, 2 shafts
Power: 29,840kW/40,000shp for 32.25 knots (deep)
Endurance: 475 tons oil for 7,130km/3,850nm at 20 knots
Protection: None
Complement: 175

LEFT: **With the "S" class came the new 55-degree 4.7in mounting, seen here in the similar *Ulster*. Savage trialled a new twin 4.5in 85-degree mounting intended for the Battles.** ABOVE: **All eight Cr-class ships found themselves under foreign flags. Four went to the Royal Norwegian Navy, the *Cromwell* (seen here) becoming the *Bergen*. Of the remainder, two each went to Canada and Pakistan.**

"Q" to "C" classes

The Third to Fourteenth Emergency Flotillas comprised 96 ships of identical hull dimensions, in 8-ship flotillas without additional leaders. Their conservative, but reliable, steam plant was heavy and bulky and, when it was thought imperative to increase endurance with the Qs, a magazine had to be sacrificed for extra fuel capacity. Endurance was now calculated at 20 knots, common for fleet operations.

Hydrodynamic efficiency was improved by the adoption of a squared-off transom. Adequate margin was left for progressive weight accumulation, making them initially exceedingly stable.

The "Q" and "R" classes retained the 40-degree 4.7in gun, succeeded by the 55-degree model from the "S" class. The *Savage* trialled a new twin 4.5in gunhouse for later use on the larger Battle class. Too large for Emergency Flotillas, it did introduce the new 4.5in calibre which, in a 55-degree shielded mounting, was standard from the "Z" class onwards.

Close-range armament was steadily improved, with 40mm Bofors taking the place of pompoms and 20mm Oerlikons replacing 0.5in machine guns. Radar now demanded pride of place at the foremast head, necessitating the reinstatement of a mainmast to support the vital HF/DF antenna. This did nothing to improve arcs, made worse when, with even more topweight, short lattice masts began to displace tripods, which had been standard since the "J" class.

Although of the same dimensions, the final four flotillas (Ca, Ch, Co and Cr classes) showed a growth of 100 tons on deep displacement. Their number included the *Contest*, the first all-welded British destroyer.

To reduce wetness, the sharply sheered bows of the "O" to "R" classes were modified and flattened, but seaworthiness of all flotillas attracted favourable comment. All were designed to be able to remove "Y" gun to convert rapidly for minesweeping or extra depth charge capacity.

ABOVE: **With rigged awnings obscuring some detail, the T-class leader *Troubridge* enters Grand Harbour. She was rebuilt as a Type 15 frigate in 1955–57, but the remaining seven Ts were given limited conversion to Type 16s, giving them a five-year shorter lifespan.**

Ca class, as built

Displacement: 1,825 tons (standard); 2,535 tons (full load)
Length: 106.1m/348ft (wl); 110.6m/362ft 9in (oa)
Beam: 10.9m/35ft 8in
Draught: 4.4m/14ft 3in (standard)
Armament: 4 x 4.5in guns (4x1); 2 x 40mm Bofors (1x2); 8 x 21in torpedo tubes (2x4)
Machinery: Single-reduction geared steam turbines, 2 boilers, 2 shafts
Power: 29,840kW/40,000shp for 32.25 knots (deep)
Endurance: 615 tons oil for 8,610km/4,650nm at 20 knots
Protection: None
Complement: 190

Weapon class

ABOVE: **Only four of a planned 20 Weapons were completed. Their sole anti-surface ship armament was their ten torpedo tubes, and they sacrificed these during the 1950s in order to ship a new mast and Type 965 long-range, air-search radar. This is *Battleaxe* at recommissioning.**

In 1942, it was decided that all new-design destroyers should have a High-Angle (HA) armament, capable of 80-degree elevation. The Weapons were the first class to be affected but, owing to the typically three-year construction span, none was completed before the cessation of hostilities.

The hull was little larger than that of the "intermediates", dimensioned so as to utilize very narrow slips or even to be built two to a slip. For main armament the ubiquitous 4in twin mounting was selected. Simple, robust and relatively light, its rate of fire made it suitable for long-range barrage fire against aircraft, yet it was just heavy enough to deal with the thick hide of a surfaced submarine.

Weapons were intended to act in the role of either fleet destroyer or of anti-submarine (AS) escort. For the former, they would carry six 4in guns, eight torpedo tubes and a Hedgehog spigot mortar. Otherwise, four 4in guns would be supplemented by ten tubes and a double Squid mortar. All would be equipped with stabilized High Angle/ Low Angle (HA/LA) directors and 40mm mountings, both twin and single.

For greater survivability, machinery was laid out on the unit system, with alternate boiler and engine rooms. This resulted in two widely spaced funnels, but deck space was conserved by leading the forefunnel up the inside of the lattice foremast. More advanced steam conditions reduced machinery size somewhat, and topside weight was reduced by incorporating some aluminium alloy into the superstructure (offset somewhat by the addition of patches of quarter-inch steel splinter protection).

Orders for 19 hulls were placed in April 1943, but the first of 15 cancellations occurred as early as September 1944.

From the late 1950s all four surviving ships served as radar pickets, their torpedoes having been traded for a large, amidships lattice mast bearing a single-mattress Type 965 antenna to extend the fleet's radar horizon.

LEFT: ***Crossbow* demonstrates the major characteristics of a radar picket Weapon-class 4in HA armament, all forward; forward boiler exhausting via foremast; amidships mast for 965 antenna; double Squid; and 40mm battery aft.**

Weapon class, as AS escorts

Displacement: 1,955 tons (standard); 2,825 tons (full load)
Length: 106.8m/350ft (wl); 111.3m/365ft (oa)
Beam: 11.6m/38ft
Draught: 4.4m/14ft 4in (standard)
Armament: 4 x 4in HA guns (2x2), 6 x 40mm guns (2x2/2x1); 10 x 21in torpedo tubes (2x5)
Machinery: Single-reduction steam turbines, 2 boilers, 2 shafts
Power: 29,840kW/40,000shp for 30 knots (deep)
Endurance: 630 tons for 9,260km/5,000nm at 20 knots
Protection: Negligible
Complement: 234

Battle class

Known as the "1942 Design" the early Battle-class were true fleet destroyers with heavier firepower than the Weapons yet all of it high angle. Their new Mk.IV twin 4.5in gunhouse, with 80 degrees of elevation, had been extensively trialled aboard the *Savage*. The so-called "between decks" mounting required space in the level below. It was heavy and was power-driven to follow the director. With pronounced ship movement this implied constant correction and consequent wear. Anti-roll stabilizers were thus specified, but quickly cancelled when it was decided that their weight/space allocation was better invested in 60 extra tons of oil fuel.

An intended third 4.5in mounting aft was never fitted, the whole after end being given to four twin 40mm mountings, individually stabilized and extremely complex.

Back-to-back boilers required only a single funnel, abaft which was a bandstand supporting a single 4in starshell gun. Two quadruple sets of torpedo tubes were fitted.

Criticism attended both the unconventional armament layout and the ships' size, although the latter was the smallest that could accommodate all the Fleet's requirements.

Orders for 24 were placed March–June 1943. Of these, only 16 were completed to the original "1942 Design", the last being launched as late as September 1945.

The final eight, of the "1943 Design", had an American Mk 37 director, topped by the same pair of nascelles, associated with the British Type 275 radar. Beam was slightly increased, the single 4in upgraded to a fifth 4.5in, and the torpedo tubes to quintuples. The considerable depth charge capacity was rearranged around a single Squid AS mortar on the quarterdeck. Increasing weight saw an enforced reduction of one twin 40mm mount, compensated somewhat by exchanging the effectively redundant starshell gun for two single 40mm.

In total, 24 Battles were completed and 16 cancelled, some well advanced.

TOP: **Three enlarged "Battle" types were completed in the UK for Venezuela, 1954–56. The *Neuva Esparta* shows her extra 4.5in gun mounting aft, and depth charges in lieu of Squid. There was only one triple torpedo tube mounting, permitting more spacious accommodation.** ABOVE: **Four later Battles were converted to full radar picket configuration. *Aisne* shows her "Double 965" on a new foremast and an associated Type 278 height-finder aft. The after 40mm mountings have been replaced by Seacat SAM.**

ABOVE: ***Trafalgar* was an earlier (1942) "Battle", and is seen in her original configuration. The main armament, located all-forward, was a direct result of the enhanced anti-aircraft battery, but it attracted much adverse comment. Unusually, as a leader, she has her pendants painted up.**

1943 Battle class, as built 

Displacement: 2,460 tons (standard); 3,420 tons (full load)
Length: 111m/364ft (wl); 115.6m/379ft (oa)
Beam: 12.4m/40ft 6in
Draught: 4.7m/15ft 4in (standard)
Armament: 5 x 4.5in guns (2x2/1x1), 8 x 40mm guns (3x2/2x1); 10 x 21in torpedo tubes (2x5)
Machinery: Single-reduction steam turbines, 2 boilers, 2 shafts
Power: 37,300kW/50,000shp for 31.25 knots (deep)
Endurance: 765 tons oil for 8,150km/4,400nm at 20 knots
Protection: Negligible
Complement: 251

LEFT: **The *Daring* was the logical three-mounting extension of the "Battle" design but, in meeting the declared deficiencies of a Battle, it became, in the opinion of most destroyer officers, too large. It was considered too valuable to hunt submarines.**
BELOW: **The *Diamond* shows the massive profile resulting from the large gunhouses. In place of the Battles' handsome soft-nose bow, the Darings reverted to a bar stem, given a somewhat unappealing curved profile.**

Daring class

The Battles were disappointing – insufficient firepower, low rate of fire, too slow. A new, lightweight twin 4.5in mounting, the Mk VI, was under development and, in contrast to the Battles' Mk IVs, it was an above-deck mounting, the penalty for which (given its 80-degree elevation) was a very high profile. This increased the height of the navigating bridge.

One Mk VI forward and one aft were planned for a new "Intermediate" destroyer (the aborted "G" class) but for the "1944 Battle", which became the Daring, three mountings were required. This, and a readoption of unit machinery layout (one boiler and one turbine in each of two separated compartments) increased hull length, but a politically acceptable displacement of 2,750 tons had to be observed. This caused design problems because the Admiralty Board also wanted two quadruple sets of torpedo tubes (quintuples were actually fitted), three twin 40mm stablized mountings and a Squid AS mortar in lieu of depth charges. With faster submarines, the latter were obsolescent, while a Daring was considered too valuable to hunt submarines as a primary requirement.

With participation in the Pacific war an increasing likelihood, a third set of torpedoes was proposed and rejected, but facilities for fighter direction were incorporated. For air-dependent operations, such as those in the Pacific, these were essential.

The Darings were the first British destroyers to be designed for assembly from all-welded modules. Improved methods of stress analysis prompted a greatly increased degree of strengthening at the discontinuity of the break of the forecastle. So heavy was this that a long-forecastle version would have been lighter, but would have raised the centre of gravity unacceptably.

Only eight of the 16 planned Darings were ever completed, and these well after the war. Not their least problem was their 330 complement. They marked the end of the gun and torpedo-armed "conventional" destroyers in the Royal Navy.

RIGHT: **The space-saving concept of the forefunnel being enclosed within the foremast was borrowed from the Weapons. *Dainty*, here, retains her original Mk VI director, in contrast to *Diamond*'s (above right) newer MRS.3.**

Daring class, as built

Displacement: 2,610 tons (standard); 3,350 tons (full load)
Length: 114.4m/375ft (wl); 119m/390ft (oa)
Beam: 13.1m/43ft
Draught: 3.4m/11ft standard
Armament: 6 x 4.5in guns (3x2), 6 x 40mm guns (3x2); 10 x 21in torpedo tubes (2x5)
Machinery: Double-reduction steam turbines, 2 boilers, 2 shafts
Power: 40,284kW/54,000shp for 31 knots (deep)
Endurance: 580 tons oil for 8,150km/4,400nm at 20 knots
Protection: Nominal
Complement: 329

County class

By 1952–53, when the Darings were completed, the Cold War was firmly established and the threat greatly changed. The Soviet Union appeared quite prepared to use tactical nuclear weapons and, deficient herself in naval terms, she was developing weapons and delivery platforms aimed at offsetting the West's pre-eminence in aircraft carrier and amphibious warfare groups. Her counter centred on Air-to-Surface Missiles (ASMs), launched from specialist bombers, and Surface-to-Surface Missiles (SSMs) deployed by small craft, destroyers and submarines.

The West focussed mainly on the ASM threat, developing Surface-to-Air Missiles (SAMs) and their complex guidance systems. These were so bulky that that the host ship was necessarily designed around them.

The Royal Navy's Seaslug had been under development since 1947. It was 6.1m/20ft long and weighed 2,000kg/4,400lb at launch. It could intercept at a slant range of up to 27,430m/30,000yd and altitudes to 15,240m/50,000ft. Eschewing the US Navy's space-saving "Coke-Bottle"-type vertical stowage, British designers stowed the missiles horizontally in a long, centreline, upper deck magazine, a feature which dictated the distinctive, high-freeboard hull of the County-class "destroyer" built to deploy it.

The ships carried a helicopter, rather than a Squid/Limbo, for AS operations. Their COmbined Steam And Gas turbines (COSAG) propulsion system was primarily steam, but supplemented by gas turbines for rapid start-up from cold or for boosting sprint speed.

The second quartette of the eight Counties built was an improved type, with superior electronics and a Mk II Seaslug, capable of carrying a nuclear-tipped warhead and with improved capability against surface targets.

All eight ships were designed with two Mk VI 4.5in twin gun mountings forward. On the last four of the second group "B" mounting was exchanged for four Exocet MM38 SSMs in unreloadable canister launchers.

TOP: **Chile purchased the second quartet of "Counties" during the 1980s. Their obsolete Seaslug systems were replaced by hangar and flight pad for two large helicopters. Finally retired in 2003, *Blanco Encalada* was originally HMS *Fife*.** ABOVE: **The four Batch I Counties carried two twin 4.5in gun mountings forward and a single Type 965 mattress. One deck in depth, the Seaslug magazine ran as far forward as the foremast, despite which only 20 missiles could be carried.**

LEFT: **In their original configurations, *Norfolk*, *Antrim* and *London* steam in formation. Note that the forward funnel exhausts the steam plant, the after the gas turbines. Unusually, the helicopter was moved athwartships in and out of its hangar.**

First group, as designed

Displacement: 5,250 tons (standard); 6,150 tons (full load)
Length: 154m/505ft (wl); 158.8m/520ft 6in (oa)
Beam: 16.5m/54ft
Draught: 4.7m/15.7in (standard)
Armament: 4 x 4.5in guns (2x2); 1 x twin Seaslug launcher; 1 x quadruple Seacat SAM launcher
Machinery: Double-reduction steam turbines and gas turbines (4), 2 boilers, 2 shafts
Power: 30,000shp/22,380kW plus 30,000shp/22,380kW for 31.5 knots (deep)
Endurance: 780 tons fuel (total) for 6,440km/3,500nm at 20 knots
Protection: Nominal
Complement: 460

LEFT: **Larger than many earlier cruisers, the *Bristol* was a "destroyer" by virtue of her status as a primarily anti-aircraft carrier escort. Her size was driven largely by the decision to accommodate both Sea Dart SAM and Ikara ASM systems.**

ABOVE: **No helicopter facilities were provided beyond a flight pad. The cumbersome twin-armed Sea Dart launcher is located forward of this. The radome of the after Type 909 missile director and the split uptakes from the gas turbine spaces are visible.**

Type 82 (*Bristol*)

In 1966 CVA-01, Britain's first post-World War II aircraft carrier, was cancelled. With her went the Type 82s, her dedicated escorts. So many novel systems were involved, however, that it was decided to construct one already designed Type 82 as a trials ship. She was launched in 1969 as HMS *Bristol*.

Her primary area air-defence system was Sea Dart. More compact than Seaslug, its missiles were fed vertically to the twin launcher from a rotating drum. Their maximum slant range was 27,430m/30,000yd at an altitude of 19,800m/65,000ft. Optimistically, it was hoped that Sea Dart would fit into a "frigate-sized" ship, the reason why the "Type 82" class identifier was from the frigate numbering sequence.

Bristol's Sea Dart was located aft, controlled by two Type 909 illuminator/tracker radars, sited forward and aft under large radomes. Forward, she carried Ikara, a stand-off (9,140m/10,000yd) AS weapon comprising a fully controllable torpedo-carrying, rocket-propelled vehicle. Right forward was the new single Mk VIII 4.5in mounting. Fully automatic, this was adopted as the Royal Navy's standard gun, serving long and reliably.

Because the T82 was designed to work with a carrier, no helicopter facilities, beyond a pad, were included.

Yet another intended new system was the Type 988 Anglo-Dutch "Broomstick" surveillance radar, whose antenna would have been housed within a very large radome atop the bridge structure. With this project's cancellation, a double Type 965 was substituted, later updated to a Type 1022.

An improved COSAG propulsion system was specified. Its Olympus gas turbines were repair-by-replacement, necessitating split after uptakes to facilitate engine changes.

The *Bristol*'s all-round capability resulted in such a large and expensive ship that it is doubtful whether the planned eight would ever have been approved. Since 1991 she was served as static harbour training/accommodation ship, a function that she still fulfils at the time of writing.

ABOVE: ***Bristol*'s Ikara launcher was housed in the "zareba" abaft the single 4.5in gun. Its missile was controlled by radars located under small domes flanking the bridge front. Note that the large radome over the forward Type 909 is removed in this view.**

Type 82, as built

Displacement: 6,300 tons (standard); 7,100 tons (full load)
Length: 149.5m/490ft (wl); 154.6m/507ft (oa)
Beam: 16.8m/55ft
Draught: 5.1m/16ft 7in (full load)
Armament: 1 x 4.5in gun; 1 x twin Sea Dart SAM launcher; 1 x Ikara AS launcher
Machinery: Double-reduction steam turbines (2) and Olympus gas turbines (2), 2 boilers, 2 shafts
Power: 22,380kW/30,000shp plus 33,272kW/44,600shp for 30 knots
Endurance: 9,260km/5,000nm at 18 knots
Protection: Nominal
Complement: 407

Type 42 (Sheffield) class

Politics left their mark heavily on the Type 42s. Built at a rate of barely one per year and to tight cost and displacement limits, most were completed "for but not with" essential systems. The intention was to house all of the T82 *Bristol's* systems (less Ikara but with a Lynx helicopter) in a hull of little more than half the displacement. The designers succeeded, but at the cost of a cramped, wet ship.

In saving weight, Batch 1 units proved inadequately stiff, resulting in the later ships being heavily reinforced along the sheer strake.

The short forecastle of the 125.7m/412ft overall Batch 1 and 2 ships put their single 4.5in gun in a very wet position and left the twin-arm Sea Dart launcher in a cramped situation between it and the bridge front.

Externally, the earlier T42s were dominated by the two Type 909 Sea Dart control radars, the double Type 965 surveillance radar atop the bridge structure, and the outsized funnel casing which exhausted the all-gas turbine drive of two Olympus and two Tynes, the latter used for cruising.

All four surviving Batch 1s were expected to have been deleted by the end of 2006, Batch 2s by 2012.

Already a tight design, the T42s gained further, post-Falklands War topweight in Vulcan Phalanx CIWS and 20mm cannon, a Type 1022 radar in place of the 965, and improved electronics. Seaboats and triple AS torpedo tubes were landed as partial compensation.

The inadequacy of the basic Type 42 design was recognized by the insertion of a considerable 15.6m/51ft section in the forward hull of the four Batch 3s. The length of the entry, plus bow bulwarks, makes for greatly improved dryness and extra missile stowage. Better lines also give an extra 1.5 knots for the same power.

ABOVE LEFT: **The cramped arrangements of the earlier Type 42s is well evident in this shot of *Exeter*. Experience in the Falklands War dictated the addition of the waist CIWS systems, installed at the expense of the original seaboats on davits.** ABOVE: **Even the lengthened Batch 3 *Manchester* can still ship solid water forward, alleviated somewhat in her sister ship *Edinburgh* by the addition of a bulwark. The low-freeboard quarter deck is also prone to wetness.**

LEFT: **Although lengthened by over 16m/52.4ft overall to improve seakeeping, endurance and habitability, the Batch 3 Type 42s, such as *Gloucester*, retain the same armament. Note the heavy strakes added amidships to reduce longitudinal stress levels.**

Batch 3 units

Displacement: 3,810 tons (standard); 5,075 tons (full load)
Length: 132.3m/434ft 3in (wl); 141.1m/463ft 2in (oa)
Beam: 14.9m/49ft
Draught: 5.8m/19ft (maximum)
Armament: 1 x 4.5in gun; 1 x twin Sea Dart launcher; 2 x 20mm Vulcan Phalanx CIWS
Machinery: 2 Olympus and 2 Tyne gas turbines, 2 shafts
Power: 40,582kW/54,400shp or 7,967kW/10,680shp for 29.5 or 18 knots
Endurance: 600 tons fuel for 8,800km/4,750nm at 18 knots
Protection: Nominal
Complement: 285

Type 45 (Daring) class

During 1995 the British, French and Italians formed a consortium to define a destroyer of a common form suitable to each. Although the British left the ship group four years later they remained committed to the French missile system. There remains also a strong family resemblance between the resulting ships – the six British Daring class, three French Forbin type and two, possibly four, Italian Bergamini.

The British ships are replacements for the rapidly aging T42s and a second set of six will be a necessity but, inevitably, their fate will be bound up with that of the Royal Navy's two projected fleet carriers, long a political football. Despite sharp lessons of the past, we once again see plans to commission ships fitted "for, but not with".

Displacing half as much again as a T42, the Darings are of a sharply sculpted, radar signature-reducing design, but laid out much like a T23 frigate. A single 4.5in gun in a new "Mod 1" enclosure is located forward of a 48-cell Vertical Launch System (VLS) containing 16 long-range Aster 30 and 32 medium-range Aster 15 Surface-to-Air Missiles (SAMs).

Despite the hugely expensive development of the capable Merlin helicopter, reports speak of the Daring "making do" with Lynxes on grounds of economy. As the ships lack any anti-ship missiles they will need to rely on the Lynx for delivery of Sea Skua ASMs as well as AS torpedoes. Neither does the ship carry a CIWS.

Two shafts are driven directly by reversible electric motors, speed-controllable over their full range. Power for them is generated by two new Anglo-American WR-21 gas turbines or, for ultra-quiet navigation, two vibration-isolated diesel alternators.

ABOVE: **First-of-class *Daring* undergoing an extended period of acceptance trials. Between the low bridge and the "Mod 1" gun mounting is the VLS housing. This may later include cells for Tomahawk cruise missiles.** LEFT: **Although all hull and superstructure modules are built in covered facilities, they are assembled and launched into the Clyde from a traditional slipway. This is *Diamond*, already in an advanced state of fitting out.**

Assembled from modules built both in Portsmouth and on the Clyde, the Daring class has been subjected to many changes and delays as naval funding becomes ever tighter.

Type 45, as projected

Displacement: 7,350 tons (full load)
Length: 152.4m/500ft (wl)
Beam: 21.2m/69ft 7in (at upper deck); 18m/59ft 1in (at wl)
Draught: Not known
Armament: 1 x 4.5in gun; 16 x Aster 30 and 32 x Aster 15 SAM; 2 x 30mm cannon (2x1)
Machinery: Gas turbine/electric, 2 shafts
Power: 40,000kW/53,650shp for 29 knots (or 4,000kW/5,365shp for quiet drive)
Endurance: 12,965km/7,000nm at 18 knots
Protection: Nominal
Complement: 190

LEFT: **Compared with the pre-war picture of *Farragut* (below), the *Macdonough* (DD.351) has shipped much extra topweight during the Pacific war, compensated by little except the loss of the mainmast and the amidships 5in gun.**

Farragut (DD.348) class

Following World War I, the US Navy had large numbers of new flush-decked destroyers, but lacked suitable flotilla leaders. Larger destroyers were favoured over light cruisers, but numerous 1920s design studies resulted in no actual ships. The London Naval Treaty of 1930 then defined maximum individual and global displacements, establishing also that gun calibres should not exceed 130mm.

Future destroyers, it was decided, should be of two basic types, designed either to screen the battle fleet or to operate offensively in independent, torpedo-centred strike squadrons.

Bethlehem Steel, a specialist destroyer yard, produced the design that resulted in the "1,500-ton" Farragut class of the early 1930s. The general layout accorded closely with that already well-established by the Royal Navy, but with displacement and 5in guns pushing more closely at Treaty-agreed maxima.

Far less conservative than the British in machinery practice, American plant had far higher power-to-weight ratios, the Farraguts being designed for a respectable maximum speed of 36.5 knots. The two closely spaced funnels indicated adjacent boiler spaces, the thicker after funnel exhausting boilers in each of the spaces.

Readopting a half-height forecastle for improved seakeeping, the Farraguts were designed with five single 5in guns, two superimposed at either end and a fifth on a bandstand immediately abaft the after funnel. The bridge was set well back to improve dryness and to reduce the blast effect of "B" gun mounting. Above it was a substantial dual-function director. There were two quadruple banks of torpedo tubes.

The design proved to be weight-critical and, in order to acquire an adequate AA armament during World War II, the ships lost their amidships 5in gun mount, the shields of the after 5in guns, the mainmast and one or more boats. Two of the class capsized during the 1944 typhoon, unable to utilize their depleted fuel tanks for water ballast.

ABOVE: **In this 1930s photograph, the Bethlehem-designed *Farragut* (DD.348) shows well the influence of the classic British layout. Although a considerable advance on the preceding flush-deckers, the design was regarded as "tight". The "E" is for "Excellent", an accolade earned over a specific period.**

Farragut, as designed

Displacement: 1,360 tons (standard); 1,585 tons (full load)
Length: 101.9m/334ft (wl); 104.2m/341ft 6in (oa)
Beam: 10.5m/34ft 3in
Draught: 2.9m/9ft 8in (deep)
Armament: 5 x 5in guns (5x1); 8 x 21in torpedo tubes (2x4)
Machinery: Single-reduction steam turbines, 4 boilers, 2 shafts
Power: 31,930kW/42,800shp for 36.5 knots
Endurance: 200 tons oil for 12,965km/7,000nm at 12 knots
Protection: None
Complement: 160

LEFT: **As built, the 1,850-tonners had massive tripod masts. These were removed, as seen here on *Phelps* (DD.360), along with the twin 5in mountings in "B" and "X" positions. A single 5in was substituted at "X", together with eight 40mm weapons.** ABOVE: **An early wartime picture of *Somers* (DD.381), lead ship of an improved Porter type. Inherently overweight, she has shed some after superstructure but still retains her original 5in mountings and rather odd, box-like director.**

Porter (DD.356) and Somers (DD.381) classes

Following on from the Farragut, the "1,850-ton" Porters were built to the treaty limit on displacement. Described as "leaders", they were intended to be large enough to act offensively. To this end, they carried eight 5in 38-calibre ("5-inch 38") guns in four twin gunhouses, superimposed at either end. While having no more torpedo tubes than the Farragut, they carried a reload for each.

Imposing in appearance, the Porters had a full-height forecastle, bulky superstructure, topped off by low-angle directors forward and aft, and substantial tripod masts. The mainmast supported an elevated platform bearing two searchlights. Superfiring "B" and "X" positions were quadruple 1.1in anti-aircraft cannon.

Unofficial policy was to build to treaty limits, with capacity to add further weight in an emergency. Even without such as depth charges and arrangements being included, however, the class was overweight (cf British Tribal). With war they landed "B" and "X" mountings, acquiring a single in "X" position. Pole masts replaced tripods and the after director was landed. Reload torpedoes were abandoned in favour of a third quadruple bank.

The five Somer class ships of the following year's (i.e. 1934's) programme were described as Improved Porter. Their machinery was completely redesigned, generating a further 1,492kW/2,000shp. This alone could drive a destroyer at 15 knots, but already on the steep part of the speed/resistance curve, it was good for only an extra half knot. A single trunked funnel served both boiler spaces. The third set of tubes was included, with the suppression of after director and tripod masts contributing to the saving of topweight. With war, however, main armament was likewise reduced to five 5in guns in order to acquire eight 40mm anti-aircraft weapons.

Only 2 of the 13 were lost, the *Porter* to a Japanese torpedo off Guadalcanal, the *Warrington* (DD.383) foundering in a Caribbean hurricane.

Somers class, as designed

Displacement: 2,010 tons (standard); 2,765 tons (full load)
Length: 113.3m/371ft 6in (wl); 116.4m/381ft 6in (oa)
Beam: 11.2m/36ft 10in
Draught: 4.1m/13ft 5in (full load)
Armament: 8 x 5in guns (4x2); 12 x 21in torpedo tubes (3x4)
Machinery: Single-reduction steam turbines, 4 boilers, 2 shafts
Power: 38,792kW/52,000shp for 37.5 knots
Endurance: 620 tons oil for 7,870km/4,250nm at 20 knots
Protection: None
Complement: 235

RIGHT: ***Porter* (DD.356) in an interim wartime condition. Compared with *Phelps* (above), she has not received 5in 38 Dual Purpose (DP) mountings, has had her original director radar-fitted and retains her original funnel profiles. The bulwark amidships is an addition.**

LEFT: **As designed, the 1,570-ton Sims class – *Anderson* (DD.411) seen here as built – packed a maximum of five 5in guns and twelve torpedo tubes, one quad on the centreline and one each beam. Note the heavy after superstructure, with boats under derricks.** BELOW: **In Pearl Harbor, December 1941, *Downes* (DD.375) is shown supporting the near-submerged *Cassin* (DD.372) in a flooded drydock. In a gesture of pride, the US Navy salvaged the machinery of both, installing it in new hulls, bearing identical names and numbers.**

Mahan (DD.364), Craven (DD.380) and Sims (DD.409) classes

Built to replace aging flush-deckers, the "1500-tonners" of the 1930s followed the Japanese lead in favouring torpedoes over gun batteries. Tactics called for high speeds, leading American practice to successively higher steam pressure and temperatures. Simpler and lighter turbines rotated at higher speeds, but with the penalty of two-stage reduction gearing. Improved power-to-weight ratios and fuel economy came at the cost of increasingly cramped machinery spaces.

Launched 1935–36, the 18 Mahans were a development of the Farraguts. Their foremasts were designed as tripods, the extra stiffness reducing rigging, which adversely affected fields of fire. It was ironic, therefore, that they were later exchanged for stayed pole masts when the acquisition of more light weapons demanded economies in topweight.

Designed for five 5in 38s, they were reduced to four, with the forward mountings in shields, the after ones unprotected. Separate funnels served the two boiler spaces. Between them was an elevated quadruple torpedo bank; two more were sided further aft.

With the 22 Cravens (otherwise termed Gridleys or Bagleys) that followed, a single, very large, trunked funnel served all four boilers. Saving both topweight and deckspace, it also removed the smoke nuisance further from the bridge. By reducing the main battery to four 5in weapons, a fourth quadruple torpedo tube bank was possible. All were sided.

As the waist abaft the break of the forecastle tended to be very wet,

bulwarks were added, extending as far aft as the forward tubes.

The final dozen of the series (sometimes referred to as the Benham subgroup) had only three boilers, resulting in a considerably smaller funnel.

The final group of single-stackers was the 12-strong Sims class. These were much the same but readopted the fifth gun (landed in wartime), with only three quadruple torpedo tube banks.

ABOVE: **Lead ship of 22, the *Craven* (DD.380) carried only four main-battery guns to compensate for a massive complement of twelve torpedo tubes, with two triples on either side. Note the prominently trunked funnel and lack of shields to after guns.**

Sims class, as built

Displacement: 1,760 tons (standard); 2,290 tons (full load)
Length: 104m/341ft (wl); 106.1m/347ft 9in (oa)
Beam: 11m/36ft 2in
Draught: 3.9m/12ft 9in (full load)
Armament: 5 x 5in guns (5x1); 12 x 21in torpedo tubes (3x4)
Machinery: Double-reduction steam turbines, 3 boilers, 2 shafts
Power: 37,300kW/50,000shp for 35 knots
Endurance: 444 tons fuel for 6,720km/3,650nm at 20 knots
Protection: Nominal
Complement: 192

Benson (DD.421) and Livermore (DD.429) classes

The single-funnelled classes evolved a multi-purpose destroyer design that provided the basis for a huge replacement programme begun in 1937. The previous design displacement of 1,500 tons had proved over-constricting and the new ships, nominally at least, would be of 1,630 tons, treaty restrictions by now being effectively a dead letter. The smaller ships were known as the Benson class, the larger as the Livermore. Externally, their funnels differed, the Livermore being round, the Benson slab-sided.

At the time of the programme's instigation a theoretical Pacific war dominated the ship's specification. By the time of the early deliveries the Atlantic war was a reality and, although neutral until late 1941, the United States became increasingly involved through the president's "Short of War" policy.

Early units commissioned with five 5in guns and ten torpedo tubes. Escorting convoys in the western Atlantic, however, required large outfits of depth charges. Following British experience, therefore, destroyers landed one gun and one bank of tubes in order to ship not only depth charges but also a respectable anti-aircraft armament.

More compact boilers allowed the Benson/Livermore class to adopt a unit machinery layout. Two each alternate boiler and engine rooms necessitated two thin, but nicely proportioned, funnels. Acceptance of centreline torpedo tubes gave the same broadside for half the weight, a bonus being the adoption of quintuple mounts.

Reduction in weight elsewhere and modifications such as lowering the director tower permitted the fitting of two twin 40mm Bofors and four 20mm Oerlikons. These complemented the main battery guns, which were Dual-Purpose (DP). Because of supply bottlenecks, however, there was a wide variety of armament fits at any time. By the end of World War II, what with acquisitions of electronics, further armament and crew, many units were running at an extra 300 tons deep, a problem common to most destroyers.

ABOVE LEFT: **Although the majority of the Bensons were given only one quintuple bank of torpedo tubes and four main-battery guns, they still came out considerably overweight. Some of the slightly enlarged Livermores took the designed five guns and ten tubes.** ABOVE: **The Benson-class *Farenholt* (DD.491) is launched from Bethlehem Steel's Staten Island yard on November 19, 1941. Typical of so many destroyers, she enjoyed barely 4 years of active service, followed by 25 years in reserve before being scrapped.**

LEFT: **Following President Roosevelt's "Short of War" directive, US Navy destroyers aggressively escorted North Atlantic convoys. On October 17, 1941, *Kearny* (DD.342) survived torpedoing by *U-568*, incurring the first fatal casualties of the US Navy's war.**

Benson class, average, as built

Displacement: 1,910 tons (standard); 2,475 tons (full load)
Length: 104.1m/341ft 3in (wl); 106.1m/348ft (oa)
Beam: 11.1m/36ft 3in
Draught: 4.2m/13ft 9in (full load)
Armament: 4 x 5in guns (4x1); 5 x 21in torpedo tubes (1x5); 4 x 40mm (2x2) guns; 4/6 x 20mm guns (4/6x1)
Machinery: Double-reduction steam turbines, 4 boilers, 2 shafts
Power: 37,300kW/50,000shp for 35 knots
Endurance: 450 tons oil for 7,223km/3,900nm at 20 knots
Protection: Nominal
Complement: 191

Fletcher (DD.445) class

The scale of American destroyer programmes meant considerable overlap in classes, with the first of 175 Fletchers commissioning long before many of the preceding Livermores. Where the latter were, nominally at least, treaty-constructed, the Fletcher located the same five 5in/ten tube outfit in a hull that was comfortable and not overloaded. Unfortunately, spare capacity always appears to be something of a challenge to evolution.

At the outset, the design successfully combined the specified main armament with Anti-Aircraft (AA) weapons, a five-pattern depth charge capacity, sufficient endurance and a sustained speed of better than 35 knots. Standard displacement as designed, however, increased from some 2,100 tons to about 2,275 tons.

Once again, designers opted for a flush-decked hull. This avoided the obvious stress concentration caused by the discontinuity at the break of the forecastle and also better suited the longitudinal framing chosen for series production. The resulting continuous sheerline gave a greater depth of hull amidships, increasing strength. Wetness remained a problem, however, the waist bulwark being retained.

Progressive weight acquisition saw some units displacing over 3,000 tons (deep) by 1944. Designed AA batteries of two 40mm and six 20mm had grown by up to ten 40mm and seven 20mm, director controlled and most in splinter-proof tubs. Superstructures that had been designed to incorporate a degree of aluminium alloy for lightness had already been worked in steel because of shortages of raw materials; these had now acquired further areas of light steel protection, 12.5–19mm/½–¾in in thickness. Complements increased from a designed 273 to about 300, putting increasing pressure on accommodation.

ABOVE LEFT: **No longer constrained by treaty restrictions, the Fletchers grew to a size well capable of carrying a five-gun, ten-tube armament. Modernized, as seen here, the *Cowell* (DD.547) was transferred to Argentina in 1971, serving until the mid-1980s.** ABOVE: **A foredeck shot of *Fletcher* (DD.445), as delivered. She is fitted with the original pole mast, topped with its SC-2 air-search radar antenna, seen near end-on. Despite their size, they were soon more than 200 tons overweight.**

Together with considerable topside electronic additions, these changes were paid for in reduced stability, greater draught and lower speed. Despite all, however, (including their enormous turning circle), the Fletchers were considered very successful.

LEFT: **A total of 39 Fletchers, including *The Sullivans* (DD.537), were modernized after the Korean War. The tripod mast supports the large SPS-6B air-search radar, the after funnel a spreader with domes for radar direction finders.**

Fletcher class, as designed

Displacement: 2,110 tons (standard); 2,700 tons (full load)
Length: 112.5m/369ft (wl); 114.8m/376ft 6in (oa)
Beam: 12.2m/39ft 9in
Draught: 4m/13ft 3in (full load)
Armament: 5 x 5in guns (5x1); 10 x 21in torpedo tubes (2x5)
Machinery: Double-reduction steam turbines, 4 boilers, 2 shafts
Power: 44,760kW/60,000shp for 35 knots
Endurance: 491 tons oil for 6,450km/3,500nm at 20 knots
Protection: Nominal
Complement: 273

Allen M. Sumner (DD.692) class

In formulating the specification for the Sumners, the successors to the Fletchers, the US Navy took account of the battle experience of the already heavily engaged Royal Navy. Torpedoes appeared to have been of far less application than an effective, dual-purpose armament. In the interests of standardization, machinery and hull length would not be changed but beam would need to be increased, at consequent cost to speed.

The Fletchers' high profile had attracted criticism, leading to the development of a twin 5in 38 gunhouse and the likely intention of siting one forward and one aft. Immediately, however, a four-gun forward battery was thought desirable and, as the arrangement of the forthcoming British 1942 Battle did not enthuse, a third mounting was sited aft in the "Y" position. For little increase in weight a further gun had been added while precious centreline space had been saved in using three mountings in place of five. The bridge was lowered one level and, on some, opened to allow better all-round visibility in the event of air attack.

Where the Fletchers' two torpedo tube banks bracketed the after funnel, the after set in the Sumners was moved aft to a location just forward of "Y" mounting. In many units, it was later exchanged for a further quadruple 40mm mounting. Two more of these were sited in staggered, sided tubs, with singles or twins also mounted on the box-like wings which added space to the bridge structure.

The Sumners were improved but overloaded; Fletchers were a half-way house to the stretched, follow-on Gearings. They had, by virtue of twin rudders, improved manoeuvrability but, due to the extra weight forward, were notably wet.

Backbone of the post-war US Navy's destroyer fleet, both Sumners and Gearings would be subjected to comprehensive modernization programmes.

ABOVE LEFT: Built for gun and torpedo attack, American destroyers had to be remodelled for Cold War anti-submarine operations by 1960. *Allen M. Sumner* (DD.692) thus underwent Fleet Rehabilitation And Modernization (FRAM). ABOVE: The Sumner-class *Walke* (DD.723) lays outboard of the Fletcher-class *Halford* (DD. 480) at the Mare Island Navy Yard in March 1945. Note the latter's temporary bows. BELOW LEFT: The FRAM-ed *Strong* (DD.758) was transferred to Brazil in 1973 as the *Rio Grande do Norte.* Although she has retained the updated electronics and DASH facilities, she has lost the large VDS visible on *Sumner* (above left).

Sumner class, as designed

Displacement: 2,535 tons (standard); 3,150 tons (full load)
Length: 112.5m/369ft (wl); 114.8m/376ft 6in (oa)
Beam: 12.5m/41ft
Draught: 4.3m/14ft 1in (full load)
Armament: 6 x 5in guns (3x2), 12 x 40mm guns (2x2/2x4); 10 x 21in torpedo tubes (2x5)
Machinery: Double-reduction steam turbines, 4 boilers, 2 shafts
Power: 44,760kW/60,000shp for 35 knots
Endurance: 504 tons oil for 6,020km/3,250nm at 20 knots
Protection: Nominal
Complement: 336

Gearing (DD.710) class

Only 58 Sumners were built (12 of them modified for minelaying) before 4.3m/14ft was added to the length to accommodate the obvious overloading. The transition was smooth, many ships ordered as Sumner being delivered as the longer Gearing. Ninety-nine of these were completed, many others being cancelled with the close of hostilities.

Although parallel construction programmes were producing large numbers of Destroyer Escorts (DEs) for Anti-Submarine (AS) operations, some Fletchers were modified post-war to Escort Destroyers (DDEs) with enhanced depth charge capacity and a full Hedgehog in place of "B" mounting. (The US Navy never adopted the more deadly Squid.) Most Fletchers, however, had short lives, although some were reactivated for the Korean War. Others exchanged their remaining torpedo tubes for two twin 3in in the waist to engage Japanese kamikaze suicide aircraft.

By the late 1950s, however, the US Navy was faced with block obsolescence of its destroyer force. As an alternative to a prohibitively expensive replacement programme, the Navy embarked on the so-called FRAM (Fleet Rehabilitation And Modernization) option. This was undertaken at three levels: FRAM I conversions, applied to 49 Gearings, were effectively total rebuilds; FRAM II, equivalent to a half-life refit, affected 113 destroyers, mostly Sumners; and FRAM III, involving only eight Sumners, replaced specific on-board systems.

By now, the fast nuclear submarine was a reality, and FRAM I ships received the ASROC (Anti-Submarine Rocket) stand-off weapon together with the ultimately abortive DASH (Drone AS Helicopter) system. They retained four 5in guns, but FRAM II conversions kept all six, receiving Variable-Depth Sonar (VDS) in addition to both long and short AS torpedo tubes. Topside, both types were notable for a mass of newly acquired electronics, including Electronic Countermeasures (ECM) to defeat incoming anti-ship missiles.

ABOVE: *Fiske* (DD.842) is seen here in the early 1950s as a DDR, i.e. radar picket, conversion. She retains her original main armament but has gained the very heavy SPS-8 height-finding radar on the after superstructure. BELOW: Steaming at high speed into a calm swell, *Rowan* (DD.782) is seen here before her FRAM I conversion. The broad, flat fronts of the twin 5in gunhouses could cause deck cracking when impacted by heavy seas.

LEFT: As the bulk of the US Navy's destroyers dated from 1943–45, in the early 1960s the service was faced with the huge problem of block obsolescence. The FRAM I modernization, seen here on *Rowan* (DD.782), extended useful life by an estimated eight years.

Gearing class, as designed

Displacement: 2,635 tons (standard); 3,480 tons (full load)
Length: 116.8m/383ft (wl); 119.3m/392ft (oa)
Beam: 12.4m/40ft 9in
Draught: 4.4m/14ft 5in (full load)
Armament: 6 x 5in guns (3x2), 16 x 40mm (2x2/2 or 3x4) guns; 5 or 10 x 21in torpedo tubes (1 or 2x5)
Machinery: Double-reduction steam turbines, 4 boilers, 2 shafts
Power: 44,760kW/60,000shp for 34.5 knots
Endurance: 740 tons oil for 8,056km/4,350nm at 20 knots
Protection: Nominal
Complement: 336

Forrest Sherman (DD.931) class

First post-war attempts to produce the ideal fleet destroyer, based on recent experience, resulted in the one-off, 5,600-ton *Norfolk* of 1951 and the four 3,675-ton Mitschers of 1952. Too large and expensive, both types were classified, firstly as "frigates", latterly as "leaders". The Mitschers, however, had advanced steam machinery which, although initially trouble-prone, was scaled-down successfully to suit the succeeding class, the Forrest Shermans.

Destroyers had, by now, moved away from their classic role in torpedo attack to become escorts capable of protecting a surface group against air and submarine attack. The Forrest Shermans, of which the nameship was laid down in October 1953, were the last gun-armed destroyers and, 7.3m/24ft longer than a Gearing, looked decidedly under-armed.

In place of the earlier twin 5in 38 gunhouses, they carried three of the new 5in, 54-calibre weapons in single, automatic mountings, one forward, two aft. The 54s had, however, twice the rate of fire and considerably greater range. At both ends they were superfired by a twin 3in 70. Flanking "B" position forward were two half-Hedgehogs. Four tubes for launching heavyweight AS torpedoes were sited in the waist, but these were later removed.

In the course of the 18-ship programme, the forward freeboard was twice increased to improve dryness. Much aluminium alloy, not then appreciated as a potential hazard, was incorporated in the superstructure.

By late 1958, when the last units commissioned, rapid advances in Surface-to-Air Missile (SAM) technology had already rendered them obsolescent. In 1967–68, therefore, four were converted to Guided-Missile Destroyers (DDGs), exchanging their after armament for a Tartar SAM system and an ASROC launcher. Eight more surrendered "X" gun, the 3in mountings and Hedgehogs in favour of ASROC, VDS and lightweight AS torpedo tubes. The class was scrapped during the 1980s.

ABOVE: **Transitional between the classic gunned destroyer and the current all-missile ships, the Forrest Shermans (the nameship shown here) had the power and seakeeping required to escort the new generation of large carriers.** BELOW: **During the late 1960s, four of the class were converted to Tartar-equipped DDGs. This is *Parsons*, originally DD.949, renumbered DDG.33. Note that she has landed her after guns for conversion but has gained an ASROC launcher amidships.**

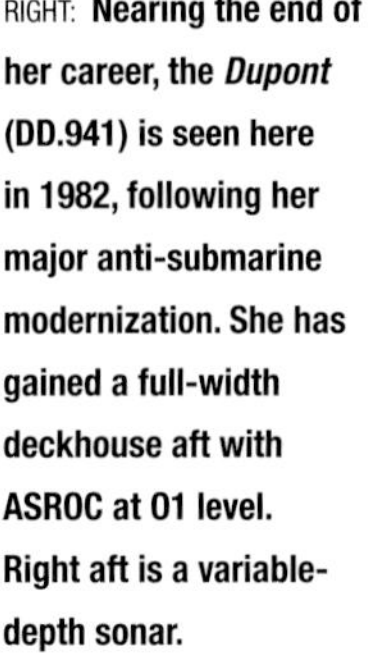

RIGHT: **Nearing the end of her career, the *Dupont* (DD.941) is seen here in 1982, following her major anti-submarine modernization. She has gained a full-width deckhouse aft with ASROC at 01 level. Right aft is a variable-depth sonar.**

Forrest Sherman class, as designed

Displacement: 2,850 tons (standard); 4,750 tons (full load)
Length: 124.1m/407ft (wl); 127.6m/418ft 6in (oa)
Beam: 13.7m/45ft
Draught: 4.6m/15ft (full load)
Armament: 3 x 5in guns (3x1), 4 x 3in guns (2x2); 4 x 21in torpedo tubes (2x2)
Machinery: Double-reduction steam turbines, 4 boilers, 2 shafts
Power: 52,220kW/70,000shp for 33 knots
Endurance: 8,335km/4,500nm at 20 knots
Protection: Nominal
Complement: 337

Charles F. Adams (DDG.2) class

Between 1956 and 1962, the Gearing-class destroyer *Gyatt* (DD.712) served as a testbed to prove the possibility of converting conventional destroyers to SAM escorts. Although feasible, it proved uneconomical. For the duration, *Gyatt* was designated DDG.1, so that the Adams, the first group of designed-to-task GM destroyers, commenced with DDG.2

Gyatt deployed the nuclear-capable Terrier missile, but the Tartar, derived from it, was built into the Adams. Each carried 42 rounds of the 32.19km/20-mile ranged weapon.

Cut by budget restrictions, the Adams class ran to 23 units. Although about 4m/13ft longer, the hull was basically that of a Forrest Sherman, as was the propulsion machinery. The extra length eased constrictions in the machinery spaces and permitted an amidships ASROC launcher. The ships remained cramped, however, which militated against subsequent major modernizations. They thus received only limited upgrading.

The final five units were fitted with the large SQS-23 sonar. Located in a forward bulb, this necessitated a more heavily raked bow and a stem anchor.

The Tartar launcher (twin-arm in the first 13 units, single-arm in the remainder) was located aft, atop a cylindrical structure that contained magazine and loading gear. Sited abaft the after 5in 54, it restricted the gun's firing arcs at lower elevations. The missile system was later modified to launch either Harpoon SSMs or Standard SM-1 MR SAMs.

ABOVE LEFT: *Charles F. Adams* (DDG.2) was lead ship for a class of 23 dating from the late 1950s. They featured a lengthened Forrest Sherman hull, with greater forward freeboard, but retaining the same machinery. ABOVE: Later units of the class were completed with improvements. The *Tattnall* (DDG.19), seen here in the Suez Canal, has the later single-arm Mk 13 launcher replacing the twin-arm Mk 11 and uprated SPS-40 air-search radar.

Two directors for target acquisition and illumination were situated abaft the after funnel. As these precluded the addition of a mainmast, the heavy, stabilized antenna for the tracking radar had to be supported on the after funnel The class was deleted during the 1990s, outlived somewhat by three modified versions built for each of the Royal Australian and German navies (*Brisbane*, *Hobart* and *Perth*, and *Lütjens*, *Mölders* and *Rommel* respectively).

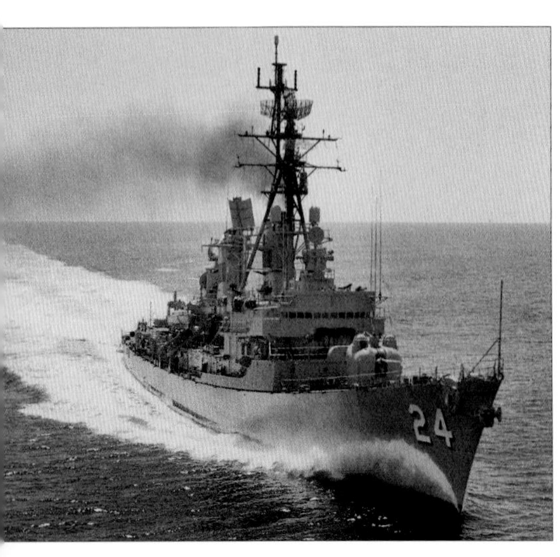

LEFT: *Waddell* (DDG.24) was the last of the US Navy's Adams, a further six being built to foreign account. This photograph well portrays the powerful sheerline and modified bow associated with the later ships' bow-mounted SQS-23 sonars. ABOVE: A Tartar missile blasts off from the single-arm Mk 13 launcher of the *Berkeley* (DDG.15). Ever-demanding of space, the revised launch system was later modified to fire the derived Standard SM-1 MR as well as Harpoon.

Adam class, as built

Displacement: 3,275 tons (standard); 4,525 tons (full load)
Length: 128.1m/420ft (wl); 133.3m/437ft (oa)
Beam: 14.3m/47ft
Draught: 5.8m/19ft (full load)
Armament: 2 x 5in guns (2x1), 0/4 x 3in guns (0/2x2); Single/twin-armed Tartar SAM launcher; 8-cell ASROC launcher
Machinery: Double-reduction steam turbines, 4 boilers, 2 shafts
Power: 52,220kW/70,000shp for 31.5 knots
Endurance: 900 tons oil for 8,335km/4,500nm at 20 knots
Protection: Nominal
Complement: 345

LEFT: **Superficially similar in appearance to an Adams, the larger Coontz type could be instantly differentiated through the considerable lattice structure before the after funnel. Ex-DLG.9 *Coontz* here shows her revised DDG.40 pendant number.**

BELOW: **With uprating from Terrier to Standard SM-2 ER missiles, the original two twin 3in gun mountings had to be sacrificed. The sole remaining anti-surface ships capability left to the *Luce* (DDG.38) is her single 5in gun.**

Coontz (DDG.40) class

Clearly from the same stable as the Adams class, which was built in parallel, the Coontz (otherwise Farragut) class ships were an imposing 21.4m/70ft longer on the waterline. Comparable with earlier gun-armed Mitschers, the ten ships were initially classified DLG.6–15, i.e. "missile-armed destroyer leaders". In 1975, however, they were regraded "GM destroyers", or DDG. They were renumbered DDG.37–46.

Designed for the area air defence of carrier groups, the class was designed around the Terrier III SAM. This was later uprated to the ER, or Extended Range, version of the Standard SM-1 (cf the Adams' MR, or Medium Range, version). Unlike the Adams', the Coontz-class launcher was located abaft the 40-round, flat-roofed missile magazine.

Only one 5in gun was fitted. This was in "A" position, superfired by an eight-cell ASROC launcher. As built, the class had a twin 3in 70 mounting on either side in the waist but, during the 1970s modernization, exchanged these for two, quadruple Harpoon SSM launchers. With the Standard missiles having terminal-phase homing, ship-end guidance electronics became simplified.

Operating facilities for a shipborne helicopter were not provided, although a touch-down pad was available right aft. Defensive armament lacking, a Close-In Weapon System (CIWS) such as Vulcan Phalanx was considered but not pursued, due to considerations of weight, cost and age.

Larger, but similar in profile to an Adams, a Coontz could be instantly differentiated by the tower-like lattice mainmast forward of the after funnel. To serve the ASROC, all had a hull-mounted (as opposed to bow-mounted) SQS-23 sonar. Later experience showed that sonars could be located within bulbous bows that could be designed to actually improve a ship's hydrodynamic performance over a given speed range. The by-now obsolete Coontz class was discarded during the 1990s.

ABOVE: **Quadruple Harpoon SSMs, visible by the *Mahan*'s (DDG.42's) after funnel, redressed the earlier deficiency. The 40-round Standard magazine is contained within the flat structure forward of the launcher.**

Coontz class, as completed

Displacement: 4,175 tons (standard); 5,650 tons (full load)
Length: 149.5m/490ft (wl); 156.3m/512ft 6in (oa)
Beam: 16m/52ft 4in
Draught: 5.4m/17ft 9m
Armament: 1 x 5in, 4 x 3in guns (2x2); 1 x twin Terrier SAM launcher, 8-cell ASROC launcher
Machinery: Double-reduction steam turbines, 4 boilers, 2 shafts
Power: 63,410kW/85,000shp for 32.5 knots
Endurance: 900 tons oil for 9,250km/5,000nm at 20 knots
Protection: Nominal
Complement: 365

Leahy (DLG.16) and Belknap (DLG.26) classes

ABOVE LEFT: **Like the Coontz-class ships, Leahys (nameship seen here) and Belknaps were originally categorized "Guided-Missile Destroyer Leaders" or DLGs. With the 1975 rationalization, however, they were upgraded to "Guided-Missile Cruisers", or CGs.**
ABOVE: **For improved seakeeping, both classes adopted a higher-freeboard, long-forecastle-style hull with a pronounced knuckle. *England* (CG.22) shows double-ended Standard SAM systems, Harpoon SSM and an ASROC launcher, but no gun.**

To boost the area air defence of high-value surface groups, the "double-ended" escort was introduced with the nine Leahy. They were completed (1962–64) with a twin-arm Terrier SAM launcher at either end. An ASROC launcher was also located forward, with AS torpedo tubes in the waist. The only medium-calibre guns were paired 3in 70s on either side of amidships.

As with the preceding Coontz class, the Leahy were initially classified DLG but, in the general 1975 reclassification were, because of their size and capability, revised upward to "GM cruisers" DLG.16–24 thus became CG.16–24.

Even on a 162.6m/533ft hull, centreline space was at a premium not least because of the necessity for a pair of missile control radars at either end. A palliative was to combine masts and funnels into so-called "macks" (i.e. mast/stacks).

A second block of DLGs, the nine Belknaps, followed on immediately. Yet another 4.3m/14ft on the waterline, they had a more balanced armament. The forward launcher could handle either Terrier or ASROC rounds. In place of an after SAM system was a hangar and pad for the ultimately aborted DASH (Drone AS Helicopter). The old missile stowage and handling area provided further much-needed accommodation while a single 5in 54 occupied the space otherwise occupied by the launcher. Commissioned as DLG.26–34, the Belknaps subsequently became CG.26–34.

Modernization during the 1970s saw both classes exchange their waist 3in mountings for two quadruple Harpoon SSM launchers. Their SAM systems were upgraded; the Leahy class to five Standard SM-1 ER, the Belknaps to the improved SM-2 ER. The old DASH facilities in the latter were remodelled to accommodate the manned LAMPS (Light Airborne Multi-Purpose System) helicopter. Both classes were stricken and scrapped about the turn of the century.

LEFT: **Although very similar to a Leahy from this angle, the Belknap-class *Josephus Daniels* (CG.27) is "single-ended", her after end being occupied by a single 5in gun and full facilities for a LAMPS (Light Airborne Multi-Purpose System) manned helicopter.**

Leahy class, as built

Displacement: 5,150 tons (standard); 7,600 tons (full load)
Length: 155.6m/510ft (wl); 162.6m/533ft (oa)
Beam: 16.3m/53ft 6in
Draught: 5.8m/19ft (full load)
Armament: 4 x 3in guns (2x2); 2 x twin Terrier SAM launchers, 8-cell ASROC launcher
Machinery: Double-reduction steam turbines, 4 boilers, 2 shafts
Power: 63,410kW/85,000shp for 32 knots
Endurance: 1,800 tons oil for 12,590km/6,800nm at 20 knots
Protection: Nominal
Complement: 396

Spruance (DD.963) and Kidd (DDG.993) classes

The 31-strong Spruance class was built by a single contractor (Litton), who was charged with producing a design to suit the requirements of the US Navy's Ship Characteristics Board (SCB) as well as setting up the associated building facility. Most unusually, the ship was specified over-large to facilitate later modernization.

Being multi-purpose, the Spruances also bucked the trend of destroyers being area air-defence platforms. Missile systems are demanding on volume and the final result appeared superficially to be under-armed.

A single 5in 54 was provided at either end. Abaft the forward gun was an eight-cell ASROC launcher. The after gun, located on a short, low quarterdeck, was superfired by a Sea Sparrow launcher. Designed for "point defence", this has a best range of 12.87km/8 miles. Forward of this were spacious facilities for a LAMPS-I (later a LAMPS-III) helicopter. An early addition was two Vulcan Phalanx CIWS, mounted high on the superstructure, forward and aft.

Propulsion was by gas turbine, two to a shaft. Machinery spaces were staggered, it being convenient to locate the enormous funnel casings to the sides of the ship. They were topped by eductors, the purpose of which was to reduce exhaust temperatures and, hence, Infra-Red (IR) signature.

Later additions added considerable, but greatly variable, weight. Most received a Vertical Launch System (VLS) forward, capable of handling both ASROC and the Tomahawk cruise missile in its anti-ship and land-attack versions. Considerable quantities of Kevlar "plastic armour" have been added to protect vital spaces.

Four modified Spruances were built to Iranian account. Completed 1981–82, they were never delivered, due to the Islamic Revolution. They were, therefore, assimilated into the US Navy as the Kidd class (DDG.993–996), their "DDG" classification resulting from their having the Standard SM-1 (later SM-2) system.

Only a handful of Spruances remain at the time of writing, mostly in reserve.

ABOVE LEFT: **Much-criticized for their apparent dearth of armament, the Spruances and Kidds were large enough to have their helicopter platform at the point of minimum accelerations. *Chandler* (DDG.996) is a double-ender of the Kidd quartet, designed for Iran.** ABOVE: **The massive, featureless bridge front and navigating bridge of the *Comte de Grasse* (DD.974) would do credit to a cruise ship but, despite its bland appearance, it pre-dates the application of Aegis fixed array radar to destroyers.** LEFT: ***Deyo* (DD.989) here shows her attractive hull lines and low-visibility number. The installation of a VLS has gathered ASROC and Tomahawk missiles together. Two quadruple Harpoons are located amidships, with Sea Sparrow aft. Note CIWS atop the bridge.**

Spruance class, as built 

Displacement: 5,830 tons (standard); 7,800 tons (full load)
Length: 161.3m/529ft (wl); 171.8m/563ft 4in (oa)
Beam: 16.8m/55ft
Draught: 6.3m/20ft 6in (full load)
Armament: 2 x 5in guns (2x1); 2 Vulcan Phalanx CIWS; 1 x 8-cell ASROC launcher; 1 x Sea Sparrow launcher
Machinery: 4 gas turbines, 2 shafts
Power: 59,680kW/80,000shp for 30 knots
Endurance: 1,600 tons fuel for 11,112km/6,000nm at 20 knots
Protection: Kevlar patches
Complement: 296

Ticonderoga (CG.47) class

Using the same hull and propulsion system as the Spruances, the Ticonderogas are complementary in providing the specialized air-defence component that the multi-purpose Spruances lacked. This was recognized in 1980 by elevating their category from DDG to CG.

Designed for future updating, the Spruances gained an average 1,850 tons over their lifetime. Beginning near the Spruance maximum displacement, the Ticonderogas have already gained a further average of 500 tons. The Spruance deep draught of 6.3m/20.5ft has thus increased to a Ticonderoga's 7.5m/24ft 6in, at a cost of over 2 knots in speed and reduced freeboard, evidenced by the addition of a forward bulwark to decrease wetness.

A major threat to a surface group is saturation missile attack using air, surface and sub-surface platforms in coordination. The Ticonderogas' phased-array radar was designed to cope with multitude simultaneous threats, its electronic scanning being more flexible than conventional rotating scanners. Her boxy superstructure is arranged around the four fixed arrays of the SPY-1A/B radar, to which are slaved four illuminators which, it is claimed, can control over a dozen ship-launched missiles simultaneously. Ship-end response has been speeded by retro-fitting two Vertical Launch Systems (VLS) in place of the earlier twin-arm launchers. VLS can handle Standard SM-2 MR, Tomahawk or ASROC, while Harpoons can be fired from two quadruple mountings located right aft.

ASROC can be targeted by the ship's LAMPS-III helicopter or by sonars, both hull-mounted and towed array. Lightweight AS torpedo tubes are located within the hull, launching through shutters. Two Vulcan Phalanx CIWS are located high in the superstructure.

ABOVE LEFT: ***Mobile Bay*** **(CG.53) and** ***Leyte Gulf*** **(CG.55) clearly show their Spruance parentage. On the same hull they have greater displacement, reducing freeboard and requiring a bulwark forward to alleviate the consequent wetness.**
ABOVE: **The four-quadrant "billboard" arrays of the SPY1A/B 3-D radar are split between the forward and after superstructures. Early units were originally equipped with Mk 26 launchers forward and aft.** ***Anzio*** **(CG.68) is shown here.**

An essential element of a coordinated area air-defence system is the ability to share real-time data between ships, the function of the so-called Tactical Distribution Link.

The first five ships of the class have already been retired.

LEFT: **The helicopter platform and after VLS are visible on this view of** ***San Jacinto*** **(CG.56). On the "fantail", a further level lower, are located the after 5in gun and two quadruple Harpoons. Note the staggered funnels.**

Ticonderoga class, as built

Displacement: 6,600 tons (standard); 8,900 tons (full load)
Length: 161.3m/529ft (wl); 171.7m/563ft (oa)
Beam: 16.8m/55ft
Draught: 7.5m/24ft 6in (full load)
Armament: 2 x 5in guns (2x1); 2 x Vulcan Phalanx CIWS; 2 x quadruple Harpoon SSM launchers, 2 x VLS with Standard SAM, ASROC AS and Tomahawk TLAM
Machinery: 4 gas turbines, 2 shafts
Power: 59,680kW/80,000shp for 30+ knots
Endurance: 2,000 tons fuel for 11,112km/6,000nm at 20 knots
Protection: Kevlar patches
Complement: 347

LEFT: **Note the beamy hull of *Curtis Wilbur* (DDG.54), whose L/B ratio is only 7.89 compared with a *Ticonderoga*'s slender 9.62. The neat octagonal forward superstructure accommodates all four fixed arrays of the SPY 1/D Aegis system.**
ABOVE: **Flight II units, such as *McFaul* (DDG.74), are indistinguishable externally from Flight Is like the *Curtis Wilbur*. The differences lay in the electronics fit.**

Arleigh Burke (DDG.51) class

A design objective for the Burke was to combine, as far as was possible, the capability of a Ticonderoga with the versatility of a Spruance. The result in two main versions, appears to be a reasonable compromise, with the added advantage of the deletion of structural aluminium alloy and the addition of a reported 130 tons of Kevlar splinter protection. Much of the structure, including the robust tripod mast, has been configured to reduce radar signature, the resulting appearance being less extreme than that of some foreign examples.

The hull form reflects an interest in the "short-fat" principle, with its generous waterplanes. Compared with a Spruance's orthodox Length-on-Breadth (L/B) ratio of 9.62, a Burke is only 7.89. The choice appears to favour volumetric capacity and ship movement.

DDG.51–71 inclusive are termed "Flight I" ships. Externally identical, "Flight II" units (DDG.72–78) have more advanced data links and Electronic Countermeasures (ECM). They are also fitted "for but not with" the ER (Extended Range) version of the Standard SM-2.

The bridge structure is a truncated, irregular octagon, whose angled faces incorporate the four fixed arrays of a modified Aegis system. This controls three illuminators. There is a 61-cell VLS aft and a 29-cell VLS forward (64 and 32 respectively in DDG.79 onwards). These can launch Standard SM-2 MR, ASROC or Tomahawk missiles. There are two quadruple Harpoon launchers, two Vulcan Phalanx CIWS and a single 5in 54-calibre gun. No helicopter is carried but a large pad and basic facilities are provided on the afterdeck.

In "Flight IIA" ships, i.e. DDG.79 onwards, the after superstructure is extended full width in order to provide a double hangar for LAMPS-III helicopters. Unusually, no Harpoons are currently carried but Sea Sparrow Basic Point Defence SAMs have been added to the VLS inventory.

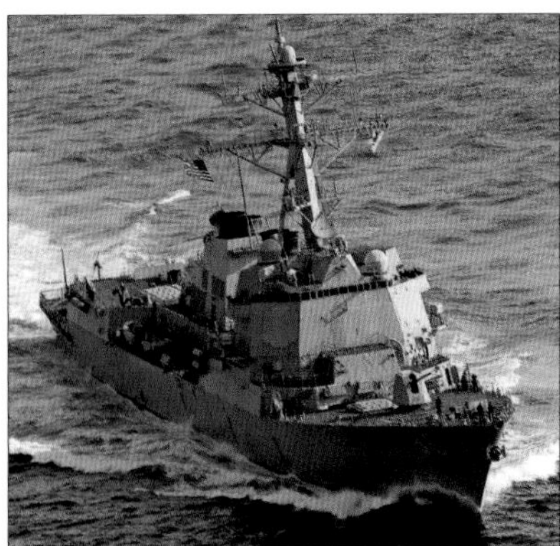

ABOVE: **The smaller forward extension of the bridge structure and the full-width helicopter hangar aft mark *Shoup* (DDG.86) as a "Flight IIA" unit. These are also 1.52m/5ft longer.**

ABOVE: ***Mustin* (DDG.89), seen early in 2007, shows less-prominent eductors atop the funnel casings. The large, low structure aft accommodates a VLS as well as a double helicopter hangar.**

Flight I, as built

Displacement: 6,820 tons (standard); 8,940 tons (full load)
Length: 142m/466ft 2in (wl); 153.8m/504ft 10in (oa)
Beam: 18m/59ft 1in on waterline
Draught: 6.3m/20ft 9in hull (full load)
Armament: 1 x 5in gun; 2 x Vulcan Phalanx CIWS; 2 x quadruple Harpoon launchers; 2 x VLS with Standard SM-2 MR, ASROC AS and Tomahawk TLAM
Machinery: 4 gas turbines, 2 shafts
Power: 67,140kW/90,000shp for 31.5 knots
Endurance: 8,150km/4,400nm at 20 knots
Protection: Kevlar patches
Complement: 337

LEFT: **As war reparation, the Japanese Navy was awarded a group of ex-German destroyers. From these it adopted the practice of locating torpedo tubes forward of the bridge. This is *Kaki* of the Momi class, as she was in the 1920s.**

Momi and Wakatake classes

Although the Imperial Japanese Navy (IJN) worked closely with the British as an ally during World War I, even operating some Royal Navy destroyers on loan, it continued with an essentially German layout in its first post-war programmes. Development built on the preceding Enoki and Momo types, with some influence from a handful of ex-German boats awarded as reparation.

Twenty-one Momi-class destroyers were built in three consecutive batches. They were the first Japanese boats to deploy 21in torpedoes, for which two twin-tube mountings were carried. The forward of these was located in a well, abaft a short, full-height forecastle. The bridge structure was now resited abaft these tubes, a dryer location for the bridge personnel, but at the expense of the forward torpedomen, regularly inundated by green water coming over the forecastle.

Three 4.7in guns were again carried, the forward one on the forecastle, the amidships and after one being elevated on bandstands for dryness. The curved, boat-shaped bow profile had now also become a distinctive feature of Japanese construction.

Completed 1919–23, the Momis were followed immediately by the 12-strong Wakatake class, of which five were cancelled. Of the same length and layout, they were given an extra 15cm/6in beam to compensate for a further 50 tons of displacement. They were also fitted to both lay and sweep mines. Not alone among Japanese warships of the time, their stability was always suspect, evidenced in 1932 by the loss of *Sawarabi* in a storm.

Both classes were active during uncontested operations in Chinese waters during the 1930s. In 1940, however, tubes, one 4.7in gun and all mine-related gear were removed in favour of depth charges, added in their conversion to convoy escorts.

Seventeen Momi served 1941–45, only seven surviving. All six of the participating Wakatakes were destroyed.

ABOVE: **Despite their apparent size, the Wakatake-class destroyers had a standard displacement of only about 900 tons, and mounted only twin torpedo tubes forward and aft. They were reckoned "Second Class" destroyers.**

Wakatake class, as built

Displacement: 900 tons (standard); 1,100 tons (full load)
Length: 83.9m/275ft (bp); 85.4m/280ft (wl)
Beam: 8.1m/26ft 6in
Draught: 2.6m/8ft 6in (standard)
Armament: 3 x 4.7in guns (3x1); 4 x 21in torpedo tubes (2x2)
Machinery: Direct-drive steam turbines, 3 boilers, 2 shafts
Power: 16,040kW/21,500shp for 36 knots
Endurance: 275 tons oil for 5,560km/3,000nm at 15 knots
Protection: None
Complement: 110

ABOVE: **Effectively lengthened Momis, the 15 Minekaze class represented a great step forward. Note that the four 4.7in guns were all at an equal height. A third pair of torpedo tubes was preferred to tripling the existing two mountings.**
LEFT: ***Mutsuki*, the nameship of a class of 12, was the ultimate development of the Momi type. Otherwise similar to the preceding Kamikaze class, the Momis mounted the 24in torpedo and were given a distinctive bow profile.**

Minekaze, Kamikaze and Mutsuki classes

Complementary to the Second Class Momis, and built in parallel were the 15 First Class Minekaze-type destroyers. Scaled-up, their extra length permitted a third pair of torpedo tubes and a fourth 4.7in gun. The latter was mounted abaft the after funnel in some, on the after deckhouse in others.

Length-on-Breadth (L/B) ratios were exceptionally fine, the earlier Wakatake 10.6 being exceeded by the Minekaze 11.0. The latter were the first Japanese boats with geared turbines and returned high trial speeds.

The nine follow-on Kamikaze class, completed between 1922 and 1925, were virtual repeats. All carried two single 4.7in guns on the after deckhouse. Their bridge structure was more substantial and the hull had a nominal increase in beam as compensation for topweight.

Considered successful, the design was developed further with the 12 Mutsuki, completed 1925–27. Their recognition feature was a bow of the new "double-curvature" profile.

This class introduced the 24in torpedo, which would develop into a much-respected weapon. These early versions were driven by compressed air (rather than oxygen) but already carried a 50 per cent heavier warhead half as far again as a standard 21in torpedo.

The Mutsukis' six tubes were better organized in two triple mountings, thus saving precious centreline space. Four reload torpedoes could be carried or, alternatively, 16 mines. Again, all carried their two after 4.7in guns on the after deckhouse all guns being located at the same height above the upper deck.

Japanese fleet destroyers were very hard-worked during World War II and, typically, ships of all three of these classes surrendered one or two 4.7in guns, some a set of torpedo tubes, in order to ship up to ten small automatic weapons and large outfits of depth charges. Widely used as transports, supporting island garrisons, they paid a high attritional price, only 7 out of 34 surviving the war, most of them damaged.

Mutsuki class, as built

Displacement: 1,315 tons (standard); 1,775 tons (full load)
Length: 97.6m/320ft (bp); 103.1m/338ft (wl)
Beam: 9.2m/30ft
Draught: 3m/9ft 9in
Armament: 4 x 4.7in guns (4x1); 6 x 24in torpedo tubes (2x3)
Machinery: Geared steam turbines, 4 boilers, 2 shafts
Power: 28,720kW/38,500shp for 37 knots
Endurance: 420 tons oil for 7,400km/4,000nm at 15 knots
Protection: None
Complement: 150

LEFT: ***Shimakaze* was a further unit of the Minekaze class. In this rather touched-up view, she carries no pendant number forward but, as was general between the wars, has her name in Japanese characters amidships.**

Fubuki and Akatsuki classes

Treated unfairly, as they saw it, by the 1921–22 Washington Conference, the Japanese sought to compensate for insufficient capital ship tonnage by building some of the world's most formidable cruisers and destroyers. Of the latter, the Fubuki class, commenced under the 1923 Programme, set a new benchmark, causing foreign fleets to upgrade their own specifications.

Over 15.2m/50ft longer than the still-building Matsukis, these "special-type" destroyers were designed for attack rather than for screening. They mounted a third triple set of 24in torpedo tubes. These were later fitted with splinter-proof shields and modified for the improved, oxygen-fuelled version of the torpedo. One reload, housed in protective casings, was provided for each of the nine tubes.

A heavier 5in calibre gun was also introduced with the class. Six were housed in three twin, fully enclosed gunhouses, another world "first". Bearing in mind British problems with introducing a High-Angle, Dual-Purpose (HA/DP) armament, it is noteworthy that the Japanese in the later Fubukis, mounted weapons of 55 degrees' elevation in 1930.

Also with a very slender hull (L/B about 11.13) the design proved to be tender. Stability was restored only by lowering funnels and bridge structure, together with substantial ballasting. This cost 4 knots in speed.

ABOVE: **When they appeared in the late 1920s, the Fubukis set a new world standard for destroyers. At the price of considerable size, they combined high speed with a heavy gun and torpedo armament. This picture shows *Uranami*.**

For the final four units of the class only three, improved boilers were fitted, in place of the earlier four. With only one boiler to exhaust, the forward funnel could be considerably, and distinctively, reduced in girth. The shorter forward boiler space also meant that the hull itself could be shortened by some 5.2m/17ft. These were termed the Akatsuki class.

With war, both classes landed "X" mounting and three spare torpedoes in favour of automatic weapons and depth charges. Just one ship of each type survived, both in a damaged condition.

ABOVE: **Generally similar to the Fubukis were the four follow-on Akatsukis, of which the *Ikazuchi* is seen here. Note the thinner forefunnel, the 5in guns twinned in enclosed gunhouses, and long forecastle. Nine 24in torpedo tubes were carried in triples.**

Fubuki class, as built

Displacement: 1,750 tons (standard); 2,090 tons (full load)
Length: 111.9m/367ft (bp); 118.5m/388ft 6in (oa)
Beam: 10.4m/34ft
Draught: 3.2m/10ft 6in
Armament: 6 x 5in guns (3x2); 9 x 24in torpedo tubes (3x3)
Machinery: Geared steam turbines, 4 boilers, 2 shafts
Power: 37,300kW/50,000shp for 38 knots
Endurance: 500 tons oil for 8,700km/4,700nm at 15 knots
Protection: None
Complement: 200

Hatsuharu and Shiratsuyu classes

TOP: *Nenohi* and *Hatsuharu* were completed in 1933 as lead ships for the class, but were found to be critically unstable. This picture shows *Nenohi* as completed, before drastic weight reduction was undertaken. ABOVE: Heavily used, the Japanese destroyer force took terrible losses, including all ten Shiratsuyus. The *Yamakaze*, here, was torpedoed by the US submarine *Nautilus* on June 25, 1942. Note the recognition panel on the turret roof.

Previously unrestricted, destroyers became limited by the 1930 London Treaty to a standard displacement of 1,850 tons. The still-completing Akatsukis, once necessarily ballasted, displaced 1,980 tons and, for Japanese designers already loading destroyers to the limit, a shift to smaller dimensions did not come easily. All-welded construction was already, however, saving considerable weight.

The 1931 Programme provided for the six Hatsuharus which, while about 7.9m/26ft shorter than an Akatsuki, contrived to carry the same armament, less one 5in gun. As built, they had a twin 5in gunhouse at either end, the forward one superfired by a single. In order to accommodate three triple 24in torpedo tube banks and their reloads the fore- and aftermost were elevated, permitting some overlap, while the after funnel was offset to starboard.

With two ships completed, stability proved deficient, necessitating the lowering of funnels and bridge structure. The aftermost tubes and reload facility were landed, enabling "B" gun to be relocated one level down, back-to-back with the after twin.

Considerable ballast was also added although the final displacement, officially at least, remained under treaty limits. Delayed by the modifications, the class overlapped the succeeding Shiratsuyus.

These ten ships, nominally of the same dimensions, took the same battery layout. To compensate for the loss of one set of tubes, the remaining two were made quadruples, the after bank reloading from the after deckhouse, the forward from a pair of angled box containers flanking the after funnel.

The class maintained an L/B ratio of 10.82 and, considering its tenderness, it is surprising that a slightly lower top speed was not accepted in exchange for a further foot of beam. Wartime modifications included removal of the single 5in gun and all torpedo reloads. All 16 ships of these classes became war losses, mostly to air and submarine attack.

ABOVE: The Shiratsuyus were redesigned to reduce topweight. Note *Kawakaze*'s third turret carried at upper deck level, aft. The bridge structure has been greatly reduced, but the massive quadruple 24in torpedo tube mountings have been retained, still comprising the major weapon system.

Shiratsuyu, as built

Displacement: 1,820 tons (standard); 2,150 tons (full load)
Length: 103.6m/339ft 7in (bp); 111.3m/365ft (oa)
Beam: 9.9m/32ft 6in
Draught: 3.5m/11ft 6in (full load)
Armament: 5 x 5in guns (2x2/1x1); 8 x 24in torpedo tubes (2x4)
Machinery: Geared steam turbines, 3 boilers, 2 shafts
Power: 31,332kW/42,000shp for 34 knots
Endurance: 500 tons oil for 11,110km/6,000nm at 15 knots
Protection: None
Complement: 180

Asashio class

In order to adequately accommodate a six-gun main battery, the ten Asashios, commenced in 1935, were over 7.6m/26ft longer than the preceding Sharatsuyu. Although larger, a compensating near-20 per cent greater installed power gave them an extra knot.

Because the twin 5in gunhouses were too heavy to permit a superimposed "B" mounting, two were located aft in "X" and "Y" positions. With just one forward mounting, it was possible to maintain a useful gap between it and the bridge front, allowing it to fire on a considerable after bearing without damage to the bridge structure.

Two quadruple torpedo tube banks were now accepted as a practical maximum. By the mid-1930s, the 24in torpedo was energized by fuel burned in an atmosphere of pure oxygen. Weighing 2,700kg/5,940lb at launch, it could carry a 490kg/1,078lb warhead to a distance of 40km/25 miles at a speed of 36 knots. Although not kept particularly secret, its performance came as something of an unpleasant surprise to the Allies during the Pacific war. Also ready to use torpedoes in large numbers, Japanese destroyers continued to be designed to carry a full set of reloads. The after deckhouse was asymmetrical in plan to accommodate four spare torpedoes, while two were stowed in each of two protected boxes flanking the forward funnel.

A simplified bridge structure, with a measure of streamlining, pointed to efforts at reducing topweight. The class introduced a new 25mm Type 96 Hotchkiss-type Anti-Aircraft (AA) gun, with a dedicated director.

With war, the usual deletion of "X" gun mounting and all spare torpedoes enabled up to 28 of the 25mm weapons to be carried, together with depth charges sufficient for six 6-charge patterns. Heavily used, every one of the class was lost.

ABOVE: **In order to return to a full six-gun 5in armament with one superimposed turret, the *Arashio* required an increase in displacement of about 25 per cent. "X" gunhouse was, nonetheless, later removed. Weight-saving measures have resulted in a "monoblock" bridge structure and very light masting.**

ABOVE: ***Arashio*, nameship of the class, in an as-completed condition. Note the Anti-Aircraft (AA) director immediately abaft the after funnel and the large, twinned 5in "X" mounting, later landed in favour of more light automatic weapons. Up to 28 25mm guns were added, at the expense of all reload torpedoes.**

Asashio class, as built

Displacement: 2,070 tons (standard); 2,530 tons (full load)
Length: 111.1m/364ft 2in (bp); 118.3m/388ft (oa)
Beam: 10.4m/34ft
Draught: 3.7m/12ft (full load)
Armament: 6 x 5in guns (3x2); 8 x 24in torpedo tubes (2x4)
Machinery: Geared steam turbines, 3 boilers, 2 shafts
Power: 37,300kW/50,000shp for 35 knots
Endurance: 500 tons oil for 8,700km/4,700nm at 15 knots
Protection: None
Complement: 200

LEFT: **Essentially modified Asashios, the *Kagero* class is represented here by *Shiranui*. As in many Japanese destroyers, the galley funnel, snaking from bridge structure to forward funnel, and crowned with a "Charlie Noble", is an art form in itself.**

Kagero and Yugumo classes

With the *Asashio*, the IJN had a destroyer design suitable both for its requirements and for series production. That it was still considered deficient in stability, however, is apparent in that the 18 follow-on Kagero-class boats, although nominally of the same length, were given an extra 50cm/20in of beam. Treaty limitations now abandoned, the Japanese recognized the inexorable increases of displacement in referring to the Kageros as a "cruiser" type, a reference to size rather than to function.

To reduce the size and bulk of machinery, the Japanese were using advanced steam conditions. There were mechanical problems but, also, those of stability. This was because machinery weight saved from low in the ship was immediately replaced by further topside equipment and weaponry.

One weight-saving feature was the exceptionally light tripod masts, yet even these were replaced by fragile, stayed pole masts in some destroyers. Radar, when it was introduced, require antennae separated on to both fore- and mainmasts, so that the latter had to be retained. Neither radar nor sonar was particularly effective, a situation not helped by the general attitude that their use was "defensive", opposing the fiercely "offensive" ethic of the IJN.

Up to eighteen 25mm weapons were later added – forward of and flanking the bridge structure, immediately abaft the after funnel, and on two levels atop the after deckhouse in place of the 5in "X" mounting, which was landed.

Considerably out-classing the contemporary American Benson, the Kageros were completed by mid-1944, the series continuing with the Yugumos, of slightly modified design but near identical in appearance. Although 28 of the latter were authorized, only 20 were actually built.

The 38 ships of these classes saw action throughout the theatre. Only one survived the war, the remaining laying in waters from Japan to the Philippines, from China to New Guinea.

ABOVE: **An interesting late picture shows the Kagero-class *Nowaki* stemmed in dry dock. Note the wartime additions of heavy degaussing cable, showing as a dark line around the hull, and the added twin AA mounting forward of the bridge.**

ABOVE: **The Yugumo-class *Kiyoshimo* as completed, with additional AA guns forward but still in possession of "X" mounting. The gantries facilitating the reloading of the heavy 24in torpedoes are becoming prominent features. Throughout the war, the Japanese regarded the torpedo as the weapon of choice.**

Yugumo class, as built

Displacement: 2,220 tons (standard); 2,690 tons (full load)
Length: 111.6m/366ft (bp); 119.3m/391ft (oa)
Beam: 10.8m/35ft 5in
Draught: 3.8m/12ft 6in
Armament: 6 x 5in guns (3x2); 8 x 24in torpedo tubes (2x4)
Machinery: Geared steam turbines, 3 boilers, 2 shafts
Power: 38,792kW/52,000shp for 35 knots
Endurance: 9,260km/5,000nm at 18 knots (Kagero class)
Protection: None
Complement: 230

Akitsuki class

During the late 1930s the major fleets became aware that the likely scale of air attack on a surface group would be such as to require dedicated Anti-Aircraft (AA) escorts. Both the Americans and British built small cruisers in response (Atlanta and Dido classes respectively), but neither was fully satisfactory in that their main calibre weapons were too heavy to enjoy the required rate of fire, yet too light for ships of their size.

A better British solution was the conversion of 20-year old, 4,290-ton C-class cruisers to carry eight or ten 4in high-angle guns with efficient direction. These could well have influenced the IJN in its choice of small AA cruiser form. The Akizukis were 3.4m/11ft 3in shorter than the elderly British ships, but considerably narrower.

They carried four twin, fully enclosed 3.9in gunhouses. The guns themselves were 65-calibre models with high muzzle velocity. With a raised forecastle and two superimposed mountings at either end, the ships certainly looked like destroyers. Also not overloaded, it was hardly surprising that a single quadruple 24in torpedo mounting was added, together with reloads. Seventy-two depth charges and their projectors completed the transformation from cruiser to destroyer.

They were instantly distinguishable from earlier Japanese destroyers by their single funnel, heavily trunked to exhaust both boiler spaces. The single casing saved a little weight and offered less obstacle to AA weapons while keeping smoke clear of the bridge structure.

Being more closely associated with battle fleet operations, the Akitsukis probably found themselves less called upon to perform the high-attrition, maid-of-all-work tasks that fell to other fleet destroyers, accounting for their relatively high 50 per cent survival rate.

Twenty-six more destroyers of the same size were cancelled or never completed, while sixteen planned larger versions were never commenced, due to a dearth of raw materials.

TOP: To meet the requirement for more fleet AA escorts, the Akitsuki class was designed with four twin 3.9in gun mountings. Only one quadruple torpedo tube bank could be accommodated. This is *Harutsuki*, which survived the war. ABOVE: *Yoitsuki* also avoided destruction by being under repair. Here, she awaits disarmament post-war, prior to being used for repatriation duties. Following these, she was ceded to China. Note the class's very fine lines.

LEFT: The Akitsukis were well designed for their task. This is *Terutsuki*, sunk by US torpedo boats in December 1942. Note the gap between the forward armament and the bridge to permit maximum clear firing arcs.

Akitsuki class, as built

Displacement: 2,700 tons (standard); 3,700 tons (full load)
Length: 126.1m/413ft 4in (bp); 134.3m/440ft 3in (oa)
Beam: 11.6m/38ft 1in
Draught: 4.1m/13ft 7in
Armament: 8 x 3.9in guns (4x2); 4 x 24in torpedo tubes (1x4)
Machinery: Geared steam turbines, 3 boilers, 2 shafts
Power: 38,792kW/52,000shp for 33 knots
Endurance: 1,100 tons oil for 15,270km/8,300nm at 18 knots
Protection: None
Complement: 290

Yamagumo/Minegumo class

Restyled the Japanese Maritime Self-Defence Force, the Japanese Navy began building destroyers in 1953. All weaponry was now American-supplied and the first pair of ships, the 1,700-ton Harukaze class, were of typical US flush-decked design.

They were followed by seven Ayanami class (1957–60), three Murasames (1958–59) and two Akizukis (1959), all of long forecastle design. Their widely spaced funnels indicated adoption of unit machinery layout, but the one-forward, two-aft gun disposition was inherited from earlier practice.

More original were the nine Yamagumos/Minegumos of 1965–77. Well removed from the classic destroyer concept, they featured advanced Anti-Submarine (AS) equipment and light, Dual-Purpose (DP) guns in place of the earlier heavy gun and torpedo batteries. With their change in function, high speed was no longer necessary, propulsion being by three diesels coupled to each of two shafts. The ships' ASW bias reflected the fact that, during the Cold War, the Japanese were the West's closest allies to the submarines of the Soviet Pacific Fleet.

Three Yamagumos, launched 1965–66, began the series. They were designed around an ASROC system, whose launcher was located amidships for minimum ship movement. A quadruple-barrelled Bofors AS mortar was carried forward and triple AS torpedo tubes sided in the after waist. Their six diesel engines were divided between two, widely separated compartments.

The following trio, termed the Minegumos (1967–69), were modelled around the abortive Drone Anti-Submarine Helicopter (DASH) system. This necessitated a compact superstructure and single funnel, with a DASH hangar and flight pad sited aft. From 1979 ASROC was retro-fitted in lieu.

DASH was already proving technically inadequate when the decision was made to complete the final group of three to the original Yamagumo design.

All hulls were identical except that the final six had knuckles forward. One ship, *Yugumo*, still exists, in a training role.

ABOVE: **Although of the same basic design as *Yamagumo* (below left), the *Minegumo* was one of three remodelled around the abortive DASH system, whose small hangar can be seen aft, adjacent to the eight-celled ASROC launcher.**

ABOVE: **The eight Yamagumo variants had their machinery divided around the ASROC arrangement amidships. With no helicopter, some had their after end raised to accommodate a Variable-Depth Sonar (VDS) installation. Note the two funnels.**

Yamagumo, as built

Displacement: 2,150 tons (normal); 2,700 tons (full load)
Length: 114.9m/377ft 2in (wl)
Beam: 11.8m/38ft 9in
Draught: 4m/13ft 2in
Armament: 4 x 3in guns (2x2); 1 x 8-cell ASROC AS launcher; 1 x 4-barrelled Bofors 375mm AS mortar; 6 x 12.7in AS torpedo tubes (2x3)
Machinery: Six 12-cylinder diesel engines, 2 shafts
Power: 19,769kW/26,500bhp for 27 knots
Endurance: 12,965km/7,000nm at 20 knots
Protection: None
Complement: 215

LEFT: **This early picture of *Kikusuki* shows her with her name painted up amidships and her after end still configured to operate DASH. The flight pad was later used for a Sea Sparrow SAM launcher, superfired by a Phalanx Close-In Weapon System (CIWS).**

Takatsuki class

Contemporary with the first group of Yamagumos, the four Takatsukis were larger and steam-propelled. Again, they had a strong ASW bias. Their flush-decked hulls, with long, sweeping sheerline, continued a more uniform "American" appearance. Superstructure was divided between two blocks with deck space being conserved by combining masts and funnels in so-called "macks".

As completed, the after end was dedicated to facilities for no less than three DASH helicopters. Forward of the bridge structure was the ASROC launcher, right forward a Bofors AS mortar. In the waist were triple tubes on either side for AS torpedoes. Bow sonar was fitted in two, VDS in the others. Except for the dual-purpose capability of the two 5in 54s, air defence, for such valuable ships, appeared deficient.

DASH was removed from 1977, along with the after 5in gun located on the hangar roof. The space so freed was used to greatly improve the ships' defensive armament. On what had been the flight deck was mounted an 8-cell launcher for the Sea Sparrow, a point-defence SAM system effective out to 12.8km/8 miles. In place of the after gun, a lofty structure was added to accommodate associated acquisition and guidance electronics.

Superfiring Sea Sparrow was added a self-contained Vulcan Phalanx, Gatling-style 20mm CIWS. Its inbuilt radars track both target and projectile stream to bring them coincident. Its range is about 1.7km/1 mile (5 seconds for a trans-sonic missile).

Between the new director tower and the after funnel was added two quadruple Harpoon canister launchers. Although this SSM has a reported range of better than 96.5km/60 miles the ships, sans helicopter, would require third party assistance to realize its full potential.

To improve the potential of the ASROC, the class was also fitted with passive towed arrays. Now specialist in neither AAW nor ASW, and with no reloads for ASROC or Harpoon, the remaining class life was limited.

ABOVE: ***Takatsuki*, nameship for the class, appears rather under-armed in the original configuration. She and *Nagatsuki* differed in having a mainmast, topped with a Tactical Air Navigation (TACAN) beacon. Note the triple ASW torpedo tubes amidships. Modernization saw the addition of Sea Sparrow and Harpoon.**

Takatsuki class, as built

Displacement: 3,200 tons (normal); 4,500 tons (full load)
Length: 136m/446ft 5in (wl)
Beam: 13.4m/44ft
Draught: 4.4m/14ft 5in
Armament: 2 x 5in guns (2x1); 1 x 8-cell ASROC AS launcher; 1 x 4-barrelled Bofors 375mm AS mortar; 6 x 12.7in AS torpedo tubes (2x3)
Machinery: Geared steam turbines, 2 boilers, 2 shafts
Power: 44,760kW/60,000shp for 32 knots
Endurance: 900 tons oil for 12,965km/7,000nm at 20 knots
Protection: None
Complement: 270

Shirane and Haruna classes

With the demise of DASH, there was an urgent requirement to get manned helicopters to sea. Where the latter had the disadvantage of extra bulk and weight they were, once equipped with an efficient data link, an intelligent extension to the ship herself. Two or more helicopters are more efficient in a submarine hunt, while also conferring a measure of redundancy.

The two Harunas (launched 1972–73), although looking very different, were logical rearrangements of the Takatsukis, with ASROC and both 5in guns forward, but without the AS mortar. Greater size was driven by the dimensions of an enormous hangar, suitable for three aircraft. Originally these were HSS-2 Sea Kings, replaced latterly by the more effective SH-60J version of the LAMPS-III Seahawk.

Launched in 1978–79, the two Shiranes are improved Harunas, some 6.1m/20ft greater in length. All four have a knuckle running the full length of the hull, to maximize deck width without increasing beam at the waterline. Both types are designed to achieve 32 knots on a relatively modest 52,220kW/70,000shp. All are steam-turbine propelled, the Haruna having one huge "mack", the *Shirane* two smaller. Uptakes on both are offset from the centreline to better utilize space.

ABOVE: ***Shirane*'s flight deck, appearing foreshortened here, occupies, with the hangar, 50 per cent of the ship's length. A helicopter dominates the layout. Note the full-length knuckle, a device to increase width at upper deck level.** LEFT: **A pretty photograph of *Kurama* leaving Yokosuka. Although she carries a modern range of electronics, she is still fitted with the old-style ASROC launcher forward, and remains essentially an ASW ship. The two funnels give the appearance of a single structure.**

As both types had the size to act as flagships, they were extensively modernized during the 1980s, with superstructures enlarged and electronics renewed and extended. Earlier deficient in AA defence, both gained a Sea Sparrow launcher on the hangar roof and a pair of Vulcan Phalanx CIWS high on the superstructure. Active stabilizers have been added to facilitate flying operations in adverse conditions and right aft, below the flight deck, is a passive towed array.

With the oldest now over 33 years in service, all four ships are due for replacement, their successors likely to be up to four 13,500-tonners with through flight decks.

Shirane class, as modernized

Displacement: 5,200 tons (normal); 6,800 tons (full load)
Length: 158.8m/521ft 3in (wl)
Beam: 17.5m/57ft 5in
Draught: 5.3m/17ft 5in
Armament: 2 x 5in guns (2x1); 1 x 8-cell ASROC IAS launcher; 1 x 8-cell Sea Sparrow SAM launcher; 2 x 20mm Vulcan Phalanx CIWS; 6 x 12.7in AS torpedo tubes (2x3)
Machinery: Geared steam turbines, 2 boilers, 2 shafts
Power: 52,220kW/70,000shp for 32 knots
Endurance: Not known
Protection: Nominal
Complement: 360

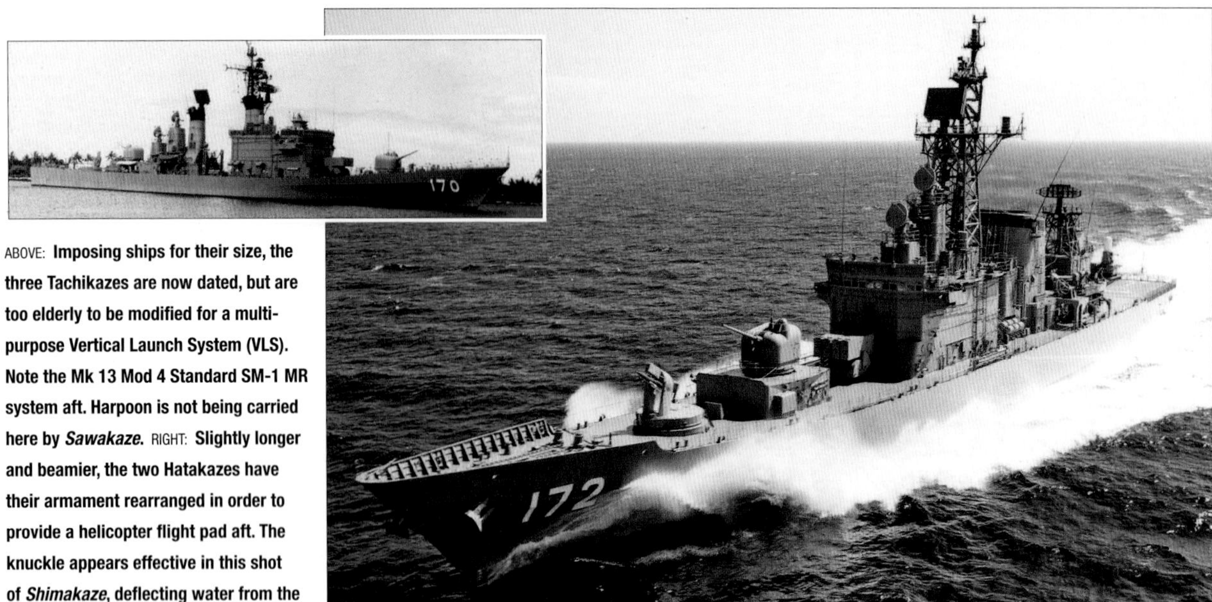

ABOVE: **Imposing ships for their size, the three Tachikazes are now dated, but are too elderly to be modified for a multi-purpose Vertical Launch System (VLS). Note the Mk 13 Mod 4 Standard SM-1 MR system aft. Harpoon is not being carried here by *Sawakaze*.** RIGHT: **Slightly longer and beamier, the two Hatakazes have their armament rearranged in order to provide a helicopter flight pad aft. The knuckle appears effective in this shot of *Shimakaze*, deflecting water from the hull as she proceeds at high speed.**

Tachikaze and Hatakaze classes

With the *Amatsukaze*, launched in 1963, the Japanese acquired their first Guided Missile Destroyer, or DDG. A single-arm launcher for Standard SM-1 MR occupied the whole after end, while the associated directors and electronics gave the ship a lofty, almost stately, appearance that made her look far larger than her 3,050 tons.

It would be a decade and more before she was followed by further DDGs in the three Tachikazes (1974–81). ASROC, located amidships in the *Amatsukaze*, was resited forward while a 5in 54, forward and aft, gave the ships more credible firepower than the earlier ship's four 3in weapons. Their launcher was later modified to fire Harpoon SSMs as an alternative, the missile total remaining a maximum 40.

Slightly lengthened, their hull forms were shared with the earlier Takatsukis, the forward sections being particularly elegant. Serving steam turbine propulsive machinery, the two widely spaced funnels were again combined with heavy, electronics-laden masts.

Again, it would be a decade before further DDGs were built. The two Hatakazes (launched 1984–87) in turn shared a lengthened hull with much the same form as the preceding Hatsuyuki-class AS destroyers.

Gas-turbine propulsion had, by now, superseded steam, greatly reducing machinery weight and bulk, and the number of engine-room personnel. They assumed the proven combination of two Olympus and two Speys, exhausted via a single large funnel.

The Standard launcher was moved forward, sharing the foredeck with one of the two 5in guns and ASROC. A forward bulwark and knuckle testify to forward wetness, the entry being fine.

Two quadruple Harpoon canister launchers are located abaft the *Hatakaze*'s funnels, allowing the full 40-round Standard outfit to be carried. Two Vulcan Phalanx CIWS have been added, but no Sea Sparrow. None of the DDGs carries a helicopter.

LEFT: **This against-the-light image gives an excellent view of *Hatakaze*'s layout. She has manned ship, has her stem anchor "a-cockbill" and has sternway. An American tug is in the foreground.**

Hatakaze class

Displacement: 4,650 tons (normal); 5,600 tons (full load)
Length: 150m/492ft 4in (wl)
Beam: 16.4m/53ft 10in
Draught: 4.8m/15ft 9in
Armament: 2 x 5in guns (2x1); 1 x single-arm launcher Standard SM-1MR SAM; 1 x 8-cell ASROC launcher; 2 x quadruple Harpoon launchers; 2 x 20mm Vulcan Phalanx CIWS; 6 x 12.7in AS torpedo tubes (2x3)
Machinery: 2 Olympus gas turbines and 2 Spey gas turbines, 2 shafts
Power: Olympus each 18,426kW/24,700hp; Spey each 9,940kW/13,325hp, in COGAG format; 56,700kW/76,000hp for 32 knots
Endurance: Not known
Protection: Nominal
Complement: 260

LEFT: **The combined mass of funnel and helicopter hangar gives the *Shimayuki* a distinctive "hump-backed" appearance. To reduce the effects of ship movement, the flight pad is located more forward than usual and is elevated one level.** ABOVE: ***Hatsuyuki*, nameship of a class of 12. The hull has no knuckle but has a slight crank level with the helicopter pad. Note the smaller 76mm gun forward. The conspicuous white dome covers the radar control for Sea Sparrow, located right aft.**

Hatsuyuki and Asagiri classes

General Purpose Destroyers (DDK) but heavily biased toward AS operations, the 12 Hatsuyukis carry a heavy equipment load on a modest displacement. Their bulky topsides were designed around the HSS-2 Sea King, now being replaced by the marginally smaller SH-60J Seahawk. Two Olympus gas turbines deliver the power for sprint speed but, for cruising, the smaller and more appropriate Tyne has been specified.

Forward, the ships mount ASROC; amidships, AS torpedo tubes. Aft, they can deploy a passive towed array to complement the hull-mounted sonar. The helicopter can deploy dipping sonar, sonobuoys and AS torpedoes.

Conventional firepower has been scaled down to a single OTO-Melara 76mm gun forward. Quadruple Harpoon SSM launchers flank the funnel, although, as is common, the full outfit appears not to be usually carried.

Defensively, a Sea Sparrow launcher is mounted aft, its director protected by the conspicuous white radome atop the hangar. Vulcan Phalanx CIWS flank the bridge structure.

Described as Improved Hatsuyukis, the eight Asagiris followed on immediately. They carry the same weapon and sonar fits, and in the same basic layout, but are approximately 5m/16ft 5in longer and 1m/3ft 2in broader. They also look very different.

The Hatsuyukis are COGOG (Combined Gas Or Gas), meaning that they can run on Olympus or Tyne, but not together. The Asagiris have adopted four Speys in a COGAG (Combined Gas And Gas), where either one or two engines can power each shaft. Here, they have been divided between two separated machinery spaces. The two funnels, Spruance-style, are offset, the forward to port, the after to starboard. Their appearance from one quarter thus differs from that from the other.

A knuckle has been added forward, suggesting that the earlier ships were wet. Proliferating electronic systems, an increasing proportion of which are domestically produced, have necessitated the addition of a substantial mainmast of complex lattice construction.

LEFT: **Only 5m/16ft 5in longer, but looking larger, the six Asagiris have four similar Spey gas turbines. Separated into two spaces, they require a second offset funnel. Note the unoccupied Harpoon cradles by the after funnel and the reversion to a forward knuckle.**

Asagiri class

Displacement: 3,500 tons (normal); 4,300 tons (full load)
Length: 136.5m/448ft 1in (wl)
Beam: 14.6m/47ft 11in
Draught: 4.5m/14ft 9in
Armament: 1 x 76mm gun; 2 x quadruple Harpoon SSM launchers; 1 x 8-cell ASROC launcher; 1 x 8-cell Sea Sparrow launcher; 2 x 20mm Vulcan Phalanx CIWS; 6 x 12.7in AS torpedo tubes (2x3)
Machinery: 4 Spey gas turbines, 2 shafts
Power: 40,209kW/53,900hp for 30 knots
Endurance: Not known
Protection: Nominal
Complement: 220

LEFT: The nine Murasames (this is *Samidare*) may easily be confused with American Arleigh Burkes, but they are not fitted with Aegis radar and can immediately be differentiated by the substantial lattice mast. ABOVE: Two VLSs are visible on *Harusame*, that abaft the gun for ASROC and that between the funnels for Sea Sparrow. Note that the stem anchor is housed in an extension to the hawsepipe, indicating a very large bow sonar.

Murasame and Takanami classes

Some 15m/50ft longer than the Asagiri design from which they were derived, the nine Murasames have an extremely capable range of weaponry.

Amidships, the two quadruple canister launchers fire not Harpoon but the new Japanese-built SSM-1B, an interim model capable of a range of 150km/93 miles. Another innovation is the inclusion of two Vertical Launch Systems (VLSs). The VLS immediately abaft the 76mm OTO-Melara gun contains 16 ASROC missiles, doubling earlier capacity. It is scheduled to be modified to fire also the Standard SM-2 MR SAM. Although without additional magazine capacity, this will allow the ships to be armed according to mission.

The second VLS, ahead of the after funnel, loads 16 Sea Sparrow SAM, obviating the need to reload under conditions of saturation attack. Sea Sparrow, too, is due to be superseded by a domestically developed derivative. The two Vulcan Phalanx CIWS are located on the centreline, forward and aft, improving their arcs of fire.

The gas turbine combination continues to change, the Murasames having two British-designed Speys and two American-designed LM-2500s.

Major electronics are concentrated on a single, very tall and heavily braced lattice mast, but separate directors, forward and aft, provide redundant control for both gun and Sea Sparrow.

Still under construction at the time of writing, the eight Takanami-class ships are modified Murasames, sharing the same hull but with a 250-ton greater displacement. The same gas turbine fit also has a similar power rating and so, on a deeper draught, a slightly reduced speed has been accepted.

The major difference is that the two VLSs of the earlier class have been combined in one of twice the capacity. This is located in a forward extension of the bridge structure. The gun has also been uprated to a 5in, but of OTO-Melara, rather than of American pattern. All carry a Seahawk helicopter.

LEFT: *Takanami* shows her differences with the Murasame class. Both ASROC and Sea Sparrow are located in a single VLS forward. An OTO-Melara 5in gun has replaced the 76mm while, not fitted, a new-style SSM has been preferred to Harpoon.

Takanami class

Displacement: 4,650 tons (normal); c.5,350 tons (full load)
Length: 145m/476ft (wl); 151m/495ft 8in (oa)
Beam: 17.4m/57ft 2in
Draught: 5.3m/17ft 5in
Armament: 1 x 5in gun; 2 x quadruple SSM-1B launchers; 1 x 32-cell VLS with variable mix of Standard SM-2 MR and ASROC; 2 x Vulcan Phalanx CIWS; 6 x 12.7in AS torpedo tubes (2x3)
Machinery: 2 LM-2500 gas turbines for sprint, 2 Spey gas turbines for cruising, 2 shafts
Power: 44,760kW/60,000hp for 32 knots
Endurance: 8,335km/4,500nm at 18 knots (*Murasame*)
Protection: Nominal
Complement: 170

LEFT: **Two of a kind, the Japanese Aegis destroyer *Myoko* in company with the American Aegis cruiser *Shiloh* (CG.67). Measures to reduce radar signature are less extreme than those in the West, the masts being particularly substantial.**

BELOW: **The VLS on the afterdeck of the *Kirishima* houses her Standard SM-2 MR system, whose twin directors appear beyond. Despite the space aft, helicopters may only touch down, there being no accommodation for them.**

Kongo and Improved Kongo classes

The four Kongos immediately invite comparison with the slightly smaller Flight I DDGs of the US Navy. Externally similar, they can be differentiated by their lattice masts and flush-decked hull, the helicopter pad right aft being one level higher.

With its octagonal plan, the bridge structure is similar, the fixed, phased arrays of the Aegis system occupying the oblique faces. Capable of undertaking long-range air search, target tracking and missile guidance an Aegis ship can, with suitable data links, control a surface group, assessing threats, selecting priority targets and, if required, launching and guiding missiles from accompanying vessels. As their Standard MRs are reputedly capable of intercepting ballistic missiles, the ships are reckoned to be part of the Japanese national defence plan, being deployed accordingly.

Vertical Launch Systems (VLSs) are fitted forward and aft, their total capacity being 90 missiles, either Standard SM-2 MR or ASROC. There is no separate Sea Sparrow point defence system, but Vulcan Phalanx CIWS are located at either end of the superstructure. The two quadruple Harpoon launchers, sited amidships, are likely to be replaced by the domestically built SSM-1B.

The single 5in gun is of OTO-Melara manufacture, favoured apparently for a higher rate of fire than the standard American Mk 42. The Improved Kongos will be slightly larger, normally displacing a further 450 tons. They, too, will have their VLS split between a 32-cell unit forward and a 64-cell unit aft. The latter will lay between the hangars provided for a pair of Seahawk (or, possibly, EH.101/Merlin) helicopters.

Both classes have bow- and hull-mounted sonars, together with passive towed arrays. Beside ASROC and Standard missiles, the improved ships' VLS can launch Sea Sparrow.

Propulsion in all is by four, licence-built LM-2500 gas turbines. Visually the improved ships differ in their solid masts and bulkier after superstructure.

LEFT: **Completed in 2007, the *Atago* was the first Improved Kongo. The two main features in which they differ from the first group are visible here: the solid mast and the larger after superstructure incorporating double hangars.**

Kongo class

Displacement: 7,250 tons (normal); 9,485 tons (full load)
Length: 150.5m/494ft (bp); 161m/528ft 6in (oa)
Beam: 20m/65ft 8in
Draught: 6.2m/20ft 4in
Armament: 1 x 5in gun; 2 x quadruple Harpoon SSM launchers; 2 x VLS with 90 Standard SM-2 MR and ASROC; 2 x Vulcan Phalanx CIWS; 6 x 12.7in AS torpedo tubes (2x3)
Machinery: 4 LM-2500 gas turbines, 2 shafts
Power: 74,600kW/100,000hp for 30+ knots
Endurance: 1,000 tons fuel for 8,335km/4,500nm at 20 knots
Protection: Nominal
Complement: 310

LEFT: **Looking very sleek for a 1920s design, the *Bourrasque* was lead ship of a class that began a series of very fine French destroyers, fated never to demonstrate their potential. Evacuating 600 troops, she was sunk by a French mine at Dunkirk.**
ABOVE: **A pre-war rendering of *Siroco* with French neutrality markings on "X" gunshield. She was another Dunkirk casualty, sunk by E-boat torpedoes while evacuating 770 troops. Of more than 900 aboard, only 252 survived.**

Bourrasque class

When French destroyer construction was resumed after World War I, it was divided primarily between the large *Contre-torpilleurs*, or Torpedo Boat Destroyers, and the medium-sized and more affordable *Torpilleurs d'Escadre*, or Flotilla Destroyers.

The first of the latter type, the 12-strong Bourrasque class, were of a design that owed less to earlier French practice than to contemporary British, with long-full-height forecastles, superimposed guns forward and aft, and two sets of centreline torpedo tubes.

As usual, the French adopted their own calibres for weaponry. Their 130mm gun fired a 32kg/70.4lb projectile and when the limits of destroyer specifications were eventually set by the 1930 London Naval Conference, this calibre was made the destroyer maximum. Torpedoes, too, were of an odd 550mm diameter that differed but marginally from the 533mm used almost universally elsewhere.

In profile, the Bourrasque presented a more rakish appearance than their British peers. The stem was sharply curved rather than raked, and the funnels were prominently capped. A very French feature was the provision of one funnel for each of the three boilers. The after pair of these were installed back-to-back in a single space, resulting in the funnels being unequally spaced. Speed in deep condition could be only 28 knots.

Those that survived to fight an active war underwent the usual modifications of landing "X" gun and one set of tubes in favour of further automatic weapons and depth charges. Mainmasts were removed and the foremast reduced in height, in some braced as a tripod.

With the division of France in 1940, the fortunes of the class were varied. Three were sunk during the Dunkirk evacuation; two more, rearmed, fought subsequently with the Royal Navy. Two, were destroyed by British action at Mers-el-Kebir. Three were variously scuttled, one later being salvaged and serving briefly under the Italian flag.

Bourrasque class, as built

Displacement: 1,320 tons (standard); 1,900 tons (full load)
Length: 105.8m/347ft 2in (oa)
Beam: 9.6m/31ft 8in
Draught: 4.2m/13ft 9in
Armament: 4 x 130mm guns (4x1); 1 x 75mm HA gun; 6 x 550mm torpedo tubes (2x3)
Machinery: Geared steam turbines, 3 boilers, 2 shafts
Power: 23,126kW/31,000shp for 33 knots
Endurance: 2,780km/1,500nm at 15 knots
Protection: None
Complement: 138

LEFT: **An interesting shot of two French destroyer flotillas swinging into a line-ahead formation. Note the two apertures for depth charges, set into the sloping, rounded stern, and the prominent range clock above "X" gun.**

L'Adroit class

As is customary, the Bourrasque design was an armament and speed specification that fitted into the smallest envelope which satisfied seakeeping and cost criteria. Almost inevitably, the compression was somewhat overdone, the end result being cramped and liable to roll heavily. A little extra length assists in the maintenance of speed at sea, while a slightly increased beam makes a marked difference in stability and steadiness. For a given power, a longer ship is potentially faster, a wider ship slower. Having lengthened and widened his original design in order to improve it, a designer will often see his efforts nullified by the larger vessel immediately being burdened with more equipment.

The 14-ship l'Adroit class, which succeeded the Bourrasque, carried the same armament (although with a newer-model 130mm gun) but were given about 1.5m/5ft more in length and 16cm/6in in beam. To maintain the same speed, however, power was necessarily increased by 10 per cent.

The unusual, pronounced forward slope of the stern made gravity release of depth charges from the quarter deck traps difficult. The charges thus fell through apertures, being guided clear by rails protruding from the counter.

The 75mm anti-aircraft gun, fitted abaft the funnels and replaced in war by two single 37mm weapons, was a modified army field artillery gun on a high-angle mounting.

ABOVE: **With the rugged ridge of Mont Faron in the background, the l'Adroit-class destroyer *la Palme* steams in company off Toulon, where she was to be scuttled in 1942. Note the later-model 130mm guns as compared with the Bourrasques.**

Ten of the class became war losses. Two joined the long list of casualties attendant upon the Dunkirk evacuation. The considerable French force based on Casablanca was loyal to the Vichy administration and allowed some freedom under the agreed Franco-German armistice conditions. In resisting the Allied invasion of November 1942, four more of the class were lost there. Following attempted German seizure, the mass scuttling of the main body claimed three more at Toulon.

ABOVE: **Manning ship, *l'Alcyon* steams by in review. French flotilla markings were unusual, here denoting that *l'Alcyon* was the second ship in the Eleventh Flotilla. Despite the ship's apparent size, only triple torpedo tubes were carried. The general appearance suggests that topweight was always a problem.**

L'Adroit class, as built

Displacement: 1,380 tons (standard); 2,000 tons (full load)
Length: 107.2m/351ft 10in (oa)
Beam: 9.8m/32ft 2in
Draught: 4.3m/14ft 1in
Armament: 4 x 130mm guns (4x1); 1 x 75mm HA gun; 6 x 550mm torpedo tubes (2x3)
Machinery: Geared steam turbines, 3 boilers, 2 shafts
Power: 25,364kW/34,000shp for 33 knots
Endurance: 2,780km/1,500nm at 15 knots
Protection: None
Complement: 138

ABOVE LEFT: **Moored to a buoy, *le Hardi* presents her magnificent profile. Note the torpedo tube layout, with a triple between the funnels and twins sided farther aft. Both gunnery rangefinders are trained on the beam.** ABOVE: **Although having seen less than three years service, it was the fate of these fine ships to be scuttled with the Mediterranean Fleet at Toulon in November 1942. This is the bridge front of *Mameluck*.** LEFT: **Completed at la Seyne, near Toulon, in June 1940, the *Fleuret* is probably seen here soon after handing over. She was almost immediately renamed *Foudroyant*.**

Le Hardi class

Having built several classes of large destroyer, the French increased the size of their next flotilla boats to meet the limits allowed by treaty. At a time when the Royal Navy was still building the four-gun "I" class of 1,370 tons, the new French le Hardi type mounted six of greater calibre on a standard displacement of (officially) 1,775 tons. They were a major factor in the British adopting the six-gun "J" type.

Nearly 19m/62ft longer than the contemporary "I" class, the French ships had four boilers in separate spaces to develop the power for a sustained 37 knots. They did, in fact, develop 7.5 per cent more power than the British Darings of 15 years later, and the largest conventional destroyers ever built for the Royal Navy.

The French gun was a new-model 130mm, dual purpose but, reportedly, unreliable. Six were mounted in three gunhouses, one forward on the raised forecastle, two superfiring aft. Abaft and above the forward mounting were located the two 37mm automatic weapons that comprised the main anti-aircraft defence. Four single 13.2mm machine guns were mounted aft. To improve fields of fire there was no mainmast, aerials being strung to a substantial frame on the after funnel. The resulting profile was handsome.

An unusual seven torpedo tubes were fitted, a triple mount on the centreline between the two funnels, and two twins sided abaft the after funnel.

Of the 12 planned ships, only 8 were complete or mobile in June 1940. All were at Toulon and scuttled in November 1942. They were subsequently salvaged by the Italians and, in slow time, were being refurbished when, in September 1943, the Armistice saw the Germans take them over. None of them was yet operational when the Germans scuttled them, finally, a second time. All were scrapped post-war.

LEFT: **With the sinking of *l'Adroit* at Dunkirk in June 1940, the new *l'Epeé*, completing at Bordeaux, assumed the name. Although salvaged by the Germans and repaired, the ship saw no further action.**

Le Hardi class, as built

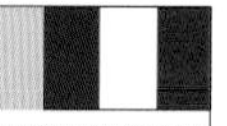

Displacement: 1,775 tons (standard); 2,420 tons (full load)
Length: 118.8m/390ft (bp)
Beam: 11.9m/39ft 1in
Draught: 3.6m/11ft 10in (standard)
Armament: 6 x 130mm guns (3x2); 7 x 550mm torpedo tubes (1x3/2x2)
Machinery: Geared steam turbines, 4 boilers, 2 shafts
Power: 43,268kW/58,000shp for 37 knots
Endurance: 470 tons oil for 5,090km/2,750nm at 20 knots
Protection: None
Complement: 187

LEFT: **A feature of the big French destroyers was their generous freeboard, as seen here with *Chacal*. This facilitated their maintaining high speed in poor conditions. The distinctive tripod mainmast was removed in surviving ships.** ABOVE: ***Chacal* again, here under the lowering skies of Portsmouth, England. Note the fifth gun amidships and the distinctive, forward-sloped profile of the stern. The horizontal bar amidships is a furled awning.**

Chacal class

The multi-national agreement resulting in the Washington Treaty of 1921–22 concealed considerable repressed resentments. Not only did Japan feel slighted by being allowed only a 5:3 ratio in capital ships compared with Britain and the United States, but France also maintained that, as she had more colonies than Italy, she should have had greater than parity. In truth, both France and Italy already had as many capital ships as either needed or, indeed, could afford, but pride and rivalry now saw them start to compete in cruisers and destroyers, of which the latter were not yet subject to limitation.

Several ex-German destroyers had been acquired by France in 1920. Larger than the war-built norm, they underlined the advantages of size in terms of speed, seakeeping and firepower.

The six-ship Chacal class were, accordingly, commenced in 1922. By the new Washington "standard" reckoning, they displaced 2,125 tons, but it was nearer 2,700 tons in seagoing trim. Although Britain had not yet recommenced destroyer construction, these "super destroyers" were far and away superior to anything being planned for the post-war fleet.

Their hulls were long in order to accommodate five boilers. The forward of these exhausted through the thin forward funnel; the others, arranged back-to-back in pairs, required two more funnels of greater girth.

Two 130mm guns were superimposed at either end, a fifth being located immediately abaft the after funnel. Two 75mm anti-aircraft guns were carried and two triple centreline torpedo tube mountings.

Two were lost at Dunkirk and two scuttled at Toulon. Another was taken intact from Toulon but, following the Italian capitulation, was returned to the French. She, together with the *Tigre*, then joined the *Léopard* as an Allied long-range escort, in which role main armament was reduced and the forward funnel and boiler removed in favour of extra fuel tanks.

ABOVE: **Carrying the coveted "11" pendants the *Tigre* is seen here probably as a new ship in 1926. Captured in June 1940, she operated under the Italian flag until October 1943. Returned to France, she served, modernized, in their post-war fleet with a modified profile, having lost her forefunnel.**

Chacal class, as built

Displacement: 2,125 tons (standard); 3,000 tons (full load)
Length: 126.8m/416ft 3in (oa)
Beam: 11.4m/37ft 5in
Draught: 4.1m/13ft 5in (standard)
Armament: 5 x 130mm guns (5x1), 2 x 75mm HA guns (2x1); 6 x 550mm torpedo tubes (2x3)
Machinery: Geared steam turbines, 5 boilers, 2 shafts
Power: 37,300kW/50,000shp for 35.5 knots
Endurance: 530 tons oil for 3,700km/2,000nm at 20 knots
Protection: None
Complement: 195

LEFT: **Not usually formed into flotillas, the large French "super destroyers" normally carried individual pendant numbers, as on *Verdun*. She is moored to a buoy, with her motor boat riding to the boat boom; there is a Bretagne-class battleship in the background.** ABOVE: **"Chamfered-up" for the occasion, the *Bison* presents immaculately clear decks. The picture is, however, dominated by the extraordinary twin 203mm pressure-tight gun mounting of the "Corsair" submarine *Surcouf*. Note the *Bison*'s boat cranes.**

Guépard class

A logical derivative of the Chacal design, the six Guépards which followed four years later were larger again, with main battery guns increased to 138.6mm. The distinction between these "super destroyers" and light cruisers now began to became somewhat blurred, not least because France, piqued at some aspects of the Washington Treaty, would refuse to accept the full limitations on the types, soon to be agreed at the 1930 London Naval Treaty.

At 130.2m/427ft 4in overall, and armed with five 138mm guns, a Guépard compared favourably with a British C-class cruiser of only ten years earlier. These mounted five 6in weapons on a length of 137.7m/451ft 6in.

Compared with a Chacal, the most obvious difference was in the adoption of two pairs of funnels. Four boilers of larger capacity were specified, with machinery arranged on the unit system for improved survivability, two pairs of adjacent boiler spaces being separated by the engine room. The 64,000 designed horsepower (60 per cent more than that of a C-class cruiser) drove the Guépards at some impressive trials speeds, several reputedly exceeding 40 knots, for a sustained speed of 35.5.

Layout was similar to that of the Chacals, with the addition of a second range finder aft. The earlier class's tripod mainmast was suppressed in favour of funnel-mounted W/T aerial spreaders.

With plenty of freeboard, the ships could maintain their speed, and the two based on Beirut during the 1942 Syrian campaign proved more that a match for the British H and J-class destroyers that tried to contain them. One of these two, before the division of France, had operated successfully with the Royal Navy. Another of the class was lost during the 1940 Norwegian campaign. The five surviving boats were scuttled at Toulon in 1942. Super destroyers had come and gone without ever proving themselves.

MIDDLE: **A pre-war picture of *Guépard* at speed. The overall impression is one of low, spare superstructure and very light masting. As was common at the time, there is no evidence of anti-aircraft guns. Her "2" pendant is at the dip.** ABOVE: ***Guépard*, wearing the flag of a rear admiral. Supporting the Allies early in 1940, *Guépard* and *Valmy* sank a German U-boat. Post-June 1940, and now siding with the Vichy government, the pair fought an action with British destroyers off Syria.**

Guépard class

Displacement: 2,435 tons (standard); 3,200 tons (full load)
Length: 130.2m/427ft 4in (oa)
Beam: 11.8m/38ft 8in
Draught: 4.7m/15ft 5in (standard)
Armament: 5 x 138mm guns (5x1); 6 x 550mm torpedo tubes (2x3)
Machinery: Geared steam turbines, 4 boilers, 2 shafts
Power: 47,744kW/64,000shp for 35.5 knots
Endurance: 580 tons oil for 4,075km/2,200nm at 20 knots
Protection: None
Complement: 230

Aigle and Vauquelin classes

Despite the usual "class" grouping of the previous "super destroyers", they were officially grouped in series, each with homogeneous names. Thus, Series A (animals) were *Bison*, *Guépard* and *Lion*; Series B ("V") were *Valmy*, *Vauban* and *Verdun*; while Series C (birds) were *Aigle*, *Albatros*, *Gerfaut* and *Vautour.* Superficial differences, as detailed, ran however in sequence, and were confined more to the "classes" (as described) rather than to "series" (as above).

To confuse matters further, neither Series D (*Milan* and *Epervier*) nor Series E (*Cassard*, *Chevalier Paul*, *Kersaint*, *Maillé Brézé*, *Tartu* and *Vauquelin*) conform. Alike, they all had a cruiser stern in place of the forward-sloped, "bevelled" arrangement of the earlier ships. Their wheelhouse was also rounded where others were angular. Their torpedo outfit was also increased to seven, with twin mountings sided between the two pairs of funnels and a triple centreline mounting farther aft.

Most of the D and E series post-dated the 1930 London Naval Treaty, which France did not ratify. The agreed destroyer upper limit of 1,850 tons standard displacement and a maximum of 130mm guns was, therefore, ignored.

British-made Asdic (Sonar) was added only in 1940, together with depth charge throwers, but the small depth charge capacity was not much improved. Neither was the ship's inadequate anti-aircraft armament.

These fine ships also suffered a war of divided loyalties. Of the Series E ships, one (*Chevalier Paul*) was sunk by British torpedo aircraft off Syria while another (*Maillé Brézé*), which sailed alongside the Royal Navy under the Free French flag, was destroyed by a torpedo explosion in the Clyde.

The remaining four were scuttled by their crews at Toulon in November 1942, to prevent them, as part of the French Mediterranean Fleet, from falling into German hands. None was salvaged in usable condition, although most were flooded rather than destroyed.

ABOVE: **The six Aigle-class destroyers were virtual repeats of the Guépards, the *Gerfaut* differing only slightly in detail of the bridge front and counter. In this pre-radar age, designers could produce ships of classic, uncluttered beauty.**

ABOVE: **The Vauquelin-class *Maillé Brézé* as a leader at about 1939. Note the modified stern profile. In a freak accident in 1940, the ship was destroyed by a torpedo fired inadvertently along her upper deck.**

Series E ships, as completed

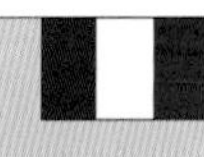

Displacement: 2,441 tons (standard); 3,140 tons (full load)
Length: 122.4m/401ft 9in (bp); 129.3m/424ft 5in (oa)
Beam: 11.7m/38ft 5in
Draught: 5m/16ft 5in (full load)
Armament: 5 x 138mm guns (5x1); 7 x 550mm torpedo tubes (1x3/2x2)
Machinery: Geared steam turbines, 4 boilers, 2 shafts
Power: 47,744kW/64,000shp for 36 knots
Endurance: 585 tons oil for 5,555km/3,000nm at 20 knots
Protection: None
Complement: 230

Le Fantasque and Mogador classes

ABOVE LEFT: **By 1936, when *le Fantasque* was completed, French and Italian superstructure design had begun to develop some "Odeon" characteristics, the hull remaining as pretty as ever. Note the main battery disposition, echoed in the later American Fletchers.** ABOVE: ***Le Fantasque* following her US refit of 1943. The great increase in Anti-Aircraft (AA) armament and electronics was compensated partially by landing one torpedo tube mounting. Despite extra topweight, she looks remarkably steady on a fast turn.**

Following criticism of the high silhouette of preceding classes, the six Fantasques, commenced in 1931, were redesigned internally. By locating their boilers in two, back-to-back pairs, the distinctive four funnels could be reduced to two short stacks of considerably greater girth. Boiler and machinery spaces were again alternated. The earlier tripod mast was reduced to a slender vertical pole, crossed with cruciform yards. The bridge front was rounded to make it difficult to estimate the ships' heading.

Five 138mm guns were again carried, the earlier amidships mounting being moved to the after deckhouse, not least to improve ammunition supply. By tripling all three torpedo mountings, the outfit was increased to nine.

The Fantasques had a standard displacement of 2,570 tons, but were hardly in the water when the first of six planned Mogadors of 2,885 tons was commenced. These were over 5m/16ft 5in longer and, by virtue of higher steam conditions, developed about 13 per cent more power. Like the Italians, the French ran trials in a very light condition, often without armament. Speeds returned were, nonetheless, impressive with some ships maintaining over 43 knots for 8 hours (at which speed their range was 700 nautical miles, or barely 16 hours' steaming). Endurance was regulated largely by Mediterranean operations.

The Mogadors were armed with four twin 138mm gun mountings. They had ten torpedo tubes, arranged in two triple and two twin mountings, all sided. Probably due to shortcomings in main battery design, only two of the projected six were actually built.

Unusually, four of the Fantasques survived to serve eventually alongside Allied forces during World War II. In the process of American refits, they were much modified to achieve logistic compatibility and to permit replenishment at sea. With added radar, sonar and much improved anti-aircraft armament, they went on to serve until 1955, still impressive, but obsolete.

LEFT: **The ultimate expression of French "super-destroyer" design were the Mogadors. This illustration highlights the major external differences, i.e. four twin 138mm gunhouses and ten torpedo tubes, with a twin and a triple on either side.**

Mogador class

Displacement: 2,885 tons (standard); 4,020 tons (full load)
Length: 137.5m/451ft 4in (oa)
Beam: 12.7m/41ft 8in
Draught: 6.6m/21ft 8in
Armament: 8 x 138mm guns (4x2); 10 x 550mm torpedo tubes (2x3/2x2)
Machinery: Geared steam turbines, 4 boilers, 2 shafts
Power: 68,632kW/92,000shp for 3 knots
Endurance: 710 tons for 5,555km/3,000nm at 20 knots
Protection: None
Complement: 264

Surcouf and Duperré classes

World War II drastically changed the role of the classic destroyer and, although still of conventional long forecastle design, France's first post-war ships, authorized in 1949, were rather smaller. The 12-strong Surcouf, or T47, class were categorized as "Fast AAW Escorts" rather than "Destroyers".

A major change was the adoption of the 5in gun calibre, reflecting American assistance through then-membership of NATO. Three twin 5in Dual-Purpose (DP) and fully automatic mountings were carried, one forward and two aft.

France preferred the heavier 57mm to the near-universal 40mm, although both were Bofors-designed weapons. One twin 57mm occupied "B" position with two more sided in the waist.

Four triple torpedo tube mountings were carried. All were of the standard French 550mm calibre, but six tubes were reserved for AS torpedoes of domestic manufacture. Main and secondary gun directors were backed by comprehensive air-and surface-search radars. Braced tripod masts for these were located near amidships to minimize effects of ship motion.

The five T53R Duperré-class ships were very similar to the above but, with even more comprehensive radar, were fitted for command and aircraft direction roles. Six tubes were sacrificed, the remainder being dual-function. A sextuple 375mm Bofors AS rocket launcher was added, as destroyers' role moved away from surface attack.

All were extensively modified during long careers. During the 1960s, four T47s exchanged their 5in gun batteries and four 57mm for an aft-mounted Tartar/Standard SM-1 system. A Bofors AS launcher was added forward. Others had their after ends heavily modified with various combinations of fixed and folding helicopter hangars and flight pads.

France rapidly developed a capable defence electronics industry and an extra ship, the T56 *la Galissonnière,* was trials vessel for an AS system incorporating a powerful Variable Depth Sonar (VDS) and the new Malafon Stand-off weapon. Several of the classes served into the 1990s.

ABOVE: ***Cassard*** **was one of three Surcoufs to be converted to "command ships". The twin 57mm in "B" position has been sacrificed for an accommodation extension, and only six lightweight AS torpedo tubes are carried.**

LEFT: **Much modified by the end of her career, *Duperré* has landed her conventional after armament in favour of full helicopter facilities, a large Variable Depth Sonar (VDS) installation and four MM38 Exocet SSMs in the waist.**

Surcouf class, as built

Displacement: 2,7500 tons (standard); 3,750 tons (full load)
Length: 128.7m/422ft (oa)
Beam: 12.7m/42ft 8in
Draught: 5m/16ft 6in
Armament: 6 x 5in guns (3x2), 6 x 57mm guns (3x2); 12 x 550mm torpedo tubes (4x3)
Machinery: Geared steam turbines, 4 boilers, 2 shafts
Power: 47,000kW/63,000shp for 34 knots
Endurance: 700 tons oil for 9,260km/5,000nm at 18 knots
Protection: None
Complement: 347

Suffren class

The difficulty of pigeon-holing modern warships was amply illustrated by the two Suffrens, whose initial prestige saw them ordered as "Guided Missile (GM) cruisers", completed as the then-current "GM frigates" before serving, more realistically, as "GM destroyers". Their significance rested in their affirmation of French independence in every aspect of ship, weapons and electronics. The distinctive radome protecting the antenna of the DBRI-23 three-dimensional air search radar could give rise to superficial confusion with the two Dutch Tromps (of a rather later date) but closer comparison reveals little further resemblance.

The ship's major system was the Masurca SAM, whose twin-arm launcher and paired tracker/illuminators were located aft. A large, stern-mounted VDS and a bow sonar provided, in the absence of a helicopter, data for targeting the Malafon stand-off AS weapon. Four launchers were mounted for domestically designed AS torpedoes. Four canister launchers for MM38 Exocet SSM were paired amidships. Forward were two single 100mm automatic guns, which calibre had replaced the 5in as standard. Both ships were fitted with the latest SENIT combat data system, enabling them to act as force flagships.

Heat and smoke from the boilers were exhausted clear of electronics via a lofty, streamlined casing that acted also as a basis for the foremast. To steady the ships as weapons platforms, three pair of active stabilizers were fitted. Being designed at the height of the Cold War, with nuclear exchanges a very real possibility, the ships had hulls devoid of scuttles, all living and working spaces being air-conditioned and slightly pressurized against ingress.

At the time of writing, both ships still exist, although the nameship has been in low-category reserve for some years. Both their major weapon systems have long been superseded and are no longer supported.

ABOVE: **Completed in 1967, The *Suffren* typifies the "new generation" destroyer, built around a 3-D air search radar and area-defence SAM, here the French-built Masurca, aft. Amidships is the Malafon stand-off AS weapon, served by the VDS.**

ABOVE: **This later view of *Duquesne* shows the Exocet SSMs added to supplement anti-surface ship armament. Not the large towfish of the DUBV 43 Variable Depth Sonar (VDS). She is flying a Dutch courtesy flag and her four-character international "number".**

Suffren class

Displacement: 5,335 tons (standard); 6,785 tons (full load)
Length: 148m/485ft 10in (bp); 157.6m/517ft 4in (oa)
Beam: 15.5m/51ft
Draught: 7.3m/23ft 9in maximum
Armament: 2 x 100mm guns (2x1); 1 x Masurca SAM system; 1 x Malafon AS system; 4 x MM38 Exocet SSM launchers
Machinery: Geared steam turbines, 4 boilers, 2 shafts
Power: 54,085kW/72,500shp for 34 knots
Endurance: 8,280km/4,500nm at 20 knots
Protection: Nominal
Complement: 349

Tourville class

In March 1970 the French launched a one-off, general-purpose "corvette" *Aconit*. Her speciality was ASW, for which purpose she carried Malafon, a quadruple mortar and AS torpedoes, supported by VDS and bow sonar. For her size, she carried also a sophisticated air surveillance radar. At 3,500 tons, she was a large corvette but was apparently felt to be limited by her size and lack of helicopter. Her builders, Lorient Dockyard, then produced an enlarged version in the trio of Tourvilles, also commenced in 1970.

Smaller than the Suffrens, they have a similar tall, tapered funnel/mainmast combination. This leaves clear arcs behind for the octuple Crotale point-defence SAM launcher, and ahead for Malafon. As the latter required a steady platform, ships so fitted exhibited a characteristic gap amidships, where its launcher was located. Now obsolete, the system has been removed from all three ships.

With their extra length, they are able to accommodate hangar and flight pad for a Lynx helicopter (or, at a squeeze, two) which constitutes a potent AS system in itself when sharing tracking and targeting data with the ship.

Where the *Aconit* was a 27-knot single-shaft vessel, the Tourvilles have reverted to relatively high power on two shafts for a more destroyer-like 32 knots.

Like the Suffrens, their low quarterdeck is dedicated to the substantial Variable Depth Sonar (VDS) towed body and its handling gear. Its bistatic sonar is the active component, "illuminating" a submerged target for the ship-end passive sonar.

During major refits, all three ships have been stiffened by the addition of a substantial external longitudinal, fitted along either sheer strake.

Duguay-Trouin, never fully modernized, has already spent some years in low category reserve. Her two sisters are now both decommissioned.

ABOVE: **The effectiveness of the Tourvilles as AS ships was increased by adding the full helicopter facilities to the Malafon/VDS combination. Lacking area defence, she is more truly a frigate, but is powered for 32 knots.**

ABOVE: **Like the *Tourville* (above), the *Duguay-Trouin* is pictured in the mid-1970s, before the after 100mm gun was replaced by a short-range Crotale SAM system. Note the triple Exocet SSMs, sided abaft the bridge structure. The line of the hull is particularly pleasing.**

Tourville, as built

Displacement: 4,580 tons (standard); 5,745 tons (full load)
Length: 142m/466ft 2in (bp); 152.8m/501ft 7in (oa)
Beam: 15.3m/50ft 2in
Draught: 5.7m/18ft 9in
Armament: 2 x 100mm guns (2x1); 1 x Malafon AS system; 6 x MM38 Exocet SSM launchers; 1 x Crotale point-defence SAM system
Machinery: Geared steam turbines, 4 boilers, 2 shafts
Power: 40,582kW/54,400shp for 32 knots
Endurance: 6,667km/3,600nm at 20 knots
Protection: Nominal
Complement: 298

FAR LEFT: **A small ship to accommodate a full Standard SM-1 MR system, the *Jean Bart* emerges atmospherically into an early sun. She has space for only one 100mm gun forward and a small helicopter aft.** ABOVE INSET: **The *Cassard* shows her unusual layout. The narrow hangar is flanked by Sadral point-defence SAM mountings. Forward of this is a gap accommodating the Standard SAM launcher. Note the offset diesel exhaust and uncovered air-search antenna.**

Georges Leygues and Cassard classes

Currently the backbone of the French *Force d'Action Navale*, the seven Leygues and two Cassards share a common hull form, the former being F70-type ASW and the latter C70 AAW escorts. All carry destroyer pendants. The F70s are CODOG-propelled (Combined Diesel Or Gas), using gas turbines for high (30 knots) speed or diesels (21 knots) for AS operations. The C70s are, unusually, of all diesel configuration for 29.5 knots.

Externally, the major difference is in the replacement of the F70s' large funnel casing with diesel exhaust in the C70s surmounted by the radome-protected, air-search radar associated with the single-arm, launcher for Standard SM-1 MR missiles. Flanking the C70s' helicopter hangar are sextuple launchers for the Sadral point-defence SAM system. Amidships are two quadruple canister launchers for the MM40 version of the Exocet SSM.

With no area-defence SAM system, the F70s have more space for the helicopter facilities, and both VDS and towed-array sonars. Both classes have a large, low-frequency bow sonar. As on other examples, the relatively shallow, highly stressed hull has exhibited fatigue cracking in service, requiring heavy remedial reinforcement along the sheer strakes. The extra topweight involved required compensatory ballast, increasing displacement by some 330 tons. This would have increased draught by nearly 50cm/20in, affecting maximum speed.

Both C70 and F70 are due for replacement, the former by the French variant of the Horizon frigate. At the time of writing, three of these have been authorized, of which the first two will resurrect the names *Forbin* and *Chevalier Paul*, and be in service by 2008.

A Franco-Italian project will produce the 4,500-ton Aquitaine class to replace the F70s. Built in both ASW and land-attack versions, they will also replace the Tourvilles.

ABOVE: **The Georges Leygues class are AS (Anti-Submarine) ships sharing a common hull with the Cassards. That of the *Dupleix*, seen here, has since been stiffened with a heavy sheer strake. Note the CODOG (Combined Diesel Or Gas) funnel/intakes, Crotale SAM, larger hangar and Variable Depth Sonar (VDS).**

Georges Leygues (F70) type, as built

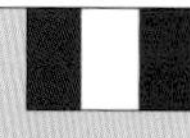

Displacement: 3,830 tons (standard); 4,170 tons (full load)
Length: 129m/423ft 5in (bp); 139m/456ft 3in (oa)
Beam: 14m/46ft
Draught: 5.6m/18ft 4in
Armament: 1 x 100mm gun; 4 x MM38 Exocet SSM launchers; 1 x Crotale point-defence SAM system
Machinery: 2 Olympus gas turbines (sprint) or 2 medium speed diesel engines (loiter/cruising)
Power: 34,316kW/46,000shp for 30 knots, or 7,982kW/10,700bhp for 21 knots
Endurance: 600 tons fuel for 18,400km/10,000nm at 15 knots (on diesel engines)
Protection: Nominal
Complement: 216

Sella and Sauro classes

Following World War I, new Italian construction first favoured what were, for the time, very large destroyers, classed as "scouts". Exceeding 1,750 tons standard displacement, the Mirabello and Leone classes carried eight guns but only four torpedo tubes. Such large and expensive craft were unsuitable for flotilla attack on an enemy line, for which smaller and more nimble craft were required.

Launched by the Pattison yard in Naples during 1925, the four Sella-class ships were thus of less than 1,000 tons. They were of orthodox design, with two closely spaced funnels. Unusually, the forecastle extended to a point between the funnels, increasing accommodation.

As with British destroyers, Italian ships carried guns of 120mm/4.7in calibre. As built, the Sellas carried a single on the forecastle and a twin mounting on the after deckhouse. Besides being a drier location, this located all weapons on a common horizontal datum, simplifying gunlaying. Shortly after their completion, their forward mountings were also twinned.

Two pairs of torpedo tubes were carried, sited back-to-back on the centreline. All units, as was customary, were fitted for minelaying, to a maximum of 32 apiece.

The Sellas were quickly followed by the four Sauros. At nearly 5m/16ft 6in longer, these were able to accommodate tripled torpedo tubes and a larger mine capacity of 52.

Very similar to the earlier ships, they could be distinguished by the profile of the hance at the break of the forecastle.

ABOVE: **Although fitted with very early examples of twinned gun mountings, the Sauros were of simple design. The bridge structure remains flimsy. Unusual features of the *Cesare Battisti* are very long forecastle and a stern modified for an alternative minelaying role.**

They later had a heavier director tower atop the bridge structure, together with a secondary director located between the banks of torpedo tubes.

Two of the Sellas (*Ricasoli* and *Nicotera*) were sold to Sweden in 1940. Following the Italian capitulation in September 1943 the *Crispi* was taken under the German flag, being sunk by British aircraft. Her sister *Sella* was sunk by a German torpedo boat. With hostilities, all four Sauros were isolated in their Red Sea bases and inevitably destroyed.

ABOVE: ***Francesco Crispi* of the earlier Sella class. Note the funnels of near-equal height, a later and improved bridge, fragile masting and different hance profile. Operated by the Germans, she was sunk by British aircraft. Early in 1940, two sister ships were acquired by the Swedish Navy.**

Sauro class

Displacement: 1,060 tons (standard); 1,600 tons (full load)
Length: 89.6m/294ft 1in (bp); 90.1m/296ft (oa)
Beam: 9.2m/30ft 2in
Draught: 2.9m/9ft 6in
Armament: 4 x 120mm guns (2x2), 2 x 40mm guns (2x1); 6 x 533mm torpedo tubes (2x3)
Machinery: Geared steam turbines, 2 shafts
Power: 26,856kW/36,000shp for 35 knots
Endurance: Not known
Protection: None
Complement: 155

Turbine class

With the Sauros, the Italians had produced a useful small destroyer which would provide the basic form for succeeding classes. It is natural law of ship design, however, that a few extra metres will solve the problems encountered with any class. The result is inevitably a creeping escalation in size. Thus, although carrying the same armament, the eight *Turbine*-class destroyers were 3m/10ft longer than the Sauros which, with the same layout, had been 5m/16ft 5in longer than the preceding Sellas. Greater length also confers improved seakeeping, manifested as reduced wetness and the ability to maintain speed in adverse conditions. The greater steadiness also makes the ship a better gun platform.

Masting was very light and not reduced during hostilities. The bridge structure appeared massive, the large tubular director tower at its forward end being overlooked by a higher observation platform, surmounted in turn by a large searchlight.

Identification of Italian destroyers was by pairs of letters rather than the more usual pendant numbers. At 2m/6ft 6in high, they were indicative of a ship's name, the surname in the cases of those named after people (e.g. the full name of *Sauro* was *Nazario Sauro*, but she carried the identifier "SU"). The Turbines were named after winds. With the outbreak of war, Italian destroyers adopted bold disruptive camouflage paint schemes to make difficult the estimation of their heading, and the hitherto black characters of their identifiers was changed to a softer red. Numbers were adopted when Italy joined NATO.

ABOVE: **Slightly enlarged Sauros, four Turbines of the Italian Prima Squadriglia are seen "Mediterranean moored", stern to jetty. Named after winds, they are (from left to right) *Espero*, *Zeffiro*, *Borea* and *Ostro*. All four came from the Ansaldo yard.**

The Italian destroyer force suffered badly during World War II. Six of the eight Turbines were lost in the first three months. Their poor anti-aircraft armament made them vulnerable to British torpedo aircraft, which claimed three.

Following the 1943 Italian Armistice the *Euro*, under the Italian colours, was destroyed by German aircraft, while the *Turbine*, in a reversal of fortune, was appropriated by the Germans and sunk by American aircraft.

LEFT: **An earlier shot of *Ostro*, which here lacks the after fire control visible in the top picture. Note the moderate flare, which would have increased pitch amplitude but hopefully reduced pitch accelerations, making a steadier gun platform.**

Turbine class, as built

Displacement: 1,090 tons (standard); 1,700 tons (full load)
Length: 92.6m/304ft 1in (bp); 93.2m/305ft 11in (oa)
Beam: 9.2m/30ft 2in
Draught: 3m/9ft 10in
Armament: 4 x 120mm guns (2x2), 2 x 40mm guns (2x1); 6 x 533mm torpedo tubes (2x3)
Machinery: Geared steam turbines, 2 shafts
Power: 29,840kW/40,000shp for 36 knots
Endurance: Not known
Protection: None
Complement: 179

Leone and Navigatori classes

In 1909 the British completed the experimental one-off "flotilla leader" *Swift*. A 35-knotter of 2,170 tons, she was enormous for her day and was meant to replace the light cruiser customarily dedicated to leading a 16-strong destroyer flotilla. She was not considered a success, but her size and duty saw her armed, not with the usual 12pdrs, but with a single forecastle-mounted 6in gun and with two single 4in secondary weapons.

Although the *Swift* proved to be an evolutionary dead end for the Royal Navy, it is interesting that the Italians commenced work on three 1,810-tonners in 1914. These, the Mirabellos, carried a single 150mm and up to seven 100mm. Again, the experiment was not repeated, but the obvious advantages of size led to the launch in 1923–24 of the three Leone-class scouts, later classed simply "destroyers". At 1,745 tons these carried a homogeneous battery of eight 120mm guns, in twin mountings, at a moderate 34 knots.

It was no coincidence that the French, even before the *Leone* launch, laid down their initial class of large *contre torpilleur* (Chacal). Larger, faster, more heavily armed they, too, carried "big cat" names, with the pointed omission of *Lion*, retained for use in the following (Guépard) class. These, laid down in 1927, were immediately matched by the 12 Italian Navigatori.

The latter's six 120mm threw a broadside of 139kg/306lb against a Guépard 202kg/445lb, but with a superior range and rate of fire. Although smaller than the French, the Italian boats well exceeded 40 knots on trials, but were very wet until their bows were modified with increased freeboard and flare.

The Navigatori class's third twin 120mm mounting was carried amidships. Machinery spaces were separated on the unit system. Torpedo tubes were mostly removed during the war, which claimed every one of the class except *Nicoloso da Recco*.

ABOVE: **Of nearly twice the displacement of preceding destroyers, the Navigatori were built as scouts. They were credited with very high trial speeds, and the two widely spaced funnels attest to the length of the machinery spaces.**

ABOVE: **Of a size, but slower than the Navigatori, the three Leones were an earlier type of scout. Their four twin 120mm guns were spaced along the ship and these, together with their four torpedo tubes, equalled the armament of a British Tribal of 14 years later.**

Navigatori class, as built

Displacement: 1,944 tons (standard); 2,580 tons (full load)
Length: 107m/351ft 3in (bp); 107.7m/353ft 3in (oa)
Beam: 10.2m/33ft 6in
Draught: 3.4m/11ft 2in
Armament: 6 x 120mm guns (3x2), 2/3 x 37mm guns (2/3x1); 4/6 x 450mm or 533mm torpedo tubes (2x2/3)
Machinery: Geared steam turbines, 2 shafts
Power: 37,300kW/50,000shp for 38 knots
Endurance: Not known
Protection: None
Complement: 224

Dardo and Folgore classes

The four Dardos followed immediately upon the completion of the Turbine-class flotilla destroyers and, like them, were designed by Odero. Not surprisingly, therefore, there was not great change, with much the same outfit on a hull a little over three metres more in length.

Claimed to be the first-ever destroyers designed with a single funnel, they achieved this with close-spaced boilers, whose uptakes were directed into a rectangular upper deck casing upon which stood the funnel proper. This was not trunked. Surprisingly, an increase of just 10 per cent in installed power was expected to realise a further two knots in maximum speed.

A new-style director tower was less bulky than its predecessor, but the bridge structure, considered as a whole, still presented a very high profile. This contrasted with the Dardos' very low-freeboard after end. The wetness of this was underlined by after twin 120mm mounting being located atop the after superstructure, and the two triple torpedo tube banks on high turntables.

The overall appearance of the class was pleasing, assisted by the adoption of a slightly raked bow with a soft nose. This was raked slightly more in the four Folgore-class boats which continued the series and which, otherwise, showed little significant external difference.

ABOVE LEFT: **With their large, single funnel and bold, clean styling, the Dardos set the pattern for Italian flotilla ships for the following 15 years. Common Italian practice, the after awning is extended to screen the accommodation ladder.** ABOVE: **Concerns about topside weight are apparent in this photograph of the Dardo-class *Strale*, which has had the shields removed from her twin 120mm guns. Note the very clear side decks for the stowage of up to 54 mines.**

Although of the same length as the Dardos, the Folgores were more than 50cm/20in less in beam. It may be assumed that this, most unusual, step was part of a refinement of hull lines to actually make the 38 knots' service speed which the Dardo class reportedly had difficulty in achieving.

None of either class survived World War II. Like their merchant fleet, many Italian warships were sunk in the resupply of Axis armies in North Africa. All four Folgores were lost in surface combat while escorting convoys.

MIDDLE: **The *Lampo* on a picturesque port visit. As is here seen, the bow profile and anchor stowage of the Folgores differed from that of the Dardos. The angular casing is clearly visible, gathering the boiler uptakes into the single funnel.** ABOVE: **Except for the angled funnel cap, the follow-on Folgore-class boats were virtually identical to the Dardos. The after freeboard is very limited, and the torpedo tubes and after guns are located relatively high. This photograph is of *Folgore* herself.**

Folgore class

Displacement: 1,240 tons (standard); 2,090 tons (full load)
Length: 94.3m/309ft 6in (bp); 96m/315ft 2in (oa)
Beam: 9.2m/30ft 2in
Draught: 3.3m/10ft 10in
Armament: 4 x 120mm guns (2x2), 2 x 37mm guns (2x1); 6 x 533mm torpedo tubes (2x3)
Machinery: Geared steam turbines, 2 shafts
Power: 32,824kW/44,000shp for 38 knots
Endurance: Not known
Protection: None
Complement: 182

LEFT: One of the very few Italian destroyers to survive World War II, the *Grecale* is seen as modernized, with a rebuilt bridge structure, tripod foremast and electronics, and new armament. Italy now being a NATO partner, she bears new-style pendant numbers. BELOW: An impression of the Oriani-class *Vincenzo Gioberti*, which usually carried the designators "GB". The class had a fifth 120mm gun amidships for starshell illumination and stowed anchors at the deck edge to reduce spray-making.

Maestrale and Oriani classes

These handsome classes, each of four ships, differed only in the latter displacing an extra 75 tons. The small extra draught was more than compensated by a 9 per cent increase in installed power, giving it a legend increase of an extra knot's maximum speed, an unsustainable 39 knots.

Unlike earlier classes, they were of commercial design and, although considerably larger than the preceding Folgores, carried the same four-gun, six-tube main armament. It might be noted that, commencing with the Navigatori, their 120mm guns were of a new 50-calibre type, throwing a slightly heavier round to an improved range of 22,000m/24,060yd. Their maximum elevation, however, was only 45 degrees, so anti-aircraft defence depended upon Italian-pattern 20mm and (in the Orianis) 37mm weapons. Both classes carried one/two short-barrelled 120mm high-angle guns dedicated to firing starshell. (This was of some irony in the case of the latter-class *Alfieri* and *Carducci*, overwhelmed by British destroyers in the night action off Cape Matapan.)

Something of an Italian trademark of the 1930s, the single funnel was prominently trunked, both to reduce topweight and to set it back somewhat from the bridge structure. A further characteristic design feature, first seen in the Navigatori, was to house anchors at the level of the deck edge, rather than in conventional hawse pipes, probably to reduce pounding and spray-making.

The Maestrale-class *Scirocco* foundered during the violent storm that was rising on March 22, 1942, at the Second Battle of Sirte.

Her sister *Libeccio* had been sunk on controversial circumstances about four months earlier. She had been engaged in rescuing survivors from the badly mauled "*Duisburg* convoy" when torpedoed by a Malta-based submarine, following a deliberate decision.

ABOVE: Reduced to reserve, this Oriani has had her identifiers painted out. Note that the tall mainmast has been struck. *Alfredo Oriani*, the lead ship, survived to be ceded to the French Navy in 1948, serving for a further six years as the fast escort *d'Estaing*.

Oriani class, as built

Displacement: 1,715 tons (standard); 2,290 tons (full load)
Length: 104.4m/341ft 4in (bp); 106.7m/350ft 4in (oa)
Beam: 10.2m/33ft 6in
Draught: 3.4m/11ft 2in
Armament: 4 x 120mm guns (2x2), 2 x 37mm guns (2x1); 6 x 533mm torpedo tubes (2x3)
Machinery: Geared steam turbines, 2 shafts
Power: 35,808kW/48,000shp for 39 knots
Endurance: Not known
Protection: None
Complement: 206

LEFT: ***Carabiniere*, of the first set of 12 Soldatis, undertakes a jackstay transfer. The early electronic additions suggest a late-1940s date. She has had an open bridge added above the wheelhouse and a breakwater about the forward gun mounting.**
BELOW: **A pretty view of *Geniere*, a light following wind lifting a haze of funnel smoke. She was nearly destroyed in March 1943 in dry dock at Palermo, when the caisson was breached during a heavy bombing raid. She was salvaged.**

Soldati class

With the obvious approach of war, the launch of the final Oriani, late in 1936, was followed by the commencement of 12 further hulls of identical size. Completed by May 1939, this group apparently satisfied the Italian Navy's requirements, for it was not until the nation's rather unanticipated entry into World War II in June 1940 that a further seven units were ordered. With shipyards already busy, the last of these was not even commenced until September 1941.

The two series differed little and were named after specialist military units, hence "Soldati". For a 1,700-tonner, an Oriani, with four guns and six torpedo tubes, was quite lightly armed. Eight of the first series were given the same outfit, the last four gaining a fifth gun, located on a bandstand between the sets of tubes. All the second group were so armed but, as some were reduced to three tubes while others lost their secondary director to ship extra automatic weapons and/or depth charges, it suggests that the displacement (grown to 1,850 tons from an Oriani 1,715) had reached a safe maximum.

When, early in 1943, Italy belatedly began to replace her considerable losses, it was with a 2,100-tonner. Named after "Gold Medal" naval heroes, twenty of these were ordered; nine were actually laid down but none ever completed. Of 120.7m/396ft 2in length, these would have rivalled the French destroyers, carrying four single 135mm guns of the type mounted also in the *Capitani Romani* light cruiser/scouts.

Of the 17 Soldatis actually completed, ten were sunk. One, *Lanciere*, foundered in the same storm that sank the *Scirocco*. Two, incomplete, were taken by the Germans at the Armistice, but destroyed. Of those remaining, three were ceded to France and two to Soviet Russia. *Carabiniere* and *Granatiere* served under the Italian flag post-war.

ABOVE: **A comparative view of *Carabiniere* as rebuilt into a fast AS escort during the early 1950s. Torpedo tubes have been landed and a single 120mm gun has replaced the earlier twin mounting forward. Note the remodelled bridge structure, depicted in better detail on *Grecale* (see previous page).**

Soldati, second series

Displacement: 1,845 tons (standard); 2,500 tons (full load)
Length: 104m/341ft 4in (bp); 106.7m/350ft 4in (oa)
Beam: 10.2m/33ft 6in
Draught: 3.6m/11ft 10in
Armament: 5 x 120mm guns (2x2/1x1), 2/3 x 37mm guns (2/3x1); 3/6 x 533mm torpedo tubes (1/2x3)
Machinery: Geared steam turbines, 2 shafts
Power: 37,300kW/50,000shp for 39 knots
Endurance: Not known
Protection: None
Complement: 217

Impavido class

ABOVE: **Although somewhat smaller, the Impavidos share some of the lofty appearance of the American Coontz type, with which they might be superficially confused. The US-sourced Tartar SAM system contrasts with the elderly twin 5in 38 gun mounting of World War II vintage.**

Somewhat reminiscent of the contemporary American Coontz class, the two Impavidos ushered in the missile age for the Italian Navy, narrowly ahead of the more handsome Andrea Doria-class GM cruisers that they were designed to complement. Their strongly "vertical" look, shared with their American peer, was due to the single-arm Tartar SAM launcher being mounted aft. In order to "gather" the missile on launch, it was necessary to locate the two SPG-51 tracker-illuminator radars just ahead, clear of the smoke resulting from launch. To carry hot exhaust gases over these, the after funnel needed to be even higher. The system's associated SPS-39 height-finding radar had then to be located on a rigid, lattice mast, to site it above the funnel exhaust.

The flush-decked hull, with its long, sweeping sheerline, also echoed American practice. Shorter-range air defence was vested in four single OTO-Melara 76mm mountings, sided in the waist. They, and the twin 5in 38-calibre, US-pattern gunhouse forward had a bridge-mounted director, with secondary directors amidships. Active fin stabilizers were added to the specification to improve system accuracies.

Both ships were equipped with American sonar and had a flight pad aft for a light AB 204 ASW helicopter, carried only until the 1970s. Triple light-weight AS torpedo tubes flanked the bridge structure. With the emphasis on stand-off weaponry, speed was no longer of primary importance.

A mid-1970s upgrade saw the SAM system adapted to fire Standard SM-1 MR missiles, housed again in the large, flat structure immediately ahead of the launcher. Domestically built surface-search radar and Selenia/Elsag gun director radars also replaced existing obsolescent equipment.

Dating from an age that showed a strong reliance on American-sourced technologies, the two Impavidos were replaced in the early 1990s by the pair of de la Penne-class GM destroyers.

ABOVE: **This view gives a good idea of the *Intrepido*'s layout. Much deck area is absorbed by the missile magazine structure ahead of the launcher. Although there is a spacious helicopter pad, there are therefore no hangar facilities.**

Impavido class, as built

Displacement: 3,200 tons (standard); 3,940 tons (full load)
Length: 131.1m/430ft 4in (oa)
Beam: 13.6m/44ft 8in
Draught: 4.4m/14ft 5in
Armament: 2 x 5in guns (1x2), 4 x 76mm guns (4x1); 1 x Tartar SAM system
Machinery: Double-reduction geared steam turbines, 4 boilers, 2 shafts
Power: 52,220kW/70,000shp for 33.5 knots
Endurance: 650 tons oil for 6,110km/3,300nm at 20 knots
Protection: Nominal
Complement: 238

LEFT: ***Audace*, as built, carried two 127mm OTO-Melara single guns, seen here. During the 1980s, "B" mounting was landed in favour of an Albatros/Aspide point-defence SAM launcher. Note the distinctive humped profile of the helicopter hangar aft.** ABOVE: **A close-up of the starboard waist gun mountings visible in the overall view at left. These are the 76mm 62-calibre OTO-Melara guns that have enjoyed remarkable export sales. The quoted rate of fire is 85 rounds per minute.**

Audace class

It would be a further nine years before the two Impavidos were joined by the pair of slightly larger Audaces which, from the outset, were designed around the Standard SM-1 MR SAM system. Although this was again located aft, the overall ship length was more compact, giving the appearance of being smaller. The funnels were less dominant, the forward one being also a structure supporting the foremast, while the after, of strangely cranked shape, provided support for the SPS-52 three-dimensional, height-finding radar.

Flanking the distinctive gap between the two main superstructure blocks were four single OTO-Melara 76mm guns. Originally of the new, fully automatic Compatto type, these were later upgraded to the "Super Rapid" variant. The gap itself was later occupied by eight canister launchers for the Italian-built Teseo/Otomat SSM, an active radar homer capable of a theoretical range of about 185km/115 miles.

The after end of the ships was better utilized than those of the Impavidos, with hangar and flight pad for two AB-212 helicopters. Four aft-facing torpedo tubes were added subsequently beneath the flight pad, firing wire-guided, heavyweight torpedoes. These were later removed, their use impeding free movement of the parent ship.

As built, two OTO-Melara 127mm dual-purpose guns occupied "A" and "B" positions. With modernization, "B" gun was landed in favour of an 8-cell launcher for the Aspide point-defence SAM system. This is an Italian-manufactured variant on the widely used NATO Sea Sparrow.

As is usual in Italian destroyers, the hull and bridge structure was devoid of scuttles as an NBCD measure. The hull itself readopted a forward knuckle to reduce wetness.

Superseded by the pair of de la Pennes and with the "Horizon" destroyers due in the short term, both Audaces are bound for retirement at the time of writing.

ABOVE: **A low morning light emphasizes the detail of *Audace*'s hull. Having sailed, she lowers her four-character "number" but retains her anchor "a-cockbill", i.e. ready to release. This is again a 1980s photograph, the ship lacking both Aspide and the Teseo SSM launchers amidships.**

Audace class, as built

Displacement: 3,950 tons (standard); 4,550 tons (full load)
Length: 140.7m/461ft 10in (oa)
Beam: 14.7m/48ft 2in
Draught: 4.6m/15ft 1in
Armament: 2 x 127mm guns (2x1), 4 x 76mm guns (4x1); 1 x Standard SM-1 MR system; 4 x 533mm torpedo tubes (4x1); 6 x 324mm AS torpedo tubes (2x3)
Machinery: Geared steam turbines, 4 boilers, 2 shafts
Power: 54,458kW/73,000shp for 33 knots
Endurance: 7,410km/4,000nm at 25 knots
Protection: Nominal
Complement: 380

Durand de la Penne class

Ordered as the *Animoso* and *Ardimentoso*, this pair of GM destroyers was, while under construction, renamed for two naval heroes of World War II. The considerable rearrangement of the two Audaces, completed in 1988, left them as near diminutives of the new vessels, upon which work had recently commenced. These are a generous 7m/23ft greater in length, not least to accommodate an EH.101 helicopter.

Similar to the Royal Navy's Merlin, their aircraft weighs more than two AB-212s together, and has a rotor diameter some 4m/13ft greater. In accordance with the general realignment of western fleets toward "littoral" warfare, only half of them will be ASW-specialist. Four more are due to be equipped with Marte air-to-surface (i.e. anti-ship) missiles and their associated search and targeting radar, while four/eight more will be configured as "assault transports". The five-hour endurance of the aircraft, together with its ability to target both its own and its ship's weapons, makes it an effective "force multiplier".

A major departure for the de la Penne is the adoption of CODOG propulsion. Two cruising-diesel engines exhaust through the centreline forward funnel, while a pair of licence-built LM-2500 gas turbines exhaust through casings angled out on either side of the Standard SM-1 MR fire control radars. The latter's associated SPS-52 3-D air-search radar has a proper mainmast to support it (the arrangement on the Audaces required later strengthening). Again, eight SSMs are located amidships, but one of the earlier four 76mm Super-Rapids has been made unnecessary by mounting one weapon centreline on the hangar roof.

The ships are shortly to be complemented by a first pair of "Horizon" frigates, closely related to the British Daring-class T45s. As the Bergamini class, they will probably more closely resemble the French *Forbin*.

ABOVE LEFT: *Francesco Mimbelli*, with *Aviere* on her quarter and the two San Giorgio LPDs in the distance. Both foreground ships have 127mm guns superfired by Albatros/Aspide launchers. Note *Mimbelli*'s angled gas turbine exhaust casing. ABOVE: Here, both Durand de la Pennes are followed in line by a pair of Artiglieres and both San Giorgios. Note the paired directors for the Aspide missile control above the wheelhouse. The crowded electronics environment requires careful arrangement. BELOW LEFT: *Luigi Durand de la Penne*'s forward funnel indicates that she is proceeding under diesel power. In a CODOG system the two types of prime mover cannot be used together. This picture pre-dates the 2005–07 upgrades, the ship lacking IRST domes.

Durand de la Penne class

Displacement: 4,500 tons (standard); 5,400 tons (full load)
Length: 135.6m/445ft 1in (bp); 147.7m/484ft 10in (oa)
Beam: 15.9m/49ft 3in
Draught: 5.1m/16ft 9in
Armament: 1 x 127mm gun, 3 x 76mm guns (3x1); 1 x Standard SM-1 MR system; 1 x 8-cell Albatros point-defence SAM system; 6 x 324mm AS torpedo tubes (2x3)
Machinery: 2 gas turbines and 2 cruising diesels in CODOG configuration
Power: 41,030kW/55,000shp for 31.5 knots or 9,400kW/12,600bhp for 21 knots
Endurance: 12,965km/7,000nm at 18 knots (on diesels alone)
Protection: Mirex/Kevlar patches
Complement: 375

Skoryi class

ABOVE: **A Skoryi (sometimes rendered Skory) in her original classic form, whose design dated from the 1940s. The broad transom with minelaying apertures echoes German wartime practice. The after 130mm guns are superfired by a twin 85mm mounting.**

Following World War II, the Soviet Union used captured German expertise and resources to develop new weapons and technologies. Until these came "on line", however, the supposed threat posed by the Western powers had to be met by conventional means. Ambitious programmes of cruisers, destroyers and submarines were, therefore, put in train. For rapid production standardization was essential.

The adopted design of destroyer was the Skoryi (or Skory), based on a pre-war class, but further influenced by German ships acquired as reparation. Not surprisingly, given the climatic conditions in which they would have to operate, the ships were large, their 2,600 tons and 121m/397ft overall length exceeding even the 2,425 tons and 119m/390ft 6in of an American Gearing. With the common occurrence of heavy topside ice accumulation, the Skoryi was less burdened with weaponry, notably carrying only two twin gunhouses to the American's three. Masting, however, was substantial and well braced.

As designed, the Skoryi profile was not unpleasing, with a conventional raised forecastle and two quintuple torpedo tube banks alternating with two squat funnels. Gunhouses, each of two 130mm guns, were fully enclosed and mounted at different levels, one forward, one aft. Superfiring the after gunhouse was a twin 85mm high-angle mounting. Manually operated, this was probably too heavy to be effective as an anti-aircraft weapon, being often replaced by 37mm weapons, of which four twins were already usually carried.

A rather Germanic, broad transom stern was fitted, improving reserve buoyancy at the after end and facilitating minelaying. Two tracks, with a capacity of about 70 mines, ran much of the length of the after deck.

Probably 64 of a planned 80 Skoryis were completed. Modest modernization was begun in the late 1950s but quickly discontinued. Upgraded units could be identified through their larger funnel caps and heavier mainmasts.

ABOVE: **Another Skoryi in its original form. Note the two sets of torpedo tubes and long, parallel afterbody. The platform forward of the bridge was later widened to accommodate sided MBU-2500 AS rocket projectors, the forward tubes landed and Anti-Aircraft (AA) armament enhanced.**

Skoryi class, as designed

Displacement: 2,600 tons (standard); 3,500 tons (full load)
Length: 121.5m/398ft 10in (oa)
Beam: 12m/39ft 4in
Draught: 4.5m/14ft 9in
Armament: 4 x 130mm guns (2x2), 2 x 85mm guns (1x2), 7/8 x 37mm guns (7x1 or 4x2); 10 x 533mm torpedo tubes (2x5)
Machinery: Geared steam turbines, 4 boilers, 2 shafts
Power: 44,760kW/60,000shp for 36 knots
Endurance: 790 tons oil for 8,520km/4,600nm at 18 knots
Protection: None
Complement: 260

Kotlin class

ABOVE: **A nice view of a Kotlin as originally built. The massive enclosed twin 130mm gun mountings are fully stabilized, as are the four quadruple 57mm weapons, two of which are sided amidships. The after torpedo tubes were later removed.**

During the course of the Skoryi programme, the Russians built a prototype destroyer leader. Launched in 1953, the *Neustrashimy* (NATO reporting name *Tallinn*) was an enormous 3,200-ton flush-decker, but carrying little more effective armament than a Skoryi. The proposed series was terminated at this one ship, but she acted as test-bed for advanced steam machinery and new stabilized gunhouses.

The Kotlins were Tallinn diminutives, wide-transomed, flush-decked and with a long, sweeping forward sheerline. Machinery was arranged on the unit system, with the resulting wide-spaced funnels alternating with quintuple torpedo tube mountings. Like the Skoryis, the heavily braced tripod mainmast was stepped between the funnels to give the anti-aircraft armament clear arcs. This powerful secondary battery comprised four quadruple 57mm mountings. Of these, one superfired the main gunhouse at either end. The other two were sided, flanking the mainmast. Separate secondary directors were provided, forward and aft.

Most units later landed the after set of torpedo tubes in favour of more superstructure and a brace of forward-firing MBU-2500 type, 12-railed AS rocket projectors.

It is believed that 28 of a planned 36 Kotlins were completed as what were probably the last-ever classic destroyers. Eight, possibly nine, of those were converted to carry the 25km/16-mile ranged, SA-N-1 (NATO reporting name "Goa") SAM system. Known as "Kotlin-SAMs", these ships sacrificed their after tubes and gun armament for a large magazine/deckhouse upon which was mounted the twin-armed launcher. Their after funnel was moved farther aft to accommodate a pyramidal "mainmast" bearing the guidance radar.

In lieu of the waist 57mm AA guns, some ships gained four of the new helmet-like, twin 30mm mountings, fully automatic and controlled in pairs by adjacent "Drum Tilt" directors. The SAM conversions lost the 70-mine capacity of the remainder.

RIGHT: **During the 1960s, several Kotlins were rebuilt aft in order to accommodate the pioneer SA-N-1 ("Goa") SAM system, whose twin-armed launcher is located here on the large 20-round magazine, added aft. Note the new pyramidal mainmast.**

Kotlin class, as designed

Displacement: 2,850 tons (standard); 3,880 tons (full load)
Length: 128m/420ft 2in
Beam: 13m/42ft 8in
Draught: 5m/16ft 5in
Armament: 4 x 130mm guns (2x2), 16 x 57mm guns (4x4); 10 x 533m torpedo tubes (2x5)
Machinery: Geared steam turbines, 4 boilers, 2 shafts
Power: 53,712kW/72,000shp for 36 knots
Endurance: 850 tons oil for 7,410km/4,000nm at 18 knots
Protection: None
Complement: 325

Kildin class

ABOVE: **The Kildins were the world's first true guided-missile destroyers but, with the discontinuation of the SS-N-1, some were given four canister-launched SS-N-11. This photograph probably shows *Bedovy.* Note the 57mm quads forward and amidships, the 76mm twins aft.**

To deal with the supposed threat from the West's carrier and amphibious forces, the Soviet Union early developed two large Ship-to-Ship Missiles (SSM). These were known to NATO as the SS-N-1 (NATO name "Scrubber") and the rather smaller SS-N-2A ("Styx"). Both were effective to horizon range, although the former, based on the German V-1 flying bomb design of World War II, had a maximum range of about 160km/100 miles. The Styx was deployed in the many minor war vessels intended to deal with amphibious forces, but the Scrubber first went to sea on four Kotlin-class conversions. The first of these was modified for the task, the others being especially built. They were known as the Kildin-class and, by pre-dating the Kotlin SAMs, were reputedly the world's first GM destroyers.

As modified, the ships retained their basic Kotlin appearance but with the afterdeck now occupied by the cumbersome, twin-rail launcher for the SS-N-1, which weighed over 3 tons at launch. Between the launcher and the after funnel was a single-level deckhouse, topped with a magazine containing two reloads.

With the necessarily more comprehensive electronics fit, masting was on a much heavier scale than that of the Kotlins. No main battery 130mm mountings were carried but the sixteen 57mm guns were retained. Two quadruple mountings were located in the centreline "A" and "B" positions, with two more flanking the mainmast. Only four torpedo tubes were shipped, these being paired on either side in the waist.

During the 1970s the Kildins were upgraded to deploy the SS-N-2C, an improved Styx. These were accommodated in canister launchers, elevated at a fixed angle and sited, two per side, abreast the after funnel. There were no reloads. Without the requirement for the earlier magazine and launcher, two 130mm gun mountings were reinstated aft.

ABOVE: **This Kildin had a machinery fire while in the Mediterranean, but the obsessively secretive Soviet Navy refused all offers of assistance. Note the size of the twin SS-N-1 launcher aft, with its magazine reportedly containing four reloads. Compare the layout with the later version (top).**

Kildin class, as built

Displacement: 3,000 tons (standard); 4,000 tons (full load)
Length: 128m/420ft 2in (oa)
Beam: 13m/42ft 8in
Draft: 5m/16ft 5in
Armament: 16 x 57mm guns (4x4); 1 x SS-N-1 SSM launcher; 4 x 533mm torpedo tubes (2x2); 2 x 12-rail MBU-2500 AS rocket launchers
Machinery: Geared steam turbines, 4 boilers, 2 shafts
Power: 53,712kW/72,000shp for 36 knots
Protection: None
Complement: 350

Krupny class

ABOVE: **A good view of a Krupny at a 1962 review. As hull numbers were constantly changed, individual identities are never certain. Note the World War II vintage "Wasp Head" director. The large gun mountings are twin 57mm.** LEFT: **There were probably no more than a couple of double-ended Krupnys created from stretched Kotlin hulls. Despite the space required by the SS-N-1 systems, this one retains her waist torpedo tubes and has a helicopter pad right aft.**

The single-ended Kildin conversions could launch only two missiles before having to reload, a process which appeared to be critically time-consuming under operational conditions. Their major function was to knock out hostile aircraft carriers and, as SSMs would need to be launched in pairs to give one of them a reasonable chance of a hit, a rapid follow-up with a second pair was obviously of advantage. The eight Krupny-class double-enders were thus a logical development.

For the sake of urgency, the long-suffering Kotlin hull form was not only lengthened by 10m/33ft but also "kippered" and widened by 1.6m/15ft 3in. This increased the Length-on-Breadth (L/B) ratio somewhat, making for a more stable weapon platform but at the cost of hydrodynamic efficiency. The resulting ships, although of higher power, were thus somewhat slower.

An interesting innovation, right aft, was a helicopter platform. The SS-N-1 had the potential to hit a target at about 160km/100 miles, but lacked the necessary on-board intelligence. A helicopter, pre-positioned beyond the horizon, would be able to order a mid-course correction sufficient to bring the missile within its own active homing range of the target.

Even 160km/100 miles is a suicidally close range to approach a carrier and, while reloading the four repeat rounds, a Krupny could expect to be under heavy air attack. Even if accompanied by a Kotlin SAM, she would need all of her sixteen 57mm anti-aircraft weapons to survive. Having exhausted her eight (although possibly more) SSMs, she would be reduced to torpedo attack, for which purpose two triple mountings were sided in the waist.

As a weapons system, the SS-N-1 failed to impress and, by 1968, a programme was initiated to convert six of the Krupnys to Kanins.

Krupny class

Displacement: 3,650 tons (standard); 4,600 tons (full load)
Length: 138m/452ft 11in (oa)
Beam: 14.6m/47ft 11in
Draught: 5m/16ft 5in
Armament: 16 x 57mm guns (4x4); 2 x SS-N-1 SSM launchers; 6 x 533mm torpedo tubes (2x3); 2 x 12-rail MBU-2500 AS rocket launchers
Machinery: Geared steam turbines, 4 boilers, 2 shafts
Power: 59,680kW/80,000shp for 34 knots
Endurance: 900 tons oil for 8,280km/4,500nm at 18 knots
Protection: None
Complement: 360

LEFT: **Late in the 1960s, the Krupnys' obsolete SS-N-1s were stripped out and the ships, now known to the West as Kanins, were rebuilt around the SA-N-1 SAM system. Note the bow profile, altered for a new sonar installation.**

Kanin class

Efforts to improve the SS-N-1 SSM continued until 1966, at which point the even larger SS-N-3 (NATO name "Shaddock") assumed the primary anti-surface ship role. The double-ended Krupnys were then taken in hand for conversion to area air defence escorts. In this guise they were redesignated Kanin by NATO.

On what had been the after SS-N-1 magazine structure was mounted the twin-armed launcher of a SA-N-1 ("Goa") SAM system. The magazine beneath stowed a reported 22 missiles. Forward of the after funnel was erected a pyramidal "mainmast" bearing the massive "Peel Group" control radar associated with the SA-N-1. Its heavy "Head Net-C" search radar antenna topped the foremast.

Forward, two quadruple 57mm gun mountings now occupied centreline "A" and "B" positions. A new structure around the after funnel supported four 30mm automatic twins, each pair of mountings being controlled by a dedicated "Drum Tilt" radar located on the mainmast. The two quintuple torpedo tube groups, sided in the waist, represented the Kanins' only defence against surface ships.

Anti-submarine capability was considerably improved. Three MBU-2500A 12-round AS rocket projectors were carried, one in a very exposed location on the foredeck, the others sided on raised platforms in the waist. A new, low-frequency bow sonar was added, necessitating an extended and more heavily raked bow to enable ground tackle to drop clear of the bulb. This added a further 1.5m/5ft to the length of the hull.

Right aft, the helicopter platform could be moved somewhat farther forward, thus reducing the amplitudes and accelerations of ship motion experienced by the aircraft. There was no hangar, the ships presumably acting as platforms for shared Kamov KA-25 "Hormone" ASW helicopters.

Apparently effective in their new role, the Kanins remained on the inventory until the 1990s. Like most Soviet warships, they occasionally changed their hull numbers. The reasons for these changes were never quite clear.

LEFT: **Soviet Black Sea units habitually spent long periods at anchor in remote offshore Mediterranean anchorages. The twin-arm SA-N-1 launcher is clearly visible here. Note the forward 57mm mounting, tracking the photographer's aircraft and the four 30mm "Dalek" mounts.**

Kanin class

Displacement: 3,675 tons (standard); 4,550 tons (full load)
Length: 139.5m/457ft 10in (oa)
Beam: 14.6m/47ft 11in
Draught: 5m/16ft 5in
Armament: 8 x 57mm guns (2x4), 8 x 30mm guns (4x2); 1 x SA-N-1 SAM launcher; 10 x 533mm torpedo tubes (2x5); 3 x 12-rail MBU-2500A AS rocket launchers
Machinery: Geared steam turbines, 4 boilers, 2 shafts
Power: 59,680kW/80,000shp for 34 knots
Endurance: 900 tons oil for 8,280km/4,500nm at 18 knots
Protection: Nominal
Complement: 350

LEFT: **An earlier Kashin with her entire above-surface armament trained on the port beam. Note the size of the 25.7km/16-mile-range SA-N-1 SAMs on the launcher rails. A total of 22 missiles were accommodated in each of the two magazines.**

Kashin class

As the Soviet fleet's first gas-turbine destroyers, the Kashins were all gas, not being combined with steam or diesel power. Probably lacking the range of engines available in the West, the designers opted for four identical M-8E units, each rated at some 18,000kW maximum. Although the ships had a distinctly "Soviet" profile, they were instantly, identifiable by their massive split funnel casings, angled to eject exhaust gases clear of electronics. These gases were first cooled to reduce the ships' Infra-Red (IR) signature, while structural surfaces also were subtly angled to reduce radar return.

The Kashins were designed as "double-ended" SAM escorts, having two SA-N-1 systems. These required two "Peel Group" control radars, one atop the strangely truncated bridge structure, the other on a short tower ahead of the after funnels. Long-range, three-dimensional air search/warning was provided by two complementary systems, known as Head Net (A or C) and Big Net, whose large and weighty antennas were located on high and substantial lattice masts.

Forward and aft were sited twin 76mm dual purpose guns, a new calibre of weapon in fully stabilized mountings, each with its own director. Only one quintuple torpedo tube mount was carried, located amidships on the centreline. A helicopter pad, again without hangar, was provided on the quarterdeck.

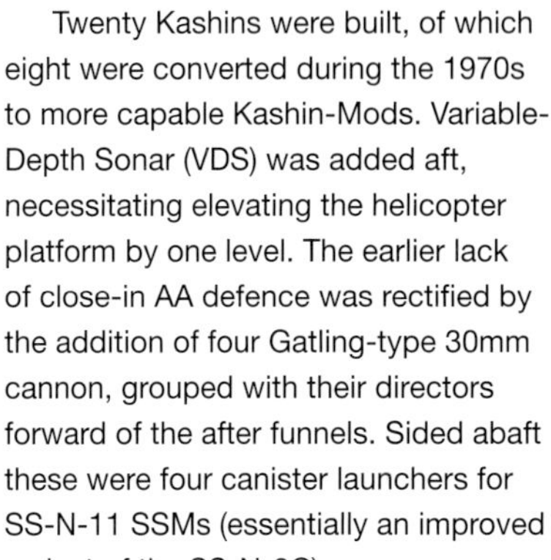

Twenty Kashins were built, of which eight were converted during the 1970s to more capable Kashin-Mods. Variable-Depth Sonar (VDS) was added aft, necessitating elevating the helicopter platform by one level. The earlier lack of close-in AA defence was rectified by the addition of four Gatling-type 30mm cannon, grouped with their directors forward of the after funnels. Sided abaft these were four canister launchers for SS-N-11 SSMs (essentially an improved variant of the SS-N-2C).

By 2007 no fully operational Kashins or Kashin-Mods remained on the inventory, joining the very considerable drawdown in the strength of the Russian fleet.

LEFT: **The Modified Kashins, as seen here, were retro-fitted with canister launchers for four SS-N-11s, here flanking the after SA-N-1 launcher. The split uptakes for the gas turbines are evident, as is the quintuple torpedo tube bank amidships.**

Kashin class, as built

Displacement: 3,750 tons (standard); 4,750 tons (full load)
Length: 144m/472ft 8in
Beam: 15.8m/51ft 10in
Draught: 4.8m/15ft 9in
Armament: 4 x 76mm guns (2x2); 2 x SA-N-1 SAM launchers; 5 x 533mm torpedo tubes (1x5); 2 x 6-rail MBU-1000 AS rocket launchers
Machinery: 4 gas turbines (COGAG), 2 shafts
Power: 71,616kW/96,000shp for 36 knots
Endurance: 940 tons oil for 5,556km/3,000nm at 20 knots
Protection: Nominal
Complement: 285

Sovremennyy class

The planned programme for these formidable-looking 8,000-tonners fell into complete disarray due to uncertain funding following the collapse of the Soviet Union. Of the original 28, only 10 are active under Russian Federation colours. Two, possibly four, have been sold to China. Some languish incomplete, others have been prematurely scrapped.

In function, the Sovremnnyys are intended primarily for surface action and area air defence, having only basic ASW capacity. Of almost twice the displacement of a Kashin, they reverted to steam turbine propulsion in order to generate a one-third increase in sustained power.

The hull has also reverted to a raised-forecastle which, like that of a Kashin, has a gentle knuckle running almost full length. A new-style 54-calibre, 130mm gun has been introduced. Fully automatic and dual-purpose, it appears in twin mountings, forward and aft. There are also four 30mm Gatlings, two forward and two aft.

Superfiring each main gun mounting is an SA-N-7 ("Gadfly") SAM launcher. First trialled on a Kashin, the weapon has a reported range of 25km/15 miles. Flanking the massive bridge structure are eight canister launchers for SS-N-22 ("Sunburn") SSMs, manoeuvrable and with a putative range of 101km/63 miles. Targetting for these is facilitated by the "Bandstand" radar within the conspicuous dome atop the bridge block, alternative targeting assistance being possible through the ship's Ka-27 ("Helix") helicopter. This is carried high on the after superstructure and is provided with a light, telescoping hangar.

The helicopter can also be used defensively against submarines, for which purpose the ship is also equipped with bow sonar and two rocket projectors. Unlike Western equivalents, the Sovremennyys retain heavyweight torpedo tubes which, presumably, could accommodate either anti-ship or anti-submarine weapons.

Finally, these very capable ships can carry up to 40 mines.

ABOVE LEFT: **Many modern warships appear under-armed; not so the Russians. Here, the *Nastoychivyy* fairly bristles. The SA-N-7 ("Gadfly") launchers forward and aft are complemented by eight canister/launchers for the 101km/63-mile SS-N-22 ("Sunburn") SSMs.** ABOVE: **Forward and aft the *Otchayannyy* is equipped with twin, 130mm guns which, as can be seen, are capable of local control. CIWS Gatling-type guns flank the wheelhouse and also the elevated helicopter pad, three-quarters aft.**

LEFT: **Mutual interest; the Northern Fleet's *Rastoropnyy* encounters the American Spruance-class *O'Bannon*. The Russian ship is not carrying her helicopter, for which the telescopic hangar has been stowed. The hull is subtly knuckled to reduce radar signature.**

Sovremennyy class

Displacement: 7,950 tons (normal); 8,500 tons (full load)
Length: 145m/475ft 11in (wl); 156m/513ft 4in (oa)
Beam: 16.3m/53ft 6in
Draught: 6m/19ft 8in
Armament: 4 x 130mm guns (2x2), 4 x 30mm Gatling guns (4x1); 2 x SA-N-7 SAM launchers; 8 x SS-N-22 SSM launchers; 4 x 533m torpedo tubes (2x2); 2 x 6-rail MBU-1000 AS rocket launchers
Machinery: Geared steam turbines, 4 boilers, 2 shafts
Power: 82,060kW/110,000shp for 33 knots
Endurance: 1,740 tons oil for 6,480km/3,500nm at 20 knots
Protection: Nominal
Complement: 296

Udaloy class

ABOVE: **The Udaloy-class destroyers have an unmistakably "chunky" appearance and are unusual these days in having superimposed gun mountings forward. The quadruple canisters are for the SS-N-14 ("Silex") anti-ship/anti-submarine SSM.**

Also affected by the distintegration of the Soviet Union were the Udaloy-class ASW destroyers. Ten are in service but at least four appear to have been cancelled, scrapped or cannibalized. The latter course is not unusual as now-separate republics bargain over single-sourced technologies.

Slightly larger than a Sovremennyy, an Udaloy is easily differentiated by her long-forecastle hull form and two paired funnel casings that indicate her gas turbine propulsion. Two boost engines and two cruise units are arranged in COGAG configuration but, even run together, develop less power than is customary in Russian ships.

The exaggerated bow overhang results from a complex bow bulb, arranged around several acoustically based systems, but adversely affecting resistance and manoeuvring. Two Ka-27 "Helix A" ASW helicopters are accommodated in hangars but the Udaloy main combat system is the SS-N-14 "Silex" missile, whose quadruple canister launchers flank the bridge structure. The 50km/31-mile weapon may be configured either to release an AS torpedo over a submerged target, or fitted with a warhead to counter surface targets, probably with mid-course correction.

To two 100mm and four 30mm Gatling guns the ships add the SA-N-9 ("Gauntlet") vertically launched SAM. Eight 8-round silos for these are divided between the forecastle and the after superstructure, each group having its own distinctive "Cross Sword" directors.

Short-range AS weapons comprise a pair of MBU-6000 rocket launchers and two quadruple banks of heavyweight torpedo tubes. Although massive in appearance, the ships are contoured to reduce radar signature.

LEFT: **The Udaloys have twinned helicopter hangars of compact design. Between them is an unoccupied "Bandstand" for the Kinzhal SAM system, presumably not fitted. Note the large stern door, through which the towed VDS is deployed.**

Of the ten extant Udaloys, one (*Admiral Chabanenko*) varies sufficiently to be classed separately as an Udaloy-II. Probably designed for the former KGB, she has an even longer forecastle, necessitating the heavy torpedo tubes being carried behind shutters. Her major weapon has been changed to eight SS-N-22 "Sunburn" anti-ship missiles, while a twin 130mm mounting replaces the single 100mms.

Udaloy class

Displacement: 6,940 tons (standard); 8,400 tons (full load)
Length: 145m/476ft (wl); 163.5m/536ft 8in (oa)
Beam: 17.2m/56ft 6in
Draught: 5.2m/17ft 1in
Armament: 2 x 100mm guns (2x1); 4 x 30mm Gatling guns (4x1); 8 x SS-N-14 SSM/AS launchers; 8 x 8-cell SA-N-9 SAM launchers; 8 x 533mm torpedo tubes (2x4); 2 x 12-rail MBU-6000 AS rocket launchers
Machinery: 2 boost and 2 cruise gas turbines, 2 shafts
Power: 2 x 16,7985kW/22,500shp and 2 x 5,595kW/7,500shp for 29.5 knots
Endurance: 1,500 tons fuel for 13,890km/7,500nm at 18 knots
Protection: Nominal
Complement: 220

LEFT: **More correctly "Z10", the *Hans Lody* was of the original Maass type. Designed for high speed and maximum firepower, these lacked the range for oceanic operations. Note the lack of forward sheer, contributing to wetness.** ABOVE: **By virtue of the incorrect funnel proportions, this impression of *Max Schultz* (Z3) gives more the appearance of a light cruiser. She also had a straight stem and rounded sheer strake to the forecastle.**

Maass and Roeder classes

A large German naval construction programme followed the naval agreement with Britain in 1935. As destroyers were required to conform to the generally adopted maxima of the London Naval Treaty of 1930, the large majority were limited to a standard displacement of 1,500 tons and a number of guns not exceeding 130mm (German 13cm) in calibre.

Twenty-two were laid down 1934–38, comprising four Type 34s and twelve Type 34As (collectively the Leberecht Maass class), followed by the six Type 36s, or Diether von Roeder, class. Their design brief emphasized seaworthiness, hull strength, speed, endurance and firepower, a conflicting set of ideals which, not surprisingly, inflated their reported displacements to well beyond the 2,000-ton treaty limit.

Types 34 and 34A differed primarily in the latter having a new bow configuration to improve seakindliness. The Type 36s were somewhat longer and beamier, otherwise not dissimilar.

All were of orthodox layout, with a raised forecastle and five 12.7cm guns in single open mountings, two forward, three aft. Masting was light, the foremast bearing a distinctive cruciform yard. Tophamper otherwise was heavy, particularly forward, making earlier units very wet. The after funnel was located between two quadruple banks of torpedo tubes, and sided mine rails ran most of the length of the afterdeck. Funnels were heavily capped.

The most contentious element in their design was the adoption of yet-untried steam conditions, far and away in advance of anything used in other major navies. The objective of compact, but powerful, plant was achieved at the cost of endless mechanical problems.

Unlike British equivalents, German destroyers never saved topweight by landing one set of torpedo tubes and when, in 1944, surviving units were given comprehensively improved "flak" defences, they became even more heavily loaded.

Although ten of the twenty-two had been destroyed by April 1940, seven succeeded in surviving hostilities.

ABOVE: **Derived directly from the Maass, or Type 34/34A, were the six Type 36 units, usually referred to as the Diether von Roeder class. *Hans Lüdemann* (Z18) shows their shorter funnels and bows with greater sheer and flare.**

Types 34 and 34A

Displacement: 2,220 tons (standard); 3,155 tons (full load)
Length: 115m/377ft 6in (bp); 120m/393ft 11in (oa)
Beam: 11.3m/37ft 1in
Draught: 4m/13ft 2in
Armament: 5 x 12.7cm guns (5x1), 4 x 3.7cm guns (2x2); 8 x 53.3cm torpedo tubes (2x4)
Machinery: Geared steam turbines, 6 boilers, 2 shafts
Power: 52,220kW/70,000shp for 36 knots
Endurance: 715 tons oil for 3.312km/1,800nm at 19 knots
Protection: None
Complement: 325

LEFT: **The 12 ships of the Z23 type were war-built, officially of the Type 36A class. They can be recognized by the twin gunhouse forward with no superfiring "B" gun, strongly curved bow profile and tripod mast.** ABOVE: **Contrasting with the French post-war paint scheme (left), this Type 36A (Mob) in Norwegian waters carries a disruptive pattern. Note the large search radar antenna.**

Z23–39

Unique in bearing names, the previous German destroyers were also allocated pendant numbers, prefixed "Z" (*Zerstörer*/Destroyer). Types 34 and 34A were thus also Z1–16, and Type 36 Z17–22 inclusive. Subsequent war-built destroyers reverted to the earlier convention of numbers only.

Concerned that large foreign destroyers, notably French, still outgunned its ships, the German Fleet Command wanted new construction to mount 15cm guns rather than 12.7cm. Throwing a much heavier projectile (45.3kg/100lb against 28kg/62lb), it was also a much heavier gun. Following various permutations of layout, and bearing in mind the need to reduce weight forward, it was decided to specify an enclosed twin gunhouse forward and three open, single mountings aft. Together with two quadruple banks of torpedo tubes, this would demand no more than a couple of metres on length, together with a small increase in beam to maintain stability.

The resulting eight Type 36A ships, numbered Z23–30 inclusive, were completed 1940–41. Their twin gunhouses being delayed, all were completed with a fourth open single mounting forward. Their appearance otherwise was similar to that of earlier vessels except for tripod foremasts, markedly greater forward sheer and curved bow profiles.

When, in 1942, a first twin 15cm mounting became available, it was fitted to Z23. It caused the ship to plunge heavily in adverse conditions and proved unreliable because of resulting water ingress.

The next group, known as Type 36A (Mob), comprised Z31–34 and Z37–39 inclusive. Retaining four guns, they differed internally.

With the 15cm gun continuing to cause problems, a batch of seven Type 36Bs, with five 12.7cm weapons was ordered in February 1941. Of this group, only Z35–36 and, eventually, Z43 were ever completed.

Plans for destroyers propelled by multiple diesel engines ended with the destruction by bombing of the prototype Z51. She was lead ship for the projected eight-strong Type 42 (Z51–58).

ABOVE: **Reversion to smaller gun mountings, in combination with a tripod foremast, mark this unidentified unit as a Type 36B, i.e. either Z35 or Z36. Both ships were destroyed in a German minefield in the Gulf of Finland, December 1944.**

Type 36A

Displacement: 2,600 tons (standard); 3,580 tons (full load)
Length: 121.9m/400ft 2in (bp); 127m/416ft 10in (oa)
Beam: 12m/39ft 3in
Draught: 3.9m/12ft 10in
Armament: 4/5 x 15cm guns (4x1 or 1x2/3x1), 4 x 3.7cm guns (2x2); 8 x 53.3cm torpedo tubes (2x4)
Machinery: Geared steam turbines, 6 boilers, 2 shafts
Power: 52,220kW/70,000shp for 36 knots
Endurance: 775 tons oil for 4,075km/2,200nm at 19 knots
Protection: Nominal
Complement: 318

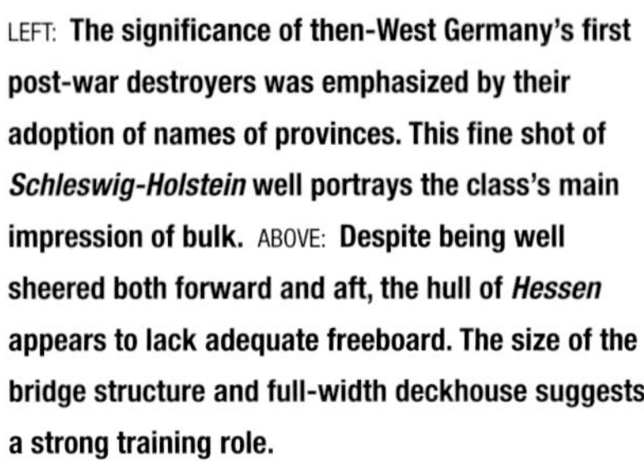

LEFT: **The significance of then-West Germany's first post-war destroyers was emphasized by their adoption of names of provinces. This fine shot of *Schleswig-Holstein* well portrays the class's main impression of bulk.** ABOVE: **Despite being well sheered both forward and aft, the hull of *Hessen* appears to lack adequate freeboard. The size of the bridge structure and full-width deckhouse suggests a strong training role.**

Hamburg class

While still the Federal Republic, or West, Germany became a member of NATO, and its first post-war destroyers were both named and given "D" pendant numbers. For their category, the four Hamburgs had a massive profile. A flush-decked hull form was readopted, somewhat disguised by the full-width lower levels of the bridge block. The bow section, with its prominent sheer and knuckle, and anchors stowed at the deck edge, was reminiscent of later war-built German destroyers. Indeed the whole hull appeared to be an extrapolation of that of the slightly earlier Köln-class frigates, which stemmed from the same yard.

For their bulk, the Hamburgs always gave the impression of being under-armed. As built, they carried four French-pattern, single 10cm guns in enclosed mountings. In the course of a major 1970s refit, "C" mounting was landed in favour of four, forward-angled MM38 Exocet canister launchers.

Five 53.3cm torpedo tubes were built into the hull, three firing forward through the stem head, and two aft through the transom. These were all removed during the 1970s refit, at which time the bridge structure was also remodelled.

The main ASW weapons were a pair of Bofors four-barrelled projectors, sited immediately forward of the bridge front, and two lightweight torpedo tubes in the waist. With the removal of the hull-mounted tubes, the latter were replaced with sided pairs of heavyweight tubes.

Masting was also heavy, bearing an array of mainly British-and-Dutch-sourced electronics. The aftermost of the three original masts was later removed. Funnels were large and heavily capped. The inadequate anti-aircraft armament of four paired 40mm Bofors weapons was later supplemented with launchers for the Rolling-Airframe Missile (RAM). All four were scrapped in the late 1990s.

LEFT: ***Bayern*'s large funnel caps were intended to protect electronics from hot, corrosive stack gases. Her "X" gun has here been landed in favour of four MM38 Exocets. The wide transom was designed to accommodate minelaying.**

Hamburg class, as built

Displacement: 3,500 tons (standard); 4,700 tons (full load)
Length: 128m/420ft 2in (bp); 133.7m/438ft 10in (oa)
Beam: 13.4m/44ft
Draught: 5.2m/17ft 1in
Armament: 4 x 10cm guns (4x1); 5 x 53.3cm torpedo tubes (5x1); 2 x AS torpedo tubes (2x1); 2 x 37.5cm Bofors AS rocket launchers (2x4)
Machinery: Geared steam turbines, 4 boilers, 2 shafts
Power: 50,728kW/68,000shp for 35 knots
Endurance: 810 tons oil for 6,297km/3,400nm at 18 knots
Protection: Nominal
Complement: 276

Holland/Friesland class

Four new destroyers, closely following classic British (Yarrow) design, were under construction in Dutch yards when the nation was invaded in 1940, Two were completed, one by the British, one by the Germans, and two were scrapped. This might have been the end of what would have been the Callenburgh class, except that four complete sets of Parsons-designed machinery, intended for them, surprisingly survived the war. Designed to deliver a continuous 33,570kW/45,020shp, these would drive the 1,600-ton Callenburgh at 36 knots. Post-war, however, they were used to power the four-ship Holland class which, at 2,215 tons, longer and beamier, could make only 32 knots.

Unusual in having a light protective belt over the length of their machinery space, the Holland were otherwise of conventional raised forecastle design. No anti-surface ship torpedo tubes were carried (although heavyweight AS tubes were unsuccessfully trialled early in their careers), destroyers by now having evolved into primarily fast AA/AS escorts.

The main gun battery was fully automatic and dual purpose, comprising two twin Bofors 120mm gunhouses, one mounted forward, one aft. There were also six 40mm Bofors weapons. Several directors were backed by a comprehensive radar fit. Beyond depth charges, AS armament consisted of two 4-barrelled, 375mm rocket projectors, also from Bofors. These fired forward from a location ahead of the bridge front. As a space-saving measure, the forward funnel was built into the foremast, as on a British Daring.

The requirement for a dozen destroyers was met by building eight more to the same basic design but with slightly enlarged dimensions to accommodate more powerful machinery, reportedly similar to that specified for the American Gearing. Appreciably faster, the eight were termed the Friesland class, also named after provinces.

Following the disposal of the Holland, the seven surviving Frieslands were sold to Peru in the early 1980s.

ABOVE: **Built post-World War II, the Frieslands were designed to counter aircraft and submarines rather than surface ships. *Rotterdam*, here, and others, if ever fitted with 21in torpedo tubes, quickly had them removed.** BELOW LEFT: ***Amsterdam*, another of the Frieslands, differed slightly in machinery and hull dimensions from the Hollands. Note the two Bofors AS rocket launchers in "B" position. Guns are also of Bofors pattern but major electronics are of Dutch design; the topmast is British.**

Friesland class, as built

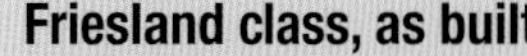

Displacement: 2,500 tons (standard); 3,075 tons (full load)
Length: 112.8m/370ft 3in (bp); 116m/380ft 9in (oa)
Beam: 11.8m/38ft 9in
Draught: 5.2m/17ft 1in
Armament: 4 x 120mm guns (2x2); 2 x 4-barrelled 375mm AS rocket launchers
Machinery: Geared steam turbines, 4 boilers, 2 shafts
Power: 44,760kW/60,000shp at 36 knots
Endurance: 6,110kW/3,300nm for 22 knots
Protection: Light vertical belt over machinery spaces
Complement: 285

Öland class

The two Ölands evolved from the Göteborgs of the late 1930s. Of only 1,140 tons, these six were orthodox destroyers with two funnels and two triple sets of torpedo tubes. One of their three single 120mm guns was located amidships. Their dominant feature was a monolithic bridge block, extending the full width of the ship.

To ensure her neutrality during World War II, Sweden expanded her small fleet. The four Visbys were slightly enlarged Göteborgs differing in having two, close-set funnels of unequal size, and the third gun moved aft to a superfiring position.

Swedish warships, not intended for blue water operation, tend to have limited endurance and, post-war, both these classes were remodelled as anti-submarine frigates.

The succeeding Ölands were also a wartime design but, incomplete in 1945, were finished in slow time. Although obviously derived from the *Visby*, they were a considerable 13.6m/44ft 7in greater in length. Where the preceding classes emphasized speed, the Ölands were powered for a more moderate 35 knots.

Their armament was designed for maximum anti-aircraft capability. At either end was a twin Bofors 120mm mounting – fully enclosed, semi-automatic and with an 80-degree elevation. Both uptakes were trunked into a single large funnel casing and the massive bridge, subsequently rebuilt, supported a stubby pole mast. As built, the ships had a seventh 40mm Bofors located right forward in the "bow-chaser" position favoured by contemporary British Hunt-class ships that frequently engaged fast enemy torpedo boats. Exposed, and with no peacetime application, these were later removed, their bases remaining.

ABOVE: At the outbreak of World War II, Sweden acquired a couple of Italian-built torpedo boats, effectively light destroyers. Their influence on layout may be discerned in the *Öland*. The ring, right forward, supports a 40mm "bow chaser" gun, when fitted. BELOW LEFT: *Uppland* at speed. Note how the depth of hull is varied to reflect bending moments. The profile is exceptionally low, Swedish ships sometimes being berthed in bomb-proof chambers hewn into solid rock.

Although not rerated as frigates, at least one of the Ölands was modified to carry a helicopter, as were some of their smaller destroyers. As part of a general drawdown of larger Swedish combatants, all three of these classes had been discarded by 1981.

Öland class, as built

Displacement: 1,880 tons (standard); 2,400 tons (full load)
Length: 107m/351ft (bp); 111.1m/364ft 2in (oa)
Beam: 11.2m/36ft 9in
Draught: 3.4m/11ft 3in
Armament: 4 x 120mm guns (2x2); 6 x 533mm torpedo tubes (2x3)
Machinery: Geared steam turbines, 2 boilers, 2 shafts
Power: 32,824kW/44,000shp for 35 knots
Endurance: 300 tons oil for 4,630km/2,500nm at 20 knots
Protection: Splinter protection
Complement: 200

LEFT: **The two Hallands were of an age with the Dutch Frieslands, and it will be noticed how the twin 120mm Bofors mountings and Dutch LW 02/03 air-search radar are common to both types.** BELOW: **Unusually, the four Östergötlands showed a reduction in size compared with the preceding Hallands. This is the nameship, breasting the wake of another vessel. Note how she lacks the twin 57mm guns in "B" position.**

Östergötland and Halland classes

Completed in 1955–56, the two Hallands must be contenders for the most handsome destroyers ever. Their two funnels were slightly tapered and well proportioned, their profiles complemented by the angled front and back faces of the otherwise monolithic bridge block.

The first Swedish destroyers of post-war design, they had raised forecastles and a fully automatic, dual-purpose, twin 120mm Bofors mounting at either end. The forward mounting was superfired by a twin 57mm, also by Bofors. The same company also supplied the two four-barrelled AS launchers on the foredeck and that for the early RB O8 SSM, located abaft the funnels. One quintuple and one triple torpedo tube mounting was also fitted. Modernization saw them acquire a large air/surface-search radar on the mainmast, and a four-rail Seacat point-defence SAM.

Two sister ships were cancelled, but were probably subsumed into the four-ship Östergötland class which followed on. Almost uniquely, these were smaller than the ships from which they were derived. Chunky and powerful looking, they lacked the classic elegance of the Halland.

The Östergötland differed primarily in having a flush-decked hull form, while their diminutive mainmast was stepped before the after funnel. The 57mm twin mounting was omitted, the forward 120mm being superfired by two of the seven single 40mm weapons that were carried. These too, were later supported by a Seacat system. No SSM was carried, and only one bank of torpedo tubes, a probably unique sextuple.

Sweden's long coastline, shallow offshore, lends itself to defensive mine warfare, and all destroyers had considerable minelaying capacity.

Geography determines that Swedish waters could be dominated by hostile, land-based air power, leading to the conclusion that major surface combatants were over-vulnerable. All were thus paid off by the early 1980s in favour of smaller, more agile warships which could be readily concealed.

ABOVE: **The *Halland* shows her complex superstructure. Note the enclosed bridge structure, with few apertures, and the transom, configured for minelaying. Abaft the after funnel is the inclined launcher for the Bofors RB 08 anti-ship missile, unique to Swedish ships.**

Östergötland class, as built

Displacement: 2,050 tons (standard); 2,600 tons (full load)
Length: 112.1m/367ft 6in (bp); 115.9m/380ft (oa)
Beam: 11.2m/36ft 9in
Draught: 3.7m/12ft
Armament: 4 x 120mm guns (2x2); 6 x 533mm torpedo tubes (1x6); 2 x 4-barrelled 375mm AS rocket projectors
Machinery: Geared steam turbines, 2 boilers, 2 shafts
Power: 29,840kW/40,000shp for 35 knots
Endurance: 330 tons oil for 4,075km/2,200nm at 20 knots
Protection: Some; extent not known
Complement: 210

4
F229

Directory of Frigates

For the purposes of this book, the term "frigate" is synonymous with "escort", including as it does the various sloops, corvettes, torpedo boats/escort destroyers/destroyer escorts that were concerned primarily with the safe passage of commerce and, by extension, taking the war to the submarines bent on its destruction. Space, regrettably, forbids the inclusion of the considerable classes of ocean minesweeper and "Admiralty trawler" which, although performing admirably as escorts, cannot be considered frigates.

The eventual employment of convoy during World War I resulted in the development of the first dedicated escorts, uncomplicated ships designed for humdrum routine, releasing destroyers to the business for which they were better suited. The Battle of the Atlantic underlined the need for "large corvettes", combining range and capacity with seaworthiness, simplicity and cheapness. Thus emerged the frigate, a further feature of which was its suitability to be series-built in large numbers.

With the formation of NATO, all primarily Anti-Submarine (AS) escorts became generically termed "frigates", in contradistinction to "destroyers", which were now configured primarily around Anti-Aircraft Warfare (AAW).

LEFT: **HMS *Lancaster*, a Type 23 frigate, passes the Thames flood barrier on a port visit to London. As a general-purpose frigate, her AS capacity resides in her helicopter and shipboard torpedo tubes. Note the Harpoon and Sea Wolf VLS forward.**

LEFT: **In a distinctive Western Approaches camouflage scheme, *Crane* is seen here "swinging compasses". The censor has deleted the HF/DF antenna at the masthead, the communications antenna at the yardarm extremities and the pendant number.** BELOW: **Badly shot-up during the "Yangtze Incident", *Amethyst* was repaired in time to participate in the Korean War. Bridge personnel and gun crews, clad in anti-flash gear, stand by in anticipation of yet another bombardment detail.**

Black Swan and Modified Black Swan classes

Fine ships, the Black Swan sloops tended to be built by destroyer yards. They were designed for the AA protection of convoys, for which they carried the very effective twin 4in high-angle (HA) Mk X1X mounting, four in the earliest examples, three in the remainder, with a quadruple 2pdr pompom in lieu of "Y" guns. Together with full director control, this amounted to a considerable aggregation of topweight and this, with the requirement for a slow, easy roll (to make a good gun platform) gave designers a challenging stability problem. Active fin stabilizers, not yet very effective, were fitted but hostilities saw a creeping increase in complement and topweight, necessitating an extra 30cm/1ft of beam in the "modified" subclass, with the omission of splinter protection and some boats.

Extra weight included a proliferation of light, automatic weapons and a lattice mainmast bearing the "lantern" of the Type 271/272 surface warning radar. Depth charge capacity also increased, from 40 with two projectors in early units to 110 and eight respectively.

The design did not readily lend itself to later modification for a forward-firing Squid mortar, taking instead a split Hedgehog, located either side of "B" mounting. Despite this, the Black Swans were deadly submarine hunters. Based mainly at Liverpool and Greenock, they were fully or partly responsible for 28 kills, many by Captain "Johnny" Walker's redoubtable 2nd Escort Group. Afterdeck arrangements were cramped by the Admiralty requirement that a proportion of the class should be capable of minesweeping.

Steam-turbine propelled, they had good acceleration and were handy in manoeuvring. At "convoy" speeds, they had an endurance of about 13,800km/7,500nm.

Thirteen original and twenty-four modified Black Swans were built, six to Indian account. Five were cancelled and, although hard-worked, only four were lost.

LEFT: **Seen shortly after World War II, the Modified Black Swan *Peacock* enters Grand Harbour, Malta. She retains her old-style "U" flag superior and the original depth charge arrangements. Split Hedgehog was carried forward but the class did not get Squid.**

Modified Black Swan class, as designed

Displacement: 1,350 tons (standard); 1,960 tons (full load)
Length: 86.3m/283ft (bp); 91.3m/299ft 6in (oa)
Beam: 11.7m/38ft 6in
Draught: 3.5m/11ft 4in
Armament: 6 x 4in guns (3x2), 4/6 x 40mm guns (2x2/2x1)
Machinery: Geared steam turbines, 2 boilers, 2 shafts
Power: 3,208kW/4,300shp for 19.5 knots
Endurance: 420 tons for 11,220km/6,100nm at 15 knots
Protection: Nominal
Complement: 210

Hunt classes

The Black Swans were officially termed Convoy Escorts; the Hunts, Fast Escorts. Where the sloops traded speed for capacity, the Fast Escorts were small destroyers, smaller but considerably faster than the sloops, carrying the same powerful AA battery but lacking their great endurance. They were intended to undertake all destroyer activities short of fleet work.

Over-worked constructive staff unfortunately made a fundamental error in stability calculation. On being inclined, the first-of-class was obliged to land "X" gun mounting, shorten the funnel and to reduce the upper structure. These measures, together with 50 tons of permanent ballast, were sufficient, and 22 of these Type I Hunts were built.

The Type Is were seen as deficient in armament, however, so that follow-on Type IIs were made a considerable 76cm/30in beamier. This cost about three knots in speed, but allowed the reinstatement of the third mounting and an improved bridge layout. This programme ran to 34 units.

As the war obliged Hunts to undertake duties for which they were not intended, torpedo tubes were demanded. This resulted in the 28 Type IIIs, with a twin 21in torpedo tube mounting, but reverting to only two twin 4in mountings, in "A" and "X" positions. Funnel and masts were set vertically, without rake.

The two Type IVs were not related, being Thornycroft "specials", Nearly 5m/16ft 5in longer, and beamier, they could carry the full specified six-gun AA battery and three of the desired four torpedo tubes. With similar machinery, however, they were slower. Their major innovation was to continue the forecastle deck three-quarters aft, making for a stronger and more comfortable (if hotter) ship. The pronounced forward knuckle was not successful.

The Hunts performed very effectively, particularly in support of English East Coast and Mediterranean convoys. Nearly one in four was lost.

ABOVE: **Steaming past an interned Italian battleship in Malta, the *Tanatside* shows the characteristics of the Type III Hunts, vertical funnel and mast, "Y" gun mounting suppressed, but with a twin torpedo tube mounting added amidships.**

ABOVE: **The Type I Hunts, typified by *Meynell*, came out badly overweight. Torpedo tubes and "X" 4in gun mounting were sacrificed, funnel shortened and director lowered. Although employed on the East Coast, she has the Type 271 radar lantern and the "Huff-Duff" aerial of an ocean escort.**

Type II Hunt class, as built

Displacement: 1,050 tons (standard); 1,420 tons (full load)
Length: 80.6m/264ft 3in (bp); 85.4m/280ft (oa)
Beam: 9.6m/31ft 6in
Draught: 3.4m/11ft (mean)
Armament: 6 x 4in guns (3x2); 1 x quadruple 2pdr pompom
Machinery: Geared steam turbines, 2 boilers, 2 shafts
Power: 14,174kW/19,000shp for 25.5 knots
Endurance: 277 tons fuel for 4,630km/2,500nm at 20 knots
Protection: Nominal
Complement: 164

LEFT: **Still looking very "mercantile", the 1941-built *Jasmine* has been given a long forecastle but still has the original flimsy bridge structure and mast ahead of it. Engaged in convoy escort, she has her whaler griped but turned out for instant use.**

Flower class

Although immortalized by their role in the Battle of the Atlantic, the Flowers were intended to be coastal escorts. Built largely to mercantile, rather than Admiralty standards, their hull was based on a stretched version of a Smiths Dock whale catcher. Their size and class meant that they could be built by many yards, British and Canadian, with no previous experience of warship construction. Already in production, they were involved in ocean warfare in the absence of anything more suitable.

Expected also to double as minesweepers, early examples had a short forecastle, with a single bandstand-mounted 4in gun. The after sheer was pronounced; the forward, less so. Like trawlers, they had a deeper after draught to give the hull "bite" and the single, large-diameter propeller adequate immersion. Propulsion was by a simple steam reciprocating engine, but lacking both redundancy and size, a Flower could not expect to survive torpedo damage.

ABOVE: ***Vetch*, as shown in 1942, has gained a more "naval" bridge structure, radar and a relocated mast. She carries her escort group number on her funnel. The 2pdr gun has a good all-round arc of fire.**

There was a distinctly mercantile air about early Flowers, with their cowl ventilators, flimsy glazed wood wheelhouse and foremast ahead of it. Later ships were improved with much longer forecastles, modified forward sections and an "Admiralty" bridge.

They were amazingly seaworthy little ships but had a rapid and pronounced movement that fatigued the best of crews. Living conditions, already spartan, were frequently made worse by flooding.

Flowers were built in yards ranging from the mighty Harland & Wolff to tiny slips up obscure Canadian creeks. With little shipbuilding tradition, the contribution of Canada to the Atlantic battle is worthy of great credit, their 121 (many improved) Flowers being just one element. The many British yards involved constructed a further 145. Most were completed by 1942, with construction moving on to frigates and the improved Castle-class corvette. Flowers are credited with sinking 53 enemy submarines; 35 became war losses.

LEFT: **HMCS *Oakville* is a reminder of the great contribution made by the Canadians to victory in the Battle of the Atlantic. In total, 121 Flowers stemmed from Canadian yards. Note the American-sourced anchor.**

Flower class, with long forecastles

Displacement: 1,015 tons (standard); 1,220 tons (full load)
Length: 58.9m/193ft (bp); 63.5m/208ft 4in (oa)
Beam: 10.1m/33ft 1in
Draught: 4.2m/13ft 9in (mean)
Armament: 1 x 4in gun; 1 x Hedgehog AS spigot mortar (later)
Machinery: 1 x 4-cylinder triple-expansion steam engine, 2 boilers, 1 shaft
Power: 2,052kW/2,750ihp for 16 knots
Endurance: 230 tons oil for 6,480km/3,500nm at 12 knots
Protection: None
Complement: 85

LEFT: **The numerical "2" on the nearest River proclaims her as French. She is ex-HMS *Windrush*, now *la Découverte*, berthed in the Penfeld at Brest. Post-war, all three have gained the heavy dish of the Type 277 radar.** BELOW: ***Swale*, producing the spray that constantly washed down ship and crew. Completed in 1942, she is still armed with Hedgehog. Squid might later have been accommodated had not the Lochs been coming into service by then.**

River class

Even as the Flowers first demonstrated their limitations under ocean conditions, a more appropriate type was under development. To pursue a surfaced submarine, or to quickly regain station, an escort really required 22 knots rather than the Flowers' 16. As this would require steam turbine propulsion, however, it was decided to compromise with a "twin-screw corvette", capable of 20 knots with a Flower-type reciprocating engine on each shaft. Only in 1942 was their extra speed and capability recognized by recoining the historic term "frigate".

Even 20 knots demanded an increase of nearly 50 per cent in hull length, so that many of the small, corvette builders could not construct the new ships, all named after British rivers. This was remedied, however, by the United States building the design as its Patrol Frigate (PF). Of these, 21 were transferred to the Royal Navy as the Colony class.

Dimensioned around full minesweeping gear, the Rivers' spacious afterdeck was able to accommodate over 200 depth charges. A full Hedgehog was carried forward, but very exposed. Later fitting of a double Squid was intended, but eventually applied to just one ship.

Larger escorts such as frigates were also expected to contribute to the AA defence of a convoy. To the single 4in low-angle guns of the surface armament was thus added an eclectic range of automatic weapons. The mix depended upon availability but only latterly included 40mm Bofors to replace pompoms and Oerlikons.

In addition to the universal "Huff-Duff" direction-finding antenna, all sported the Type 271 "lantern", later superseded by the tilting "dish" antenna of the improved Type 277.

In all, there were 57 British-built Rivers, 45 Canadian and 22 Australian. There were 77 American PFs. Five Rivers were lost, but accounted for 18 submarines.

River class, as designed

Displacement: 1,400 tons (standard); 1,925 tons (full load)
Length: 86.3m/283ft (bp); 91.9m/301ft 4in (oa)
Beam: 11.1m/36ft 6in
Draught: 3.9m/12ft 10in (mean)
Armament: 2 x 4in guns (2x1/1x2); 1 x Hedgehog AS mortar
Machinery: 2 x 4-cylinder triple-expansion steam reciprocating engines, 2 boilers, 2 shafts
Power: 4,103kW/5,500ihp for 20 knots
Endurance: 646 tons for 13,335km/7,200nm at 12 knots
Protection: Nominal
Complement: 114

RIGHT: ***Antigonish* was one of 70 Rivers built in Canada. Following post-war modification, she has been built up aft to create a well for Squid, has a twin 4in gun forward and an enclosed bridge, more appropriate to Canadian weather conditions.**

LEFT: **In a late World War II paint scheme, *Leeds Castle* shows her clear Flower ancestry. With a full frigate-type bridge structure and long, easy sheer, there is little "mercantile" left except, perhaps, the cowl ventilators over the machinery space.** ABOVE: **It is 1946, but *Bamborough Castle* still looks weather-worn and carries her wartime-style pendant number. The robust lattice mast still supports a Type 272, where *Leeds Castle* (left) has a later Type 277, its dish laid horizontally.**

Castle class

Designed to rectify the shortcomings of the Flowers, the Castles were some 15m/50ft longer, placing them halfway between a Flower and a River. Still to be built by many small, unsophisticated yards, they were designed for construction by traditional methods, rather than by the pre-fabrication then becoming general.

Dating from late 1942, the Castle design was able to incorporate features proven by early Rivers. The forward end had a sweeping flare and sheer, with the forecastle deck continued well aft. The quarterdeck, made more spacious by an adaptation of the Rivers' triangular transom, was enclosed by a solid bulwark. There was a full naval bridge structure, and an amidships lattice mast supporting the Type 272 (later 277) radar antenna at an effective height. Visually, the Castles were very attractive.

The class was designed around the new Squid mortar, the *Hadleigh Castle* being the first to take it to sea operationally, in August 1943. Only a single Squid could be accommodated, located in the elevated "B" position and superfiring an improved single 4in gun. Because of the (fully justified) confidence placed in Squid, the depth charge arrangements were much reduced.

Unseen, the Castles accommodated their major advantage, the Type 147Q Asdic (Sonar) that could continuously feed the Squid system with range, bearing and depth, "holding" a submerged target up to the mount of firing three, fast-sinking bombs.

For simplicity of production, the propulsion unit was the same type of reciprocating engine that powered both the Flowers and Rivers, though with improved, water-tube boilers.

Maturing rather late in the war, the Castle programme was drastically curtailed, only 39 being completed as corvettes. Fifteen from British yards were cancelled, as were all thirty-six ordered from Canadian yards. Twelve British-built Castles were transferred to Canada, and one to the Norwegian flag.

ABOVE: ***Hadleigh Castle* as a new ship in late 1943. The single Squid, on the platform forward of the bridge, is not obvious. Although few depth charges needed to be carried, she had a wide, uncluttered afterdeck.**

Castle class

Displacement: 1,080 tons (standard); 1,580 tons (full load)
Length: 68.6m/225ft (bp); 76.9m/252ft (oa)
Beam: 11.1m/36ft 6in
Draught: 4.1m/13ft 6in (mean)
Armament: 1 x 4in gun; 1 x 3-barrelled Squid AS mortar
Machinery: 1 x 4-cylinder triple-expansion, steam-reciprocating engine, 2 boilers, 1 shaft
Power: 2,051kW/2,750ihp for 16.5 knots
Endurance: 480 tons oil for 11,480km/6,200nm at 15 knots
Protection: Nominal
Complement: 100

ABOVE LEFT: **This picture of *Loch Killisport* shows that only a single 4in gun is carried, located on a bandstand. There is no director, but a quadruple 2pdr pompom is sited aft.** ABOVE: **For philatelic artwork, this rendering of *St. Austell Bay* is surprisingly accurate. It indicates well the crank level with the bridge at the commencement of the straight line sheer. Lapped plates are, however, shown where the hull was, in fact, all-welded.** LEFT: **The Bays were AA variants of the Lochs. As can be seen here on *Mounts Bay*, the double Squid was suppressed in favour of a Hedgehog in "A" position. Two twin 4in guns are carried, together with full director control and Type 293 radar.**

Loch and Bay classes

The Rivers confirmed the optimum size for a North Atlantic escort, but there continued to exist the urgent need for numbers. These could be produced only by redesigning for construction from prefabricated modules, fitted out to rigidly standard specification. The resulting Loch-class frigates thus comprised large numbers of elements, none heavier than 3 tons, produced by non-shipbuilding concerns and transported to dedicated assembly and fitting-out facilities. Complex curvature was avoided, the result retaining River-class characteristics but with greater sheer and flare forward.

Larger, of course, than a Castle (to which there was a distinct resemblance), a Loch could accommodate a double Squid in the elevated "B" position. The associated Asdic, which made the system so deadly, was situated adjacently, in an office extending from the bridge front. As the depth charge outfit was, again, much reduced, it left adequate space aft for the first crude countermeasures ("Foxers"), designed to meet the threat of the acoustic torpedoes with which U-boats were now targeting convoy escorts specifically.

Only one 4in gun was carried, on a bandstand where it could be depressed easily to engage very close-range targets. The after centreline position was occupied by a quadruple 2pdr pompom with an excellent field of fire.

By the time that the first-of-class, *Loch Fada*, was completed at the end of 1943, the conventional U-boat was a spent force. Only 31 hulls were, therefore, completed as Lochs but, despite their limited numbers, they still accounted for 16 of the enemy.

With emphasis shifting to Pacific operations, the next 19 hulls were completed as Bay-class AA escorts, with Squids suppressed in favour of a Hedgehog, but with a twin 4in mounting at either end and two sided twin 40mm Bofors. These proved their worth during the Korean War, which involved considerable bombardment details.

Loch class, as built

Displacement: 1,430 tons (standard); 2,260 tons (full load)
Length: 87.2m/286ft (bp); 93.7m/307ft 4in (oa)
Beam: 11.7m/38ft 6in
Draught: 3.8m/12ft 4in (mean)
Armament: 1 x 4in gun; 1 x quadruple 2pdr pompom; 2 x 3-barrelled Squid AS mortars
Machinery: 2 x 4-cylinder triple-expansion, steam-reciprocating engines, 2 boilers, 2 shafts
Power: 4,103kW/5,500ihp for 19.5 knots
Endurance: 725 tons oil for 12,965km/7,000nm at 15 knots
Protection: Nominal
Complement: 114

ABOVE: **Six surplus Lochs were acquired by the Royal New Zealand Navy in 1948. Here, a pristine *Rotoiti* retains her original Royal Navy pendant number as *Loch Katrine*. Post-war, all frigates took an "F" flag superior.**

Types 15 and 16

Although the German fast submarine programme was delayed sufficiently for it to have little effect on World War II, the Soviet Union's acquisition and exploitation of the associated technology posed a new threat, the more real with the outbreak of the Korean War. Faced again with the prospect of general war, the Royal Navy needed a new generation of escort, fast enough to deal with high-speed submarines. Funds, however, were sufficient only for the conversion of war-built fleet destroyers to "fast AS frigates".

Full conversions, eventually numbering 23, were known as Type 15s, the programme running from 1949 to 1956. Remodelling was very thorough, the selected hulls being razed to upper-deck level. To tolerate the requirement of being driven into a head sea at 25 knots, the bow section was stiffened and the forecastle extended to over 80 per cent aft. At its after end were two staggered pockets housing Squid AS mortars, later replaced by Limbos.

ABOVE: **AS high-speed convoy escorts, the Type 15s were designed to co-operate with aircraft in countering the fast submarine. *Wakeful* here, has the full standard outfit. Note how the line of the original destroyer hull can be clearly discerned.**
LEFT: **An ice-dusted *Virago* is seen in the Arctic during the 1950s. The conditions point to the weakness of having the wheelhouse set so low. A double Squid and twin 4in guns were located aft, with only a twin 40mm gun forward.**

The Bikini A-bomb trials had highlighted the effect of nuclear blast, so superstructure was restricted to just one level above the forecastle deck. All needed to be enclosed, causing bridge personnel difficulties in navigation.

Cleared of all except anchor gear, foredecks were given two breakwaters and a curved bridge front. Armament was reduced to a twin 4in mounting aft and a twin 40mm Bofors atop the bridge. Ships were fitted for, rarely with, up to eight sided tubes for homing torpedoes. Much of the new topside structure was in aluminium alloy. The original machinery and funnel were retained.

Less thoroughly rebuilt were the ten Type 16s. These had higher, frigate-style bridges and a twin 4in in "B" position. Their forecastles were not extended, the original forward set of tubes being retained for AS torpedoes. Two Squids were located aft.

ABOVE: **The Type 16 limited conversions were just that. The ships retained their destroyer-like characteristics being able, as this picture of *Termagent* shows, even to remount their torpedo tubes. Gun armament has, however, been drastically reduced, the after deckhouse accommodating a Double Squid.**

U-class destroyer, as Type 15 AS frigate

Displacement: 2,200 tons (standard); 2,700 tons (full load)
Length: 103.5m/339ft 6in (bp); 110.6m/362ft 9in (oa)
Beam: 10.9m/35ft 9in
Draught: 4.9m/16ft
Armament: 2 x 4in guns (1x2); 2 x 3-barrelled Limbo AS mortars; 8 x heavyweight (8x1) or 6 x lightweight (2x3) AS torpedo tubes
Machinery: Geared steam turbines, 2 boilers, 2 shafts
Power: 29,840kW/40,000shp for 36.5 knots
Endurance: 585 tons for 5,370km/2,900nm at 20 knots
Protection: Nominal
Complement: 185

LEFT: **Termed "Second Rate" frigates to differentiate them from such as the big Type 12s, the Type 14s (or Blackwoods*)* were really an updated and (relatively) cheap corvette. Despite single screw and rudder, *Hardy* shows her manoeuvring qualities.** ABOVE: **The Type 14s were often criticized for being under-armed and, as this picture of *Duncan* shows, there was little to see beyond the two Limbo mortars. Disposal of a damaged, surfaced submarine would have been a problem.**

Type 14

Budgets boosted by the threat posed by the Korean War, the Royal Navy embarked on a relatively ambitious frigate building programme during the 1950s. To the "de luxe", but stop-gap, Type 15/16s needed to be added a simple convoy AS escort, capable of being produced in quantity in emergency. Earlier, the Type 14 or Blackwood, would have been called a "corvette"; in new terminology, it was classed a Second-Rate Frigate.

Designed to a cost limit, the Type 14 was the smallest that could accommodate a double Limbo and full sonar outfit, while being large and fast enough to deploy them effectively against a 17-knot (submerged) submarine. The result looked, and was, utilitarian.

A raised forecastle extended 50 per cent of her length, topped by a full-width house upon which was set the diminutive bridge. This arrangement resulted in a two-level transition to the bridge deck, which made the after end appear to lack freeboard. A single, vertical funnel served to two boilers of the half-frigate propulsion plant. For compactness, diesel engines were considered, but rejected on cost grounds. There was a single shaft and rudder.

The two Limbos, which occupied the after end, were protected by bulwarks and deckhouse, but wetness was such that an overhead catwalk connected after superstructure and forecastle, while a solid bulwark was provided right forward. Anchors were recessed.

Controversially, the Type 14s did not carry a medium-calibre gun. Submarines forced to the surface would thus need to be finished by torpedo, for which paired tubes, unusually of large calibre, were sided in the waist.

Although only 12 of a planned 23 were built, they were deemed successful although, by today's standards, service aboard was spartan. Fine-lined and fast, if somewhat fragile, they made their mark in fishery protection.

LEFT: **In the late 1960s, *Exmouth* was converted into a trials ship for gas turbine propulsion. One sprint Olympus and two cruise Proteus were installed COGOG fashion. Note how the ducting dominated the topsides of so small a ship.**

Type 14, as designed

Displacement: 1,100 tons (standard); 1,460 tons (full load)
Length: 91.5m/300ft (bp); 94.6m/310ft (oa)
Beam: 10.1m/33ft
Draught: 3.1m/10ft
Armament: 3 x 40mm guns (3x1); 2 x 3-barrelled Limbo AS mortars; 4 x 21in AS torpedo tubes (2x2)
Machinery: Geared steam turbines, 2 boilers, 1 shaft
Power: 11,190kW/15,000shp for 24.5 knots
Endurance: 260 tons oil for 8,335km/4,500nm at 12 knots
Protection: None
Complement: 111

LEFT: **Types 41 and 61 shared a common hull, being fitted out either for anti-aircraft (Type 41) or aircraft-direction duties. Designed for convoy duties, both were diesel-propelled. *Salisbury*, a Type 61, shows her comprehensive electronics fit.**

Types 41 and 61

Even with the end of hostilities in 1945, the defence of trade, specifically convoys, still loomed large with the Admiralty Board. The dual-function Loch/Bay programme had impressed, producing numerous hulls quickly and relatively cheaply. They had, however, already been rendered obsolete by the arrival of the fast submarine and jet aircraft. ASW would need to be addressed by faster ships, but the Board also required a hull that could be fitted out for AAW or for the control of carrier-borne or shore-based aircraft. As both of these functions were aimed primarily at the defence of convoys, a 25-knot maximum speed would suffice, with emphasis being placed instead on endurance and good seakeeping.

Endurance was conferred with diesel propulsion. Three machinery spaces accommodated no less than ten engines, four of which could be coupled to each of two shafts. The remaining pair powered generators.

A high-freeboard hull took the forecastle deck right aft to a point just forward of a short quarterdeck. Forward of the break was a pocket containing a single Squid. The chosen medium-calibre weapon was the new Mk VI twin 4.5in gun. The size and weight of this mounting resulted in the unusually cranked forward sheerline. This gave the required freeboard while lowering the weight of the gunhouse in relation to the hull for stability purposes. It also allowed the personnel in the new-style, low-level bridge to see over it. There were no conventional funnels, the diesel exhausts led up the inside of the lattice masts.

Only four of each type were built for the Royal Navy. The AAW version (Type 41/Leopard class) was roll-stabilized with two twin 4.5in guns. The AD (Aircraft-Direction Type 61/Salisbury class) had half the firepower but an impressive array of electronics, later extensively modernized.

LEFT: **This is the Type 41 *Puma*, as completed, with a second twin 4.5in gunhouse aft. The mainmast was later plated-in to support a single 965 radar. Note the "two ball" daymark to indicate that she is engaged in towage.**

Type 41

Displacement: 2,225 tons (standard); 2,525 tons (full load)
Length: 100.7m/330ft (wl); 103.7m/339ft 11in (oa)
Beam: 12.2m/40ft
Draught: 3.3m/10ft 10in (mean)
Armament: 4 x 4.5in guns (2x2); 1 x 3-barrelled Squid AS mortar
Machinery: 8 diesel engines, 2 shafts
Power: 11,190kW/15,000bhp for 23 knots
Endurance: 230 tons fuel for 8,335km/4,500nm at 15 knots
Protection: Nominal
Complement: 221

INSET RIGHT: **Built as essentially general-purpose frigates, the Leanders were also given major conversions for specialization in either surface or AS warfare. Here, *Penelope* of the former group shows Exocets and a shrouded Sea Wolf launcher.** RIGHT: **The basic Leander design, an Improved Type 12, sold well for export. Here, the Royal New Zealand Navy's *Wellington* prepares to refuel from the replenishment tanker *Endeavour*. Note her sister *Canterbury* in the background.**

Type 12/Leander class

To run alongside the Types 41/61 frigates, a new ASW ship was required, fast enough to counter the expected Soviet HTP (High Test Peroxide) closed-cycle submarines. The best compromise was the 28-knot Type 12, essentially a similar hull form, but with an extended and fine-sectioned bow. Steam-driven with a standardized and compact machinery outfit, these required a conventional funnel, initially thin and vertical, later, and less successfully, larger.

Excellent Sonar was teamed with two Limbos, located in a deep pocket where the long forecastle terminated, well aft. Sided in the waist were, initially, no less than 12 heavyweight AS torpedo tubes but, with the failure of the weapon itself, these were replaced by tripled small-calibre tubes, not always carried.

From 1966 the Wasp helicopter became the delivery platform for highspeed, stand-off reaction to submerged contacts. The Type 12's forward Limbo was landed and part of the well decked-over to provide a flight deck. The after superstructure was converted to a hangar and topped with the four-rail Sea Cat point-defence SAM, a not-too successful replacement for the 40mm Bofors.

The Improved Type 12, or Leander, class used the same hull form (later units were given 61cm/2ft more beam) and machinery. Full freeboard extended right aft, but with a transom notch for VDS. A solid, compact superstructure had plated-in masts, the mainmast supporting a "single bedstead" of the Type 965 air warning radar. A small helicopter, Sea Cat and a single Limbo were incorporated from the outset.

Of the twenty-six Leanders built for the Royal Navy, eight were later converted to deploy the Australian Ikara stand-off AS missile. Seven more were remodelled around the MM38 Exocet SSM, with a further five taking both Exocet and the Sea Wolf point-defence SAM.

Magnificent seaboats, the Leanders also sold well abroad.

ABOVE: **An early Type 12, *Scarborough*, with the original small funnel. To minimize the effects of nuclear blast, the upperworks were deliberately made very low. The long, high-freeboard bow design made them magnificent seaboats. She is seen at Malta with an American Coontz-class DDG.**

Leander class, as designed

Displacement: 2,305 tons (standard); 2,875 tons (full load)
Length: 109.8m/360ft (wl); 112.9m/370ft (oa)
Beam: 12.5m/41ft
Draught: 4.1m/13ft 4in (mean)
Armament: 2 x 4.5in guns (1x2); 2 x Sea Cat 4-rail SAM launchers; 6 x 325mm AS torpedo tubes (2x3)
Machinery: Geared steam turbines, 2 boilers, 2 shafts
Power: 22,380kW/30,000shp for 28 knots
Endurance: 480 tons oil for 8,335km/4,500nm at 12 knots
Protection: Nominal
Complement: 258

Type 21

The Admiralty's own resources being at full stretch, Vosper-Thornycroft's gas turbine Mark 5 frigates, built for Iran, were made the starting point for the new Type 21, intended as a replacement for the aging Types 41 and 61 and, possibly as a follow-on to the Leanders. The Admiralty Board was convinced that it could thus acquire a cheaper, but equally capable, ship. It couldn't, but the reduced complement resulting from gas-turbine propulsion certainly effected a real through-life saving.

Two Olympus engines were supplied for sprint speeds, and two Tynes for cruising. Even derated, the former delivered power for an unusually high speed of 30 knots. The forward end, otherwise conventional, was thus given a pronounced knuckle to throw water clear, while the anchors were set high and in pockets.

Rakish rather than handsome, the Type 21s had a full-width superstructure deck which dropped to a broad-transomed afterdeck, giving relatively generous space for a small helicopter. Much of the superstructure was of load-bearing aluminium alloy which, in service, proved liable to fatigue cracking, weakening the hull girder.

Forward was a single 4.5in gun of the new fully automatic Mk VIII design. Superfiring it, on most of the eight ships, were four MM38 Exocet SSM launchers. On the hangar roof was a quadruple Sea Cat SAM launcher. The primary ASW system was the Lynx helicopter, capable of carrying a limited combination of weapons, sensors and datalink. It was supported by its ship's sonar and two sets of AS torpedo tubes.

A single, plated-in mast was located amidships and the after superstructure was dominated by the single large funnel and its associated downtakes. Accommodations were spacious, adding to the ships' popularity.

The design proved to have little margin for updating, and all six survivors were sold to Pakistan in 1993–94.

ABOVE: **Safeguarding vital tanker traffic during the Iran–Iraq War was but one of the Royal Navy's duties, discharged here by *Active*. The controversial industry-designed Type 21s were the first British all-gas turbine frigates.**

LEFT: **The class lead ship, *Amazon*, replenishes at sea. Four Exocets superfire the forward 4.5in gun, and the Sea Cat mounting is visible aft. All structure above upper deck level was of aluminium alloy, the hull requiring subsequent stiffening.**

Type 21, as designed

Displacement: 2,750 tons (standard); 3,250 tons (full load)
Length: 109.8m/360ft (wl); 117.1m/384ft (oa)
Beam: 12.7m/41ft 8in
Draught: 5.9m/19ft 6in (maximum)
Armament: 1 x 4.5in gun; 4 x Exocet MM38 SSMs (4x1); 1 x quadruple Sea Cat SAM; 6 x 325mm AS torpedo tubes (2x3)
Machinery: 2 Olympus and 2 Tyne gas turbines, 2 shafts
Power: 37,300kW/50,000shp for 30 knots
Endurance: 7,410km/4,000nm at 17 knots
Protection: Nominal
Complement: 175

LEFT: **One of the Batch I Type 22s, *Brazen*'s dimensions were limited by home dockyard covered facilities. Designed as successors to the Leanders, they were gas-turbine driven and carried fewer crew members, but were considerably larger.** BELOW: **Built as a replacement for Falklands War losses, *London* was a Batch II ship whose major differences, besides upgraded electronics, were a remodelled bow section to accommodate improved sonar, and facilities for a larger helicopter. Note the lack of a gun.**

Type 22

Originally as Anglo-Dutch project, from which the Dutch withdrew, the Type 22 was intended as close escort for high-value vessels. The hull was designed around the two 45.8x3.1m/150x10ft arrays of the Type 2016 sonar, one of which was located on either side of the keel. The primary AS weapons delivery system was the helicopter (one/two Lynx or one Sea King), backed by shipboard AS torpedo tubes.

At either end was a Sea Wolf point-defence SAM system, capable of engaging incoming missiles as well as aircraft. There was no space for a medium-calibre gun but four MM38 Exocets were located forward.

Two Olympus and two Tyne gas turbines were again arranged COGOG fashion, exhausting through a single funnel of considerable dimensions.

Only four of these "Batch I" units were built before it was decided to significantly upgrade capability by adding both towed array and new (Type 2015) bow-mounted Sonars. The former required a widened transom, enabling helicopter facilities to be extended, possibly for the future Merlin. The bow Sonar dictated a heavily raked bow profile and stem anchor.

Electronic Counter and Support Measures (ECM/ESM) were also greatly improved. The machinery fit was changed to a more economic pair of Spey gas turbines for sprint with two Tynes retained for cruising. Termed "Batch IIs", six were built.

Following the loss of two Type 42s and two Type 21s during the Falklands War, four further Type 22s were built as replacements. These, known as "Batch IIIs", added a 4.5in gun (found indispensable in the shore support role) and Harpoon SSMs in place of Exocets. These were relocated amidships.

Only the Batch IIIs remain in the Royal Navy. The four Batch Is were sold to Brazil and two Batch IIs each to Chile and Romania. One has been scrapped and one expended as a target.

ABOVE: **Sharing a common hull form with the Batch IIs, the Batch III *Cornwall* has been given a 4.5in gun. Exocets have been replaced by Harpoon, relocated abaft the bridge and thus releasing valuable space on the foredeck. The carrier is the American CVN.74 *John C. Stennis*.**

Type 22, Batch III

Displacement: 4,280 tons (standard); 4,850 tons (full load)
Length: 135.7m/445ft 4in (bp); 148.1m/486ft 2in (oa)
Beam: 14.8m/48ft 5in
Draught: 6.4m/21ft (max)
Armament: 1 x 4.5in gun; 8 x Harpoon SSM (2x4); 2 x sextuple Sea Wolf SAM; 1 x 30mm Goalkeeper CIWS; 6 x 325mm AS torpedo tubes (2x3)
Machinery: 2 Spey and 2 Tyne gas turbines (COGOG), 2 shafts
Power: 35,957kW/48,200shp for 30 knots.
Endurance: 700 tons fuel for 12,965km/7,000nm at 18 knots
Protection: Nominal
Complement: 232

LEFT: **Designed for quiet operation, the Type 23 is driven by electric motors coupled directly to the shafts, eliminating gearing. Power for the motors is generated by separate vibration-isolated units. This is *Northumberland.*** ABOVE: **The class lead ship, *Norfolk*, on builders' trials, and wearing Red Ensign and Yarrow's flag. Forward, she has a 4.5in gun, a VLS for Sea Wolf SAM and eight Harpoon SSMs, the latter missing on the *Northumberland* (left).**

Type 23

The Type 23 began as an austere vessel, designed around the major task of deploying a passive towed array sonar for sustained periods. Such has been the pace of the Royal Navy's retrenchment, however, that the design grew into a full-specification frigate, necessarily filling the gap left by Leander disposals. Size and cost escalation nonetheless demanded that, where there were 26 Leanders, there were but 16 Type 23s. These were launched over a 13-year period, with early units being sold abroad just five years after the last ones hit the water.

The remainder are capable, multi-purpose frigates whose subtle, signature-reducing features have resulted in an appearance both pleasing and business-like. Their major combat system is the Merlin ASW helicopter, whose size demands a generously dimensioned flight pad, from beneath which the towed array is streamed. Anti-submarine torpedo tubes are carried, as is an active, bow-mounted sonar.

The single 4.5in dual-purpose gun forward is backed by eight Harpoon SSMs, sited forward of the bridge. Between is the Vertical-Launch System (VLS) containing 32 Sea Wolf point-defence SAMs, whose all-round control is exercised by directors both forward and aft. Two 30mm cannon flank the structure forward of the large, angular funnel, which is wider than it is long.

Two Spey gas turbines drive generators to provide the power for the electric propulsion motors built around the shafts. Emergency, get-you-home power may also be diverted from the ships' four diesel generators. Because the electric propulsion units may be reversed, variable-pitch propellers are not necessary, their fixed-pitch alternatives being optimized to run most quietly over the ships' most sensitive speed range. The final ten of the class have a 25 per cent greater propulsion power, increasing speed by possibly 2 knots. Every effort has been made to minimize crew strength.

ABOVE: **Type 23s have a much-reduced radar signature, even to giving the hull a flare over its full length. *Lancaster* has the well-tried Mk VIII 4.5in gun, but all will receive the new Mod. 1 version with the "radar-reduced" angular shield. These will be issued to all units as they come to major refit.**

Final ten of Type 23 class 

Displacement: 3,600 tons (standard); 4,300 tons (full load)
Length: 123m/403ft 9in (bp); 133m/436ft 7in (oa)
Beam: 15m/49ft 3in
Draught: 5.5m/18ft 1in (maximum)
Armament: 1 x 4.5in gun; 8 x Harpoon SSM (2x4); 1 x 32-cell Sea Wolf SAM VLS; 6 x 325mm AS torpedo tubes (2x3)
Machinery: 2 Spey gas turbine/generators driving electric propulsion motors, 2 shafts
Power: 39,015kW/52,300shp for 30 knots
Endurance: 800 tons fuel for 14,445km/7,800nm at 17 knots
Protection: Nominal
Complement: 185

LEFT: **During the course of their careers, the E50s and E52s underwent so many modifications that they became difficult to differentiate. *Le Corse*, here, shows the E50s' early "trademark" of four triple AS torpedo tubes forward.**

Le Corse and Le Normand classes

Much of a size with the British-sourced River-class frigates that they superseded, these were the first significant post-war classes built by the French with funding supplied partially by the Americans under their Mutual Defence Assistance Programme.

The four le Corse (E50) types and the 14 le Normands (E52) had a common hull and machinery fit, differing only in their armament disposition. Both types were classified "fast escorts" and carried both AA and AS outfits of considerable potency for the size of ship.

Their hulls were flush-decked, with pronounced forward sheer, a form possibly influenced by the ex-American Destroyer Escorts (DEs) which were also still serving under French colours. In line with the then-current assumptions on the likelihood of nuclear exchanges, neither the monolithic bridge structure nor the hulls were pierced for scuttles.

Besides a quadruple or sextuple mortar (two in the E50s) the major AS weapons resided in four triple torpedo tube mountings. In the E50s, these were all forward of the bridge at 01 level, backing on to structures containing reloads. The E52s carried theirs in a more orthodox arrangement, sided in the waist. This created space for a forward-mounted mortar.

Both classes carried three twin 57mm dual-purpose gun mountings, one forward and two in superfiring arrangement aft. Steam turbine propulsion gave a good turn of speed, and the taller, prominently capped funnel located close to the mast differentiated them immediately from Commandant Rivière-class frigates with which they could be confused.

During 20 years of service, individual units began to differ widely in detail, *le Brestois* for instance acting as trials ship for the single 100mm gun that went on to be widely adopted in French warships, and *l'Agenais* trialling a large VDS installation in lieu of the after guns.

By 1981, none of either class remained on the active list.

ABOVE: ***Le Picard* was an E52, this photograph showing clearly that the four triple AS torpedo tubes are located in more protected positions, sided in the after waist. Note the sextuple AS launcher forward. The 57mm armament was effective only against aircraft.**

E52 type, as built

Displacement: 1,295 tons (standard); 1,795 tons (full load)
Length: 95m/311ft 10in (bp); 99.3m/325ft 11in (oa)
Beam: 10.3m/33ft 10in
Draught: 4.1m/13ft 6in (maximum)
Armament: 6 x 57mm guns (3x2); 1 x 4- or 6-barrelled 305mm AS mortar; 12 x AS torpedo tubes (4x3)
Machinery: Geared steam turbines, 2 boilers, 2 shafts
Power: 14,920kW/20,000shp for 28.5 knots
Endurance: 310 tons oil for 8,335km/4,500nm at 12 knots
Protection: Nominal
Complement: 175

FAR LEFT: **The *Commandant Rivière* class followed the E52s quickly and, while only slightly larger, differed considerably. The dual-purpose 100mm guns were effective against aircraft and surface craft, while diesel propulsion conferred greater range.** ABOVE: **During the early 1970s, the *Balny* acted as the trials ship for gas turbine propulsion. Although echoing *Exmouth*'s role in the Royal Navy, she had a gas turbine and diesel (COGAD) arrangement as opposed to the British ship's COGOG.**

Commandant Rivière class

Specialist in series small-ship production, Lorient naval dockyard, which had built eight of the E50/52s, went on to construct all nine of the Commandant Rivière-type follow-ons.

The later ships were to act in peace time as "avisos", station ships in the still-numerous French colonies. In this sense, they were the lineal descendants of the colonial cruisers, the sailing corvettes of a different era.

For the sake of required speed, the E50/52s were relatively fine, while their pronounced forward sheer would have translated somewhat uncomfortably to the accommodation deck below. The Rivières' hull was made about 4m/13ft 2in longer but proportionately more beamy. Unlike that of the preceding class, the deckhouse extended to the ships' sides, the foredock accommodating a 100mm gun. The extra space was required to transport and support up to 80 troops, for whom two small Landing Craft, Personnel (LCP) could be carried under davits.

Essential to colonial duty was extended endurance and reliability. For this reason, they were powered by four medium-speed diesel engines. These were coupled two to a shaft, making it possible to run with any combination of one to four units. Any could thus be taken off-line for routine maintenance while, together, they could power the ships for 25.5 knots, sufficient for them to act as useful escorts in wartime.

The *Commandant Bory* and *Balny* performed the same role as the *Exmouth* of the Royal Navy in being trials platforms for gas turbine propulsion. Work concluded, they were refitted with standard diesel units.

As built, the Rivières had three of the new 100mm guns, in single, automatic, enclosed mountings, in place of the earlier ships' twin 57mm mountings. From the late 1970s most exchanged "X" gun for four MM38 Exocet SSMs. An enclosed quadruple AS mortar occupied "B" position. The class was scrapped during 1988–92.

MIDDLE: ***Doudart de Lagrée* at her full 25-knot speed. Note the "X" gun replaced by four Exocets, the French-built quadruple AS mortar and reload facility in "B" position, and the triple AS torpedo tubes sided abaft the funnel.** ABOVE: **Oblique lighting picks out the effects of years of stress on the hull of *Enseigne de Vaisseau Henry.* The large full-width deckhouse allows the carriage of an 80-man marine unit or, in their absence, spacious accommodation, welcome on what frequently acted as station ships.**

Commandant Rivière class, as designed

Displacement: 1,750 tons (standard); 2,250 tons (full load)
Length: 98m/321ft 8in (bp); 103.7m/340ft 4in (oa)
Beam: 11.6m/38ft 1in
Draught: 4.6m/15ft 2in (maximum)
Armament: 3 x 100mm guns (3x1); 1 x 4-barrelled 305mm AS mortar; 6 x AS torpedo tubes (2x3)
Machinery: 4 diesel engines, 2 shafts
Power: 11,936kW/16,000bhp for 25.5 knots
Endurance: 210 tons for 13,890km/7,500nm at 16 knots
Protection: Nominal
Complement: 166

LEFT: **A one-off, the *Aconit* was very unusual for a ship of her size in having single-shaft propulsion. In this early picture she mounts an AS projector forward of the bridge and Malafon (not visible) amidships.**

Aconit

Her original status indicated by her name, one of the British-built Flower-class corvettes manned by Free French crews, the *Aconit* nonetheless carried full frigate capability, indicated by an "F" identifier. Despite her single shaft and anti-submarine configuration, however, she looked more like a destroyer, and soon adopted a "D" flag superior. Her task was, primarily, to act as a trials platform for the larger Tourville-class destroyers then building.

Aconit's hull was flush-decked, dropping one level to a short afterdeck, whereon was accommodated the large winch/towfish assembly of the DUBV 43 Variable Depth Sonar (VDS). The bows showed the pronounced overhang associated with a large bow sonar, also incorporating the flattened sheerline that enabled the forward gun to work at slight depression for close ranges.

She was the first to be designed around the Malafon AS stand-off system, following its satisfactory trials in the converted destroyer *La Galissonnière*. Destined for the new Tourville and Suffren classes, Malafon was a small, rocket-propelled, aerodynamic vehicle that could release a homing torpedo on coordinates determined by the ship's sonars.

For self-defence, *Aconit* had launchers for AS torpedoes and, forward of the bridge, an enclosed quadruple AS mortar. The latter was removed during the early 1980s in favour of eight updated MM40 Exocet SSMs, grouped in two quadruple protective boxes.

Although lacking an AA missile system, the *Aconit* was dominated by the large tower and dome associated with the DRBV 13 (later DRBV 15) surveillance radar, and the antenna of the DRBV 22A targeting radar on the lattice mast on the after superstructure.

Being steam propelled, *Aconit* had a conventional funnel although, in order to conserve centreline deck space, this had to support a lofty, and complex foremast, an ungainly arrangement.

Along with the Malafon system itself, the *Aconit* was retired in the mid-1990s, her name being quickly reassigned to a La Fayette-class frigate, perpetuating a unique Anglo-French naval link.

LEFT: **With modernization during 1984–85, the *Aconit* had eight MM40 Exocets fitted, visible here inside protective boxes. Malafon remained as there was no helicopter, but a new VDS and passive towed array were installed aft.**

Aconit, as built

Displacement: 3,500 tons (standard); 3,840 tons (full load)
Length: 127m/416ft 10in (oa)
Beam: 13.4m/44ft
Draught: 5.5m/18ft 1in (maximum)
Armament: 2 x 100mm guns (2x1); 1 x Malafon AS stand-off system; 1 x quadruple 305mm AS mortar; 2 x launchers for AS torpedoes
Machinery: Geared steam turbines, 2 boilers, 1 shaft
Power: 21,373kW/28,650shp for 27 knots
Endurance: 9,260km/5,000nm at 18 knots
Protection: Nominal
Complement: 255

D'Estienne d'Orves class

Although twin-screwed and carrying "F" pendants, the d'Estienne d'Orves, or A69, class are strictly corvettes, designed for inshore AS operations. They began to commission in 1976 as the first E50/52s reached about 21 years of age and, thereafter, replaced them on a near one-for-one basis. Considerably smaller, however, they are also less capable, their design being strongly driven by the requirement for economical operation. Through-life costs have been reduced considerably by their diesel propulsion and a crew of only 100. Classed as "avisos", their lack of size has, nevertheless, been a drawback in that their additional full 18-man military detachment apparently cannot, in practice, be supported.

Compact little ships, their single 100mm gun looks disproportionately large. The low bridge structure is integral with a long, full-width deckhouse. Not having space for a helicopter, their AS capability is, by current standards, weak. Four fixed AS torpedo tubes are built into the after superstructure, but the quadruple AS mortar on top has now been removed in favour of light AA missiles, either the capable Crotale or the much lighter, two-rail Simbad. Only one, hull-mounted sonar is fitted.

Originally termed A70s, some units were fitted with two MM38 Exocets. This variant disappeared as all were gradually fitted for, but not always with, two of the later MM40s which would, however, require a third party in order to realize their full over-the-horizon potential. This greater emphasis on light escort ("*frégate légère*") function is underlined by the addition of defensive anti-missile and anti-torpedo decoy systems.

TOP: **An early picture of *d'Estienne d'Orves*, lead ship of an excellent class of twin-screw corvette. The 100mm gun was standard throughout the French Navy and was a useful yardstick in estimating a ship's size.** ABOVE: **Unusually carrying no pendant number, the nameship here looks more weatherworn and retains her short funnel. Note the caps of the AS torpedo tubes in the after deckhouse, atop which is a sextuple Bofors-pattern AS rocket launcher.**

Ordered originally by South Africa, two more units were purchased by Argentina, which then built a third. Seven have now been retired and one transferred to Turkey. All of the remainder are due to be paid off by 2016.

ABOVE: **During Operation "Desert Shield" in 1990, the *Commandant Ducuing* is seen with the later raised funnel and mast. She lays alongside repair ship *Jules Verne*, with a Durance AOR beyond (right) and Clemenceau carrier (left). In Gulf conditions, large-ship facilities are welcome to small-ship crews.**

A69, as built

Displacement: 1,050 tons (standard); 1,250 tons (full load)
Length: 76m/249ft 6in (bp); 80m/262ft 7in (oa)
Beam: 10.3m/33ft 10in
Draught: 5.3m/17ft 4in (maximum)
Armament: 1 x 100mm gun; 1 x quadruple/sextuple AS mortar; 4 x fixed AS torpedo tubes
Machinery: 2 diesel engines, 2 shafts
Power: 8,335kW/12,000bhp for 23 knots
Endurance: 8,280km/4,500nm at 15 knots
Protection: Nominal
Complement: 100

LEFT: **Larger and more comfortable for lengthy seatime than the d'Estienne d'Orves type, the Floréal-class corvettes are designed more as offshore patrol vessels. The Moroccan *Mohammed V* was one of two built to a reduced export specification.** ABOVE: **Here, the Moroccan *Mohammed V* is led by her sister the *Hassan II*. In armament and electronics, they have a lower capability than the French Floréals but are similar otherwise. Note the 76mm guns and rather dated WM-25 fire control.**

Floréal class

With ever-fewer front-line warships available, their use can no longer be justified for low-risk duties such as fishery protection or colonial policing. Rather limited as "avisos", the A69s were more useful as escorts in the Mediterranean. The Floréals, which effectively replaced them in patrolling the overseas territories, were built more cheaply to mercantile standards, constructed at St. Nazaire but fitted with their military equipment in the Lorient naval dockyard. Named after months of the New Revolutionary Calendar, all were commissioned in 1992–94.

In length, the Floréals are pitched between the A69s and the E50/52s that preceded them in colonial duties. Being designed for only 20 knots, however, they are relatively beamy (L/B 6.09 compared with the 23-knot A69's 7.38 and the 26-knot E50's 8.31), with a capacious hull. This allows the A69's major shortcomings to be addressed. Up to 24 military personnel may be carried, along with an LCP under davits. Where smaller, utility helicopters are usually deployed, the hangar has the capacity to accommodate either an AS.332 Super Puma transport helicopter or, if required, an NH-90 AS machine. The ships are not fitted with sonar or AS weapons but can carry two MM38 Exocets and a Simbad/Mistral SAM system.

The aircraft hangar runs forward between the sided uptakes which have mercantile-style tops. The hull is flush-decked, a form much disguised by the long, full-width "centre-castle". This terminates short of the stern, suggesting that, in emergency, the ships could be fitted with a large towed array passive Sonar for surveillance purposes. Forward, the rather limited freeboard is compensated by a pronounced flare. Active stabilizers reduce ship motion.

All six carry a single 100mm automatic gun with optronic fire control. They are fitted to ship two MM38 Exocets and/or one Simbad/Mistral point-defence SAM mounting.

ABOVE: **"Regular" Floréals carry a 100mm gun, more modern electronics and are fitted for, but not necessarily with, two Exocet SSMs. Their considerable internal space results in a bulky hull that gives the effect of low-freeboard bows. This is *Prairial*, the "month of meadows" and ninth in the New Calendar.**

Floréal class, as built

Displacement: 2,600 tons (standard); 2,950 tons (full load)
Length: 85.2m/279ft 8in (bp); 93.5m/306ft 11in (oa)
Beam: 14m/45ft 11in
Draught: 4.4m/14ft 5in
Armament: 1 x 100mm gun; 2 x MM38 Exocet SSM; 1 x twin-rail Simbad SAM
Machinery: 4 diesel engines, 2 shafts
Power: 6,565kW/8,800shp for 20 knots
Endurance: 390 tons fuel for 18,520km/10,000nm at 15 knots
Protection: Nominal
Complement: 83

LEFT: **Lead ship of the class, *la Fayette* has lowered shutters covering the mooring ports forward. The boat aperture may also be screened. A pair of Exocets are visible amidships and, to their left, the launcher for the Crotale point-defence SAM.**
ABOVE: **The latest of many French warships to bear the name *Surcouf* is seen in the Gulf in 2002, serving as part of a multinational force. Note how the hull and upperworks are not pierced with scuttles, and also the newly profiled 100mm gunhouse.**

La Fayette class

Although much of a size with a British Type 42, a la Fayette appears somewhat smaller by virtue of her radically different appearance and lack of detail. There had been a growing trend toward inclining surfaces in order to reduce radar return, particularly to defeat the active homing radar of anti-ship missiles. The la Fayettes took the concept a stage further, with an outer shell configured to screen all the many minor protuberances that, collectively, define a ship's radar signature. Their hulls have a continuous flare and the extensive inclined planes of the superstructure are fabricated from a radar-absorbent sandwich. All apertures, such as those for access, for boat stowage, anchor pockets, etc are covered by flush-fitting doors as tightly engineered as those of an automobile, and likely as vulnerable to contact damage.

Diesel propulsion has again been specified, considerably simplifying problems associated with hot exhaust emissions while improving both economy and endurance. The cost, however, is a mediocre maximum speed.

Like the smaller Floréals, the la Fayettes normally carry no AS sensors or armament. They can accommodate a 25-strong military detachment and are fitted for colonial duties. Current peacetime armament comprises a 100mm gun forward (its enclosure reconfigured to further reduce reflection), two quadruple MM40 Exocet SSM launchers (behind deep bulwarks amidships) and an 8-cell Crotale point-defence SAM mounting on the hangar roof. A Panther multi-purpose helicopter is normally carried, but facilities are adequate to accommodate the larger NH-90 AS helicopter if required for specific tasking.

The half deck between gun and bridge front marks a covered cavity into which can be slotted a double 8-cell VLS for the smaller type of ASTER SAMs, probably not normally fitted.

Six modified and more heavily armed versions were built for Taiwan (1994–96) and three for Saudi Arabia (2000–02).

ABOVE: **Model-like in her simplicity of form, the *la Fayette* sheers away from the American Fast Combat Support Ship *Seattle* (AOE.3). Her low radar signature is to fool incoming SSMs as much as to avoid detection.**

La Fayette class, as built

Displacement: 3,200 tons (standard); 3,600 tons (full load)
Length: 115m/377ft 6in (bp); 124.2m/407ft 8in (oa)
Beam: 13.6m/44ft 8in
Draught: 4.8m/15ft 9in (maximum)
Armament: 1 x 100mm gun; 8 x MM40 Exocet SSM (2x4); 1 x 8-cell Crotale SAM launcher
Machinery: 4 diesel engines, 2 shafts
Power: 15,666kW/21,000bhp for 25 knots
Endurance: 350 tons fuel for 12,965km/7,000nm at 15 knots
Protection: Nominal
Complement: 153

LEFT: **A good beam shot of *Manju* of the Etorofu class, whose elegant destroyer-like hull belies her humbler status. Later units had hulls almost devoid of double-curvature plating. Her low-elevation 4.7in guns date from World War I.**

Shumushu and Etorofu classes

Although the Imperial Japanese Navy viewed convoy as "defensive" and, therefore, of low priority, it did produce during the late 1930s the four-strong Shumushu (or Shimushu) class of general-purpose escorts. Basically of sound design, they proved suitable for later series production and for further development. With some uncertainty as to their exact role, they were fitted initially for minesweeping.

Unlike the British and American navies, which disliked diesel propulsion (not least because it was then very noisy in an AS escort, which needed to minimize self-generated noise), the Japanese adopted it readily. Its advantages included compactness and few engine room staff, against which it required highly refined fuel, which would become difficult to obtain.

In length comparable with a British Castle-class corvette, a Shumushu was somewhat narrower, with a 3-knot speed advantage. Like a small destroyer, with no torpedo tubes, she had a very short forecastle which terminated short of the simple bridge structure, reminiscent of German World War I practice, illustrated elsewhere.

For their size, these escorts were relatively heavily gunned, i.e. with an eye to resisting surface attack rather than the threat from submarine and aircraft which actually developed. Both the Shumushus and the 14 virtually identical Etorofu type, that followed somewhat later, carried three single 4.7in guns, one forward, two aft. All were on low elevation mountings removed from destroyers scrapped after World War I.

As built, the early ships carried only a handful of automatic weapons and a dozen depth charges (without associated sound equipment) but, under pressure of combat experience, minesweeping gear and other topweight was landed in favour of up to 60 depth charges and a dozen or more 25mm automatic weapons. They also gained sonar and radar although, at this time, these were of indifferent quality.

ABOVE: **The Etorofus (Type A) were the first derivative class, similar but of slightly greater displacement. This is *Kasodo* at an unknown date, fitted with a temporary bow, not an unfamiliar sight in the Pacific.**

ABOVE: **Although having the appearance of a wartime emergency design, the four Shumushus were completed pre-war. They were successful, and provided the basis for the extended classes of anti-submarine escorts that succeeded them.**

Etorofu class, as built

Displacement: 870 tons (standard); 1,020 tons (standard)
Length: 73m/239ft 7in (bp); 77.5m/254ft 4in (oa)
Beam: 9.5m/31ft 10in
Draught: 3.1m/10ft
Armament: 3 x 4.7in guns (3x1)
Machinery: Geared diesel engines, 2 shafts
Power: 3,133kW/4,200bhp for 19.5 knots
Endurance: 14,816km/8,000nm at 16 knots
Protection: None
Complement: 147

LEFT: **Where the earlier classes had been configured as general-purpose escorts with minesweeping gear, the Mikuras (Type B) were fitted primarily for AS duties. This is *Awaji*, early in 1944, with reduced surface armament and clear quarterdeck.**

Mikura and Ukuru classes

A major weakness of the Japanese high command was its inflexible attitude to planning so that, as the Pacific war developed into a protracted test of attrition, it was unwilling to adapt. Because a short war had been hypothesized, escorts came low on the construction priority list. This remained the case even when the Japanese merchant marine, upon which the sustenance of the newly acquired empire depended, was targeted by a growing infestation of American submarines. Thus, although the four Shumushus were launched in 1939–40, it would be late in 1942 before the first of the follow-on Etorofus entered the water. This class of 14 was then launched over a 14-month period with apparently little urgency even though, up to December 1943, over 2.9 million tons of mostly unconvoyed shipping had been lost.

From October 1943 the yet-incomplete Etorofu programme overlapped that for the eight Mikura type, modified and slightly enlarged. Their forecastles extended aft to the bridge block and the funnel was placed much farther aft. Although configured primarily for AS operations, with a 120 depth charge capacity and sonar gear, they were still burdened with three 4.7in guns, the after weapons in an open twin mounting. An interesting response to the lack of a purpose-designed, ahead-throwing weapon was to mount a 75mm Army-pattern mortar ahead of the bridge. Again, AA weaponry was augmented as opportunity offered.

The Mikuras, launched between July 1943 and February 1944, could be built in as little as six months. During this period, however, mercantile losses were causing some concern. The Mikura design was thus redrawn to cut out all complex, or double, curvature, even deck camber, in order to facilitate construction through the assembly of prefabricated modules. Thirty-three of these Ukuru-class variants were built.

ABOVE: **Later versions of the Mikuras were known as the Ukuru class, or Modified Type B. Of similar design, they began to incorporate single-curvature plating, as apparent in the bow section of the *Ukuru* herself, seen here post-war.**

Ukuru type, as built

Displacement: 940 tons (standard); 1,020 tons (full load)
Length: 72m/236ft 4in (bp); 78m/256ft (oa)
Beam: 9m/29ft 7in
Draught: 3.1m/10ft
Armament: 3 x 4.7in guns (1x2/1x1); 1 x 75mm mortar
Machinery: Geared diesel engines, 2 shafts
Power: 3,133kW/4,200bhp for 19.5 knots
Endurance: 9,260km/5,000nm at 16 knots
Protection: None
Complement: 150

LEFT: **Far too late, the Japanese began series production of escorts to screen their fast-diminishing merchant marine. The Kaibokans were smaller versions of the preceding classes. This example is a diesel-propelled Type C.**
ABOVE: **The Kaibokans were much smaller than Western AS escorts, and this unidentified Type D has succumbed quickly to the mining effect of several near missiles. As she rolls over, her crew can be seen evacuating.**

Kaibokan classes

Far too late, the Kaikobans were the major series-built, emergency escorts. They were known commonly as "Type C", Types "A" and "B" being the Shumushu/Etorofu and Mikura/Ukuru classes respectively. Although the "Type C" design was approved early in 1943, production began only late in that year. Despite its being given higher priority, the programme suffered from the generally poor organization and decision-making process that was a feature of a Japan unready for an extended war. There was a chronic lack of skilled workers and increasing shortages of essential, imported raw materials.

ABOVE: **Due to a dearth of suitable diesel engines, the Type D Kaikobans were fitted with single-screw steam turbine machinery, evidenced by the smoke and taller funnel of this example, known simply as "No. 8".**

Types "A" and "B" were of about 78m/256ft overall length, their production confined to just five yards. The emergency Kaikoban programme involved an initial order of over 130 hulls. Many more yards needed to be involved, and it was probably to utilize smaller facilities that the "Type C" design was limited to 67.5m/221ft 6in. Less just one medium-calibre gun, however, they carried the same armament as the still-building "Type Bs".

Apparently too numerous to name, Kaikoban were simply numbered. With diesel engine production inadequate, some later units were given steam turbine propulsion. Twin-shaft, diesel-driven units (odd numbers) remained "Type C" but the slightly larger, single-shaft, turbine-driven ships (even numbers) were known as "Type Ds". Externally, these differed in having a taller, more slender funnel of round section, placed further forward than the hexagonal-sectioned stacks of the diesel ships.

Building times varied between three and eight months, and the programme was successful in that upwards of 90 units were definitively completed, many others existing as partly assembled modules. Although even the oldest saw barely a year of hostilities, it bears testimony to the, by then, overwhelming superiority of the Americans by sea and air that 55 of them became war losses. Orders for hundreds more, many half-complete, were cancelled.

Type C, as built

Displacement: 745 tons (standard); 810 tons (full load)
Length: 63m/206ft 7in (bp); 67.5m/221ft 7in (oa)
Beam: 8.5m/27ft 10in
Draught: 2.9m/9ft 6in
Armament: 2 x 4.7in guns (2x1); 1 x 75mm mortar
Machinery: Geared diesel engines, 2 shafts
Power: 1,417kW/1,900bhp for 16.5 knots
Endurance: 12,040km/6,500nm at 14 knots
Protection: None
Complement: 136

LEFT: **This view of the *Oi* emphasizes the high forward freeboard of the Isuzu design. Anchors are partly recessed to reduce slamming and spray-making. Note the Bofors-type AB rocket launcher.**

Ikazuchi and Isuzu classes

Reconstructed as the Japanese Maritime Self-Defence Force (JMSDF), the Japanese navy was, during the early 1950s, permitted to build its first new ships. Closely controlling Japan's regeneration, the United States was also concerned at Soviet Russia's naval building in the Pacific. Japan's ability to defend herself, or even act as an ally, was to be encouraged.

A major perceived threat was from Russian high-speed conventional submarines, derived from captured German technology. These were capable of bursts of 15 to 17 knots submerged and, to engage them, it was reckoned that contemporary escorts needed to have a 10-knot speed advantage.

In December 1954 Japan laid down her first trio of new frigates. The Ikazuchis were smaller than the ex-American escorts that the JMSDF was already running, but showed the latter's influence in that armament and electronics were all American sourced. Unambitious, flush-decked vessels, they were armed with a pair of 3in guns, a Hedgehog and depth charges. There was a single, braced tripod mast, replaced by a lattice on the Isuzus.

All were twin-screwed, but *Akebono* (slightly the largest and with two funnels) was steam-turbine propelled, while the other single-funnelled pair had diesel engines, Mitsubishi in *Ikazuchi* and Mitsui/B&W in *Inazuma.*

Although the 28-knot *Akebono* was a clear 3 knots faster, she also required 30 more crew, and diesel propulsion was selected for the four Isuzus, launched in two pairs in 1961 and 1963. All four had differing types of diesel engine layout.

As long as a DE, but narrower, the Isuzu was an obvious derivative of the Ikazuchi, but differed in having fore- and mainmasts, both of lattice construction. Four 76mm/3in guns were carried, in twin mountings forward and aft. There was a forward-firing Bofors-type quadruple AS mortar and, later, AS torpedo tubes and VDS. They were very dependent upon standard American equipment but although capable, would have had difficulty in tackling a fast submarine.

LEFT: **Inheriting the name of a notable heavy cruiser of World War II, the *Mogami* shows her deck layout. Of an essentially simple design, suitable for series production, she carries her name amidships, a custom briefly revived post-war.**

Isuzu class, as built

Displacement: 1,490 tons (standard); 1,700 tons (full load)
Length: 94m/308ft 6in (oa)
Beam: 10.4m/34ft 2in
Draught: 3.5m/11ft 6in (mean)
Armament: 4 x 3in guns (2x2); 1 x quadruple AS mortar
Machinery: 4 diesel engines, 2 shafts
Power: 11,936kW/16,000bhp for 25 knots
Endurance: Not known
Protection: None
Complement: 180

LEFT: **Japan's increasing value as a Western ally was evident in the further sophistication of transferred weapons technology. Acquisition of ASROC was a major step forward, *Ayase* of the Chikugos being among the smallest vessels to deploy it.** ABOVE: **The Chikugo design – this is *Chitose* – was of a size with the Isuzus and directly derived from them. The layout appears less cluttered, but the bridge structure is, in proportion, rather more bulky.**

Chikugo class

Developed Isuzus, the Chikugos followed after a lapse of seven years. They were slightly shorter, but beamier, continuing the trend to the deployment of increasingly sophisticated sensors and weaponry. From the Ikazuchis' already out-moded Hedgehog, the Isuzus tried the Americans Mk 108 launcher (Weapon Able) before adopting the Bofors quadruple mortar. With the Chikugos came ASROC, they being reputedly the smallest ships to carry it. Previous weapons had been forward-firing, and were located in "B" position, forward of the bridge. Depending upon sonar conditions, ASROC could range effectively to 9.6km/6 miles and could, therefore, be mounted aft of amidships where its large Mk 16, 8-cell launcher was better protected, dominating the ship's profile. ASROC could deliver either a homing torpedo or a nuclear depth charge, although the latter are most likely never to have been supplied.

In layout, the Chikugos closely followed that of the Isuzus but, in overall appearance, had lost some of the latter's Japanese characteristics. The sharply cut-off funnel was replaced by a more conventional "flower-pot", while the traditional curved stem profile gave way to the heavily overhung, straight stem and anchor that advertised the bow-mounted sonar which necessarily complemented the ASROC. Later, the class would gain also a towed VDS, located in a well in the transom, offset to starboard. In order to reduce wetness, the forward hull had a long knuckle, a feature then used extensively in the US Navy and, for designers, of debatable effectiveness.

Diesel propulsion was again specified and, once again, was sourced from two separate manufacturers. To reduce radiated noise, diesel engines were, by this time, being raft-mounted and supported on flexible mounts to decouple their noise and vibration from a ship's hull. AS torpedo tubes could also be shipped but, otherwise, the Chikugos were weakly armed.

All 11 were discarded between 1996 and 2003.

ABOVE: **Lacking a helicopter for targeting, the *Chikugo*'s ASROC depended upon another ship or her own sonar to supply coordinates. A medium-frequency Variable Depth Sonar (VDS) is installed aft and a lower-frequency unit under the sharply raked bows.**

Chikugo class, as designed

Displacement: 1,510 tons (standard); 1,760 tons (full load)
Length: 93m/305ft 3in (oa)
Beam: 10.8m/35ft 5in
Draught: 3.5m/11ft 6in (mean)
Armament: 2 x 3in guns (1x2); 1 x 8-cell ASROC launcher; 6 x 324mm AS torpedo tubes (2x3)
Machinery: 4 diesels, 2 shafts
Power: 11,936kW/16,000bhp for 25 knots
Endurance: 19,816km/10,700nm at 12 knots
Protection: Nominal
Complement: 165

LEFT: ***Ishikari* was lead ship for a class of small multi-purpose frigates which, apparently, proved to be too small to meet their designated requirements. Note the Harpoon SSMs aft and a reversion to the Bofors pattern AS rocket launcher forward.**

Ishikari and Yubari classes

By virtue of not being designed to operate shipborne helicopters, Japanese frigates tend to be small and compact but, by the standards of their peers, are more general-purpose combatants than specialist anti-submarine escorts. A Chikugo was less than half the displacement of, say, a British Type 23 but at 93m/305ft was obviously thought over-large, for the one-off *Ishikari*, launched in 1980, was a considerable 8.5m/27ft 10in shorter.

A consistent feature of Japanese frigates was a 25-knot maximum speed, achieved in the *Ishikari* with a Combined Diesel Or Gas (CODOG) turbine installation. Her two shafts are driven from a common gearbox, powered either by a single diesel (for cruising speeds up to 19 knots) or by a single, licence-built Olympus gas turbine. Although more compact, the arrangement lacks to a degree the versatility.

Externally, a major departure was to increase internal volume by the addition of a long, full-width deckhouse of an otherwise flush-decked hull. The bridge-mast-funnel arrangement is much the same, the large funnel casing resulting from the requirement of the gas turbine.

A considerable amount of aluminium alloy is reportedly incorporated in the upper structure. As such alloys can melt and fail in the event of a serious fire, this is not considered very good practice.

Apparently over-compact, the *Ishikari* was followed by the two Yubaris, near-identical but some 6.5m/21ft greater in length. Like her, their AS capability is limited to small-calibre torpedo tubes and a Bofors quadruple mortar. There is no bow sonar.

The gun calibre remains the same, but firepower is limited to a single weapon of OTO-Melara manufacture. A planned Vulcan/Phalanx CIWS appears never to have been fitted. There being no VDS, the low afterdeck is occupied by four to eight Harpoon SSMs.

LEFT: ***Yubetsu* was the second of a pair of slightly enlarged Ishikari derivatives. The gearing arrangements were such that both shafts could be powered by either a single gas turbine or a single diesel engine.**

Yubari type

Displacement: 1,470 tons (standard); 1,760 tons (full load)
Length: 91m/298ft 8in (oa)
Beam: 10.8m/35ft 5in
Draught: 3.6m/11ft 10in (mean)
Armament: 1 x 76mm gun; 4/8 x Harpoon SSM; 1 x quadruple 375mm AS mortar; 6 x 324mm AS torpedo tubes (2x3)
Machinery: 1 Olympus gas turbine and 1 diesel engine, 2 shafts
Power: 21,179kW/28,390shp for 25 knots or 3,730kW/5,000bhp for 19 knots
Endurance: Not known
Protection: Nominal
Complement: 98

Abukuma class

Terminated at just two units, the Yubari type was probably an exercise in producing a lean-crewed, small escort that could be series-built in an emergency. Too limited for peacetime activities, it was succeeded by the Abukuma class, six units that harked back to the earlier Chikugos.

The most important influence on the Abukumas was the decision to increase maximum speed to 27 knots. This required an increase in length, a full 16m/52ft 5in greater than that of a Chikugo. A necessary two-thirds increase in power is developed by a pair of Spey SM-1C gas turbines, whose size gives them a more economical operating range than the larger Olympus. For cruising, there are two diesel engines. Arranged CODOG-fashion, each shaft can be driven by one gas turbine or one diesel. The machinery is located in two, well-separated spaces, each served by a large, square-sectioned funnel.

The hull is of the long forecastle type, without a forward knuckle. The upper deck is continued right aft, over the short, open afterdeck. This gives the impression that the ships have both VDS and a helicopter pad. The former, however, is only a possible future option, while a helicopter can only be "vertically replenished" (VERTREP) while hovering.

The space between the funnels is occupied by an 8-cell ASROC launcher. ASROC rounds are now launched more commonly from a Vertical Launch System (VLS). The considerable space between the bridge front and the gun suggests that a small VLS could well be another future option.

Ahead of the VERTREP area are two pairs of Harpoon SSMs and a Vulcan/Phalanx CIWS. Lack of a second CIWS and the usual complement of SSMs suggests topweight problems. The foremast is a truly massive lattice structure and there had yet appeared few concessions to radar invisibility.

ABOVE: **Unusual in modern frigates, the Abukumas have no shipborne helicopter. The area right aft, abaft *Chikuma*'s Phalanx CIWS, is fitted for the "vertical replenishment" (VERTREP) of helicopters, which have to remain on the hover.** BELOW RIGHT: **The large gap between *Chikuma*'s gun and the bridge front suggests that space has been reserved for the later addition of a small Vertical-Launch System (VLS). At present, ASROC is launched from an amidships Mk 112 mounting.**

ABOVE: ***Oyodo* is seen fitted with two pairs of Harpoon SSMa aft, whereas *Chikuma* (top) has only empty cradles. It is now unusual for such small ships to be fitted with two funnels, whose black caps are something of a Japanese trademark.**

Abukuma class, as built

Displacement: 2,050 tons (standard); 2,550 tons (full load)
Length: 109m/357ft 10in (oa)
Beam: 13.4m/44ft
Draught: 3.8m/12ft 6in (mean)
Armament: 1 x 76mm gun; 4 x Harpoon SSMs (2x2); 1 x 8-cell ASROC launcher; 1 x Vulcan/Phalanx CIWS; 6 x 324mm AS torpedo tubes (2x3)
Machinery: 2 gas turbines, 2 diesel engines, 2 shafts
Power: 20,142kW/27,000shp for 27 knots or 7,460kW/10,000shp for 19 knots
Endurance: Not known
Protection: Nominal
Complement: 115

LEFT: **Of 268 Rudderow type ordered, only 81 were actually completed, the programme being curtailed by the war's end. Compared with the Buckleys' 3in guns, the Rudderows' 5in 38 at either end look somewhat outsized.**
ABOVE: **No less than 152 Buckleys were completed, this being *Wilmarth* (DE.638). One of the "long-hull" types, the Buckleys accommodated machinery for a respectable 24 knots. Note the prominent trunking to the funnel and the triple-torpedo tubes, carried high.**

Destroyer Escort (DE) classes

As early as 1939 the US Navy was considering specifications for an escort vessel suitable for production in large numbers, which would release destroyers for the duties for which they had been designed. Protracted consideration of the conflicting merits of speed and armament, endurance and seakeeping indicated, however, that a larger number of standard destroyers would be better value.

A near-moribund project was then kick-started in June 1941 by an urgent request for escorts from a hard-pressed British Admiralty. All the necessary design work had been done for a small, destroyer-like vessel of some 91.5m/300ft overall, about the same size as a River-class frigate. Like British corvettes, these new "Destroyer Escorts", or DEs, would be built in yards not used to naval orders, although naval standards would apply.

The US Navy, now itself at war, realized the utility of DEs and the numbers involved became staggering. Over 1,000 were ordered, of which about 450 were eventually cancelled. Of 565 actually completed, 90 were transferred during hostilities, 78 of them to the Royal Navy.

The DEs' flush-decked hulls, with their pronounced forward sheer, were diminutives of those of American destroyers. The open-topped bridge, with its all-round visibility, was adopted from British practice. They were excellent seaboats but, designed with an unusually large metacentric height, they had a rapid and vicious motion until extra weight was moved topside and larger bilge keels fitted to dampen rolling.

US Navy practice stressed relatively high speeds, the DE's specification calling for steam turbines and 24 knots. With the numbers involved, machinery production could not keep pace, necessitating some units being diesel powered. Various combinations of machinery were used, resulting in six major variants of DE being recognized.

Experience with British Hunt classes had demonstrated the occasional value of torpedo tubes, and a triple bank was fitted to the Edsall, Buckley and Bostwick classes. In those transferred to the Royal Navy, all of the Evarts and Buckley types, the extra speed and tight turning circle were much appreciated (as were the relatively high-class accommodation and facilities). Although an excellent dual-purpose weapon, the 3in gun was considered by the British to be inadequate to quickly dispose of a surfaced submarine.

ABOVE: **DEs were transferred widely with the end of World War II, the French-flag *Touareg* being one of 14 acquired in two batches. One of the 21-knot diesel-electric Bostwick type, she served originally as the USS *Bright* (DE.747).**

Type	Length (oa) (m/ft)	Beam (m/ft)	Propulsion type	Power (kW/h)	Speed (knots)	Armament
Evarts	88.3/289.5	10.7/35	Diesel-electric	4,476/6,000	21	3 x 3in
Edsall	93.3/306	11.3/37	Geared diesel	4,476/6,000	21	3 x 3in
Buckley	93.3/306	10.7/35	Turbo-electric	8,952/12,000	24	3 x 3in
Bostwick	93.3/306	10.7/35	Diesel-electric	4,476/6,000	21	3 x 3in
Butler	93.3/306	10.7/35	Turbo-electric	8,952/12,000	24	2 x 5in
Rudderow	93.3/306	10.7/35	Turbo-electric	8,952/12,000	24	2 x 5in

Two 3in guns were superimposed forward, "A" gun being very wet in a seaway. Abaft "B" gun was a full Hedgehog. Effective in its day, it proved to be the DE's weakness in that the highly efficient Squid (never adopted by the US Navy) could not be retro-fitted. The slower, but more roomy, British Lochs thus became the better U-boat killers.

The adoption of diesel drive was expedited by utilizing the standard 1,500hp diesel generator/motor combination already used in submarines. No less than eight of the sets were to have been installed to generate the required 12,000shp but, owing to conflicting demands of submarine and amphibious craft programmes, only four diesel engines per ship could be spared. Diesel-powered ships thus enjoyed only half the propulsive power of steamers, the speed penalty being 3 knots. In the Edsalls (only) diesels drove the shafts through gearing rather than electrically.

Post-war, 94 DEs were converted to high-speed transports (APDs), with accommodation for 162 troops and their equipment, with four LCVPs under davits. About 45 more became radar pickets, both types reflecting experience gained in the Pacific war. Many were transferred abroad post-war, some serving into the 1960s.

ABOVE LEFT: **Resulting from the massed air attacks of World War II, the US Navy modified considerable numbers of destroyers and DEs to Radar Pickets for the purposes of providing early warning. *Calcaterra* (DER.390) was one of 34 Edsall-class conversions.** ABOVE RIGHT: ***Sellstrom* (DER.255) was another Edsall-class conversion. Note the full-width amidships deckhouse and modified bridge. She has been given an unshielded, twin 3in 50 forward and retains her Hedgehog, here uncovered.** BELOW: **During the south-west Pacific campaign, suitably modified "four-pipers", then DEs, proved to be invaluable as fast transports/troop carriers (APDs). *Ruchamkin* (APD.89) shows her assault landing craft and 5in gun for supporting fire.**

LEFT: **The diesel-electric *Dobler* (DE.48) of the short-hulled Evarts type was one of the original large British order that was retained by the US Navy. Two forward guns were appreciated, but at the cost of a very wet "A" position.**

Buckley type, as built

Displacement: 1,400 tons (standard); 1,685 tons (full load)
Length: 91.5m/300ft (wl); 93.3m/306ft (oa)
Beam: 10.7m/35ft
Draught: 3.2m/10ft 6in (maximum)
Armament: 3 x 3in guns (3x1); 3 x 21in torpedo tubes (1x3); 1 x Hedgehog AS mortar
Machinery: Turbo-electric, 2 boilers, 2 shafts
Power: 8,952kW/12,000shp for 24 knots
Endurance: 11,112km/6,000nm at 12 knots
Protection: Nominal
Complement: 213

Dealey/Courtney and Claude Jones classes

Built to rigid standard specification in order to facilitate series production, DEs faced mass obsolescence by 1945 because of the rapid parallel advance of the fast, deep-diving submarine. As early as 1947, studies began for a DE replacement. Again, it had to be inexpensive and suitable for series production in an emergency.

A 27-knot speed, together with good seakeeping, demanded a hull of comparable dimensions. Because of the limited training angles of ahead-throwing weapons, a fast helm response and tight tactical diameter were important. In this respect, the US Navy favoured its Weapon Able (or Alfa) over the British Squid.

Based on the reasonable argument that wartime experience demonstrated that damaged ships survived by circumstance rather than by redundancy, single-screw propulsion was chosen, necessitating only one set of machinery and fewer personnel.

Not surprisingly, the indistinguishable Dealey and Courtney classes closely resembled earlier DEs, but with twin 3in 50s forward and aft, and a Weapon Able forward. A substantial lattice mast supported a comprehensive range of electronics, while much of the upper structure was in aluminium alloy. All 13 of the class were completed between 1954 and 1958, subsequent to the Korean War.

Some of the class were later converted to deploy the ultimately abortive DASH (Drone Anti-Submarine Helicopter) system but, even without this failure, they had been less than impressive with their high cost and insufficient range.

A long-forecastle, diesel-driven variant was thus developed in the four-ship Claude Jones class, completed 1958–60. These had four diesels, two shafts and two funnels. A 21.5 knot maximum was offset by an extra 1,852km/ 1,000nm endurance at the range of speed normally expected of a convoy escort. With very similar salient-dimensions, they had a reduced specification of two single 3in guns, two trainable Hedgehogs and two triple AS torpedo tubes. All four were transferred to Indonesia in 1973–74.

ABOVE LEFT: **Because of priorities in machinery production, many of the war-built DEs were powered for only 21 knots. They were, nonetheless, so valuable that the DE concept was updated post-war. This is the 25-knot *Courtney* (DE.1021).** ABOVE: **The post-war DE design proved to be useful for construction by allied NATO navies, the Portuguese building three Dealeys with mainly US offshore funding. *Almirante Gago Coutinho* has twin Bofors AS launchers in place of the usual Mk 108, Weapon "Able".**

LEFT: **The four Claud Jones-class DEs were a post-war attempt to produce an inexpensive, diesel-driven escort. They proved to be too small and were transferred to Indonesia. This is the nameship *Monginsidi*. Note the two funnels.**

Dealey class, as built

Displacement: 1,450 tons (standard); 1,880 tons (full load)
Length: 93.9m/308ft (wl); 96.1m/325ft (oa)
Beam: 11.2m/36ft 8in
Draught: 3.7m/12ft
Armament: 4 x 3in (2x2); 1 x Able AS rocket launcher; 6 x AS torpedo tubes (2x3)
Machinery: Geared steam turbines, 2 boilers, 1 shaft
Power: 14,920kW/20,000shp for 25 knots
Endurance: 400 tons oil for 11,112km/6,000nm at 12 knots
Protection: Nominal
Complement: 173

Bronstein, Garcia and Brooke classes

With the introduction of the nuclear submarine came the requirement for a new type of escort, fast enough to be able to screen a task group, and capable of detecting and engaging a submerged target at a safe range. The key element for this was the low frequency SQS-26 sonar, necessarily housed in a large bulbous forefoot that required a telltale overhung bow profile.

The resulting sonar data would be used to control a Drone Anti-Submarine Helicopter (DASH). Theoretically, this could place a homing torpedo over a target at out to 9,144m/10,000yd but, proving unreliable, was effectively abandoned in 1968 in favour of the LAMPS (Light Airborne Multi-Purpose System) manned helicopter. This left the escorts with only ASROC, which had only half the range but which had the option of compensating for its lack of accuracy by carrying a nuclear warhead, capable of "sanitizing" a considerable area.

Completed in 1963, the two prototype Bronsteins were designed with the smallest hull that could efficiently accommodate a SQS-26 system. Even powered with only 20,000shp, they were some 21.3m/70ft longer than earlier DEs. With adequate freeboard, their long forecastle-deck hulls did not require a pronounced forward sheer. A "mack" exhausted boiler uptakes via a plated-in mast and a generously dimensioned helipad was located about three-quarters aft. The 8-cell ASROC launcher was sited forward of the bridge.

The Bronstein design proved to be too tight and the derived Garica class were a further 13.1m/43ft longer. Guns were upgraded from four 3in to two 5in, the DASH facility being moved right aft. In the six-ship Brooke subgroup the amidships 5in gun was exchanged for a modified Tartar SAM system. All had 35,000shp, but still with a single shaft. ASROCs were reloadable and heavy, wire-guided torpedoes could be launched through the transom.

ABOVE LEFT: **The two Bronsteins (this is the *McCloy*) were the forerunners of a second-generation DE designed around the new ASROC stand-off missile. Larger and more expensive, they could target ASROC with both low-frequency bow sonar or helicopter-deployed sensors.** ABOVE: ***Albert David* (DE.1050) of the Garcia class executing a tight turn. Derived directly from the Bronsteins, the Garcias are significantly longer by virtue of shipping two 5in 38 guns and being equipped with a helicopter hangar, initially for the aborted DASH.** LEFT: ***Bronstein* (DE.1037) quietly proceeding at listening speed. The sheer size of her bow-mounted sonar dome requires her bower anchor to be stowed nearly abreast the 3in 50 gun mounting. Note that there is no hangar or ASROC reload facility.**

Garcia class, as designed

Displacement: 2,625 tons (standard); 3,480 tons (full load)
Length: 121.8m/400ft (wl); 126.3m/414ft 8in (oa)
Beam: 13.5m/44ft 3in
Draught: 7.9m/25ft 11in (maximum)
Armament: 2 x 5in guns (2x1); 1 x 8-cell ASROC launcher; 4 x AS torpedo tubes (2x2); 2 x 21in torpedo tubes (2x1)
Machinery: Geared steam turbine, 2 boilers, 1 shaft
Power: 26,110kW/35,000shp for 27+ knots
Endurance: 600 tons oil for 7,410km/4,000nm at 20 knots
Protection: Nominal
Complement: 209

ABOVE: ***Talbot* (FFG.4) was one of the six Garcia-class derivatives which exchanged the amidships 5in mounting for a Mk 22 launcher, intended for Standard SM-1 MR (Medium-Range) SSM.**

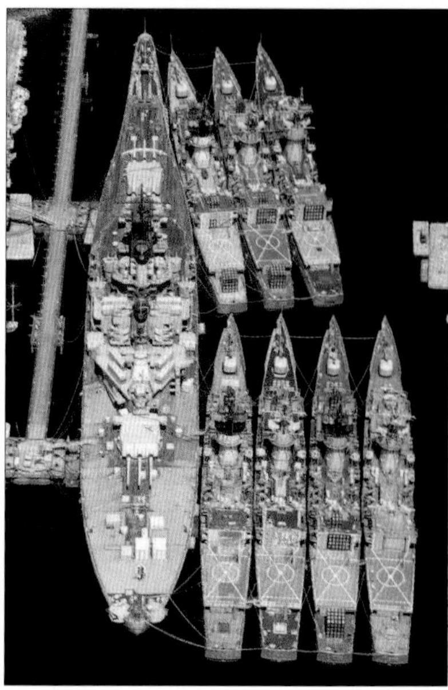

Knox class

ABOVE LEFT: **The Knox-class ships took the title "frigate" and designator "FF", FF.1054 being the *Gray*, seen here leading a Newport-class Tank Landing Ship. Her sonar dome, visible through the clear water, is smaller than those on preceding classes.** ABOVE: **The Knox class ran to 46 units, more than could usefully be employed in a peacetime navy, and many quickly found themselves reduced to reserve fleet status. Seven, showing remarkably few preservation measures, lay here alongside the veteran battleship *New Jersey*.**

The cost differential between the Tartar-armed Brooke-class DEGs and the non-missile, but otherwise similar, Garcia-class DEs was considerable and, for the planned successors, would be higher, To reduce unit cost in order to obtain the numbers required, the Knox-class ships did not receive an area defence SAM. Their programme overlapped that of the Garcias and, resulting from considerable effort to clean up the rather "bitty" appearance of earlier ships, they were reasonably handsome, if functional.

The truncated conical "mack" was located exactly amidships to minimize ship motion, bearing as it did a short lattice mast supporting the ships' electronics. Earlier classes carried a stem anchor, with the second stowed, submarine-style, in the keel. The Knoxes were given a keel and a port-side anchor, the latter of Danforth pattern. It appears improbable that this feature created the wetness for which the class was noted, but both spray rails and bow bulwarks were added to most.

By the time that the lead ship entered service in 1969, DASH was a dead letter, the class being adapted for LAMPS. Its helipad was sited slightly forward of the after end and, to economize on length, was fitted with a telescopic hangar.

Much of the superstructure was made full width to increase internal volume. Forward was a 5in gun of the new, 54-calibre, type. The adjacent 8-cell ASROC launcher could be reloaded from a facility in the bridge front. Two cells were adapted to launch Harpoon SSMs as an option. Right aft, the originally fitted Sea Sparrow point-defence launcher was replaced by a single Vulcan-Phalanx CIWS. The large bow sonar was complemented by VDS and/or towed array sonars.

The class extended to a respectable 46 units, all of which were disposed of by the mid-1990s. At the time of writing, a dozen or more are still serving under foreign flags.

LEFT: **The Knox class quickly acquired a reputation for wetness, and each was fitted with forward bulwarks and spray rail, as seen here on *Aylwin* (FF.1081). Note the CIWS added aft. Two cells of the ASROC launcher have been modified to launch Harpoon SSMs.**

Knox class, as designed

Displacement: 3,075 tons (standard); 4,070 tons (full load)
Length: 126.6m/415ft (wl); 133.6m/438ft (oa)
Beam: 14.3m/47ft
Draught: 7.6m/24ft (maximum)
Armament: 1 x 5in gun; 1 x 8-cell ASROC/Harpoon launcher; 1 x Sea Sparrow BPDMS; 4 x fixed AS torpedo tubes; 2 x fixed 21in torpedo tubes (2x1)
Machinery: Geared steam turbine, 2 boilers, 1 shaft
Power: 35,000shp/26,110kW for 27+ knots
Endurance: 750 tons oil for 8,100km/4,400nm at 20 knots
Protection: Nominal
Complement: 224

LEFT: **Derived directly from the Knox design, the Perrys differ in being built around a Standard/ Harpoon system forward (relying on a single launcher) and facilities aft for a LAMPS-III helicopter and TACTASS towed array. They are classified "FFG".** BELOW: **Executing a zig-zag trials manoeuvre, *Kauffman* (FFG.59) shows her layout. Note the squat, round funnel casing exhausting the gas turbines, the single 76mm gun amidships and CIWS aft.**

Oliver Hazard Perry class

By 1970, the US Navy was faced with the mass retirement of modernized, war-built hulls. To maintain the required number of hulls, it appeared an attractive option to build "for but not with", creating a pool which could, at a later date, be fitted out specifically for AAW, ASW or surface warfare. The resulting 51 Perry-class missile frigates (FFG) were considerably upgraded Knoxes.

Procured under the strictest of cash-control regimes, the ships have a bow form capable of accepting a large Sonar, which never materialized. The hull itself is Knox-like, but topped by a continuous, two-level boxy superstructure. Its after end extends full-width to provide a hangar for a pair of LAMPS-III, SH-60B Seahawk helicopters, not always carried. Their required operating area, however, necessitated the transom to be given a pronounced rake.

Because of the effectiveness of a double LAMPS-III, ASROC is not provided. All were fitted originally with a single-arm Mk 13 launcher forward, giving them "FFG" status. The launcher could handle Standard SM-1 MR SAMs or Harpoon SSMs. With the demise of the former in 2003, however, the launcher was removed. Not replaced with a VLS, the class has been down-graded to "FF" and 18 of the earlier units sold out to friendly flags.

Despite their capacious appearance, Perrys have little reserve capacity and are now up to 500 tons overweight. Despite this, they are criticized (unreasonably) for their under-armed appearance, not helped by the adoption of a single 76mm OTO Melara for general-purpose firepower. Most have received a Vulcan Phalanx CIWS in addition. Some have their hull sonar complemented by a towed array.

The single shaft is driven by a pair of LM-2500 gas turbines, a pair of azimuth thrusters providing a measure of "get-you-home" redundancy.

A modernization programme for the 24 newest units has been proposed.

LEFT: **The SM-1 version of the Standard SAM having reached retirement, the Perrys had the Mk 13 launcher removed, as in this photograph of *Elrod* (FFG.55). The newest 24 units are slated to receive an extensive modernization.**

Earlier units, as designed

Displacement: 2,770 tons (standard); 3,660 tons (full load)
Length: 124.4m/408ft (wl); 135.7m/445ft (oa), or later 138.8m/455ft 7in (oa)
Beam: 15.2m/50ft
Draught: 8.6m/28ft 3in (maximum)
Armament: 1 x 76mm gun; 1 x standard SAM/Harpoon SSM launcher; 1 x Vulcan-Phalanx CIWS; 2 x AS torpedo tubes (2x1)
Machinery: 2 gas turbines (COGAG), 1 shaft
Power: 29,840kW/40,000shp for 29 knots
Endurance: 587 tons fuel for 7,730km/4,200nm at 20 knots
Protection: Splinter protection over vital spaces
Complement: 176 (now up to 225)

Spica class

The category of "torpedo boat", as opposed to "destroyer" was, as in the German Navy, only a matter of scale. Italian destroyers built during the early 1920s were of a maximum 876 tons and, being greatly outclassed by the 1,640-tonners of the mid-1930s, were downgraded to torpedo boats.

For the relatively short distances involved in Mediterranean operations, ships of this size were useful and, after over a decade's lapse, the 32-strong 800-ton Spica class were laid down from 1934. They resembled the contemporary Oriani-class fleet destroyers but could be quickly differentiated by their smaller, capped funnel, that of an Oriani being broad, trunked and not capped. The Italian love of 1930s streamlining was evident in the compact bridge structure and funnel being combined in a single entity, teardrop-shaped in plan.

They were not over-gunned, their three 100mm weapons being split between one on the forecastle and two superfiring aft. As built, some had four, sided 450mm torpedo tubes, each provided with a deck-mounted reload. Others had one centreline twin and two, sided reloadable tubes. During World War II all are believed to have had two twin centreline mountings. Heavily used as convoy escorts, particularly on the bitterly contested North Africa route, they were also fitted with shields on "A" and "Y" guns, their 20mm armament being increased to 16 barrels. They could carry up to 20 mines or their equivalent weight in depth charges.

LEFT: **One of the 16-strong Alcione type, *Libra* is seen here raising steam during World War II. Note the paravane, deployed by a powered davit. Three read-use depth charges are in the trap, while, forward of the canvas dodger, are two loaded throwers with reloads.**

ABOVE: ***Cassiopea* belonged to the Climene subgroup of the Spica class. She is seen here in the early 1950s, modified with a new bridge structure, as a "fast corvette". The attractive lines of her light destroyer pedigree remain in evidence.**

With twin-shaft, steam turbine propulsion, the Spicas could, with a clean hull and calm conditions, raise 34 knots but their speed fell off rapidly in the "deep and dirty" condition.

Two of the class were sold to Sweden in 1940 and 23 more were to become war losses. Survivors served as "fast corvettes" until the late 1950s, armed with Hedgehog but no torpedo tubes.

Spica class, as built

Displacement: 794 tons (standard); 1,020 tons (full load)
Length: 78.5m/257ft 8in (bp); 83.5m/274ft 1in (oa)
Beam: 8.1m/26ft 10in
Draught: 2.6m/8ft 6in
Armament: 3 x 100mm guns (3x1); 4 x 450mm torpedo tubes (4x1)
Machinery: Geared steam turbines, 2 boilers, 2 shafts
Power: 14,174kW/19,000shp for 34 knots
Endurance: 215 tons oil for 3,520km/1,900nm at 15 knots
Protection: None
Complement: 99

Ariete class

War estimates provided for no less than 42 Improved Spica, or Ariete, class torpedo boats. Italy's ability to carry through her emergency programmes was, however, already badly eroded and, by January 1942 when the first keel was laid, ten of the earlier class had already been lost. Only three yards were involved, all situated in the north and farthest removed from Allied interference. Despite this, only 16 had been laid down by September 1943, when Italy negotiated an armistice.

Ansaldo at Genoa had laid down its full six-ship allocation on the same day in July 1942. The two furthest advanced, *Ariete* and *Arturo*, were launched during March 1943, the former being delivered in the August. Ten more were launched and fitting out, but the *Ariete* would be the only one to serve in the Italian Navy.

Because of the remoteness of the yards from the battle front, the Germans succeeded in completing the remainder. They thus became war losses under the German flag. Only the *Ariete*, together with two damaged on the slip, survived the war, all three being ceded to the fleet of then-Yugoslavia.

The Arietes differed little from the original Spica class. The bridge front was squared-off rather than rounded. With 100mm guns in "A" and "X" positions only, and a larger, uncapped funnel, they could easily be confused visually with a fleet destroyer. A minesweeping winch and two sets of permanent minelaying rails were provided aft.

The main deck was no longer pierced for scuttles. This was probably a damage-control feature.

The class was officially referred to as "attack torpedo boats", a reference presumably to their two triple 450mm torpedo tube mountings and the 16 per cent increase in installed power, providing for a sustained sea speed of 31.5 knots.

TOP: The Italian port of Fiume was incorporated into post-war Yugoslavia as Rijeka. The incomplete hull of the *Balestra*, already renamed TA 47 by the Germans, was captured there. She was completed as the Yugoslav *Ucka* to a modified design. ABOVE: As the only unit of the class to be completed for the Italian Navy, the *Ariete* is seen here in the original form. Note the ungainly squared-off bridge structure and lack of main deck scuttles, as compared with *Ucka* (above).

Ariete class, as designed

Displacement: 757 tons (standard); 1,127 tons (full load)
Length: 81.1m/266ft 3in (bp); 83.5m/274ft 1in (oa)
Beam: 8.6m/28ft 3in
Draught: 3.1m/10ft 2in (mean)
Armament: 2 x 100mm guns (2x1); 6 x 450mm torpedo tubes (2x3)
Machinery: Geared steam turbines, 2 boilers, 2 shafts
Power: 16,412kW/22,000shp for 31.5 knots
Endurance: 214 tons oil for 2,780km/1,500nm at 16 knots
Protection: None
Complement: 150

LEFT: **Completed only shortly before the Italian capitulation, *Aliseo* survived only to be ceded to Yugoslavia. As can be seen, the Ciclone/Animosos lowered the silhouette and landed "Y" gun for an increased depth charge capacity.**

Pegaso and Ciclone classes

A further variant of the Spica design was that of the four-strong Pegaso class. Although of much the same dimensions and appearance, the hulls were refined hydrodynamically for improved seakeeping and endurance. A small bulbous forefoot, common on Italian cruisers, was designed for optimal flow conditions over a specific speed band, allowing either higher speed for the same power, or greater economy at the same speed.

Instead of the Spicas' flattish cut-up, under the after end, typical of current destroyer practice, the Pegasos had a "cruiser" stern. Besides giving more buoyancy right aft, this would probably have given a more uniform flow over the propeller disc, reducing vibration and increasing propeller efficiency. Forward, a slight knuckle was introduced to reduce wetness. Very wet aft, the Spicas had a centreline catwalk connecting the forecastle deck to the light automatic gun positions and "X" gun. On the Pegasos, the underside of this was filled in to create safe fore-and-aft access at upper deck level. Because of this, the two twin torpedo tube mountings had to be sided, halving the maximum salvo. Three depth charge projectors were provided on either side.

The 16 Ciclone-class "destroyer escorts" (*torpediniere di scorta*) were derived directly from the Pegasos.

LEFT: ***Pegaso*, one of four, has had a second depth charge trap added, forward of the propeller guard, allowing for larger patterns. The small crane, right aft, was a feature of these classes, and was provided to assist recovery of the paravanes.**

Mostly laid down before disruption and shortages bit too hard, most were completed before the armistice.

Looking similar to Pegasos but, in some cases, with a third 100mm gun added amidships, the Ciclones in general arrived too late to experience the worst of the North African convoy run. The only ones, therefore, to be lost in surface action with Allied forces were two of the three commandeered by the Germans following the separate Italian Armistice. With three being ceded to Soviet Russia and two to then-Yugoslavia none remained to Italy post-war.

LEFT: **Already in an advanced state of completion, the Ciclone-class *Monsone* is seen here on the slip at Castellammare di Stabia. Note the adoption of a knuckle forward and the aftward extension of the forecastle deck.**

Pegaso class, as designed 

Displacement: 855 tons (standard); 1,600 tons (full load)
Length: 82.5m/270ft 1in (bp); 89.3m/293ft 2in (oa)
Beam: 9.7m/31ft 10in
Draught: 3.7m/12ft 2in (full load)
Armament: 2 x 100mm guns (2x1); 4 x 450mm torpedo tubes (2x2)
Machinery: Geared steam turbines, 2 boilers, 2 shafts
Power: 11,936kW/16,000shp for 28 knots
Endurance: 390 tons oil for 9,385km/5,100nm at 14 knots
Protection: None
Complement: 154

Albatros and de Cristofaro classes

ABOVE: **With a 19-knot speed and dimensions significantly less than those of war-built escorts, the Albatros class was near the bottom end of capability for an AS corvette. *Albatros* herself shows her Italian ancestry in "boat" bow and anchor stowage.**

In the early 1950s, the Italian Navy's escort forces comprised World War II survivors and three ex-American DEs, transferred under the Mutual Defence Assistance Programme. This last arrangement also funded Italy's first post-war corvettes, a series of eight providing much-needed employment.

Only three of these (the Albatros class) were to Italian account, four going to Denmark and one to the Netherlands. The Dutch, with limited use for a one-off, transferred theirs back to Italy after five years, when she was renamed *Aquila*.

Perhaps with a nod toward its source of funding, the Albatroses' hull abandoned the more usual Italian raised-forecastle arrangement in favour of a flush-deck with a pronounced forward sheer. The compact superstructure was based on a full-width amidships deckhouse and there was a transom stern. No funnel was provided, the relatively low-power diesels exhausting through the hull.

Not much admired, the quartette were nonetheless useful 21-knot AS escorts, carrying two Hedgehogs and two 76mm guns (later replaced by 40mm weapons). Modest though they were, it would be seven years from their completion before Italy could embark on an improved version in the de Cristofaros, of which a fifth planned unit was cancelled.

About 4m/13ft longer, the hull of the de Cristofaros reverted to a raised forecastle design, the hance at the break of the forecastle being very long to increase the modulus at the hull discontinuity. A retained feature was the unusual "boat" bow profile. The higher-powered diesel engines exhausted through a small, tapered pot of a funnel. The two 76mm guns also gained a proper director.

The out-dated Hedgehogs and depth charges of the earlier class were here replaced by tripled AS torpedo tubes and a domestically developed, single-barrelled "Menon" AS mortar. VDS was added to a hull-mounted sonar.

ABOVE: **A decade later, but little larger, the four de Cristofaros were higher-powered and faster, with two improved 76mm guns and an Italian-designed Menon single-barrelled AS launcher in place of the Albatroses' two Hedgehogs. Note the reinstatement of a raised forecastle.**

de Cristofaro class

Displacement: 850 tons (standard); 1,020 tons (full load)
Length: 75m/246ft 2in (bp); 80.3m/263ft 7in (oa)
Beam: 10.3m/33ft 9in
Draught: 2.8m/9ft 2in
Armament: 2 x 76mm guns (2x1); 1 x 305mm Menon AS mortar; 6 x 324mm AS torpedo tubes (2x3)
Machinery: 2 diesel engines, 2 shafts
Power: 6,266kW/8,400bhp for 23 knots
Endurance: 100 tons fuel for 7,410km/4,000nm at 18 knots
Protection: None
Complement: 130

LEFT: **Nameship of the class, *Centauro* is seen here as originally completed with a unique but trouble-prone solution to twin 76mm gun mountings. She has American electronics but no modern director. The tripod and topmast are an interesting combination.**

Centauro class

Also funded by the American mutual defence "offshore" programme were the four ships of the Centauro class. As ordered, they carried numbers from the US Navy DE series, starting with DE.1020, but, looking like destroyers, they took "D" pendant numbers on completion. With a speed of only 25 knots and no anti-surface ship torpedo tubes, however, they were later reclassified with "F" identifiers.

Although exceeding 1,800 tons displacement, they had features in common with the Albatros type, the hull being flush-decked, with a triangular, flat transom. Because of the greater length, the forward sheer did not appear to be so pronounced.

Since the early 1930s, Italian destroyers had been designed with adjacent boiler spaces and a single, large, trunked funnel. The arrangement was compact but vulnerable to a single hit. Since 1951, the Italians had been operating two ex-American destroyers. Their boiler spaces were separated for survivability, resulting in two funnels, with the Centauros following suit.

Forward and aft, the Centauros carried a totally new style of 76mm gun mounting, with two barrels arranged in a common vertical plane and elevating together. Although credited with a high rate of fire they proved to be over-complex and were replaced by a simpler single mounting.

Two paired 40mm mountings originally flanked the superfiring "X" position, their firing arcs reduced somewhat by the rather superfluous pole mainmast. Both mast and 40mm were latter suppressed in favour of a third 76mm gun.

In addition to an American-sourced sonar, there were two large-diameter AS torpedo tubes and depth charges, with a triple-barrelled Menon AS mortar in "B" position. This triple-barrelled version also proved to be relatively short-lived.

Not lending themselves easily to economical conversion to true AS frigates, the class began the process of disposal in 1980 with the sale of *Castore.*

ABOVE: **Modernization saw the Centauro class receive more orthodox single 76mm guns with proper director control. Further electronics tried the mast's stiffness, resulting in the addition of cross-bracing. Note that *Canopo*'s flag superior has been changed from "D" to "F".**

Centauro class, as designed

Displacement: 1,680 tons (standard); 2,120 tons (full load)
Length: 96.9m/317ft 8in (bp); 103.2m/338ft 4in (oa)
Beam: 11.6m/38ft
Draught: 3.5m/11ft 6in
Armament: 4 x 76mm guns (2x2); 2 x 21in torpedo tubes; 1 x 3-barrelled AS mortar
Machinery: Geared steam turbines, 2 boilers, 2 shafts
Power: 16,412kW/22,000shp for 25 knots
Endurance: 360 tons oil for 6,760km/3,650nm at 20 knots
Protection: None
Complement: 207

LEFT: ***Alpino* (seen here) and her sister *Carabiniere* were developments of the Centauro design and, indeed, were originally to have taken "C" names. They have diesel engines of far higher output than their predecessor's steam plant, two helicopters and six 76mm guns.**

ABOVE: **The four Bergaminis show a different and cheaper line of development from the Centauro design. They have two 76mm guns and a mortar forward, like the Alpinos, but just one helicopter and half the engine power. This is *Luigi Rizzo.***

Carlo Bergamini and Alpino classes

Launched in 1960, the four Bergaminis were frigate versions of the de Cristofaro corvettes. For an extra 10m/33ft, they shipped a helicopter and a third gun, and gained 2.5 knots.

Again, a flush-decked hull was topped with a full-width deckhouse, now supporting at its after end a telescopic hangar for a small Agusta-Bell 47 helicopter. A light, elevated extension of the 01 level served as a flight pad. Active fin stabilizers were fitted to assist flight operations through roll reduction.

During the late 1960s, helicopter facilities were upgraded for the more capable AB.212. A larger hangar and extended flight pad meant the landing of the after 76mm guns and a single-barrelled Menon AS launcher. The uptakes from the four diesels exhausted via a funnel/mast combination. Beyond further upgrading, the Bergaminis were discarded in the early 1980s.

Some 20m/65ft 7in longer than the Bergaminis, the two Alpinos took the concept a stage further. This pair were to have been named *Circe* and *Climene*, continuing the astronomical names associated with torpedo boats. Before launch, however, they took *Alpino* and *Carabiniere*, old destroyer names that better reflected their size.

Their propulsion was by two small gas turbines and four diesels in CODAG combination. The resulting large funnel had proportions which greatly enhanced the ships' appearance. To the usual Menon launcher and two 76mm guns mounted forward were added four more 76mms, sided along the superstructure. Accommodation, originally for two small AB 204B helicopters, was later adequate for a single AB.212.

Two further units were cancelled but both Alpinos still exist (at the time of writing) as special-purpose auxiliaries and trials ships. They have been reduced to diesel propulsion only and their armament cut to three guns and their helicopter. Both now carry "A", auxiliary pendant numbers.

ABOVE: **Lead ship *Carlo Bergamini* in historic surroundings. Her small helicopter is demanding on space, which has been economized by the combination of mast and funnel, and a telescopic hangar. The flight pad is well forward to minimize movement and accelerations.**

Alpino class, as designed

Displacement: 2,000 tons (standard); 2,690 tons (full load)
Length: 106.4m/349ft 3in (bp); 113.3m/371ft 10in (oa)
Beam: 13.3m/43ft 8in
Draught: 3.8m/12ft 5in
Armament: 6 x 76mm guns (6x1); 1 x single-barrelled AS mortar; 6 x 324mm AS torpedo tubes (2x3)
Machinery: 2 gas turbines, 4 diesels, 2 shafts
Power: 11,488kW/15,400hp plus 12,533kW/16,800bhp for 28 knots
Endurance: 275 tons fuel for 7,780km/4,200nm at 17 knots
Protection: Nominal
Complement: 247

LEFT: **With massive gas turbine sprint power in a relatively small hull, the Lupos had an un-frigate-like 35-knot top speed, but cruised on diesel engines. *Sagittario*'s four starboard-side Otomat SSM cradles are unoccupied.**

Lupo and Artigliere classes

Although of the same length as the preceding Alpinos, the Lupos, most unusually, were significantly narrower. The reason, probably, lay in the adoption of CODOG (as opposed to CODAG) propulsion. Two diesel engines were installed for cruising (up to 20 knots) but, for sprint power, there were two licence-built LM-2500 gas turbines, capable of a joint 37,300kW/50,000hp output. This represented a 25 per cent increase in propulsive power compared with an *Alpino*, and which, with an improved hull form, translated into a 4-knot increase in sustained speed.

Some sacrifice was necessary in topweight and a single 127mm gun, and tube- and helicopter-launched topedoes were able to replace the earlier six 76mm weapons and Menon AS launcher, now obsolete. Modern missile systems are bulky but not heavy, the Lupos carrying both an 8-cell Sea Sparrow point defence SAM and eight canister-launchers for Otomat SSMs.

That the Lupo design was too tight was evident in the class being curtailed in favour of the longer Maestrale type, all being scrapped by 2003. Handsome ships, they sold well for export, however, with six being built to Venezuelan account and four each to Peru and Iraq. The last named, laid down 1981–84, ran foul of a generally imposed embargo on West-supplied war materials. With no potential buyers, they were taken into the Italian Navy as the Artigliere class.

All remain on the inventory and are effectively identical with the late Lupo class, with the important difference that acceptance was conditional upon all ASW weaponry and sensors being removed. This was presumably a budgetary manoeuvre, the ships being officially "Fleet Patrol Ships" rather than frigates. To compensate for their lack of ASW armament (which, presumably, could be added), their helicopters have enhanced capability for over-the-horizon direction for the ships' SSMs.

LEFT: **Between 1980 and 1982, Italy completed six standard Lupos for Venezuela. Here, the *Mariscal Antonio José de Sucre* crosses the stern of the stationary *General Bartolomé Salom*. Both are carrying their full outfit of Otomat SSMs.**

Lupo class, as designed

Displacement: 2,210 tons (standard); 2,525 tons (full load)
Length: 106m/347ft 11in (bp); 113.6m/372ft 10in (oa)
Beam: 12m/39ft 4in
Draught: 3.5m/11ft 7in
Armament: 1 x 127mm gun; 8 x Otomat SSM (8x1); 1 x 8-cell Sea Sparrow SAM launcher; 6 x 324mm AS torpedo tubes (2x3)
Machinery: 2 gas turbines, 2 diesels, 2 shafts
Power: 37,300kW/50,000hp or 5,968kW/8,000bhp for 35 or 20 knots
Endurance: 8,060km/4,350nm at 16 knots
Protection: Nominal
Complement: 194

Maestrale class

The limitations of the Lupo design were recognized early, for the first half-dozen of the improved version, the Maestrales, were ordered nine months before the lead ship, *Lupo*, even commissioned. Although 10m/33ft longer, they were even finer (L/B *Lupo* 8.83; *Maestrale* 9.04) and further reduction of weapon topweight was evident. A Lupo's Sea Sparrow launcher and its director were mounted on the hangar roof at 02 level. On a Maestrale the launcher has been moved to 01 level, superfiring the 127mm gun from "B" position. The compact Italian-built RTN-30X director above the bridge serves both weapons. A Lupo carried eight Otomat SSMs at 01 level. A Maestrale carries only four, in a less cramped 02 location, a net gain offset by the shift of the two twin 40mm mountings from main deck to 01 level.

The small increase in beam allowed the hangar to be widened sufficiently to accommodate a second helicopter. For ASW, these work in conjunction with the ships' VDS and towed array, deployed from a handling deck and well situated beneath the flight deck.

Although rather more powerful cruising diesels are fitted, higher speeds remain dependent upon a pair of LM-2500 gas turbines. Given the greater length it is, perhaps, surprising that they are credited with being upwards of 2 knots slower than a Lupo.

It is reported that the Maestrales were designed with no capacity for mid-life modernization and that their retirement is planned for 2011–15. The planned replacement for both the Maestrales and the already defunct Lupos is a new ten-ship class of general-purpose frigate, the lead ship of which will be named, rather confusingly, *Carlo Bergamini*. At 5,000 tons displacement and 135m/443ft 2in overall length, these will mark a considerable advance in size, capability and adaptability. They will be similar to the projected French Aquitaine class.

ABOVE LEFT: Easily mistaken for a Lupo (opposite), a Maestrale differs primarily in having her SAM launcher forward of the bridge and in having a distinct gap between funnel casing and mainmast. This is *Libeccio*. ABOVE: This overhead view of *Maestrale* emphasizes the complexity of the modern funnel, whose contents are critical to the functioning of the ship's gas turbines as well as exhausting the cruising diesels and auxiliaries. It needs to be carefully cooled.

LEFT: In the later stages of fitting out, *Grecale* presents her unusual stern configuration. The transom, very wide to support the helicopter deck above, is deeply notched to facilitate deployment of the variable depth sonar.

Maestrale class, as designed

Displacement: 2,700 tons (standard); 3,040 tons (full load)
Length: 116.4m/382ft 1in (bp); 122.7m/402ft 10in (oa)
Beam: 12.9m/42ft 4in
Draught: 6m/19ft 6in (maximum)
Armament: 1 x 127mm gun; 4 x Teseo/Otomat SSM (4x1); 1 x 8-cell Aspide/Sea Sparrow SAM launcher; 2 x 533mm AS torpedo tubes (2x1); 6 x 324mm AS torpedo tubes (2x3)
Machinery: 2 gas turbines, 2 diesels, 2 shafts
Power: 37,300kW/50,000hp or 7,572kW/10,150bhp for 33 or 21 knots
Endurance: 11,110km/6,000nm at 15 knots
Protection: Nominal
Complement: 225

LEFT: **Rather like a cut-down Maestrale in appearance, the *Minerva* differs in having a low afterdeck not overlaid with the helicopter flight pad. The practice of painting discharge areas black gives a rather tatty appearance.** ABOVE: ***Fenice* is seen here with the original lower funnel, which affected helicopter operation. The latter's pad has been moved forward to reduce the effect of ship motion, itself reduced by active stabilizers.**

Minerva class

Classed officially as "light frigates" (FFL), the Minervas, slightly larger than a torpedo boat (light destroyer) of World War II, are configured as general-purpose escorts. Their hulls have relatively high freeboard and are of long forecastle type with a knuckle forward. Although the bridge structure is of full width, it is not elongated as in earlier classes. Forward is a single 76mm OTO-Melara Super Rapid gun, a dual-purpose weapon supported by an 8-cell Sea Sparrow/Aspide SAM launcher, a point-defence weapon that occupies premium space on the low afterdeck. Standard AS capability is thus limited to small-calibre torpedo tubes and a keel-mounted sonar. Space, however, has been allocated for the addition of a VDS.

Conflicting priorities are evident in that four units have landed their SAM system and torpedo tubes in favour of a projected helicopter facility. A helicopter and VDS would greatly enhance the AS qualities of the ships, but at the expense of self-defence (or that of any vessel under escort).

A further designed option is to ship both SAM system and a reload facility, together with four Otomat/Teseo SSMs, giving flexibility for fitting out according to likely operational requirements.

Between 2002 and 2004 were completed six more corvettes classed, probably for funding purposes, as patrol ships (Sirio class) or EEZ patrol ships (Fulgosi class). Built on a common, 88.4 x 12.2m/290 x 40ft hull, they are slightly longer than a Minerva but proportionately beamier. Their hulls follow contemporary fashion, with highly sculpted, low-signature features. As patrol vessels, most have a reduced armament.

Where the Sirio type is powered for only 22 knots, the Fulgosis are as fast as a Minerva (although requiring 58 per cent more installed power due to a fuller hull form). Both types already carry a 76mm gun and facilities (with telescopic hangar) for a large helicopter.

ABOVE: **Like most of the class, *Urania* is operating without either helicopter or Aspide/Albatros launcher which, if shipped, are alternatives. The ships are at the low end of displacement to effectively operate either.**

Minerva class, as designed

Displacement: 1,030 tons (standard); 1,285 tons (full load)
Length: 80m/262ft 7in (bp); 86.6m/284ft 3in (oa)
Beam: 10.5m/34ft 6in
Draught: 4.8m/15ft 9in (maximum)
Armament: 1 x 76mm gun; 1 x 8-cell Aspide/Sea Sparrow SAM launcher; 6 x 324mm AS torpedo tubes (2x3)
Machinery: 2 diesel engines, 2 shafts
Power: 8,206kW/11,000bhp for 25 knots
Endurance: 6,480km/3,500nm at 18 knots
Protection: Nominal
Complement: 133

Kola class

Designed shortly after World War II, the Kola-class fast escorts remained on the active list until the late 1970s. Between six and ten were built, their design borrowing features from German fleet torpedo boats (light destroyers), particularly the T25–36 group of 1941–42, commonly known as Elbings, and of much the same size. The low-set, spray-deflecting knuckle forward was typically German, as was the configuration of the wide transom stern. The latter was specifically to facilitate the laying of mines, tracks for which extended on either side as far as the forward funnel.

The profile of a Kola was pleasing, with two single 100mm guns in open mountings superimposed at either end. Two well-separated, strongly raked and capped funnels indicated boiler spaces divided by the engine room. Between the funnels was a centreline, triple torpedo tube mounting. Grouped around the after funnel were four twin automatic gun mountings, two of 37mm, two of 25mm. That most units appeared to lack two of these, together with the usual MBU AS rocket launchers, reinforced the general suspicion that the design was rather tender. Certainly, the dangers of ice accretion and extreme weather were avoided by assigning the class generally to the Black Sea fleet.

The length of the permanent mine rails suggested a capacity of at least 80. This considerable extra load could have been accepted only at the expense of landing other armament to compensate.

A feature of the main gun disposition was the lack of protection for the crews of "A" and "Y" guns, exposed to the muzzle blast from "B" and "X" guns.

The comparatively large, enclosed bridge structure was topped by a heavy "Wasp Head" director (derived from the stabilized German "Wackeltopf") to the front of which was attached the "Sun Visor" radar antenna. Only one triple 21in mounting was ever fitted.

ABOVE: **With the Soviet system then at its most secretive, good photographs of Kolas are scarce, identities of individual vessels rendered uncertain through change of pendant numbers. The Kolas' light armament classed them as "escorts" rather than destroyers.**

LEFT: **Although heavily retouched, this image of a Kola shows her major features, particularly the long, unobstructed side decks and wide transom associated with minelaying. The flush deck reduces stress concentrations in the hull.**

Kola class, as designed

Displacement: 1,500 tons (standard); 1,900 tons (full load)
Length: 96m/315ft 2in (oa)
Beam: 10.4m/34ft 2in
Draught: 3.5m/11ft 6in
Armament: 4 x 100mm guns (4x1); 3 x 21in torpedo tubes (1x3); 2 x quadruple MBU-900 AS rocket launchers
Machinery: Geared steam turbines, 2 boilers, 2 shafts
Power: 22,380kW/30,000shp for 30.5 knots
Endurance: 300 tons oil for 6,480km/3,500nm at 12 knots
Protection: Not known
Complement: 190

Riga class

With more the characteristics of destroyers than the escorts that were required, the Kolas were too much configured for speed and insufficiently for capacity. Their programme was thus curtailed in favour of the Riga, a more frigate-like type whose design was, in many respects, a reduced Kola.

Overall length was reduced by 4.5m/14ft 9in, but the beam was little changed. By accepting a 28 knot (as opposed to 30.5 knot) speed, installed power could be reduced by one third. The shorter hull required the boilers to be located in adjacent spaces, reducing survivability but requiring only one large funnel to exhaust both.

Although it retained the broad, minelayer's transom, the Riga hull already showed more "Russian" characteristics, flush-decked with a long, sweeping sheerline, the anchor pocket set well back. There was no knuckle but an enhanced flare. To further reduce wetness, a short bulwark was added right forward and an American-style, full-width screen abreast "B" gun. A solid bulwark ran from the screen to the funnel; with the 01 level continued to the ship's sides, this created a covered way.

Three 100mm guns were fitted, two superimposed forward, one aft at upper deck level. Two MBU AS rocket launchers, of various types, flanked "B" mounting at 01 level. Immediately abaft the funnel was a triple torpedo tube mounting. Permanent rails ran along either side as far forward as the funnel, their capacity about 50 mines if the tubes were landed as partial compensation.

ABOVE: **Finland acquired two Rigas from the Soviet Union in 1964. This is the *Hameenmaa*. Note the height of the 100mm guns in their trunions, indicating high elevation angles.**

Originally fitted with braced tripod masts, Rigas eventually gained a lattice structure to support increased electronic equipment.

Roughly equivalent to a British Hunt, the Riga proved to be rugged and seaworthy. Sixty-six were reportedly built, of which sixteen were transferred to including states from Finland to Indonesia. Some, fitted for intelligence gathering, gained a stub mainmast. All were discarded by the late 1980s, some having served for over 30 years.

Riga class

Displacement: 1,080 tons (standard); 1,400 tons (full load)
Length: 91.5m/300ft 4in (oa)
Beam: 10.1m/33ft 2in
Draught: 3.3m/10ft 10in
Armament: 3 x 100mm guns (3x1); 3 x 21in torpedo tubes (1x3); 2 x MBU-2500 AS rocket launchers
Machinery: Geared steam turbines, 2 boilers, 2 shafts
Power: 14,920kW/20,000shp for 28 knots
Endurance: 230 tons oil for 4,075km/2,200nm at 15 knots
Protection: Not known
Complement: 177

ABOVE: **In an attitude typical of the Cold War era, the Wasp Head director and "A" gun of this unidentified Riga are tracking the photographer's aircraft, although the gun crews are not closed up. Note the broad transom and clear side decks. The funnel casing is louvred to direct gases away from the electronics.**

LEFT: **Designed for coastal escort duties, this Petya I shows her broad range of armament: two enclosed twin 76mm gun mountings, two shrouded MBU-2500 AS rocket launchers forward of the bridge and two aft, and a covered quintuple torpedo tube bank amidships.** ABOVE: **An interesting close-up of a Petya fitted with two of the later MBU-2500A AS weapons. The bowl over the bridge is the Hawk Screech fire control radar for the 76mm guns. The casual "rig of the day" suggests that she is a Black Sea unit.**

Petya and Mirka classes

Produced in parallel with the Poti programme were 46 of the larger and more capable Petya class. Multi-role craft, they were triple-screwed, the centreline shaft being driven by two cruising diesels, and each wing shaft by a gas turbine. The hull was flush-decked, with marked forward sheer and a forward bulwark. Mine rails terminated at the broad transom.

As designed, Petyas had an enclosed twin 76mm gun mounting forward and aft, a quintuple 400mm AS torpedo tube bank abaft the low, square stack, and four of the flat-form MBU-2500s AS rocket launchers. Two of these were located aft and two on the bridge structure in a position that appeared perilously close to the wheelhouse windows.

Later units, known as Petya IIs, exchanged the after MBU-2500s for a second quintuple torpedo tube mounting, the bridge-mounted launchers being upgraded to the round-form MBU-2500-A.

A third variant, known variously as a Modified Petya I, or a Petya III, landed the after torpedo tubes in favour of various configurations of deckhouse, enclosing a VDS.

Of virtually the same size as a Petya, the succeeding Mirka varied mainly in its propulsion system. Two shafts were each usually powered by a cruising diesel engine. The propellers ran in tunnels, configured to as to act also as water jets when powered by the alternative gas turbines. The latter were housed, Poti-style, in the raised after end of the hull. Lacking a funnel, the Mirka had their lattice mast relocated amidships to minimize motion.

The raised after end prevented Mirkas being mine-capable, but two MBU-2500-As were sided both forward and aft. A Mirka II variant, however, exchanged the after pair for a second quintuple set of torpedo tubes. Nine of each type were constructed.

Some Petyas were transferred, but no Mirka. Units of both classes served into the 1990s.

ABOVE: **Successors to the Petyas, the Mirkas had their gas turbines relocated right aft. Note the raised deckline and large air intakes. This is a Mirka II, with two quintuple torpedo tubes but no MBUs aft.**

Mirka II

Displacement: 950 tons (standard); 1,120 tons (full load)
Length: 78m/256ft (bp); 82.4m/270ft 6in (oa)
Beam: 9.2m/30ft 2in
Draught: 2.9m/9ft 6in
Armament: 4 x 76mm guns (2x2); 10 x 400mm AS torpedo tubes (2x5); 2 x MBU-2500-A AS rocket launchers
Machinery: 2 gas turbines, 2 diesel engines, 2 shafts
Power: 22,380kW/30,000shp for 33 knots or 8,952kW/12,000bhp for 20 knots
Endurance: 150 tons fuel for 5,555km/3,000nm at 20 knots
Protection: None
Complement: 92

LEFT: **A slightly confusing picture with the two Potis overlapping. Their flat 16-barrelled MBU-2500 projectors are also staggered, the forward one to port, the superimposed one to starboard. The hump over the gas turbine space is even more pronounced.**

Poti class

Although, in the early 1960s, Soviet Russia posed an enormous threat to the West through its considerable submarine fleet, the Russians themselves faced a similar threat. This ranged from nuclear attack boats, and SSBNs deploying the Polaris ICBM, to conventional diesel-electric boats, and resulted in a range of specialist Russian ASW vessels, varying in size from large helicopter carriers to corvette-sized craft designed for inshore AS operations.

Smallest of the latter type, and surely among the least attractive warships of all time, were the Poti class. Slightly smaller than a British Flower-class corvette of World War II, the Potis had CODAG propulsion with two diesel engines ahead, and two small gas turbines. Each drives a separate shaft, partly enclosed within tunnels. With all four engines coupled, the top speed was probably nearer 30, rather than the 34 knots sometimes claimed. The latter figure appears excessive for a small, non-planing hull.

Otherwise flush-decked, with marked sheer, the hull had a raised after section to accommodate the air ingestion units for the gas turbines, whose large, shrouded intakes were arranged in tandem. An unintentional bonus was that the odd profile made it, from a distance, difficult to estimate the ship's heading.

On two levels forward, and staggered about the centreline, were two MBU-2500A AS rocket launchers. Looking outsize on so small a ship, these could lay six-or-twelve bomb salvoes out to about 6.4km/4 miles' range. In the waist, firing outboard at fixed angles to the centreline, were four long, medium-calibre tubes for the launching of wire-guided AS torpedoes.

For self-defence a Poti depended upon the radar-directed, twin 57mm mounting amidships.

Over 60 Poti were believed built, several being transferred within the Warsaw Pact navies. Most served well into the 1980s.

ABOVE: **With its darkly painted after end, this Poti looks distinctly ungainly, but paint schemes varied from ship to ship. Visible amidships is the twin 57mm gun mounting with its associated Muff Cob director. To its left can be seen the two starboard 400mm torpedo tubes.**

Poti class

Displacement: 530 tons (standard); 615 tons (full load)
Length: 60.7m/199ft 3in (oa)
Beam: 8.2m/26ft 11in
Draught: 2.9m/9ft 6in
Armament: 2 x 57mm guns (1x2); 4 x 400mm AS torpedo tubes (4x1); 2 x MBU-2500-A AS rocket launchers
Machinery: 2 gas turbines, 2 diesel engines, 4 shafts
Power: 17,904kW/24,000shp plus 5,968kW/8,000bhp for 30+ knots
Endurance: 125 tons fuel for 4,815km/2,600nm at 16 knots
Protection: None
Complement: 80

LEFT: **At about 71.5m/234ft 7in, a Grisha lies somewhere between a Poti and a Mirka, but is a much neater design. This unit, the Lithuanian-flag *Aukstaitis*, was one of two acquired from Russia in 1992. Note the NATO-style number.** ABOVE: ***Aukstaitis* again. This variant is termed a Grisha III, which appears to vary only in the addition of a six-barrelled, Gatling-type 23mm gun, whose helmet-like containment is visible between the after 57mm gun mounting and its director.** BELOW: **A late-model Grisha V. The circular cover on the forecastle screens a "pop-up" SA-N-4 ("Gecko") SAM launcher, whose control is through the Pop Group director atop the bridge. Her main surface/air search radar is an updated Half Plate-B.**

Grisha class

At around 1,000 tons full load displacement, the Grishas are considered corvettes. They were built in considerable numbers, probably about 70 in all. While they were follow-ons to the Poti class, they are 11m/36t longer and constitute a new design rather than a derivative.

The hull has the same pronounced sheerline, but here flattened somewhat right forward to allow any forward guns to depress. The bridge structure is based on a full-width deckhouse, abaft which is a low, square-sectioned funnel, offset slightly to port and exhausting both the gas turbine and the two diesels of the CODAG propulsion system. Broad after waterplanes permit mine rails to run along either side from the after superstructure to the wide transom.

Grishas are, depending upon armament fit, divided into several sub-types. Grisha I had a retractable SA-N-4 ("Gecko") twin SAM launcher on the foredeck, superfired by two MBU-6000 12-barrelled AS rocket launchers. Sided in the waist were twin heavyweight torpedo tubes, and aft there was a twin 57mm gun mounting. Grisha IIs differed in having a second twin 57mm forward in place of the SA-N-4. All surviving examples of Types I and II reportedly serve with the Federal Border Guard in its large quasi-military fleet.

Grisha IIIs replicate Type Is but have a modified after deckhouse, which accommodates a VDS system and supports a six-barrelled 30mm Gatling. Grisha IVs appear never to have existed, the follow-ons being Grisha V. Probably 20 of these are still active. They have improved electronics while, aft, the twin 57mm mounting has been replaced by a single 76.2mm. Only one MBU-6000 is carried forward, indicating possible topside weight limitation.

The defensive firepower of all surviving Grishas has been augmented significantly by their being equipped with shoulder-launched Strela-3 close-range SAMs. Despite considerable variation, the Grisha classes are collectively termed MPK, an acronym for "Small AS Ship".

Grisha V

Displacement: 880 tons (standard); 1,030 tons (full load)
Length: 66.9m/219ft 4in (wl); 71.2m/233ft 5in (oa)
Beam: 9.5m/31ft 2in
Draught: 3.6m/11ft 9in
Armament: 1 x 76.2mm gun; 1 x 6-barrelled 30mm Gatling; 1 x SA-N-4 twin SAM launcher; 2 x shoulder-launched SA-N-8; 4 x 533mm torpedo tubes (2x2); 1 x MBU-6000 AS rocket launcher
Machinery: 1 gas turbine, 2 diesels, 3 shafts
Power: Gas turbine 13,428kW/18,000shp; diesels 7,460kW/10,000bhp each; total CODAG configuration 28,348kW/38,000shp for 32 knots
Endurance: 143 tons fuel for 4,630km/2,500nm at 14 knots
Protection: Nominal
Complement: 86

Krivak class

Powerfully armed for their size and often categorized as "destroyers", the Krivaks were built for the Soviet Navy as "large anti-submarine ships" and are, therefore, more correctly frigates.

The Krivak hull is of long forecastle type, with adequate freeboard. A slight knuckle over the centre section results from a gentle flare at the waterline. The sharply overhung stem betokens provision for a large bow sonar. On the low afterdeck a centreline casing covers a VDS, flanked by the usual mine rails.

The bridge structure is sited to place both it and the major electronics close to amidships, to minimize the effects of ship motion. The foredeck is dominated by a quadruple SS-N-14 ("Silex") launcher. This missile is dual purpose, capable of being fitted to carry either warhead or torpedo, for use against surface ship or submarine out to a 50km/31 mile range. With no embarked helicopter, the ship may require assistance in targeting.

Forward and aft are the unobtrusive silos for the pop-up SA-N-4 ("Gecko") launcher. Each has its own director. Forward of the bridge are the usual pair of MBU-6000 AS rocket launchers, while at the break of the forecastle deck are superimposed gun mountings, twin 76.2mm in Krivak Is and single 100mm in Krivak IIs. Forward of the stumpy funnel is a square deckhouse supporting radar directors for both the guns and the after SA-N-4. Sided abreast the amidships gap are quadruple heavyweight torpedo tubes. Propulsion is by gas turbine, cruise and boost units being run in COGAG configuration for maximum output on two shafts.

Of about 34 Krivaks built, probably only ten remain operational at the time of writing. At least four were late new-builds for Border Guard service. Known as Krivak IIIs, these have a single 100mm gun forward and helicopter facilities aft.

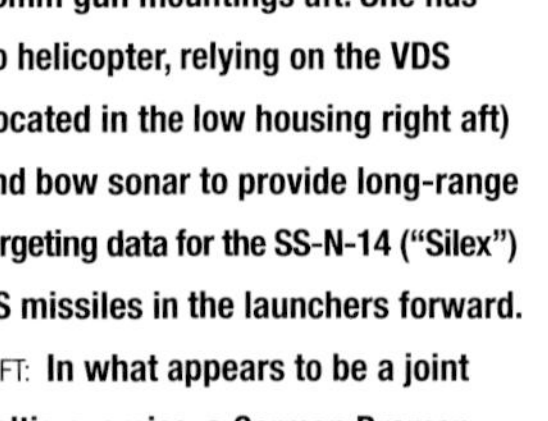

ABOVE: **A Krivak I identifiable by her 76mm gun mountings aft. She has no helicopter, relying on the VDS (located in the low housing right aft) and bow sonar to provide long-range targeting data for the SS-N-14 ("Silex") AS missiles in the launchers forward.**

LEFT: **In what appears to be a joint Baltic exercise, a German Bremen-class frigate lays astern of a Krivak I. SA-N-4 SAM launchers are housed forward and aft, the directors for each being visible. The SS-N-14 also has an anti-ship capability.**

Krivak II, as built

Displacement: 3,075 tons (standard); 3,500 tons (full load)
Length: 113m/370ft 11in (wl); 123.1m/403ft 7in (oa)
Beam: 13.2m/43ft 3in
Draught: 4.6m/15ft 1in
Armament: 2 x 100mm guns (2x1); 1 xquadruple SS-N-14 SSM launcher; 2 x twin SA-N-4 SAM launchers; 8 x 533m torpedo tubes (2x4); 2 x MBU-6000 AS rocket launchers
Machinery: 2 boost gas turbines, 2 cruise gas turbines, 2 shafts
Power: 2 x 14,920kW/20,000shp and 2 x 5,595kW/7,500shp maximum; 41,030kW/55,000shp for 30.5 knots
Endurance: 7,220kW/3,900nm at 20 knots
Protection: Nominal
Complement: 210

LEFT: **The radar-signature reduction features of *Stereguschchiy* combine to make her appear larger than her true size. Note how the masting arrangements on the ship vary from those on the official model (below).**

Stereguschchiy class

Following the collapse of the Soviet Union, cuts in defence funding saw the apparent abandonment of several interesting warship classes. These included a helicopter-equipped Krivak replacement in the 3,200-ton Neustrashimyy type, of which only two appear to have been completed, and the 1,600-ton Gepard-class "utility frigate", a concept reminiscent of the British Type 14s and also curtailed at two units.

Looking rather more hopeful, with plans for 10, even 25, ships is the slightly larger Stereguschchiy type, which appears to have been aimed at the export market. About 250 tons greater than a Gepard, it can operate a helicopter of the size of a Kamov Ka-27 (Helix A), for which a permanent hangar is provided.

The hull is of the long forecastle type, the low afterdeck being occupied largely by an enclosed VDS, which is roofed over to full hull width by the helipad. The VDS is complemented by a large, low-frequency sonar at the forefoot (of a size that could cause headaches when stemming the vessel in a small dry dock).

Backing up the helicopter for AS operations, the ship carries two twin heavyweight torpedo tubes, reportedly able to launch the Type 84R Vodopad-NK anti-submarine missile as well as wire-guided torpedoes.

The earlier planned large funnel has been reduced to a stump. A single, dual-purpose 100mm gun is mounted forward. Between it and the bridge front is a low casing which can accommodate a VLS for eight SS-N-25 ("Switchblade") SSMs or a gun/missile CIWS.

Unobtrusively recessed into the deck adjacent to the hangar are silo-housed SA-N-11 ("Grison") close-in anti-aircraft missiles, apparently optional, while flanking the after superstructure are two six-barrelled 30mm Gatling-type weapons.

ABOVE: **Virtually complete, the *Stereguschchiy* presents a workmanlike appearance. Note the Kortik-M CIWS fitted abaft the gun in place of the reported VLS. This may indicate an export version.**

Armament ard electronics fits appear to be flexible, while models indicate optional redesigned upperworks for signature reduction.

LEFT: **Although there are minor differences, the appearance of the official model is true to that of the ship herself. The very deep fairing around the bow sonar results in deep submergence and a reduced liability to damaging slamming.**

Stereguschchiy class

Displacement: 1,850 tons (standard); 2,100 tons (full load)
Length: 111.6m/365ft 10in (oa)
Beam: 14m/45ft 10in
Draught: 3.7m/12ft 2in
Armament: 1 x 100mm gun; 2 x 30mm Gatling guns; 8 x SS-N-25 SSM; 64 x SA-N-11 CIWS SAM; 4 x 533mm torpedo tubes (4x1)
Machinery: 4 diesel engines, 2 shafts
Power: 24,767kW/33,200bhp for 26 knots
Endurance: 6,667km/3,600nm at 15 knots
Protection: Not known
Complement: 100

LEFT: **Like their Italian counterparts, German designers preferred a flush-decked small frigate with accommodation gained by a full-width, non-structural deckhouse. Amidships, *Augsburg* is dominated by gas turbine requirements, with outsize funnel and casings.**

Köln class

Products of the same yard as the Hamburg-class destroyers, the six Köln were, in basic respects, diminutives of them. They were the first domestically built fast escorts permitted after 1945, and their designers naturally drew on their earlier experience, both types featuring bow sections remarkably similar to those of post-1943 torpedo boats and destroyers – sharply flared and knuckled, with anchors stowed high up at the deck edge to reduce impact and spray formation.

The Kölns were contemporary with the British Type 81s ("Tribal") and, like them, incorporated the still-new technology of gas-turbine propulsion. Of lower power, the single-screwed British ships cruised on steam, using the gas turbine (which represented only 37.5 per cent of installed power) in COSAG combination only for high-speed boost and getting under weigh from cold. The Germans installed a CODAG arrangement, coupling a pair of diesel engines and a gas turbine, singly or in combination, to either shaft. The gas turbines here generated some 68 per cent of maximum combined power. The four diesels resulted in somewhat complex gearing arrangements for either shaft but probably were the best available choice from a still-recovering heavy manufacturing industry.

The Kölns' hull was flush-decked, with full-width deckhouse, a form that was repeated with reduced crew on the Hamburgs. A French-sourced single 100mm dual-purpose gun was located at either end, the forward mounting superfired by two quadruple Bofors AS rocket launchers, sited immediately forward of the bridge.

Although fast, bettering 30 knots in service, the Kölns were cramped and had no scope for the addition of a helicopter. With the new Bremen-class frigates entering service from 1982 (confusingly with some repeated names) the Kölns began to be retired. *Karlsruhe* and *Emden* were acquired by Turkey; *Augsburg* and *Lübeck* served into the 1990s. The MEKO frigates that superseded them began an entirely new trend.

LEFT: **Portland, Dorset, where *Lübeck* is seen pierside in company with a British Hecla-class survey ship, a gun-armed Leander and a distant Type 42. Portland long served as a working-up base for newly commissioned European-NATO warships.**

Köln class, as built

Displacement: 2,150 tons (standard); 2,620 tons (full load)
Length: 105m/344ft 3in (bp); 109.9m/360ft 4in (oa)
Beam: 10.8m/35ft 5in
Draught: 3.6m/11ft 6in
Armament: 2 x 100mm guns (2x1); 2 x 4-barrelled 375mm AS rocket launchers; 4 x 533mm torpedo tubes (4x1)
Machinery: 2 gas turbines, 4 diesels, 2 shafts
Power: 2 x 9,698kW/13,000bhp and 4 x 2,238kW/3,000bhp; maximum in CODAG combination; 28,348kW/38,000shp for 30 knots
Endurance: 330 tons fuel for 5,370km/2,900mm at 22 knots
Protection: Nominal
Complement: 210

LEFT: **Best described as corvettes, the five Thetis-class AS vessels were built at Bremen during 1961–63. All, including *Najade* seen here, carried the patrol-craft "P" flag superior. A funnel would appear unusual on a diesel-propelled craft of this size.** BELOW: **Designed for shallow-water anti-submarine operations, the *Najade* has a four-barrelled Bofors-type AS launcher on the foredeck and four sided heavy torpedo tubes, two of which are visible abaft the bridge structure.**

Thetis class

German waters are notable for their shallowness, limiting the size of ships intended to operate specifically within them. This is particularly true of the Baltic, something of a maritime backwater except that during the early 1960s, the Cold War was at its height. For the not-inconsiderable Soviet naval force based on Leningrad/Kronstadt, the Baltic exits represented the only route to the open sea, and control of the Belts separating the Danish islands could expect to be contested. Considerable numbers of German wooden-hulled minesweepers were under construction (these shallow waters being ideal for mining) but further, offensively armed, units were required to dispute the passage of hostile surface ships and submarines, and for the escort of friendly traffic. Surface-to-surface missiles (once available) and torpedoes were weapons of choice to counter the former, and would eventually be deployed on large numbers of steel- and later composite-hulled fast patrol boats. These, however, were still in the future when the Thetis class was built to address the shallow-water anti-submarine requirement.

As was usual at the time, all five were contracted with a single yard. Again, the design featured the flush-decked hull, full-width deck house and knuckled forward sections that were common to most types of German warships of the period. The flat bridge front was extended in some to provide additional space for the operations room.

No medium-calibre gun was carried. The foredeck was occupied by a quadruple Bofors AS rocket launcher. Four single, heavyweight torpedo tubes were sided abaft the main superstructure, while either depth charges or mines could be accommodated aft. Defensive armament was limited to a twin 40mm mounting, located aft with its control system.

Useful as multi-purpose ships in peacetime, the Thetis class served through to the 1990s.

ABOVE: **Rather late in her career, *Triton* has been renumbered for patrol craft duties. She retains the twin 40mm mountings in the elevated aft position, but has landed her torpedo tubes. Note the broad, flat hull form.**

Thetis class

Displacement: 575 tons (standard); 660 tons (full load)
Length: 65.5m/214ft 9in (bp); 69.8m/228ft 10in (oa)
Beam: 8.2m/26ft 22in
Draught: 2.7m/8ft 10in
Armament: 2 x 40mm guns (1x2); 1 x Bofors 375mm quadruple AS rocket launcher; 4 x 533mm torpedo tubes (4x1)
Machinery: 2 diesel engines, 2 shafts
Power: 5,073kW/6,800bhp for 23.5 knots
Endurance: 78 tons oil for 5,090km/2,750nm at 15 knots
Protection: Nominal
Complement: 48

Bremen class

Known officially as Type 122s when built, but Type 122As since modernization, the Bremen resulted from a co-operative venture with the Dutch, the latter building the Kortenaer in parallel. While there are external similarities, the Bremens differ in their masting, notably with the lofty "Eiffel Tower" construction in place of the Kortenaers' rather bare pole mainmast. Dutch ancestry is evident also in the flush-decked hull, with its long, double-curvature sheer, where succeeding German design favours a raised forecastle, having adequate freeboard with little or no sheer.

LEFT: **Except for their masting, the Bremens closely resemble the Dutch Kortenaers, built as a cooperative venture. Unlike earlier classes, the Type 122/Bremens stemmed from five different yards. This photograph is of the nameship.**

The Bremens are of orthodox layout, with distinct gaps between the three (i.e. bridge, funnel-mainmast and hangar) superstructure blocks. Forward of the bridge is a single OTO-Melara 76mm gun, superfired by the rectangular NATO Sea Sparrow SAM launcher. Prominent atop the bridge are the WM-25 and optical/infra-red fire control system. Immediately abaft the bridge block, two quadruple Harpoon SSM launchers are aligned athwartships.

Where the Kortenaer are all-gas-turbine propelled, the Bremen cruise on diesel engines. The Dutch have Rolls-Royce gas turbines, the Germans Fiat-built American LM 2500s.

Together with a full updating of electronics, the 1990s modernizations saw two fast-reaction RAM (Rolling Airframe Missile) point-defence launchers added to the corners of the hangar roof, the space shared with the low structure supporting the air-search radar antenna. Conspicuous, the full-width hangar is configured for a pair of Super Lynx helicopters. Their airborne "dunking" sonars are complemented by a large, low-frequency unit at the ships' forefoot. There is also, reportedly, a mine-detecting sonar capability.

ABOVE: **A later addition to *Lübeck*'s armament was the two 21-cell RAM launchers prominent atop the hangar. The slightly longer-ranged Sea Sparrow is seen forward, and one of two quadruple Harpoon launchers abaft the bridge structure.**

To the helicopters' AS torpedoes can be added those from four, fixed 324mm tubes aboard the ships.

No further modernization being considered practical, the Bremens will be retired from 2010.

Type 122A

Displacement: 2,950 tons (standard); 3,800 tons (full load)
Length: 121.8m/399ft 4in (wl); 130m/426ft 3in (oa)
Beam: 14.4m/47ft 3in
Draught: 4.3m/14ft 1in
Armament: 1 x 76mm gun; 8 x Harpoon SSM launchers (2x4); 1 x 8-cell launcher for Sea Sparrow SAM; 2 x 21-round RAM launchers; 4 x 324mm AS torpedo tubes
Machinery: 2 gas turbines, 2 diesels, 2 shafts
Power: 38,046kW/51,000shp or 8,206kW/11,000bhp for 30 knots
Endurance: 610 tons fuel for 10,555km/5,700nm at 17 knots
Protection: Nominal
Complement: 200

LEFT: ***Schleswig-Holstein* (left) makes an interesting contrast with the rather smaller Spanish Knox-class *Estremadura* (centre) and the Turkish Perry-class *Gökçeada* (right). The German's powerful shoulders and high freeboard are evident.** ABOVE: ***Brandenburg* shows her speed. Note how Sea Sparrow is now accommodated in a VLS forward, abaft the RAM launcher which superfires the gun.**

Brandenburg class

The four Brandenburgs were designed in accordance with the MEKO principles developed by Blohm and Voss, whose yard led the construction consortium. MEKO (MEhrzweck KOmbination or, roughly, multi-purpose) see as many armament and electronics systems as possible modularized into discrete blocks which can, literally, be dropped into a ship's pre-wired system, being added or removed as required. Ships are thus delivered "for", but not necessarily "with", and can be, in theory at least, outfitted for specific missions.

An obvious drawback is that, with so much of the structure removable, the remaining hull requires to be rather more capacious, and compensated to maintain structural strength. Not surprisingly, therefore, the Brandenburgs, with much the same specification as the preceding Bremens, are of about 25 per cent greater displacement, and are proportionately more beamy to compensate for greater topweight and future growth.

The overall result is a ship which is not only structurally strong but, with its considerable depth, looks it. Freeboard is such that sheer is not required and, as a "stealth" measure, the hull has two gentle knuckles running along the greater part of the length.

The foredeck 76mm gun is superfired by one of the two RAM launchers. Between this and the bridge is a VLS with 16 Sea Sparrow SAM cells. Space is reserved to double this number.

Between the bridge block and the divided uptakes of the CODOG propulsion system are, surprisingly, four MM38 Exocet SSM launchers. A second RAM launcher is located atop the hangar roof, while two fixed AS torpedo tubes fire obliquely through apertures on either side of the hull at upper deck level. There are two Super Lynx helicopters.

Officially termed Type 123s, the Brandenburg are all named after German provinces, or *Länder*, with town/city names now apparently being reserved for smaller vessels such as corvettes.

LEFT: ***Brandenburg*'s hull, built to MEKO principles, maintains its high freeboard over the greater part of its length, contrasting with the more traditional form of the Bremens (opposite). Note the torpedo tube aperture amidships.**

Brandenburg class

Displacement: 3,600 tons (standard); 4,490 tons (full load)
Length: 126.9m/416ft 1in (bp); 138.9m/455ft 4in (oa)
Beam: 15.7m/51ft 6in
Draught: 4.4m/14ft 5in
Armament: 1 x 76mm gun; 4 x Exocet SSM launchers (4x1); 1 x VLS launcher for Sea Sparrow SAM; 2 x 21-round RAM launchers; 4 x 324mm AS torpedo tubes (2x2)
Machinery: 2 gas turbines, 2 diesels, 2 shafts
Power: 38,046kW/51,000shp or 8,206kW/11,000bhp 29.5 knots
Endurance: Over 7,410km/4,000nm at 18 knots
Protection: Nominal
Complement: 219

Sachsen class

Slightly larger than the Brandenburgs, the Type 124, or Sachsen, class share maximum commonality. Enclosed space has been gained by extending both bridge block and hangar to the deck edge. These now complement the subtly angled planes of the shell plating to give a very low radar return. To this end, the apertures for boats, torpedo tubes and accommodation ladders can be blanked off. The process is continued with the carefully configured "masts" supporting the advanced electronics which, for the first time, include three-dimensional, phased-array target designation and tracking radar with four-quadrant fixed antennas.

Although a 155mm modularized gun has been trial-fitted, a 76mm weapon is currently carried forward. Abaft it is the forward RAM mounting and a VLS with a mixed load-out of 24 Standard SM-2 and 32 Sea Sparrow SAMs. Amidships, the Sachsens have reverted to eight Harpoon SSMs. AS torpedo tubes have been tripled and are above deck.

Two Super Lynxes are currently carried, but the hangar is dimensioned to accept the larger NH-90 helicopter flown by the French and Italians.

The machinery layout has been considerably revised to a CODAG configuration, with two diesel engines but only one gas turbine. The diesels now account for about 30 per cent of total power and are used to supplement the gas turbine at maximum speed as well as for cruising.

Active fin stabilizers were fitted in the Brandenburgs, but the Sachsens use actively controlled rudders for the purpose. This is likely to lead to increased wear of steering mechanism and rudder bearings.

ABOVE LEFT: **The sculpted form of the tower bearing the four faces of the APAR radar immediately identify a Sachsen, or Type 124, frigate. Unusually, the faces are orientated along the main axes rather than at 45 degrees.** ABOVE: **On diesels alone, the Sachsens can maintain 18 knots. The machinery configuration is CODAG, i.e. combined diesel and gas turbine. With the latter on-line in combination, 29 knots can be exceeded.**

Probably another "first" for the Sachsens is the provision of dedicated accommodation for female crew members, a measure which, taken to its logical conclusion, will be a major contributor to the increase of warship size and, inevitably, expense.

German frigates work in four-ship squadrons but the fourth Sachsen (*Thüringen*) is yet to be ordered.

LEFT: **In peacetime, port visits, naval occasions and generally "showing the flag" occupy a considerable part of a warship's schedule, and here *Hessen* is dressing overall. The light clearly shows the subtle planes of the hull plating.**

Sachsen class

Displacement: 4,500 tons (standard); 5,690 tons (full load)
Length: 132.2m/433ft 3in (wl); 143m/468ft 10in (oa)
Beam: 16.7m/54ft 9in
Draught: 5m/16ft 4in
Armament: 1 x 76mm gun; 8 x Harpoon SSMs (2x4); 1 x VLS launcher for Standarad SM-2 and Sea Sparrow SAMs; 2 x 21-round RAM launchers; 6 x 324mm AS torpedo tubes (2x3)
Machinery: 1 gas turbine, 2 diesels, 2 shafts
Power: 23,500kW/31,500shp and 15,000kW/20,100bhp for 29.5 knots
Endurance: Over 7,360km/4,000nm at 18 knots
Protection: Nominal
Complement: 242

LEFT: The diesel-propelled *Braunschweig* has dispensed with a funnel, always a potential target for an IR seeker. Exhaust in early trials, however, has blackened the hull, resulting in a panel being painted black, as seen on the right.
BELOW: The class has adopted the Pool-type high holding power anchor. Although lighter, it is stowed low down and is not pocketed. Even in a calm sea, as shown here, it is the cause of spray formation. This, again, is *Braunschweig*.

Braunschweig class

Now firmly established as both a European and a NATO power, a united Germany is increasing its profile at a global level, her navy consequently undertaking more foreign deployments. Its large, capable, and very expensive frigates are its new capital ships, and there is room for smaller and simpler general-purpose vessels. The considerable flotillas of missile-armed fast patrol boats, built primarily to contest the Baltic exits have, with the relaxation of East–West tensions, lost much of their major role. The newest is also 25 years of age, old for a minor warship. Their replacements, not surprisingly, are light frigates/corvettes of considerably greater size and capability, a consequence of which has already been the reduction of the programme from a planned 15 units to just 5.

The early design favoured the flexibility of the MEKO concept but, on so small a scale, the weight penalty was excessive. The Braunschweig, or Type 130, hull is of long forecastle type, the low afterdeck forming a helipad large enough to handle a Lynx or NH-90, but with only basic facilities. Hangar space is provided only for two drone helicopters, used primarily in surveillance.

ABOVE: *Erfurt* is seen here fitting out alongside at her Emden builders. Although classed as corvettes, ships of this class are very capable. They can deploy a Lynx-sized helicopter but can hangar only two small drone machines.

Seemingly unsettled in their choice of SSM, the Germans, having already deployed Exocet and Harpoon on their frigates, have specified the 100km/62-mile Saab RBS-15 for the Braunschweigs. Dynamically programmable, this weapon is virtually a cruise missile, and can be used in land attack against designated targets.

A 76mm gun and a pair of RAM launchers are common with larger ships, but, for propulsion, the Type 130s are all-diesel, with one engine on either shaft. There is no funnel, exhaust gases being sea water-cooled to reduce IR signature.

The data stream from the drone helicopters is fused with that from the shipboard electronics systems for target designation and guidance.

Braunschweig class

Displacement: 1,690 tons (full load)
Length: 82.8m/271ft 6in (bp); 88.8m/290ft 11in (oa)
Beam: Not known
Draught: Not known
Armament: 1 x 76mm gun; 4/12 x Saab RBS-15 SSMs; 2 x 21-round RAM launchers
Machinery: 2 diesel engines, 2 shafts
Power: 14,920kW/20,000bhp for 26.5 knots
Endurance: Over 7,410km/4,000nm at 15 knots
Protection: Nominal
Complement: 65

Van Heemskerck/Kortenaer class

As already noted, the Kortenaer had a common ancestry with the German Bremens but differed visually, particularly in having a pole mainmast and a solid pyramid supporting the fire control radar atop the bridge. Both classes had gas turbine main machinery, but where the Bremens cruised on diesels, the Kortenaers used Tyne gas turbines, with the machinery arranged COGOG fashion.

The Dutch do not use the RAM point-defence system favoured by the Germans. Complementing the Sea Sparrow launcher in "B" position, the earlier Kortenaers had a second 76mm gun on the hangar roof. Later ships had light automatic weapons until Goalkeeper 30mm CIWS was acquired and fitted throughout the class. Eight Harpoon SSMs were located immediately abaft the bridge and four lightweight AS torpedo tubes could be shipped when required.

Two Lynx-sized helicopters could be accommodated in the full-width hangar, upon whose roof was located the conspicuous antenna of the long range air search radar.

Two of the ten Kortenaers were sold new to Greece in 1981 and were replaced by *Jacob van Heemskerck* and *Witte de With*, completed to a modified specification as guided-missile frigates, commissioning several years after the remainder of their near-sisters.

The van Heemskercks sacrificed their AS air component for a Standard SM-1 area defence SAM system, whose launcher is located atop the long, low superstructure that replaced the hangar. No 76mm gun is carried, while the Goalkeeper has been relocated right aft. In contrast with the standard Kortenaers, the stern is fully plated-in.

Between 1993 and 2002, the remaining eight Kortenaers were also acquired by Greece and a current rolling modernization programme seeks to extent their lives by 15 years. It was speculated that the two Heemskercks, retired early, would follow the remainder of the class, but they were acquired by Chile complete with Standard.

ABOVE LEFT: The Kortenaers were of compact but pleasing appearance, dominated aft by a large, near full-width hangar, upon whose roof *Abraham Crijnssen* has a Goalkeeper CIWS. Harpoon is just visible forward of the funnel. ABOVE: Two Kortenaers were completed as Guided Missile Frigates. The Standard SM-1 MR magazine and launcher have here replaced the helicopter hangar and flight pad on *Witte de With*. She lacks a 76mm gun forward but has CIWS aft.

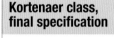

LEFT: *Jacob van Heemskerck* has a more complex electronics fit than a standard Kortenaer. The larger dishes forward and aft are for Standard SM-1 control, while the smaller dish on the "foremast" gives guidance for the adjacent Sea Sparrow.

Kortenaer class, final specification

Displacement: 3,000 tons (standard); 3,785 tons (full load)
Length: 121.8m/399ft 4in (bp); 130.2m/426ft 10in (oa)
Beam: 14.4m/47ft 3in
Draught: 4.4m/14ft 5in
Armament: 1 x 76mm gun; 8 x Harpoon SSM launchers (2x4); 1 x 8-cell Sea Sparrow SAM launcher; 4 x 324mm AS torpedo tubes (2x2)
Machinery: 2 Olympus gas turbines, 2 Tyne cruise gas turbines, 2 shafts
Power: 38,494kW/51,600shp for 30 knots or 7,311kW/9,800shp for 20 knots
Endurance: 8,705km/4,700nm at 16 knots
Protection: Nominal
Complement: 200

De Zeven Provinciën class

The gradual transfer of Kortenaers to Greece was offset by the construction of the six Karel Doorman general-purpose frigates and four larger Zeven Provinciëns, described as Air Defence and Command Frigates. The latter were to have been another co-operative project with Germany, in this case joined by Spain. The latter partner withdrew, although the resulting four Alvaro de Bazan class obviously owe much to work already done, but are heavily influenced by American Aegis technology. Germany then pulled out, her four Sachsens being based on preferred MEKO principles. Where both classes have a recognizable common ancestry with the Dutch ships, the latter reflect current French practice.

The Zeven Provinciëns are of long forecastle design, but this is not immediately apparent as the extremities are linked by a continuous knuckle, whose elegant curve divides the slight outward flare of the hull plating from the inwardly inclined, and virtually unbroken, sides of the superstructure blocks. These signature-reducing measures are continued in every "vertical" surface, and particularly in the towers incorporating the APAR phased-array radar and SMART-L early warning radar, both products of Dutch technology.

Somewhat hindered in depression by an inclined forward bulwark, the gun has been upgraded to a 127mm OTO-Melara weapon, abaft which are the flush-fitting covers of a 40-cell Vertical Launch System (VLS), designed for mixed load-outs of Standard SM-2 and Improved Sea Sparrow SAMs.

Equally unobtrusive are the eight Harpoon SSMs, concealed amidships behind inclined panels. One Goalkeeper CIWS is located over the bridge, another aft on the hangar roof.

Paired AS torpedo tubes fire through small apertures in the shell plating immediately forward of the hangar, which is dimensioned to accommodate a single NH-90 helicopter.

Propulsion is of CODAG configuration, the ships cruising on diesels but using a pair of Spey gas turbines for high speed.

LEFT: The distinctive faceted tower housing the APAR three-dimensional, phased-array, target designation and tracking radar dominates *Tromp*'s profile. Abaft the 127mm gun she is fitted with a 40-cell VLS.

ABOVE LEFT: Frigate designers are currently suffering from a bad attack of "radar invisibility", resulting in ships of closely similar appearance. Although a trifle bland, *de Zeven Provinciën*'s sharply sculpted form is still quite pleasing. ABOVE: A study in shapes: in the foreground, the elegant lines of the US Aegis cruiser *Normandy* framing the Dutch *Evertsen*; and beyond, a Danish Niels Juel corvette. The inclined black rectangle of *Evertsen*'s SMART-L radar also appears on British Darings.

De Zeven Provinciën class

Displacement: 5,870 tons (standard); 6,050 tons (full load)
Length: 130.2m/426ft 11in (bp); 144.2m/472ft 11in (oa)
Beam: 17.2m/56ft 4in
Draught: 5.2m/17ft 1in
Armament: 1 x 127mm gun; 8 x Harpoon SSM launchers (2x4); 1 x 40-cell VLS for Standard SM-2 and Improved Sea Sparrow SAMs; 2 x 30mm Goalkeeper CIWS; 4 x 324mm AS torpedo tubes (2x2)
Machinery: 2 gas turbines, 2 diesels, 2 shafts
Power: 39,000kW/52,280shp for 30 knots or 8,400kW/11,260bhp for 19 knots
Endurance: 9,260km/5,000nm at 18 knots
Protection: Nominal
Complement: 202

Karel Doorman class

Representing the "Lo" end of the "Hi-Lo" frigate force were the eight so-called "M"-class ships, effectively scaled-down Kortenaers. In service, they adopted the name of the lead ship. As in the UK, government policy is to reduce naval strength while having to recognize that the rump of a great shipbuilding industry no longer has work sufficient to justify its existence. The Ms, therefore, were ordered ahead of schedule, which served only to accelerate the disposal of the Kortenaers in compensation. At the time of writing, the Ms – the latest just 13 years in service – are themselves slated for transfer abroad.

Pre-dating the more capable de Zeven Provinciën class by some years, the Doormans lack the extreme profiling adopted to reduce radar and IR signatures. The hull has a gentle knuckle, running the greater part of its length, but the superstructure, despite its "vertical" surfaces being slightly inclined, remains conventional in layout.

The solidly plated mast is unusually tall, and is flanked by two prominent radomes for SATCOM antennas. There is a 76mm gun forward and, abaft the funnel, space for two quadruple Harpoon SSMs, rarely carried. Within the after superstructure are two pairs of lightweight AS torpedo tubes.

The hangar is dimensioned for only one Lynx-sized helicopter as it is flanked by eight Sea Sparrow launcher cells on either side. There is no capacity for Standard SM-2 missiles. This after superstructure is dominant, bearing on its roof the large standard antenna of the Dutch-built LW-08 early warning radar and, on its starboard after corner, a single Goalkeeper CIWS, again not always fitted. Later units can deploy towed array passive sonars.

Currently, two of the class are to be transferred to each of Belgium, Chile and Portugal. The remaining pair will undoubtedly follow.

ABOVE: **Originally termed M-class frigates, the Karel Doormans have an unusual Sea Sparrow SAM arrangement, 16 missiles being located in pairs on the port side of the hangar. *Van Amstel* has hers partly concealed by a radar-reflecting panel.**

LEFT: **Only 12 years of age, *Abraham van der Hulst* was one of two M-class ships sold to Chile in 2004. Unchanged except for modified helicopter arrangements, she is seen here en route to a new career in South America as the *Almirante Blanco Encalada*.**

Karel Doorman class

Displacement: 2,800 tons (standard); 3,320 tons (full load)
Length: 114.4m/375ft 1in (bp); 122.2m/400ft 9in (oa)
Beam: 13.1m/43ft
Draught: 4.3m/14ft 1in
Armament: 1 x 76mm gun; 8 x Harpoon SSM launchers (2x4); 2 x 8-cell VLS launchers for Improved Sea Sparrow SAM; 1 x 30mm Goalkeeper CIWS; 4 x 324mm AS torpedo tubes (2x2)
Machinery: 2 gas turbines, 2 diesels, 2 shafts
Power: 36,000kW/48,257shp for 29 knots or 6,300kW/8,450bhp for 21 knots
Endurance: Over 9,260km/5,000nm at 18 knots
Protection: Nominal
Complement: 154

St. Laurent class

This extended class of 20 frigates replaced the last of the war-built anti-submarine force. Their enclosed design emphasized operations in hostile northern waters and low temperatures. The hull was flush-decked and of high freeboard, the after end encompassing a long, open well containing two Limbo mortars and, with later modernization, a VDS. Except in way of the full-width deckhouse under the bridge, the sheerstrake was radiused over the entire length of the ship. Most of the anchor gear was located below the forecastle deck, clear of ice formation. The anchors themselves were recessed into pockets, with covers to reduce spray formation and further ice accretion. As this can add dangerously to topweight, this may have influenced the decision to construct the superstructure mainly in aluminium alloy.

As designed, the ships mounted two 3in 50 mountings, but the after one was landed during later modifications. The forward mounting was situated on a low, raised platform, behind a breakwater.

The extended timescale, with construction shared between six yards, saw modifications introduced to the extent that few ships were alike, and these quickly changed with further updates during their long careers.

In the original Limbo-armed version there was a single, tapered funnel and a short, plated-in mast with lattice extensions. Some later landed one Limbo, along with the after gun mounting, in order to accommodate an 8-cell ASROC launcher amidships. Half the class lost both Limbos, the well being covered with an elevated flight pad for a single Sea King helicopter. The provision of its amidships hangar required the uptakes to be split, with a separate casing on either side. To the helicopter's "dunking" sonar and AS torpedoes, the ship added VDS and six AS torpedo tubes.

The ships proved to be remarkably durable, most serving into the 1990s.

ABOVE LEFT: ***Fraser* shows something of the St. Laurents' magnificent seakeeping qualities in a short Atlantic swell. Her 3in gun mounting is trained aft to minimize water ingress. She was remodelled in the early 1980s to operate a large AS helicopter.** ABOVE: ***Terra Nova* of the Restigouche group has retained much of her original configuration, but with an ASROC (not visible here) replacing one of her Limbo mortars. Note the unusually lofty mast and the anchor pocket shuttered to reduce spray formation.**

ABOVE: **Following her 1980s DELEX modernization, *Restigouche* has acquired a reloadable ASROC installation. Most of her Limbo well has been plated-over, but her stern has been modified to accept a large American VDS. During their long careers, the ships acquired many individual characteristics.**

St. Laurent class, as designed

Displacement: 2,260 tons (standard); 2,800 tons (full load)
Length: 111.6m/366ft (oa)
Beam: 12.8m/42ft
Draught: 4m/13ft 3in
Armament: 4 x 3in guns (2x2); 2 x Limbo 3-barrelled AS mortars
Machinery: Geared steam turbines, 2 boilers, 2 shafts
Power: 22,380kW/30,000shp for 28.5 knots
Endurance: 8,800km/4,750nm at 14 knots
Protection: None
Complement: 230

LEFT: **Very considerably modernized during the early 1990s, the Iroquois class emerged as capable ships. *Algonquin*'s VLS, visible forward of the 76mm gun, is configured for Standard SM-2 SAMs. CIWS is atop the hangar and AS torpedo tubes are abreast the flight pad.** BELOW: **The Halifax class is fitted with a Bofors 57mm gun forward. Visible abreast of the funnel of *Charlottetown* is the port side, vertical-launch Sea Sparrow installation, obscuring the Harpoon launchers.**

Iroquois and Halifax classes

Carrying some of the "Tribal" names made famous during World War II, the four Iroquois of the early 1970s introduced gas turbine propulsion to the Royal Canadian Navy. Considerably larger than the St. Laurents, more heavily armed and with some command facilities, they were classed as destroyers, although still primarily AS vessels.

Their dimensions were driven by the then-bold decision to accommodate two large, Sea King-sized helicopters. Hulls were sufficiently spacious to install a passive anti-rolling system, effective at low speeds when there is inadequate flow over active stabilizing fins.

During the 1990s they were considerably updated. In place of the 5in gun appeared a recessed VLS, accommodating 29 Standard SM-2 SAMs, superfired by a 76mm OTO-Melara weapon. Cruising gas turbines were upgraded and the split exhaust casings replaced by a single large funnel. A Vulcan Phalanx CIWS was installed atop the hangar and a VDS aft.

Meanwhile, the 12-strong Halifax class was built to replace the aging St. Laurents. Despite their "frigate" label, they carry only one helicopter but are as large, and virtually as fast, as the Iroquois. They also carry Harpoon SSMs and, given small differences in layout, are comparable with the Royal Navy's Type 23s.

For improved physical protection, the Harpoons are located immediately forward of the hangar, while the VLS for the Sea Sparrow SAMs is a split, above-deck installation, flanking the enormous funnel, screened by a reflective panel.

The main propulsion units have been changed from the Iroquois' Pratt & Whitneys to the more widely used General Electric LM-2500 while, in CODOG configuration, a medium-speed diesel is used for cruising. Despite budget cuts, the class is due for thorough upgrading, including the addition of a Dutch-sourced three-dimensional search radar and an active/passive towed array sonar.

Halifax class, as built

Displacement: 4,300 tons (standard); 4,760 tons (full load)
Length: 124.5m/408ft 2in (bp); 135.5m/444ft 3in (oa)
Beam: 14.8m/48ft 6in
Draught: 4.9m/16ft 1in
Armament: 1 x 57mm gun; 8 x Harpoon SSM launchers (2x4); 2 x 8-cell VLS for Sea Sparrow SAM; 1 x Vulcan Phalanx CIWS; 4 x 324mm AS torpedo tubes (2x2)
Machinery: 2 gas turbines, 1 diesel, 2 shafts
Power: 35,435kW/47,500shp for 29 plus knots or 6,472kW/8,675shp for 18 knots
Endurance: 550 tons fuel for 8,335km/4,500nm at 20 knots
Protection: Nominal
Complement: 224

LEFT: **Nameship of an eight-strong class, *Anzac* is seen off a Gulf oil terminal, her MEKO 200 origin clearly recognizable. She is fitted with two quadruple Harpoon SSM forward and abaft the funnels, a VLS for Sea Sparrow.** ABOVE: ***Anzac* again, this time leaving Portsmouth, England, without Harpoon and the Vulcan Phalanx CIWS on the hangar roof. Electronics are a Franco-British/German/Swedish/American mix.**

Anzac class

Previously dependent upon British and American designs, Australia and New Zealand turned to Germany for the Anzacs. These were intended to replace both Adams-class destroyers and River-class (i.e. modified Type 12/ Leander) frigates, two very different types of ship. Their role could be high-risk as part of a multinational force, or low-risk in policing very long coastlines and large areas of ocean. Although Australia currently faces no obvious external threat, she is increasingly prepared to shoulder the responsibilities of regional power.

Short-listed for consideration were the German MEKO 200 (of which three had been recently and fortuitously completed for Portugal), the Dutch Karel Doorman and the "Yarrow frigate". The first-named won because of its "for, but not with" design, making it capable of being fitted for specific missions. Australia contracted for eight units, with New Zealand opting for just a pair. All were Australian-built.

On a more limited scale, the Anzacs follow the general MEKO principles featured above in the Germany section. It is worth remembering that a module for, say, a 5in 54 gun is as large for a 3,300-tonner as it is for a ship of 5,700 tons.

As delivered, the ships for both navies were similarly equipped. Forward is a 5in gun, abaft the split funnel an 8-cell VLS for Sea Sparrow SAMs. For these, space is allocated for a second 8-cell block. Margins are also provided for both eight Harpoon SSMs and a Vulcan Phalanx CIWS. Only the New Zealanders currently carry the latter.

All carry an American Super Sea Sprite LAMPS helicopter but, currently, no AS torpedo tubes. For economy, only one LM-2500 gas turbine is fitted for boost, limiting maximum speed to about 27 knots.

ABOVE: **Australian-built in the same series were two near-identical Anzacs for New Zealand. This is *Te Kaha*, with NATO-series numbering, in contrast to the Australian's US Navy style.**

Anzac class, with full planned outfit

Displacement: 3,250 tons (standard); 3,550 tons (full load)
Length: 109.5m/359ft (bp); 117.5m/385ft 3in (oa)
Beam: 13.8m/45ft 3in
Draught: 4.2m/13ft 9in
Armament: 1 x 5in gun; 8 x Harpoon SSMs (2x4); 1 x 8-cell VLS for Imp. Sea Sparrow; 1 x Vulcan Phalanx CIWS; 6 x 324mm AS torpedo tubes (2x3)
Machinery: 1 gas turbine, 2 diesels, 2 shafts
Power: 22,500kW/30,160shp for over 27 knots or 6,600kW/8,847bhp for 20 knots
Endurance: 423 tons fuel for 11,040km/6,000nm at 18 knots
Protection: Nominal
Complement: 148

Class lists

Page 60 Early torpedo boats: Numbered TB.1–T117 inclusive.
Page 61 27-knotters/"A" class: *Ardent, Banshee Boxer, Bruiser, Charger, Conflict, Contest, Dasher, Dragon, Fervent, Handy, Hardy, Hasty, Hart, Haughty, Hunter, Janus, Lightning, Opossum, Porcupine, Ranger, Rocket, Salmon, Shark, Snapper, Spitfire, Starfish, Sturgeon, Sunfish, Surly, Swordfish, Teazer, Wizard, Zebra, Zephyr.*
Page 62 30-knotters/"B" class: *Albacore, Bonetta, Earnest, Griffon, Kangaroo, Lively, Locust, Myrmidon, Orwell, Panther, Peterel, Quail, Seal, Sparrowhawk, Spiteful, Sprightly, Success, Syren, Thrasher, Virago, Wolf,* "C" class: *Avon, Bat, Bittern, Brazen, Bullfinch, Chamois, Cheerful, Crane, Dove, Electra, Fairy, Falcon, Fawn, Flirt, Flying Fish, Gipsy, Greyhound, Kestrel, Lee, Leopard, Leven, Mermaid, Osprey, Ostrich, Otter, Racehorse, Recruit, Roebuck, Star, Sylvia, Thorn, Tiger, Vigilent, Violet, Vixen, Vulture, Whiting.* "D" class: *Angler, Ariel, Coquette, Cygnet, Cynthia, Desperate, Fame, Foam, Mallard, Stag.*
Page 63 River/"E" class: *Arun, Balckwater, Boyne, Chelmer, Cherwell, Colne, Dee, Derwent, Doon, Eden, Erne, Ettrick, Exe, Foyle, Gala, Garry, Itchen, Jed, Kale, Kennet, Liffey, Moy, Ness, Nith, Ouse, Ribble, Rother, Stour, Swale, Test, Teviot, Ure, Usk, Velox, Waveney, Wear, Welland.*
Page 64–65 Beagle/"G" class: *Basilisk, Beagle, Bulldog, Foxhound, Grampus Grasshopper, Harpy, Mosquito, Pincher, Racoon, Rattlesnake, Renard, Savage, Scorpion, Scourge, Wolverine.* Acorn/"H" class: *Acorn, Alarm, Brisk, Cameleon, Comet, Fury, Goldfinch, Hope, Larne, Lyra, Martin, Minstrel, Nemesis, Nereide, Nymphe, Radpole, Rifleman, Ruby, Scheldrake, Staunch.* Modified Acorn/"I" class: *Acheron, Archer, Ariel, Attack, Badger, Beaver, Defender, Druid, Ferret, Firedrake, Forester, Goshawk, Hind, Hornet, Hydra, Jackal, Lapwing, Lizard, Lurcher, Oak, Phoenix, Sandfly, Tigress.*
Page 66 Tribal/"F" class: *Afridi, Amazon, Cossack, Crusader, Ghurka, Maori, Mowhawk, Nubian, Saracen, Tartar, Viking, Zulu.*
Page 67 Acasta/"K" class: *Acasta, Achates, Ambuscade, Ardent, Christopher, Cockatrice, Contest, Fortune, Garland, Hardy, Lynx, Midge, Owl, Paragon, Porpoise, Shark, Sparrowhawk, Spitfire, Unity, Victor.*
Page 68 Laforey/"L" class: *Laertes, Laforey, Lance, Landrail, Lark, Laurel, Laverock, Lawford, Legion, Lennox, Leonidas, Liberty, Linnet, Llewellyn, Lookout, Louis, Loyal Lucifer, Lydiard, Lysander.*
Page 69 "M" class: *Manly, Mansfield, Mastiff, Matchless, Mentor, Meteor, Milne, Minos, Miranda, Moorsom, Morris, Murray, Myngs.*
Page 70 Leanders/Lightfoots: *Abdiel, Gabriel, Ithuriel, Kempenfelt, Lightfoot, Marksman, Nimrod.* Leanders/1916/17: *Anzac, Grenville, Hoste, Parker, Saumarez, Seymour.*
Page 71 Emergency "M" class Group 1: *Maenad, Magic, Mandate, Manners, Marmion, Marne, Martial, Mary Rose, Menace, Michael, Milbrook, Minion, Mons, Moresby, Munster, Mystic.* Group 2: *Mameluke, Marvel, Mindful, Mischief, Negro, Nepean, Nereus, Nerissa, Nessus, Nonsuch.* Group 3: *Nestor, Nizam, Noble, Nomad, Nonpareil, Norman, North Star, Northesk, Nugent, Obdurate, Obedient, Octavia, Onslaught, Onslow, Opal, Ophelia, Opportune, Oracle, Orestes, Orford, Orpheus, Ossary.* Group 4: *Napier, Narborough, Narwhal, Nicator, Norseman, Oberon, Observer, Offa, Orcadia, Oriana, Oriole, Osiris, Paladin, Parthian, Partridge, Pasley, Patrician, Patriot.* Group 5: *Medina, Medway, Pelican, Pellew, Penn, Peregrine, Petard, Peyton, Pheasant, Phoebe, Pigeon, Plover, Plucky, Portia, Prince, Pylades, Rapid, Ready, Relentless, Rival.*
Page 72 "R" Class, Group 6: *Radiant, Radstock, Raider, Recruit, Redgantlet, Redoubt, Restless, Retriever, Rigorous, Rob Roy, Rocket, Romola, Rosalind, Rowena, Sable, Sabrina, Salmon, Sarpedon, Sceptre, Setter, Sorceress, Strongbow, Sturgeon, Surprise, Sybille, Sylph.* Group 7: *Satyr, Sharpshooter, Simoon, Skate, Skilful, Springbok, Starfish, Stork, Taurus, Teazer.* Group 8: *Tancred, Tarpon, Telemachus, Tempest, Tenacious, Tetrarch, Thisbe, Thruster, Tormentor, Tornado, Torrent, Torrid, Truculent, Tyrant, Ulleswater.* Modified "R" class: *Tirade, Tower, Trenchant, Tristram, Ulster, Ulysses, Umpire, Undine, Urchin, Ursa, Ursula.*
Page 73 "S" class. Group 11: *Sabre, Saladin, Scimitar, Scotsman, Scout, Senator, Sepoy, Serpah, Shamrock, Shark, Shikari, Sikj, Simoon, Sirdar, Somme, Sparrowhawk, Speedy, Splendid, Steadfast, Sterling, Success, Swallow, Swordsman, Tobago, Tomahawk, Torch, Tribune, Trinidad, Tryphon, Tumult, Turquoise, Tuscan, Tyrian.* Group 12: *Sardonyx, Scythe, Seabear, Seafire, Searcher, Seawolf, Serapis, Serene, Sesame, Spear, Spindrift, Sportive, Stalwart, Stonehenge, Stormcloud, Strenuous, Stronghold, Sturdy, Tactician, Tara, Tasmania, Tattoo, Tenedos, Thanet, Thracian, Tilbury, Tintagel, Torbay, Toreador, Tourmaline, Trojan, Truant, Trusty, Turbulent.*
Pages 74–75 V & W classes Group 9: *Vancouver, Vanessa, Vanity, Vanoc, Vanquisher, Vectis, Vega, Vehement, Velox, Vendetta, Venetia, Venturous, Verdun, Versatile, Verulam, Vesper, Viceroy, Vidette, Vimiera, Violent, Viscount, Vittoria. Vivacious, Vivien, Vortigen.* Group 10: *Voyager, Wakeful, Walker, Walpole, Walrus, Warwick, Watchman, Waterhen, Wessex, Westcott, Westminster, Whirlwind, Whitley, Winchelsea, Winchester, Windsor, Wolfhound, Wolsey, Woolston, Wrestler, Wryneck.* Modified V & W class. Group 13: *Vansittart, Venomous, Verity, Volunteer, Wanderer, Whitehall, Wishart, Witch, Wren.* Group 14: *Veteran, Whitshed, Wild Swan, Witherington, Wivern, Wolverine, Worcester.*
Page 76 Early torpedo boats. Schichau-built: S.7–23, S.24–31, S.32, S.33–41, S.42, S.43–57, S.58–65, S.66, S.67–73, S.74, S.75–81, S.82–87.
Page 77 *Divisionsboote*. Schichau-built: D.1–2, D.3–4, D.5–6. D.7–8, D.9.
Page 78 *Grosse Torpedoboote*. Schichau/Germania–built: S.90–96, S.97, S.98–101, S.102–107, G.108–113, S.114–119, S.120–124, S.125, S.126–131, G.132–136, G.137.
Page 79 *Grosse Torpedoboote*. Schichau–Germania/Vulcan-built: S.138–149, V.150–160, V.161, V.162–164, S.165–168, G.169–172, G.173, G.174–175, S.176–179, V.180–185, V.186–191, G.192–197.
Page 80–81 V.25–30, S.31–36, G.37–40, G.41–41, V.43–46, V.47–48, S.49–52, S.53–66, V.67–84, G.85–95.
Page 82 G.101–104.
Page 83 S.113–115, V.116–118, G.119–121, B.122–124.
Page 84 Early Torpedo boats: *Cushing, Ericsson, Foote, Rodgers, Winslow, Porter, Dupont, Rowan, Dahlgren, Craven, Farragut, Davis, Fox, Morris, Talbot, Gwin, Mackenzie, McKee, Stringham, Goldsborough, Bailey, Somers, Manley, Bagley, Barney, Biddle, Blakeley, DeLong, Nicholson, O'Brien, Shubrick, Stockton, Thornton, Tingey, Wilkes.* (TB.1–35 inclusive).
Page 85 Bainbridge class: *Bainbridge, Barry, Chauncey, Dale, Decatur, Paul Jones, Perry, Preble, Stewart.* Near sisters: *Hopkins, Hull, Truxtun, Whipple, Worden, Lawrence, MacDonough.*
Page 86 Smith class: *Flusser, Lamson, Preston, Reid, Smith,* Paulding class: *Ammen, Beale, Burrows, Drayton, Fanning, Henley, Jarvis, Jenkins, Jouett, McCall, Mayrant, Monaghan, Patterson, Paulding, Perkins, Roe, Sterett, Terry, Trippe, Walke, Warrington.*
Page 87 Cassin Class: *Aylwin, Balch, Benham, Cassin, Cummings, Cushing, Downes, Duncan, Ericsson, McDougal, Nicholson, O'Brien, Parker, Winslow.* Tucker Class: *Allen, Conyngham, Davis, Jacob Jones, Porter, Rowan, Sampson, Shaw, Tucker, Wadsworth, Wainwright, Wilkes.*
Pages 88–89 Flush-deckers. Caldwell class: *Caldwell, Conner, Craven, Gwin, Manley, Stockton.* Wickes class: *Aaron Ward, Abbot, Anthony, Babbitt, Badger, Bagley, Barney, Bell, Bernadon, Biddle, Blakeley, Boggs, Breckinridge, Breese, Buchanan, Burns, Bush, Champlin, Crew, Claxton, Cole, Colhoun, Cowell, Crane, Crosby, Crowninshield, DeLong, Dent, Dickerson, Dorsey, Dupont, Dyer, Elliot, Ellis, Evans, Fairfax, Foote, Gamble, Greer, Gregory, Gridley, Hale, Hamilton, Haraden, Harding, Hart, Hazelwood, Herbert, Hogan, Hopewell, Howard, Ingraham, Israel, J. Fred Talbott, Jacob Jones, Kalk, Kennison, Kitty, Kimberley, Lamberton, Landsdale, Lea, Leary, Little, Luce, Ludlow, Mackenzie, McKeen, McKee, Maddox, Mahan, Maury, Meredith, Montgomery, Mugford, Murray, O'Bannon, Palmer, Philip, Radford, Ramsay, Rathburne, Renshaw, Ringgold, Rizal, Robinson, Roper, Schenck, Schley, Sigourney, Sproston, Stansbury, Stevens, Stribling, Stringham, Talbot, Tarbell, Tattnall, Taylor, Thatcher, Thomas, Tillman, Twiggs, Upshur, Walker, Ward, Waters, Wickes, Williams, Wooley, Yarnall.* Clemson class: *Abel P. Upshur, Alden, Aulick, Bailey, Bainbridge, Ballard, Bancroft, Barker, Barry, Belknap, Billingsley, Borie, Branch, Breck, Brooks, Broome, Bruce, Bulmer, Case, Chandler, Charles Ausburn, Chase, Chauncey, Childs, Clemson, Coghlan, Converse, Corry, Dahlgren, Dale, Dallas, Decatur, Delphy, Doyen, Edsall, Edwards,*

Farenholt, Farquhar, Farragut, Flusser, Ford, Fox, Fuller, George E. Badger, Gillis, Gilmer, Goff, Goldsborough, Graham, Greens, Hatfield, Henshaw, Herndon, Hopkins, Hovey, Hulbert, Hull, Humphreys, Hunt, Isherwood, James K. Paulding, John D. Edwards, John Francis Burnes, Kane, Kennedy, Kidder, King, La Vallette, Lamson, Lardner, Lamb, Lawrence, Litchfield, Long, McCalla, McCawley, McCook, McCormick, McDermut, McDonough, McFarland, McLanahan, MacLeish, Marcus, Mason, Meade, Melvin, Mervine, Meyer, Moody, Morris, Mullany, Nicholas, Noa, Osborne, Osmond Ingram, Overton, Parrott, Paul Hamilton, Paul Jones, Peary, Percival, Perry, Pillsbury, Pope, Preble, Preston, Pruitt, Putnam, Reid, Reno, Reuben James, Robert Smith, Rodgers, S. P. Lee, Sands, Satterlee, Selfridge, Semmes, Sharkey, Shirk, Shubrick, Sicard, Simpson, Sinclair, Sloat, Smith Thompson, Somers, Southard, Stewart, Stoddart, Sturtevant, Sumner, Swasey, Thompson, Thornton, Tingey, Toncey, Tracy, Trever, Truxtun, Turner, Wasmuth, Welborn C. Wood, Welles, Whipple, William B. Preston, William Jones, Williamson, Wood, Woodbury, Worden, Yarborough, Young, Zane, Zeillin.

Page 90 Torpedo cruisers: *Tripoli, Confienza, Goito, Montebello, Monzambano, Aretusa, Calatafimi, Caprera, Euridice, Iride, Minerva, Partenope, Urania.*

Page 91 High Seas Torpedo Boats. Safo class: *Saffo, Sagittario, Scorpione, Serpente, Sirio, Spica,* Perseo class: *Pallade, Pegaso, Perseo, Procione.* Cigno class: *Calipso. Calliope, Canopo, Cassiopea, Centauro, Cigno, Climene, Clio.* Alcione class: *Airone, Albatros, Alcione, Ardea, Arpia, Astore.* Orione class: *Olimpia, Orfeo, Orione, Orsa.*

Page 92 Coastal torpedo boats: *Condore, Pellicano, Gabbiano,* 1PN–12PN, 33PN–38PN, 130S–240S, 25AS–32AS, 39RM, 40PN–45PN, 460S–510S, 52AS–57AS, 580L–630L, 64PN–69PN, 700LT–750LT, 76CP–79CP.

Page 93 Lampo class: *Dardo, Euro, Lampo, Ostro, Strale.*

Page 94 Nembo class: *Aquilone, Borea, Espero, Nembo, Turbine, Zeffira.*

Page 95 Soldati class. Group 1: *Artigliere, Bersagliere, Corazziere, Garibaldino, Granatiere, Lanciere.* Group 2: *Alpino, Carabiniere, Fuciliere, Pontiere.*

Page 96 Indomito class: *Impavido, Impetuoso, Indomito, Insidioso, Intrepido, Irrequieto.* Ardito class: *Ardente, Ardito.* Animoso class: *Animoso, Audace.*

Page 97 Sirtori class: Francesco Stocco, Giovanni Acerbi, Giuseppe Sirtori, *Vincenzo Giordano Orsini.* La Masa class: *Agostino Bertani, Angelo Bassini, Benedetto Cairolo, Giacinto Carini, Giacomo Medici, Giuseppe la Farina, Giuseppe la Masa, Nicola Fabrizi.*

Page 98 Early torpedo boats. Cyclone class: *Audacieux, Borée, Bourrasque, Cyclone, Mistral, Rafale, Simoun, Siroco, Tramontane, Trombe, Typhon.* Second-class torpedo boats: Numbered 1–369.

Page 99 Arquebuse class: *Arbalete, Arc, Baliste, Belier, Bombarde, Carabine, Catapulte, Dard, Epieu, Francisque, Fronde, Harpon, Javeline, Mousquet, Mousqueton, Pistolet, Sabre, Sagaie, Sarbacane.* Claymore class: *Carquois, Claymore, Cognée, Coutelas, Fleuret, Hache, Massue, Mortier, Obusier, Pierrier, Stylet, Trident, Tromblon.* Branlebas class: *Branlebas, Etendard, Fanfare, Fanion, Gabion, Glaive, Oriflamme, Poignard, Sabretagne, Sape.*

Page 100 Saphi class: *Aspirant, Herber, Carabinier, Enseigne Henry, Hussard, Lansquenet, Mameluk, Saphi.* Voltigeur class: *Tirailleur, Voltigeur.* Chasseur class: *Cavalier, Chasseur, Fantassin, Janissaire.*

Page 101 Bouclier class: *Bouclier, Boutefeu, Capitaine Mehl, Casque, Cimeterre, Commandant Bory, Commandant Rivière, Dague, Dehorter, Faulx, Fourche, Francis Garnier.* Bisson class: *Bisson, Commandant Lucas, Magon, Mangini, Protet, Renaudin.*

Page 102 Arabe class: *Algérien, Annamite, Arabe, Bambara, Hova, Kabyle, Marocain, Sakalave, Sénégalais, Somali, Tonkinois, Touareg.*

Page 103 Early torpedo boats: Numbered 1–75. Various builders.

Page 104 Harusame class: *Arare, Ariake, Asagiri, Fubuki, Harasame, Hayatori, Murasame.* Asakaze class: *Asakaze, Asatsuyu, Ayanami, Harakaze, Hatsuharu, Hatsushima, Hatsuyuki, Hayate, Hibiki, Isonami, Kamikaze, Kikuzuki, Kisaragi, Matsukaze, Mikazuki, Minazuki, Nagatzuki, Nenohi, Nowake, Oite, Shiqure, Shiratsuyu, Shirayuki, Shirotae, Uranami, Ushio, Uzuki, Wakaba, Yayoi, Yudachi, Yugure, Yunagi.*

Page 105 Kaba class: *Kaba, Kaede, Kashiwa, Katsura, Kiri, Kusunoki, Matsu, Sakaki, Sugi, Ume.* Momo class: *Hinoki, Kashi, Momo, Yanagi.* Enoki class: *Enoki, Kawa, Keyaki, Maki, Nara, Tsubaki.*

Page 108 "A" class: *Acasta, Achates, Acheron, Active, Antelope, Anthony, Ardent, Arrow.* "B" class: *Basilisk, Beagle, Blanche, Boadicea, Boreas, Brazen, Brilliant, Bulldog.* "C" class: *Comet, Crescent, Crusader, Cynet.* "D" class: *Dainty, Daring, Decoy, Defender, Delight, Diamond, Diana, Duchess.* "E" class: *Echo, Eclipse, Electra, Encounter, Escapade, Escort, Esk, Express.* "F" class: *Fame, Fearless, Firedrake, Foresight, Forester, Fortune, Foxhound, Fury.* "G" class: *Gallant, Garland, Gipsy, Glowworm, Grafton, Grenade, Greyhound, Griffin.* "H" class: *Hasty, Havock, Hereward, Hero, Hostile, Hotspur, Hunter, Hyperion.* "I" class: *Icarus, Ilex, Imogen, Imperial, Impulsive, Intrepid, Isis, Wanhoe.*

Page 109 Tribal class: *Afridi, Ashanti, Bedouin, Cossack, Eskimo, Gurkha, Maori, Mashona, Matabele, Mohawk, Nubian, Punjabi, Sikh, Somali, Tartar, Zulu.*

Page 110 "J" class: *Jacak, Jaguar, Janus, Javelin, Jersey, Jervis, Juno, Jupiter.* "K" class: *Kandahar, Kashmir, Kelly, Kelvin, Khartoum, Kimberley, Kingston, Kipling.* "N" class: *Napier, Nepal, Nerissa, Nestor, Nizam, Noble, Nonpareil, Norman.* "L" class: *Laforey, Lance, Larne, Legion, Lightening, Lively, Lookout, Loyal.* "M" class: *Mahratta, Marne, Martin, Matchless, Meteor, Milne, Muskateer, Myrmidon.*

Page 111 "O" class: *Obdurate, Obedient, Offa, Onslaught, Onslow, Opportune, Oribi, Orwell.* "P" class: *Packenham, Paladin, Panther, Partridge, Pathfinder, Penn, Petard, Porcupine.*

Page 112 "Q" class: *Quadrant, Quail, Qualify, Queenborough, Quentin, Quiberon, Quickmatch, Quilliam,* "R" class: *Racehorse, Raider, Rapid, Redoubt, Relentless, Rocket, Roebuck, Rotherham,* "S" class: *Saumarez, Savage, Scorpion, Scourge, Serapis, Shark, Success, Swift.* "T" class: *Teazer, Tenacious, Termagent, Terpsichore, Troubridge, Tumult, Tuscan, Tyrian.* "U" class: *Grenville, Ulster, Ulysses, Undaunted, Undine, Urania, Urchin, Ursa.* "V" class: *Hardy, Valentine, Venus, Verulam, Vigilent, Virago, Vixen, Volage.* "W" class: *Kempenfelt, Wager, Wakeful, Wessex, Whelp, Whirlwind, Wizard, Wrangler.* "Z" class: *Myngs, Zambesi, Zealous, Zebra, Zenith, Zephyr, Zest, Zodiac.* "Ca" class: *Caesar, Cambrian, Caprice, Carron, Carysfort, Casandra, Cavalier, Cavendish.* "Ch" class: *Chaplet, Charity, Chequers, Cheviot, Chevron, Chieftain, Childers, Chivalrous.* "Co" class: *Cockade, Comet, Comus, Concord, Consrot, Constance, Contest, Cossack.* "Cr" class: *Creole, Crescent, Crispin, Cromwell, Crown, Croziers, Crusader, Crystal.*

Page 113 Weapon class: *Battleaxe, Broadsword, Crossbow, Scorpion.*

Page 114 Battle class: *Agincourt, Aisne, Alamein, Armada, Barfleur, Barrosa, Cadiz, Camperdown, Corunna, Dunkirk, Finisterre, Gabbard, Gravelines, Hogue, Jutland, Lagos, Matapan, St. Kitts, St. James, Saintes, Sluys, Solebay, Trafalagar, Vigo.*

Page 115 Daring class: *Dainty, Daring, Decoy, Defender, Delight, Diamond, Diana, Duchess.*

Page 116 County class: *Antrim, Devonshire, Fife, Glamorgan, Hampshire, Kent, London, Norfolk.*

Page 117 Type 82: *Bristol.*

Page 118 Type 42: *Birmingham, Cardiff, Exeter, Glasgow, Liverpool, Newcastle, Nottingham, Southampton.* "Stretched Type 42": *Edinburgh, Gloucester, Manchester, York.*

Page 119 Type 45: *Daring, Dauntless, Defender, Diamond, Dragon, Duncan.*

Page 120 Farragut class: *Aylwin, Dale, Dewey, Farragut, Hull, MacDonough, Monaghan.*

Page 121 Porter class: *Balch, Clark, McDougal, Moffett, Phelps, Porter, Selfridge, Winslow.* Somers class: *Davis, Jouett, Samspon, Somers, Warrington.*

Page 122 Mahan class: *Case, Cassin, Conyngham, Cummings, Cushing, Downes, Drayton, Dunlap, Fanning, Flusser, Lamson, Mahan, Perkins, Preston, Reid, Shaw, Smith, Tucker.* Craven class: *Bagley, Benham, Blue,*

***Worden*, Bainbridge class**

***Neuva Esparta*, Battle class**

Craven, Ellet, Gridley, Helm, Henley, Jarvis, Lang, McCall, Maury, Mayrant, Mugford, Patterson, Ralph Talbot, Rhind, Rowan, Stack, Sterrett, Trippe, Wilson. Sims class: *Anderson, Buck, Hammann, Hughes, Morris, Mustin, O'Brien, Roe, Russell, Sims, Walke, Wainwright.*
Page 123 Benson class: *Bailey, Bancroft, Barton, Benson, Boyle, Caldwell, Champlin, Charles F. Hughes, Coglan, Farenholt, Frazier, Gansevoort, Gillespie Hilary P. Jones, Hobby, Kalk, Kendrick, Laffey, Lansdale, Laub, Mackenzie, McLanahan, Madison, Mayo, Meade, Murphy, Nibleck, Nields, Ordronaux, Parker, Woodworth.* Livermore class: *Aaron Ward, Baldwin, Beatty, Bristol, Buchanan, Butler, Carmick, Corry, Cowie, Davison, Doran, Doyle, Duncan, Forrest, Frankford, Gherardi, Glennon, Grayson, Gwin, Hambleton, Harding, Herndon, Hobson, Ingraham, Jeffers, Kearny, Knight, Lansdowne, Lardner, Livermore, Ludlow, McCalla, McCook, Macomb, Maddox, Meredith, Mervine, Monsson, Nelson, Nicholson, Plunkett, Quick, Rodman, Satterlee, Shubrick, Stevenson, Stockton, Swanson, Thompson, Thorn, Tillman, Turner, Welles, Wilkes, Woolsey.*
Page 124 Fletcher class: *Abbot, Abner Read, Albert W. Grant, Ammen, Anthony, Aulick, Bache, Beale, Bearss, Bell, Benham, Bell, Benham, Bennett, Bennison, Black, Boyd, Bradford, Braine, Brown, Brownson, Bryant, Bullard, Burns, Bush, Callaghan, Caperton, Capps, Cassin Young, Charles Ausburne, Charles J. Badger, Charrette, Chauncey, Chevalier, Clarence K. Bronson, Claxton, Cogswell, Colahan, Colhoun, Connor, Converse, Conway, Cony, Cotton, Cowell, Cushing, Daly, Dashiell, David W. Taylor, De Haven, Dortch, Dyson, Eaton, Erben, Evans, Fletcher, Foote, Franks, Fullam, Gatling, Gregory, Guest, Haggard, Hailey, Hale, Halford, Hall, Halligan, Halsey Powell, Haraden, Harrison, Hart, Hazelwood, Healy, Heermann, Heywood L. Edwards, Hickox, Hoel, Hopewell, Howorth, Hudson, Hunt, Hutchins, Ingersoll, Irwin, Isherwood, Izard, Jarvis, Jenkins, John D. Henley, John Hood, John Rodgers, Johnston, Kidd, Killen, Kimberly, Knapp, La Vallette, Laws, Leutze, Lewis Hancock, Little, Longshaw, Luce, McCord, McDermut, McGowan, McKee, McNair, Marshall, Melvin, Mertz, Metcalfe, Miller, Monssen, Morrison, Mullany, Murray, Newcomb, Nicholas, Norman Scott, O'Bannon, Owen, Paul Hamilton, Philip, Picking, Porter, Porterfield, Preston, Prichett, Pringle, Radford, Remey, Renshaw, Richard P. Leary, Ringgold, Robinson, Rooks, Ross, Rowe, Saufley, Schroeder, Shields, Sigourney, Sigsbee, Smalley, Spence, Sproston, Stanly, Stembel, Stephen Potter, Stevens, Stevenson, Stockham, Stockton, Stoddard, Strong, Taylor, Terry, Thatcher, The Sullivans, Thorn, Tingey, Trathen, Turner, Twiggs, Twining, Uhlmann, Van Valkenburgh, Wadleigh, Wadsworth, Walker, Waller, Wedderburn, Wicks, Wiley, William D. Porter, Wren, Yarnall, Young.*
Page 125 Sumner class: *Alfred A. Cunningham, Allen M. Sumner, Ault, Barton, Beatty, Blue, Borie, Bristol, Brush, Buck, Charles S. Sperry, Collett, Compton, Cooper, DeHaven, Douglas H. Fox, Drexler, English, Frank E. Evans, Gainard, Hank, Harlan R. Dickson, Harry E. Hubbard, Hugh Purvis, Hugh W. Hadley, Haynsworth, Hyman, Ingraham, James C. Owens, John A. Bole, John R. Pierce, John W. Thomason, John W. Weeks, Laffey, Lofberg, Lowry, Lyman K. Swenson, Maddox, Mannert L. Abele, Mansfield, Massey, Meredith, Moale, O'Brien, Purdy, Putnam, Robert K. Huntington, Samuel N. Moore, Soley, Stormes, Strong, Taussig, Waldron, Wallace L. Lind, Walke, Willard Keith.*
Page 126 Gearing class: *Abner Read, Agerholm, Arnold J. Isbell, Basilone, Baussell, Benner, Bordelon, Brinkley Bass, Brownson, Carpenter, Castle, Charles H. Roan, Charles P. Cecil, Charles R. Ware, Chevalier, Cone, Corry, Damato, Dennis J. Buckley, Duncan, Dyess, Epperson, Ernest G. Small, Eugene A. Greene, Everett F. Larson, Eversole, Fechteler, Fiske, Floyd B. Parks, Forrest Royal, Frank Knox, Fred. T. Berry, Furse, Gearing, George K. Mackenzie, Glennon, Goodrich, Gurke, Gyatt, Hamner, Hanson, Harold J. Ellison, Harwood, Hawkins, Henderson, Henry W. Tucker, Herbert J. Thomas, Higbee, Hoel, Holder, Hollister, James E. Kyes, John R. Craig, Johnston, Joseph P. Kennedy Jnr., Kenneth D. Bailey, Keppler, Lansdale, Leary, Leonard F. Mason, Lloyd Thomas, McCaffery, McKeen, Meredith, Myles C. Fox, New, Newman K. Perry, Noa, Norris, O'Hare, Orleck, Ozbourne, Perkins, Perry, Power, Rich, Richard B. Anderson, Richard E. Kraus, Robert A. Owens, Robert H. McCard, Robert L. Wilson, Rogers, Rowan, Rupertus, Samuel B. Roberts, Sarsfield, Seaman, Seymour D. Owens, Shelton, Southerland, Steinacker, Stickell, Stribling, Theodore E. Chandler, Timmerman, Turner, Vesole, Vogelgesang, Warrington, William C. Lawe, William M. Wood, William R. Rush, Wiltsie, Witek, Woodrow R. Thompson.*
Page 127 Forrest Sherman class: *Barry, Bigelow, Blandy, Davis, Decatur, Du Pont, Edson, Forrest Sherman, Hull, John Paul Jones, Jonas Ingram, Manley, Morton, Mullinnix, Parsons, Richard S. Edwards, Somers, Turner Joy.*
Page 128 Charles F. Adams class: *Barney, Benjamin Stoddert, Berkeley, Buchanan, Charles F. Adams, Claude V. Ricketts, Cochrane, Conyngham, Goldsborough, Henry B. Wilson, Hoel, John King, Joseph Strauss, Lawrence, Lynde, McCormick, Richard E. Byrd, Robinson, Sampson, Sellers, Semmes, Tattnall, Towers, Waddell.*
Page 129 Coontz class: *Coontz, Dahlgren, Dewey, Farragut, King, Luce, Macdonough, Mahan, Preble, William V. Pratt.*
Page 130 Belknap class: *Belknap, Biddle, Fox, Horne, Josephus Daniels, Jouett, Sterett, Wainwright, William H. Stanley.* Leahy class: *Dale, England, Gridley, Halsey, Harry E. Yarnell, Leahy, Reeves, Richmond K. Turner, Worden.*
Page 131 Spruance class: *Arthur W. Radford, Briscoe, Caron, Comte de Grasse, Conolly, Cushing, David R. Ray, Deyo, Elliot, Fife, Fletcher, Harry W. Hill, Hayler, Hewitt, Ingersoll, John Hancock, John Rodgers, John Young, Kinkaid, Leftwich, Merrill, Moosbrugger, Nicholson, O'Bannon, O'Brien, Oldendorf, Paul F. Foster, Peterson, Spruance, Stump, Thorn.* Kidd class: *Callaghan, Chandler, Kidd, Scott.*
Page 132 Ticonderoga class: *Antietam, Anzio, Bunker Hill, Cape St. George, Chancellorsville, Chosin, Cowpens, Gettysburg, Hue City, Lake Champlain, Lake Erie, Leyte Gulf, Mobile Bay, Monterey, Normandy, Philippine Sea, Port Royal, Princeton, San Jacinto, Shiloh, Thomas S. Gates, Ticonderoga, Valley Forge, Vella Gulf, Vicksburg,* Yorktown.
Page 133 Arleigh Burke class (Flight I): *Arleigh Burke, Barry, Benfold, Carney, Cole, Curtis Wilbur, Fitzgerald, Gonzalez, Hopper, John Paul Jones, John S. McCain, Laboon, Milius, Mitscher, Paul Hamilton, Ramage, Ross, Russell, Stethem, Stout, The Sullivans.* Arleigh Burke class (Flight II): *Decatur, Donald Cook, Higgins, McFaul, Mahan, O'Kane, Porter.* Arleigh Burke class (Flight II A): *Bainbridge, Bulkeley, Chafee, Chung-Hoon, Dewey, Farragut, Forrest Sherman, Gridley, Halsey, Howard, James E. Williams, Kidd, Lassen, McCampbell, Mason, Momsen, Mustin, Nitze, Oscar Austin, Pinckney, Prebel, Roosevelt, Sampson, Shoup, Sterrett, Truxtun, Wayne E. Meyer, Winston S. Churchill.*
Page 134 Momi class: *Hasu, Kaya, Kuri, Momi, Nashi, Tsuga, Warabi.* Wakatake class: *Asagao, Basho, Botan, Huyo, Karukaya, Kijiko, Kuretake, Nadeshiko, Omadaka, Sanae, Sawarabi, Wakatake.*
Page 135 Minekaze class: *Akikaze, Hakaze, Hokaze, Minekaze, Namikaze, Nokaze, Numakaze, Okikaze, Sawakaze, Shiokaze, Tachikaze, Yakaze. Yukaze.* Kamikaze class: *Asakaze, Asanagi, Harukaze, Hatakaze, Hayate, Kamikaze, Matsukaze, Oite, Yunagi.* Mutsuki class: *Fumitsuki, Kikutsuki, Kisaragi, Mikatsuki, Minatsuki, Mochitsuki, Mutsuki, Nagatsuki, Satsuki, Uzuki, Yayoi, Yuzuki.*
Page 136 Fubuki class: *Akebono, Amagiri, Asagiri, Ayanami, Fubuki, Hatsuyuki, Isonami, Miyuki, Murakumo, Oboro, Sagiri, Sazanami, Shikinami, Shinonome, Shirakumo, Shirayuki, Uranami, Ushio, Usugumo, Yugiri.* Akatsuki class: *Akatsuki, Hibiki, Ikazuchi, Inadzuma.*
Page 137 Hatsuharu class: *Ariake, Hatsuharu, Hatsushimo, Nenohi, Wakaba, Yugure.* Shiratsuyu class: *Harusame, Kawakaze, Murasame, Samidare, Shigure, Shiratsuyu, Suzukaze, Umikaze, Yamakaze, Yudachi.*
Page 138 Asashio class: *Arare, Arashio, Asagumo, Asashio, Kasumi, Michishio, Minegumo, Natsugumo, Ooshio, Yamagumo.*
Page 139 Kagero class: *Amatsukaze, Arashi, Hagikaze, Hamakaze, Hatsukaze, Hayashio, Isokaze, Kagero, Kuroshio, Maikaze, Natsushio, Nowake, Oyashio, Shiranuhi, Tanikaze, Tokitsukaze, Urakaze, Yakikaze.* Yugumo class: *Akigumo, Akishimo, Asashimo, Fujinami, Hamanami, Hayanami, Hayashimo Kawagiri, Kazegumo, Kishinami, Kiyokaze, Kyonami, Kiyoshimo, Makigumo, Makinami, Murakze, Naganami, Okinami, Onami, Satokaze, Suzunami, Taekaze, Takanami, Tamanami, Tanigiri, Umigiri, Yamagiri, Yugumo.*
Page 140 Akitsuki class: *Akitsuki, Fuyutsuki, Hanatsuki, Harutsuki, Hatsutsuki, Hazuki, Kiyotsuki, Michitsuki, Natsusuki, Niitsuki, Ootsuki, Shimotsuki, Suzutsuki, Terutsuki, Wakatsuki, Yoitsuki.*

Page 141 Yamagumo class: *Akigumo, Aokumo, Asagumo, Makigumo, Yamagumo, Yugumo.* Minegumo class: *Minegumo, Murakumo, Natsugumo.*
Page 142 Takatsuki class: *Kikizuki, Mochizuki, Nagatsuki, Takatsuki.*
Page 143 Shirane class: *Kurama, Shirane.* Haruna class: *Haruna, Hiei.*
Page 144 Tachikaze class: *Asakaze, Sawakaze, Tachikaze.* Hatakaze class: *Hatakaze, Shimakaze.*
Page 145 Hatsuyuki class: *Asayuki, Hamayuki, Haruyuki, Hatsuyuki, Isoyuki, Matsuyuki, Mineyuki, Sawayuki, Setoyuki, Shimayuki, Shirayuki, Yamayuki.* Asagiri class: *Amagiri, Asagiri, Hamagiri, Sawagiri, Setogiri, Umigiri, Yamagiri, Yungiri.*
Page 146 Takaname class: *Makinami, Onami, Sazanami, Takaname* (plus 2). Murazame class: *Akebono, Ariake, Harusame, Ikazuchi, Inazuma, Kirisame, Murasame, Samidare, Yadachi.*
Page 147 Kongo class: *Chokai, Kirishima, Kongo, Myoko.* Atago class: *Atago, Ashigara.*
Page 148 Bourrasque class: *Bourrasque, Cyclone, Mistral, Orage, Ouragan, Simoun, Siroco, Tempête, Tornade, Tramontane, Trombe, Typhon.*
Page 149 L'Adroit class: *L'Adroite, L'Alcyon, Basque, Bordelais, Boulonnaise, Brestois, Forbin, Le Fortuné, Foudroyant, Fougueux, Frondeur, Le Mars, La Palme, La Railleuse.*
Page 150 Le Hardi class: *L'Adroite, L'Aventurier, Bison, Casque, Le Cyclone, Foudroyant, Le Hardi, L'Intrepide, Mameluke, L'Opiniâtre, Siroco, Le Temeraire.*
Page 151 Chacal class: *Chacal, Jaguar, Léopard, Lynx, Panthère, Tigre.*
Page 152 Guépard class: *Bison, Guépard, Lion, Vauban, Verdun, Valmy.*
Page 153 Aigle class: *Aigle, Albatros, Epervier, Gerfaut, Milan, Vautour.* Vauquelin class: *Cassard, Chevalier Paul, Kersaint, Maillé, Brezé, Tartu, Vauquelin.*
Page 154 Le Fantasque class: *L'Audacieux, Le Fantasque, L'Indomptable, Le Malin, Le Terrible, Le Triomphant.* Mogador class: *Desaix, Hoche, Kléber, Marceau, Mogador, Volta.*
Page 155 Surcouf class: *Bouvet, Casabianca, Cassard, Chevalier Paul, D'Estrées, Du Chayla, Dupetit Thouars, Guépratte, Kersaint, Maillé Brezé, Surcouf, Vauquelin.* Duperré class: *La Bourdonnais, Duperré, Forbin, Jauréguiberry, Tartu.*
Page 156 Suffren class: *Duquesne, Suffren.*
Page 157 Tourville class: *De Grasse, Duguay-Trouin, Tourville.*
Page 158 Georges Leygues class: *Dupleix, Georges Leygues, Jean de Vienne, La Motte-Picquet, Latouche-Tréville, Montcalm.* Cassard class: *Cassard, Jean Bart.*
Page 159 Sella class: *Francesco Crispi, Quintino Sella.* Sauro class: *Cesare Battisti, Daniele Manin, Francesco Nullo, Nazario Sauro.*
Page 160 Turbine class: *Aquilone, Borea, Espero, Euro, Nembo, Ostro, Turbine.*
Page 161 Leone class: *Leone, Pantera, Tigre.* Navigatore class: *Alvise de Mosto, Antonio da Noli, Nicoloso da Recco, Giovanni da Verazzano, Lanzerotto, Malocello, Leone Pancaldo, Emanuele Pessagno, Antonio Pigafetta, Luca Tarigo, Antoniotto Usodimare, Ugolino Vivaldi, Nicoló Zeno.*
Page 162 Dardo class: *Dardo, Freccia, Saetta, Strale.* Folgore class: *Baleno, Folgore, Fulmine, Lampo.*
Page 163 Maestrale class: *Grecale, Libeccio, Maestrale, Scirocco.* Oriani class: *Vittorio Alfieri, Giosue Carducci, Vincenzo Gioberti, Alfredo Oriani.*
Page 164 Soldati class, Group I: *Alpino, Artigliere, Ascari, Aviere, Bersagliere, Camicia Nera, Carabiniere, Corazziere, Fuciliere, Geniere, Granatiere, Lanciere.* Soldalti class Group II: *Bombardiere, Carrista, Corsaro, Legionario, Mitragliere, Squadrista, Velite.*
Page 165 Imparvido class: *Impavido, Intrepido.*
Page 166 Ardito class: *Ardito, Audace.*
Page 167 Mimbelli class: *Francesco Mimbelli, Luigi Durand de la Penne.*
Page 168 Skoryi class: About 75 in class. Names not certain.
Page 169 Kotlin class: About 18 in class. Names not certain.
Page 170 Kildin class: Four in class. Names not certain.
Page 171 Krupnyi class: *Gnevny, Gordy.*
Page 172 Kanin class: *Boyky, Derzky, Gnevny, Gordy, Gremyashchy, Uporny, Zhguchy, Zorky.*
Page 173 Kashin class: *Komsomolets Ikrainyi, Krasnyi, Kavkaz, Krasnyi Krym, Obraztsovyi, Odarennyi, Reshitelnyi, Skoryi, Smetlivyi, Soobrazitel'nyi, Sposobnyi, Sterequshchiy, Strogiy.* Modified Kashin class: *Ognevoy, Sderzhannyi, Slavnyi, Smel'yi, Smyshlennyi, Stroyni.*
Page 174 Sovremennyi class: *Admiral Ushakov, Aleksandr Nevskyi. Bespokoynyi, Bezboyaznennyi, Bezuderzhanyi, Bezuprechniyi, Boyevoy, Burnyi, Bystryi, Gremyashchiy, Nastoychivyi, Okrylennyi, Osmotritel'nyi, Otchayannyi, Otlichnyi, Rastoropnyi, Sovremennyi, Stroikiy, Yekaterinburg.*
Page 175 Udaloy class: *Admiral Kharlamov, Admiral Levchenko, Admiral Panteleyev, Admiral Tributs, Admiral Vinogradov, Marshal Shaposhnikov, Marshal Vasil'yevskiy, Severomorsck, Vitse-Admiral Kulakov.*
Page 176 Maass class: *Bernd von Arnim, Bruno Heinemann, Erich Giese, Rich Koellner, Erich Steinbrinck, Friedrich Eckoldt, Friedrich Ihn, Georg Thiele, Hans Lody, Hermann Schoemann, Leberecht Maass, Max Schultz, Paul Jacobi, Richard Beitzen, Theordor Riedel, Wolfgang Zenker.* Von Roeder class: *Anton Schmitt, Diether von Roeder, Hermann Kunne, Hans Ludemann, Karl Galster, Wilhelm Heidkamp.*
Page 177 Z23–34, Z35–36, Z37–39.
Page 178 Hamburg class: *Bayern, Hamburg, Hessen, Schleswig-Holstein.*
Page 179 Groningen class: *Amsterdam, Drenthe, Friesland, Groningen, Limburg, Overijssel, Rotterdam, Utrecht.* Holland class: *Gelderland, Holland, Noord Brabant, Zeeland.*
Page 180 Ölland class: *Ölland, Uppland.*
Page 181 Östergötland class: *Gästrikland, Hälsingland, Östergötland, Södermanland.* Halland class: *Halland, Smaland.*
Page 184 Black Swan class: *Black Swan, Erne, Flamingo, Ibis, Whimbrel, Wild Goose, Woodcock, Woodpecker, Wren.* Modified Black Swan class: *Actaeon, Alacrity, Amethyst, Chanticlear, Crane, Cygnet, Hart, Hind, Kite, Lapwing, Lark, Magpie, Mermaid, Modeste, Nereide, Opossum, Peacock, Pheasant, Redpole, Snipe, Sparrow, Starling.*
Page 185 Hunt class Type I: *Atherstone, Berkeley, Cattistock, Cleveland, Cotswold, Cottesmore, Eglinton, Exmoor, Fernie, Garth, Hambledon, Holderness, Mendip, Meynell, Pytchley, Quantock, Southdown, Tynedale, Whaddon.* Type II: *AvonVale, Badsworth, Beaufort, Bicester, Blackmore, Blankney, Blencathra, Brocklesby, Calpe, Chiddingfold, Cowdray, Croome, Dulverton, Eridge, Farndale, Grove, Heythrop, Hurworth, Lamerton, Lauderdale, Ledbury, Liddesdale, Middleton, Puckeridge, Southwold, Tetcott, Oakley, Wheatland, Wilton, Zetland.* Type II: *Airedale, Albrighton, Aldenham, Belvoir, Blean, Bleasdale, Derwent, Easton, Eggesford, Goathland, Haydon, Holcombe, Limbourne, Melbreak, Penylan, Rockwood, Stevenstone, Talybont, Tanatside, Wensleydale.* Type IV: *Brecon, Brissenden.*
Page 186 Flower class UK-built, 1939 Programme: *Anemone, Arbutus, Asphodel, Aubretia, Auricula, Begonia, Bluebell, Campanula, Candytuft, Carnation, Celandine, Clematis, Columbine, Convolvulus, Coreopsis, Crocus, Cyclamen, Dianella, Dahlia, Delphinium, Dianthus, Gardenia, Geranium, Gladiolus, Godetia, Heliotrope, Hollyhock, Honeysuckle, Hydrangea, Jasmine, Jonquil, Larkspur, Lavender, Lobelia, Marguerite, Marigold, Mignonette, Mimosa, Myosotis, Narcissus, Nigella, Penstemon, Polyanthus, Primrose, Salvia, Snapdragon, Snowdrop, Sunflower, Tulip, Verbena, Veronica, Wallflower, Zinnia.* UK-built, 1939 Emergency Programme: *Acanthus, Aconite, Alyssum, Amaranthus, Arabis, Bellwort, Borage, Burdock, Calendula, Camellia, Campion, Clarkia, Clover, Coriander, Coltsfoot, Erica, Fleur de Lys, Freesia, Gentian, Gloxinia, Heartsease, Heather, Hybiscus, Hyacinth, Kingcup, La Malouine, Loosestrife, Lotus (I), Lotus (II), Mallow, Meadowsweet, Nasturtium, Orchis, Oxlip, Pennywort, Peony, Periwinkle, Petunia, Picotee, Pimpernel, Renunculus, Rhododendron, Rockrose, Rose, Samphire, Saxifrage, Spiraea, Starwort, Stonecrop, Sundew, Violet.* UK-built, 1940 Programme: *Abelia, Alisma, Anchusa, Armeria, Aster, Bergamot, Bryony, Buttercup, Chrysanthemum, Cowslip, Eglantine, Fritillary, Genista, Vervain, Vetch.* Supplementary Programmes: *Arrowhead, Balsam, Bittersweet, Eyebright, Fennel, Godetia, (II), Hepatica, Hyderabad, Mayflower, Monkshood, Montbretia, Pink, Poppy, Potentilla, Quesnell, Snowberry, Sorrel, Spikenard, Sweetbriar, Tamarisk, Thyme, Trillium, Windflower.* UK-built Modified Flower class, 1941–42: *Arabis, Arbutus, Betony, Buddleia, Bugloss, Bulrush, Burnet, Candytuft, Ceanothus, Charlock.* Canadian-built, Flower class, 1939–40 Programme: *Agassiz, Alberni, Algoma, Amherst, Arrowhead, Arvida, Baddeck, Barrie, Battleford, Brandon, Buctouche, Camrose, Chambly, Chicoutimi, Chilliwack, Cobalt, Collingwood, Dauphin, Dawson, Drumheller, Dunvegan, Edmondston, Galt, Kamloops, Kamsack, Kenogami, Lethbridge, Levis, Louisburg, Lunenburg, Matapedia, Moncton, Moosejaw, Morden, Nanaimo, Napanee, Oakville, Orillia, Pikton, Prescott, Quesnel, Rimouski, Rosthern, Sackville, Saskatoon, Shawinigan, Shediac, Sherbrooke, Sorel, Subbury,*

Summerside, The Pas, Wetaskiwin, Weyburn. Revised Canadian Flower class 1941–42 Programme: *Calgary, Charlottetown, Dundas, Fredericton, Halifax, La Malbaie, Port Arthur, Regina, Ville de Quebec, Woodstock.* 1942–43 Programme: *Athol, Coburg, Fergus, Frontenac, Guelph, Hawksbury, Lindsay, Norsyd, North Bay, Owen Sound, Rivière du Loup, St. Lambert, Trentonian, Whitby.* 1943–44 Programme: *Asbestos, Beauharnois, Bellville, Lachute, Merrittonia, Parry Sound, Peterborough, Smith's Falls, Stellaton, Strathroy, Thorlock, West, York.* Canadian-built for USN: *Comfrey, Cornel, Flax, Mandrake, Milfoil, Musk, Nepeta, Privet.* Canadian-built to RN via USN: *Dittany, Honesty, Linaria, Rosebay, Smilax, Statice, Willowherb.*

Page 187 River class 1940 Programme: *Balinderry, Bann, Chelmer, Dart, Derg, Ettrick, Exe, Itchen, Jed, Kale, Lagan, Moyola, Ness, Nith, Rother, Spey, Strule, Swale, Tay, Test, Teviot, Trent, Tweed, Waveney, Wear.* 1941 Programme: *Aire, Braid, Cam, Deveron, Dovey, Fal, Frome, Helford, Helmsdale, Meon, Nene, Plym, Ribble, Tavy, Tees, Torridge, Towy, Usk, Windrush, Wye.* 1942 Programme: *Avon, Awe, Halladale, Lochy, Mourne, Nadder, Odzani, Taff.* Canadian-built for RN: *Barle, Cuckmere, Evenlode, Findhorn, Inver, Lossie, Parret, Shiel.* Canadian-built River class 1942–43 Programme: *Beacon Hill, Cap de la Madeleine, Cape Breton, Charlottetown, Chebogue, Dunver, Eastview, Gron, Joliette, Jonquière, Kirkland Lake, Kokanee, La Hulloise, Longuenil, Magog, Matane, Montreal, New Glasgow, New Waterford, Orkney, Outremont, Port Colborne, Prince Rupert, St. Catherines, St. John, Springhill, Stettler, Stormont, Swansea, Thetford Mines, Valleyfield, Waskesiu, Wentworth.* 1943–44 Programme: *Antigonish, Buckingham, Capilano, Carlplace, Coaticook, Fort Erie, Glace Bay, Hallowell, Inch Arran, Lanark, Lasalle, Levis, Penetang, Poundmaker, Prestonian, Royal Mount, Runnymede, St. Pierre, St. Stephan, Ste. Thérèse, Seacliff, Stonetown, Strathadam, Sussexvale, Toronto, Victoriaville.*

Page 188 Castle class, 1942 Programme: *Allington Castle, Bamborough C., Caistor C., Denbigh C., Farnham C., Hadleigh C., Hedingham C., Hurst C., Kenilworth C., Lancaster C., Oakham C.* 1943 Programme: *Alnwick Castle, Amberley C., Berkeley C., Carisbrooke C., Dumbarton C., Flint C., Knaresborough C., Launceston C., Leeds C., Morpeth C., Oxford C., Pevensey C., Portchester C., Rushen C., Tintagel C.* Transferred to RCN: *Guildford Castle, Hedingham C., Hever C., Norham C., Nunnery C., Pembroke C., Rising C., Sandgate C., Sherborne C., Tamworth C., Walmer C., Wolvesey C.* Transferred to Norway: *Shrewsbury Castle.*

Page 189 Bay class: *Bigbury Bay, Burghead Bay, Cardigan Bay, Carnarvon Bay, Cawsand B., Enard B., Largo Bay, Morecambe B., Mounts B., Padstow B., Porlock B., St. Bride's B., St. Austell B., Start B., Tremadoc B., Veryan B., Whitesand B., Widemouth B., Wigtown Bay.* Loch class, 1942 Programme: *Loch Achanalt, Loch Dunvegan, Loch Eck, Loch Fada.* 1943 Programme: *Loch Achray, L. Alvie, L. Arkaig, L. Craggie, L. Fyne, L. Glendhu, L. Gorm, L. Insh, L. Katrine, L. Killin, L. Killisport, L. Lomond, L. More, L. Morlich, L. Quoich, L. Ruthwen, L. Scavaig, L. Shin, L. Tarbert, L. Tralaig, Loch Veyatie.* Transferred to RCN: *Loch Achanalt, L. Alvie, L. Morlich.* Transferred to South Africa: *Loch Ard, L. Boisdale, L. Cree.*

Page 190 Type 15 conversions: *Rapid, Relentless, Rocket, Roebuck, Troubridge, Grenville, Ulster, Ulysses, Undaunted, Undine, Urania, Urchin, Ursa, Venus, Verulam, Vigilant, Virago, Volage, Wakeful, Whirlwind, Wizard, Zest.* Type 16 conversions: *Orwell, Paladin, Petard, Teazer, Tenacious, Termagent, Terpsichore, Tumult, Tuscan, Tyrian.*

Page 191 Type 14: *Blackwood, Duncan, Dundas, Exmouth, Grafton, Hardy, Keppel, Malcolm, Murray, Palliser, Pellew, Russell.*

Page 192 Type 41: *Jaguar, Leopard, Lynx, Puma.* Type 61: *Chichester, Lincoln, Llandaff, Salisbury.*

Page 193 Type 12: *Berwick, Blackpool, Brighton, Eastbourne, Falmouth, Londonderry, Lowestoft, Plymouth, Rhyl, Rothesay, Torquay, Whitby, Yarmouth.* Leander class: *Ajax, Arethusa, Argonaut, Aurora, Cleopatra, Danae, Euryalus, Galatea, Juno, Leander, Minerva, Naiad, Penelope, Phoebe, Sirius.* Improved Leander class: *Achilles, Andromeda, Apollo, Ariadne, Bacchante, Charybdis, Diomede, Hermione, Jupiter, Scylla.*

Page 194 Type 21: *Active, Alacrity, Amazon, Ambuscade, Antelope, Ardent, Arrow, Avenger.*

Page 195 Type 22: *Battleaxe, Brazen, Brilliant, Broadsword.* Batch II: *Beaver, Boxer, Brave, Coventry, London, Sheffield.* Batch III: *Campbeltown, Chatham, Cornwall, Cumberland.*

Page 196 Type 23: *Argyll, Grafton, Iron Duke, Kent, Lancaster, Marlborough, Monmouth, Montrose, Norfolk, Northumberland, Portland, Richmond, St. Albans, Somerset, Sutherland, Westminster.*

Page 197 Le Corse class: *Le Bordelais, Le Boulonnais, Le Brestois, Le Corse.* Le Normand class: *L'Agenais, l'Alsacien, Le Basque, Le Béarnais, Le Bourguignon, Le Breton, Le Champenois, Le Gascon, Le Lorrain, Le Normand, Le Picard, Le Provençal, Le Savoyard, Le Vendéen.*

Page 198 Commandant Rivière class: *Amiral Charner, Balny, Commandant Bory, Commandant Bourdais, Commandant Rivière, Doudart de la Grée, Enseigne Henry, Protet, Victor Schoelcher.*

Page 199 *Aconit.*

Page 200 D'Estienne d'Orves class: *Amyot d'Invilles, Commandant Birot, Commandant Blaison, Commandant Bouan, Commandant de Pimodan, Commandant Ducuing, Commandant l'Herminier, D'Estienne d'Orves, Detroyat, Drogou, Enseigne de Vaisseau Jacoubet, Jean Moulin, Lieutenant de Vaisseau Lavallée, Lieutenant de Vaisseau le Henaff, Premier Maître l'Her, Quartier-Maître Anquetil, Second Maître le Bihan.*

Page 201 Floréal class: *Floréal, Germinal, Nivôse, Prairial, Vendémiaire, Ventôse.*

Page 202 La Fayette class: *Aconit, Courbet, Guépratte, La Fayette, Surcouf.*

Page 203 Shumushu class: *Hachijo, Ishigaki, Kunashiri, Shumushu.* Etorofu class: *Amakusa, Etorofu, Fukue, Hirato, Iki, Kanju, Kasado, Manju, Matsuwa, Mutsure, Oki, Sado, Tsushima, Wakamiya.*

Page 204 Mikura class: *Awagi, Chiburi, Kurahashi, Kusagaki, Mikura, Miyake, Nomi, Yashiro.* Ukuru class: *Aguni, Amani, Chikubu, Daito, Habushi, Habuto, Hiburi, Hodaka, Ikara, Ikino, Ikuna, Inagi, Iwo, Kanawa, Kozu, Kuga, Kume, Mokuto, Murotsu, Oga, Okinawa, Otsu, Sakito, Shiga, Shinnan, Shisaka, Shonan, Takane, Tomoshiri, Uku, Ukuru, Urumi, Yaku.*

Page 205 Kaibokan Type I: Odd numbers 1–235. Kaibokan Type II: Even numbers 2–204. Matsu class: *Azusa, Enoki, Hagi Hatsuyume, Hatsuzakura, Hinoki, Hishi, Kaba, Kaede, Kaki, Kashi, Katsura, Kaya, Keyaki, Kiri, Kusunoki, Kuwa, Kuzu, Maki, Matsu, Momi, Momo, Nara, Nashi, Nire, Odake, Sakaki, Sakura, Shi, Sugi, Sumire, Tachibana, Take, Tochi, Tsubaki, Tsuta, Ume, Wakazakura, Yadake, Yaezkura, Yanagi.*

Page 206 Ikazuchi class: *Ikazuchi, Inazuma.* Isuzu class: *Isuzu, Kitakami, Mogami, Oi.*

Page 207 Chikugo class: *Ayase, Chitose, Chikugo, Iwase, Kumano, Mikuma, Niyodo, Noshiro, Teshio, Tokachi, Yoshino.*

Page 208 Ishikari/Yubari class: *Yubari, Yubetsu.*

Page 209 Abukuma class: *Abukuma, Chikuma, Jintsu, Oyodo, Sendai, Tone.*

Page 210–211 Buckley class: *Ahrens, Alexander J. Luke, Amesbury, Barber, Barr, Bates, Blessman, Borum, Bowers, Buckley, Bull, Bunch, Burke, Charles Lawrence, Chase, Cofer, Coolbaugh, Cronin, Currier, Damon M. Cummings, Daniel T. Griffin, Darby, Donnell, Durik, Earl V. Johnson, Eichenberger, England, Enright, Fechteler, Fieberling, Fogg, Foreman, Foss, Fowler, Frament, Francis M. Robinson, Frybarger, Gantner, Gendreau, George, George W. Ingram, Gillette, Greenwood, Gunason, Haines, Harmon, Hayter, Henry R. Kenyon, Hollis, Holton, Hopping, Ira Jeffery, J. Douglas Blackwood, Jack W. Wilke, James E. Craig, Jenks, Jordon, Joseph C. Hubbard, Joseph E. Campbell, Kephart, Laning, Lee Fox, Liddle, Lloyd, Loeser, Lovelace, Loy, Major, Maloy, Manning, Marsh, Neuendorf, Newman, Osmus, Otter, Paul G. Baker, Raby, Reeves, Reuben James, Rich, Robert I. Paine, Runels, Schmitt, Scott, Scroggins, Sims, Solar, Spangenberg, Spangler, Tatum, Thomason, Underhill, Vanmen, Varian, Weber, Weeden, Whitehurst, William C. Cole, William T. Powell, Willmarth, Wiseman, Witter.* Cannon class: *Acree, Alger, Amick, Atherton, Baker, Baugust, Baron, Booth, Bostwick, Breeman, Bright, Bronstein, Burrows, Cannon, Carroll, Carter, Cates, Christopher, Clarence E. Evans, Coffman, Cooner, Curtis W. Howard, Earl K. Olsen, Ebert, Eisner, Eldridge, Gandy, Garfield Thomas, Gaynier, George M. Campbell, Gustafson, Hemminger, Herzog, Hilbert, John J. van Buren, Kyne, Lamons, Levy, McAnn, McClelland, McConnell, Marts, Micka, Milton Lewis, Muir, Neal A. Scott, O'Neill, Osterhaus, Oswald, Parks, Pennewill, Reybold, Riddle, Rinehart, Roberts, Roche, Russell M. Cox, Samuel S. Miles, Slater, Snyder, Stern, Straub, Sutton, Swearer, Thomas, Thornhill, Tills, Trumpeter, Waterman, Weaver, Wesson, Wingfield.* Edsall class: *Blair, Brister, Brough, Calcaterra, Camp, Chambers, Chatelain, Cockrill, Dale W. Peterson, Daniel, Douglas L. Howard, Durant, Edsall, Falgout, Farguqhar, Fessenden, Finch, Fiske, Flaherty, Forster, Frederick C. Davis, Frost, Hammann, Harveson, Haverfield, Herbert C. Jones, Hill, Hissem, Holder, Howard D. Crow, Hurst,*

Huse, Inch, J.R.Y. Blakely, J. Richard Ward, Jacob Jones, Janssen, Joyce, Keith, Kirkpatrick, Koiner, Kretchmer, Lansing, Leopold, Lowe, Marchand, Martin H. Ray, Menges, Merrill, Mills, Moore, Mosley, Neunzer, Newell, O'Reilly, Otterstetter, Peterson, Pettit, Pillsburn, Poole, Pople Price, Pride, Ramsden, Rhodes, Richey, Ricketts, Robert E. Peary, Roy O. Hale, Savage, Sellstrom, Sloat, Snowden, Stanton, Stewart, Stockdale, Strickland, Sturtevant, Swasey, Swenning, Thomas L. Gary, Tomich, Vance, Wilhoite, Willis. Evarts class: *Andres, Austin, Bebas, Brackett, Brennan, Burden R. Hastings, Cabana, Canfield, Carlson, Charles R. Greer, Cloues, Connolly, Crouter, Crowley, Decker, Deede, Dempsey, Dionne, Dobler, Doherty, Donaldson, Doneff, Duffy, Edgar C. Chase, Edward C. Daly, Eisele, Elden, Emery, Engstrom, Evarts, Fair, Finnegan, Fleming, Halloran, Gilmore, Greiner, Griswold, Harold C. Thomas, Lake, Le Hardy, Lovering, Lyman, Manlove, Martin, Mitchell, Rall, Reynolds, Sanders, Sederstrom, Seid, Smartt, Stadtfeld, Steele, Tisdale, Walter S. Brown, Whitman, Wileman, William C. Millar, Wintle, Wyffels, Wyman.* John C. Butler class: *Abercrombie, Albert T. Harris, Alvin C. Cockrell, Bivin, Cecil J. Doyle, Charles E. Brannon, Chester T. O'Brien, Conklin, Corbesier, Cross, Dennis, Douglas A. Munro, Doyle C. Barnes, Dufilho, Edmonds, Edward H. Allen Edwin A. Howard, Eversole, Formoe, Francovich, French, Gentry, George E. Davis, Gilligan, Goss, Grady, Haas, Hanna, Henry W. Tucker, Heyliger, Howard F. Clark, Jaccard, Jack Miller, Jesse Rutherford, John C. Butler, John L. Williamson, Johnnie Hutchins, Joseph E. Connolly, Kendall C. Campbell, Kenneth M. Willett, Keppler, Key, Kleinsmith, La Prade, Lawrence C. Taylor, Le Ray Wilson, Leland E. Thomas, Lewis, Lloyd E. Acree, Lloyd Thomas, McCoy Reynolds, McGinty, Mack, Maurice J. Manuel, Melvin R. Nawman, Naifeh, O'Flaherty, Oberrender, Oliver Mitchell, Osberg, Pratt, Presley, Raymond, Richard M. Rowell, Richard S. Bull, Richard W. Suesens, Rizzi, Robert Brazier, Robert F. Keller, Rolf, Rombach, Samuel B. Roberts, Shelton, Silverstein, Stafford, Steinaker, Straus, Tabberer, Thaddeus Parker, Traw, Tweedy, Tulvert M. Moore, Vandivier, Wagner, Walter C. Wann, Walton, Weiss, William C. Lawe, William Sieverling, Williams, Woodrow R. Thompson, Woodson.* Rudderrow class: *Bray, Chaffee, Charles J. Kimmel, Coates, Daniel A. Joy, Day, DeLong, Eugene E. Elmore, George A. Johnson, Hodges, Holt, Jobb, Leslie L.B. Knox, Lough, McNulty, McTivier, Parle, Peiffer, Riley Rudderow, Thomas F. Nickel, Tinsman.*

Page 212 Dealey/Courtney/Claud Jones class: *Bauer, Bridget, Charles Berry, Claud Jones, Courtney, Cromwell, Dealey, Evans, Hammerberg, Hartley, Hooper, J.K. Taussig, John R. Perry, John Willis, Lester, McMorris, Van Voorhis.*

Page 213 Bronstein class: *Bronstein, McCloy,* Garcia class: *Albert David, Bradley, Brumby, Davidson, Edward McDonnell, Garcia, Koelsch, O'Callaghan Sample, Voge.* Brooke class: *Brooke, Julius A. Furer, Ramsey, Richard L. Page, Schofield, Talbot.*

Page 214 Knox class: *Ainsworth, Aylwin, Badger, Bagley, Barbey, Blakeley. Bowen, Brewton, Capodanno, Connole, Cook, Donald B. Beary, Downes, Elmer Montgomery, Fanning, Franic Hammon, Gray, Harold E. Holt, Hepburn, Jesse L. Brown, Joseph Hewes, Kirk, Knox, Lang, Lockwood, McCandless, Marvin Shields, Meyercord, Miller, Moinester, Ouellet, Patterson, Paul, Pharris, Rathburne, Reasoner, Roark, Robert E. Peary, Stein, Thomas C. Hart, Trippe, Truett, Valdez, Vreeland, W.S. Sims, Whipple.*

Page 215 Oliver Hazard Perry class: *Antrim, Aubrey, Fitch, Boone, Carr, Clark, Clifton Sprague, Copeland, Crommelin, Curts, De Wert, Doyle, Duncan, Elrod, Estocin, Fahrion, Flatley, Ford, Gallery, Gary, George Philip, Halyburton, Hawes, Ingraham, Jack Williams, Jarrett, John A. Moore, John L. Hall, Kauffman, Klakring, Lewis B. Puller, McCluskey, McInerney, Mahlon S. Tisdale, Nicholas, Oliver Hazard Perry, Reid, Rentz, Reuben James, Robert G. Bradley, Rodney M. Davis, Samuel B. Roberts, Samuel Eliot Morison, Sides, Simpson, Stark, Stephen W. Groves, Taylor, Thach, Underwood, Vandegrift, Wadsworth.*

Page 216 Spica class: *Airone, Alcione, Aldebaran, Altair Andromeda, Antares, Aretusa, Ariel, Calipso, Calliope, Canopo, Cassiopea, Castore, Centauro, Cigno, Circe, Climene, Clio, Libra, Lince, Lira, Lupo, Pallade, Partenope, Perseo, Pleiadi, Polluce, Sagittario, Sirio, Vega.*

Page 217 Ariete class: *Alabarde, Ariete, Arturo, Auriga, Balestra, Daga, Dragone, Eridano, Fionda, Gladio, Lancia, Pugnale, Rigel, Spada, Spica, Stella Polare.*

Page 218 Orsa class: *Orione, Orsa, Pegaso, Procione.* Animoso class: *Aliseo, Animoso, Ardente, Ardimentoso, Ardito, Ciclone, Fortunale, Ghibli, Groppo, Impavido, Impetuoso, Indomito, Intrepido, Monsone, Tifone, Uragano.*

Page 219 Albatros class: *Airone, Albatros, Alcione, Aquila.* De Cristofaro class: *Licio Visintini, Pietro de Cristofaro, Salvatore Todaro, Umberto Grosso.*

Page 220 Centauro class: *Canopo Centauro, Cigno, Castore.*

Page 221 Bergamini class: *Carlo Margottini, Luigi Rizzo, Virginio Fasan.* Alpini class: *Alpini, Carabiniere.*

Page 222 Lupo class: *Lupo, Orsa, Perseo, Sagittario.*

Page 223 Maestrale class: *Aliseo, Espero, Euro, Grecale, Libeccio, Maestrale, Scirocco, Zeffiro.* Artigliere class: *Artigliere, Aviere, Bersagliere, Granatiere.*

Page 224 Minerva class: *Chimera, Danaide, Driade, Fenice, Minerva, Sfinge, Sibilla, Urania.*

Page 225 Kola class: Names uncertain.

Page 226 Riga class: Known names: *Astrakhan'skiy Komsomolets, Arkhangel'skiy, Komsomolets, Bars, Barsuk, Bobr, Buyvol, Byk, Gepard, Giena, Komsomolets Litviy, Krasnogarskiy, Komsomolets, Kunitsa, Leopard, Lev, Lisa, Medved, Pantera, Rys, Rosomakha, Shakal, Sovetskiy, Azerbaydzhan, Sovetskiy, Dagestan, Sovetskiy Turkmenistan, Strau, Tigr, Tuman, Volk, Voron, Yaguar.*

Page 227 Mirka and Petya classes: Names unconfirmed.

Page 228 Poti class: Names unconfirmed.

Page 229 Grisha classes: Names unconfirmed.

Page 230 Krivak I class: *Bditel'nyi, Bezukoriznennyy, Bezzavetnyy, Bodryy, Deyatel'nyy, Doblestnyy, Dostonyy, Druzhnyy, Ladnyy, Leningradski Komsomolets, Letuchiy, Poryvistyy, Pylkiy, Razumnyy, Razayshchiy, Restivyy, Sil'nyy, Storozhevoy, Svirepyy, Zadornyy, Zharkyy.* Krivak class II: *Bessmennyy, Gordelivyy, Gromkiy, Grozyashchiy, Neukrotimyy, Pytlivyy, Razitel'nyy, Revnostnyy, Rezkiy, Rezvyy, Ryanyy.* Krivak class III: *Anadyr, Dzerzhinskiy, Kedrov, Menzhinskiy, Orel, Pskov, Vorovskiy.*

Page 231 Steregushchiy class: *Boiky, Soobrziltel'nyy, Steregushchiy, Stoiky.*

Page 232 Köln class: *Augsburg, Braunschweig, Emden, Karlsruhe, Köln, Lübeck.*

Page 233 Thetis class: *Hermes, Naiade, Theseus, Thetis, Triton.*

Page 234 Bremen class: *Augsberg, Bremen, Emden, Karlsruhe, Köln Lübeck, Niedersachsen, Rheinland-Pfalz.*

Page 235 Brandenburg class: *Bayern, Brandenburg, Mecklesnburg-Vorpommern, Schleswig-Holstein.*

Page 236 Sachsen class: *Hamburg, Hessen, Sachsen.*

Page 237 Braunschweig class: *Braunschweig, Erfurt, Magdeburg, Oldenburg.*

Page 238 Van Heemskerck class: *Jacob van Heemskerck, Witte de With.* Kortenaer class: *Abraham Crijnssen, Banckert, Bloys van Treslong. Callenburgh, Jan van Brakel, Kortenaer, Philips van Almonde, Piet Heyn, Pieter, Florisz, Van Kinsbergen.*

Page 239 De Zeven Provinciën class: *De Ruyter, De Zeven Provinciën, Evertsen, Tromp.*

Page 240 Karel Doorman class: *Abraham van der Hulst, Karel Doorman, Van Amstel, Van Galen, Van Nes, Van Speijk.*

Page 241 St Laurent classes, Annapolis type: *Annapolis, Nipigon.* Mackenzie type: *Mackenzie, Qu'appelle, Saskatchewan, Yukon.* Restigouche type: *Chaudière, Columbia, St. Croix.* Improved Restigouche type: *Gatineau, Kootenay, Restigouche, Terra Nova.* St. Laurent type: *Assiniboine, Fraser, Margaree, Ottawa, Saguenay, Skeena.*

Page 242 Iroquois class: *Algonquin, Athabaskan, Huron, Iroquois.* Halifax class: *Calgary, Charlottetown, Fredericton, Halifax, Montreal, Ottawa, Regina, St. John's, Toronto, Vancouver, Ville de Quebec, Winnepeg.*

Page 243 Anzac class (Australia): *Anzac, Arunta, Ballarat, Parramatta, Perth, Stuart, Toowoomba, Warramunga.* Anzac class (New Zealand): *Te Kaha, Te Mana.*

***Scarborough*, Type 12**

Glossary

AA(W) Anti-Aircraft (Warfare).
AS Anti-Submarine.
Asdic Early British term for Sonar.
ASM Air-to-Surface Missile.
ASROC Anti-Submarine Rocket. American stand-off weapon.
AS(W) Anti-Submarine (Warfare).
ballast Material taken aboard to improve or correct draught, trim, stability or ship motion.
beam In this book, the maximum width of the hull at the waterline at standard displacement. With flare, a ship may be wider at higher levels.
belt Vertical armour protection of a ship's hull. Rare in smaller ships.
bhp Brake horsepower. The power output of a (usually) internal combustion engine.
bunkers Compartments for the stowage of fuel. May refer loosely to the fuel itself.
CAP Combat Air Patrol.
calibre Bore diameter of a gun barrel. Also measure of barrel length, e.g. a 3in 70 will be of 3 x 70 = 210in length.
camber Athwartships convex curvature to a ship's deck.
casing (funnel) Outer plating surrounding exhaust end of uptake.
centre of buoyancy The point through which the resultant of all upward, or buoyant, forces act. It is directly below the centre of gravity in a surface ship.
centre of gravity The point through which the resultant of all downward, or weight-related, forces act.
C-in-C Commander-in-Chief.
CIWS Close-In Weapons System. Self-contained, fully-automatic, "last-ditch" defensive system, typically comprising several high rate-of-fire cannon and/or short-range SAMs.
CODAG Combined Diesel And Gas.
CODOG Combined Diesel Or Gas.
COGAG Combined Gas And Gas.
COGOG Combined Gas Or Gas.
COSAG Combined Steam And Gas.
contra-rotating propellers Propellers, as in a torpedo, mounted on coaxial shafts and rotated in opposite directions to nullify side forces.
Controller Earlier, Comptroller. In the British Board of Admiralty, the Third Sea Lord, responsible for the design, provision and upkeep of HM warships.
crank Lacking initial stability and easily inclined by external forces, such as wind and sea.
CVE Escort carrier. Usually converted from mercantile hull.
DASH Drone Anti-Submarine Helicopter.
DDG Guided Missile Destroyer.
DDK General Purpose Destroyer.
DE Destroyer Escort.
DEG Destroyer Escort with an anti-aircraft missile system.
DESRON In the US Navy, a Destroyer Squadron.
dipping sonar Small sonar lowered by cable from a hovering helicopter. Sometimes "dunking sonar".
displacement (fl) Full load, or deep, displacement of a ship which is fully equipped, stored and fuelled.
displacement (std) Standard displacement. Actual weight of a ship less fuel and other deductions allowed by treaty.
Division Boat In Imperial German Navy, a larger type of Torpedo Boat, equivalent to a flotilla leader.
DP Dual-Purpose, i.e. a gun suitable for engaging both aerial or surface targets.
draught (or "draft") Mean depth of water in which a ship may float freely. In frigates particularly, mean draught (quoted) may be considerably less than that over protruding sonars.
ECM Electronic Counter Measures.
ER Extended Range.
ESM Electronic Support Measures.
flare Outward curvature or angle of hull plating.
flotilla Standard operational unit of destroyers or frigates, particularly in the Royal Navy.
forefoot Junction of stem with keel line.
foxer World War II countermeasure to acoustic torpedoes.
FRAM Fleet Re-habilitation And Modernization. An updating programme applied to many US destroyers.
freeboard In a warship, the vertical distance between the water to any particular point on the weather deck. Unlike merchant ships, warships do not have a designated freeboard deck.
GM Guided Missile.
Grand Fleet Title carried by the British battle fleet during World War I.
gross registered tons (grt) Measure of the volumetric capacity of a merchant ship. One gross ton equals $100ft^3$ ($2.83m^3$) of reckonable space.
gunhouse A relatively light, enclosed containment for guns, usually not extending more than one deck below. In contradistinction to a *turret*, a usually protected containment located atop a barbette or deep armoured trunk.
HA High Angle. Usually with reference to a gun's elevation.
HA/LA High Angle/Low Angle.
hard-lying A reference to the spartan conditions inseparable from early destroyers and escorts. Recognized (sometimes) by a supplement of "hard-lying money".
Hedgehog Forward-firing AS weapon of World War II, in the form of a spigot mortar projecting 12 or 24 fast-sinking bombs in an elliptical pattern.
High Sea(s) Fleet Title carried by German Battle Fleet during World War I.
horsepower Unit of power equal to 746 Watts.
Huff-Duff Popular term for HF/DF, or High Frequency Direction Finding, used by Allied AS forces to obtain bearings of a transmitting U-boat.
ihp Indicated horsepower. The power delivered by the pistons of a reciprocating steam engine.
IR Infra-Red.
Jeune École Late 19th-century French naval movement espousing the ideas of Admiral Théophile Aube, who advocated torpedo platforms as a counter to a battle fleet.
kite balloon Aerostat deployed by ships for observation or spotting.
LAMPS Light Airborne Multi-Purpose System.
L/B Length-to-Breadth.
LCA Landing Craft, Assault. Large enough to carry an equipped platoon; small enough to be carried under davits.
LCPR Landing Craft, Personnel, Ramped.
LCT Landing Craft, Tank.
length (bp) Length between perpendiculars. Customarily the distance between forward extremity of waterline at standard displacement and the forward side of the rudder post. For American warships, lengths on design waterline and between perpendiculars are synonymous.
length (oa) Length overall.
length (wl) Length on waterline at standard displacement.
Limbo British triple-barrelled AS mortar, designed to supersede Squid.
locomotive boiler Early form of boiler in which hot products of combustion were forced through tubes to heat a surrounding water mass.
LSM Landing Ship, Medium.
LST Landing Ship, Tank.
MR Medium-Range.
NATO North Atlantic Treaty Organization. Effectively a counter to the Warsaw Pact.
NBCD Nuclear, Biological and Chemical Defence.
neutrally buoyant Having density identical with that of surrounding water, tending neither to sink nor to float.

paravane A kite-like device, streamed from either bow, whose lines deflect those of moored mines, preventing the ship from striking them.
PDMS Point-Defence Missile System.
PF In US Navy, a Patrol Frigate. Category for British River-class frigates built in the United States.
phased-array radar A radar whose beam depends not upon a rotating antenna but upon sequential switching of a matrix of fixed, radiating elements.
Plan "Orange" American war plan for potential use against Japan.
protection In this book, usually described as "nominal", comprising only patches of splinter-proof, or radiation-proof, plating covering essential areas may be of "plastic", e.g. Kevlar, or of sandwich construction.
protective deck Either flat, or incorporating side slopes or pronounced curvature, it shields spaces beneath from projectiles or fragments.
QF Quick-Firing. Applied to guns with "fixed" ammunition with projectile and charge combined.
RAS Replenishment-At-Sea.
RCN Royal Canadian Navy.
SAM Surface-to-Air-Missile.
scantlings A scale of dimensions governing the size of all structural parts incorporated in a ship.
schnorkel (or "snort") A hollow mast enabling a submerged submarine to ingest atmospheric air and exhaust engine gases.
seakeeping/seakindliness/seaworthiness All applicable to a ship's ability to cope with weather conditions in discharging her functions as an efficient, but habitable, weapons platform.
sheer Curvature of deck line in fore-and-aft direction, usually upward toward either end.
shell plating General term for all outer plating of a hull.
shp Shaft horsepower. Power measured at point in shaft ahead of the stern gland. Does not include losses incurred in stern gland and A-bracket, if fitted.
sided Situated toward the sides of a ship, usually as opposed to a centreline location.
Sonar Equipment using sound to establish range, bearing or depth of a submerged object. May be "active", i.e. emitting pulsed energy, or "passive", i.e. listening only.
spar torpedo Warhead mounted on long spar protruding ahead of a small, fast launch. Operated by ramming target.
"Specials" Within the envelope of a class specification, the British Admiralty allowed key builders to incorporate non-standard features worth evaluation.
squat Tendency to trim by the stern at speed. Particularly noticeable in shallow water.
Squid British triple-barrelled, ahead-firing AS mortar. Precursor to Limbo. Designed to supersede the Hedgehog but not adopted by the US Navy.
SSBN Nuclear Ballistic Missile Submarine.
SSM Surface-to-Surface Missile.
SSN Nuclear-Propelled Attack Submarine.
stability range The range through which a ship may list while still maintaining a positive righting moment. If exceeded, capsize will follow.
stiffness The measure of the resistance of a ship to list under the action of external forces. "Stiff" is effectively the opposite to "crank".
superimposition If a gun is "superimposed" on another, i.e. located at a higher level, it is said to "superfire" it.
TACAN Tactical Air Navigation.
TBD Torpedo Boat Destroyer.
tender Tending to be "crank", but not so extreme.
TGB Torpedo Gun Boat.
ton As an imperial unit of weight, equal to 2,240lb.
tophamper Commonly, all structure above the weather deck. More specifically, masting.
towed array Sonar, typically passive, taking the form of a streamed neutrally buoyant hose containing multiple hydrophones and their cabling. The length of the array permits a reasonable bearing to be established on a noise source.
trim Amount by which a ship deviates, in the fore-and-aft axis, from her designed draught.
turbo-electric Propulsion system in which a steam turbine drives an electrical generator. This supplies energy via cable to a propulsion motor coupled to the propeller shaft.
Ultra Codeword applied to high-grade intelligence derived from Enigma signals decrypts.
uptake Conduit conducting products of combustion to the funnel.
VDS Variable Depth Sonar.
VLS Vertical Launch System.
volume critical Of a ship whose design is driven by needs of space rather than weight, e.g. aircraft carrier.
Warsaw Pact Defunct Eastern military bloc, essentially a counter to NATO.
water-tube boiler Boiler in which water is carried in tubes surrounded by hot products of combustion. Effectively a reverse, and more efficient, concept to that of the earlier Locomotive Boiler.
Weapon "Able" (Alfa) US Navy's post-war successor to Hedgehog. Trainable stabilized mounting to fire 12 rounds per minute.
weight critical Of a ship whose design is driven by considerations of weight rather than volume, e.g. a heavily armoured battleship.

Key to flags

For the specification boxes, the national flag that was current at the time of the vessel's use is shown.

 **Australia**

 **Canada**

 **France**

 **Germany: World War I**

 **Germany: World War II**

 **Germany: post-World War II**

 **Italy**

 **Japan**

 **Netherlands**

 **Russia**

 **Sweden**

 **United Kingdom**

 **United States**

 **USSR**

Index

***Minegumo*, Minegumo class**

***Curtis Wilbur*, Arleigh Burke class**

***Nastoychivyy*, Sovremennyy class**

***Mohammed V*, Floréal class**

***Abraham van der Hulst*, M class**

Acknowledgements

Research for the images used to illustrate this book was carried out by Ted Nevill of Cody Images, who supplied the majority of pictures. The publisher and Ted Nevill would like to thank all those who contributed to this research and to the supply of pictures:

AgustaWestland
ArtTech
BAE SYSTEMS
Blohm & Voss
General Dynamics
Japanese Maritime Self-Defense Force
Koninklijke Marine (Royal Netherlands Navy)
Marina Militare, Republica Italiana (Italian Navy)
NATO
Naval Historical Center, USA
National Archives & Records Administration, USA
Thomas Reyer
Ulis Fleming
US Naval Institute
US Navy
US Department of Defense

1054